The Perestroika Deception

The world's slide towards
THE 'SECOND OCTOBER REVOLUTION' ['WELTOKTOBER']

By the same author:

'New Lies for Old'
completed in 1980 and published in 1984,
New York, Dodd, Mead and Co.
London, The Bodley Head.
Paperback Edition, 1986
by Wheatsheaf Books.

The Perestroika Deception

Memoranda to the
CENTRAL INTELLIGENCE AGENCY
ANATOLIY GOLITSYN

EDWARD HARLE
London & New York

First published in Great Britain and the United States in 1995 by:

Edward Harle Limited
108 Horseferry Road
Westminster
London SW1P 2EF
United Kingdom
Telephone: 0171-222 2635
Facsimile: 0171-233 0185

Edward Harle Limited
Suite 1209
280 Madison Avenue
New York NY 10016-0802
United States
Telephone: 212-697 7212
Facsimile: 212-599 4561

ISBN 1 899798 00 5

Library of Congress Catalog Card Number: 95–76304.

British Library Cataloguing in Publication Data.
A catalogue record for this book is available
from the British Library.

Designed by Christopher Story FRSA
Typeset in Palatino, Century, Futura, Frutiger and Univers by:
Lithofax Limited, 108 Horseferry Road, Westminster, London SW1P 2EF.
Printed in Great Britain by:
Lithofax Limited, 108 Horseferry Road, Westminster, London SW1P 2EF.

In Memory of

Jim Angleton
Founder and outstanding chief
of the Central Intelligence Agency's
Counter-intelligence,
a man of vision and courage,
a warrior and comrade-in-arms,
who recognised the dangers of
the Soviets' new strategic challenge

ABOUT THE AUTHOR

Anatoliy Golitsyn was born in the Ukraine in 1926. While a cadet in military school, he was awarded a Soviet medal 'For the defence of Moscow in the Great Patriotic War' for digging anti-tank trenches near Moscow. At the age of fifteen, he joined the Komsomol (League of Communist Youth) and, at nineteen, he became a member of the Communist Party.

In the same year, he joined the KGB, in which he studied and served until 1961. He graduated from the Moscow School of Military Counter-espionage, the counterintelligence faculty of the High Intelligence School, and the University of Marxism-Leninism and completed a correspondence course with the High Diplomatic School. In 1952 and early 1953 he was involved with a friend in drawing up a proposal to the Central Committee on the reorganisation of Soviet intelligence.

In connection with this proposal he attended a meeting of the secretariat chaired by Stalin and a meeting of the Presidium chaired by Malenkov and attended by Khrushchev, Brezhnev and Bulganin. In 1952-53 he worked briefly as head of a section responsible for counter-espionage against the United States. In 1959 he graduated with a law degree from a four-year course at the KGB Institute (now the KGB Academy) in Moscow.

From 1959 to 1960, at a time when Soviet long-range strategy was being formulated and the KGB was being reorganised to play its part in it, he served as a senior analyst in the NATO section of the Information Department of the Soviet intelligence service. He served in Vienna and Helsinki on counterintelligence assignments from 1953 to 1955 and from 1960 to 1961, respectively.

He defected to the United States in December 1961. Subsequently, his contribution to the national security of leading Western countries was recognised by the award of the United States Government Medal for Distinguished Service.

He was made an Honorary Commander of the British Empire (CBE). A promise of membership of the Légion d'Honneur made when President Pompidou was in power was not fulfilled owing to the change of government.

Since 1962, the Author has spent much of his time on the study of Communist and international affairs, reading both the Communist and the Western press. In 1980 he completed, and in 1984 he published, 'New Lies for Old', a study of the Soviet long-range strategy of deception and disinformation.

For over thirty years, the Author has submitted Memoranda to the Central Intelligence Agency, in which he has provided the Agency with timely and largely accurate forecasts of Soviet Bloc developments and on the evolution of Soviet/Russian/Communist strategy. By applying the dialectical methodology which drives the strategy, the Author has been able to score innumerable 'bulls-eyes'. This unparalleled track record reflects the Author's personal experience of four years in the KGB's strategy 'think tank', together with his deep understanding of the dialectical nature of the strategy and the Leninist mentality of its originators and implementers.

The Author is a citizen of the United States. ∎

Contents

CONTENTS

CONTENTS

‘ All warfare is based on deception. Therefore, when capable, feign incapacity; when active, inactivity. When near, make it appear that you are far away;
when far away, that you are near. Offer the enemy a bait to lure him; feign disorder and strike him. When he concentrates, prepare against him; where he is strong,
avoid him. Anger his general and confuse him. Pretend inferiority and encourage
his arrogance. Keep him under strain and wear him down. When he is united,
divide him. Attack where he is unprepared; sally out when he does not expect you.
To subdue the enemy without fighting is the supreme skill... Disrupt his
alliances... Therefore I say: ‘[If you] know the enemy and know yourself, in a hun-
dred battles you will never be in peril. When you are ignorant of the enemy but
know yourself, your chances of winning or losing are equal; if ignorant of both
your enemy and yourself, you are certain in every battle to be in peril ’.

SUN TZU, 'The Art of War ', Oxford University Press Edition.

‘ ... n'oubliez jamais... que la plus belle des ruses du diable est de vous
persuader qu'il n'existe pas! ’.

CHARLES BAUDELAIRE, 'Le Spleen de Paris'.

‘ A ruling class which is on the run, as ours is, is capable of every fatuity. It
makes the wrong decisions, chooses the wrong people, and is unable to recognise
its enemies – if it does not actually prefer them to its friends ’.

MALCOLM MUGGERIDGE, 'Tread Softly for You Tread on My Jokes'.

ACKNOWLEDGMENTS

I wish to express my deep gratitude to Edward Harle Limited and to Christopher Story for publishing my manuscript. They deserve my admiration for their grasp of the significance of the manuscript and for having the courage to publish such a controversial book. I am especially grateful to Christopher Story who made the final editing of the manuscript.

I also wish to express my gratitude to my friends and retired intelligence officials for their encouragement and assistance; to "N" for editing my typescript; to other friends who read it and gave me valuable advice, with special thanks to Newton S. Miler, Arthur Martin, CBE, John Leader, Esq., the late Mary Leader, John Walker, Frank F. Friberg and William Hood. I also thank Mark Riebling who showed interest in my ideas and made valuable suggestions.

I am especially grateful to my wife, Svetlana, for her support and encouragement.

BEHIND AND BEYOND 'PERESTROIKA': SOVIET STRATEGY

Convinced from the early days after his arrival in the United States in December 1961 that conventional Western interpretations of developments in the Communist world were seriously defective, the Author embarked on a study of Soviet strategy including the use of strategic disinformation. The results of his researches were embodied in a book, 'New Lies for Old', completed in 1980 and published, with seven additional pages, in 1984. Since then, he has contributed a number of Memoranda on the subject to the Central Intelligence Agency. The selections in this book are edited versions of some of these Memoranda. ■

FOREWORD BY THE AUTHOR

This collection of my Memoranda to the Central Intelligence Agency is about Soviet grand strategy and the new dimensions of the threat to the Western democracies.

There is a marked difference between the American and the Communist use of the term 'strategy'. Americans tend to think of strategy in short-range terms in relation to presidential election campaigns, in football or baseball games or in such instances as the 'strategy of stone-walling' during the Watergate investigations. For Russian Communists on the other hand, strategy is a grand design or general Party line which governs the Party's actions over a long period and contains one or more special manoeuvres designed to help the Party achieve its ultimate objectives – the seizure of power in Russia in 1917, the subsequent expansion of the Communist camp and the final world-wide victory of Communism.

This book shows that the essence of the special manoeuvre in the present grand strategy for Communism lies, internally, in the creation and use of controlled 'political opposition' to effect a transition to new 'democratic', 'non-Communist', 'nationalist' power structures which remain in reality Communist-controlled. Internationally, the essence of the manoeuvre lies in the use of the political potential of these new power structures to develop contacts and promote solidarity with the Western democracies as a means towards the achievement of world Communist victory through the convergence of the Communist and non-Communist systems.

The main purpose of my defection at the end of 1961 was **(a)** to warn the American Government about the adoption of the current grand strategy for Communism and the political rôle of the KGB and the use of disinformation and controlled political opposition which the strategy entailed, and **(b)** to help the West neutralise KGB penetration of their governments.

On arrival in Washington, I asked to be received by President Kennedy. I was assured by General Taylor, the President's security adviser, that the President would see my appropriate contributions. Mr Robert Kennedy, the Attorney General, told me that in due time a meeting with the President would be arranged.

General Taylor wrote to me in the following terms:

THE WHITE HOUSE WASHINGTON, **21 December 1961**

Dear Mr. Golitsyn,

I have your letter of December 19, 1961, addressed to the President of the United States. The subject matter is one of considerable interest to this government and your request has received careful consideration.

I wish to assure you that the officials with whom you are now in contact have the full authority and responsibility for handling matters of this nature, and I therefore request that you give them your complete cooperation.

I have asked that I be kept informed of developments in this matter, and you may be confident that information concerning your contribution will be brought to the attention of the President if and when appropriate.

MAXWELL D. TAYLOR

While waiting for the meeting, I limited my cooperation with the CIA, FBI and allied services to the problems of KGB penetration of the American, British and French governmental institutions. After Present Kennedy's assassination, I briefed the head of the CIA and the head of that agency's counterintelligence staff about Communist long-range strategy, the creation of the disinformation department and Shelepin's reorganisation of the KGB into a *political arm of the Party*.

On many subsequent occasions, I had opportunities to brief other leading Western services on the subject of Soviet long-range strategy and the new rôle of the KGB, recommending a reassessment of the Communist problem. A few counterintelligence officials in the CIA and the British and French services began to understand and accept the validity of my views. For me, the most encouraging development was the understanding I received from Count de Marenches, the Chief of the French intelligence service under the late President Pompidou. Count de Marenches provided me with opportunities to work with his service on the reassessment of Communist developments in terms of Soviet strategy. In the presence of a dozen senior officials of his service, Count de Marenches stated that he was in agreement with my views on the existence of the strategy and of disinformation but I was unable to explain my ideas in detail because my project with his service was terminated.

This growing awareness about disinformation and the political rôle of the KGB in implementing the strategy was interrupted by the Watergate hearings (which weakened the American services) and by the unfortunate death of President Pompidou (which weakened the position of the French service).

Despite adverse circumstances, I have made a consistent attempt to analyse important developments in the USSR and other Communist countries through the prism of Communist long-range strategy, strategic disinformation and the political rôle of the KGB. I continued to submit my Memoranda to the CIA about significant Communist developments and made suggestions on how to improve the Agency's understanding of Communist strategy.

In 1984, I published a book, *'New Lies for Old'*, about Communist strategic political disinformation. In the book and in my Memoranda, I made several significant predictions about future developments in the Communist world. I predicted that the Communist strategists would *go beyond Marx and Lenin* and would introduce economic and political reforms in the USSR and Eastern Europe. I predicted the legalisation of Solidarity in Poland, the return to 'democratisation' in Czechoslovakia and the removal of the Berlin Wall. I warned about a political offensive to promote a neutral socialist Europe which would work to Soviet advantage. I also warned that the West was acutely vulnerable to the coming major shift in Communist tactics.

It is axiomatic that political ideas should be tested out in practice. And it is a fact that many of my predictions, particularly about the coming economic and political reforms in the USSR and Eastern Europe, passed the test and were confirmed by subsequent events, particularly in Poland and Czechoslovakia.

It remains also a fact that leading Soviet experts like Mr Zbigniew Brzezinski failed to make accurate predictions about these developments. This failure on the part of Mr Brzezinski and other experts in Washington was noticed by an 'independent observer' in *'The New York Times'* of 12 September 1989.

Since then, I have submitted new Memoranda to the CIA and American policymakers in which I explained Soviet grand strategy and its strategic designs against the West, the essence of *'perestroika'* (the final phase of the strategy), the new use of the Bloc's political and security potential for introducing new deceptive controlled 'democratic', 'nationalist' and 'non-Communist' structures in the Communist countries, and the deployment of the political and security potential of the renewed 'democratic' régimes for the execution of the strategic design against the West.

In the Memoranda, I provided seven keys for understanding *'perestroika'*, explained the danger of Western support for it and proposed a reassessment of the situation and a re-thinking of that support as priority items of business. I suggested also how the West should respond to the challenge of *'perestroika'* and its destabilising effect on the Western democracies.

Since the Central Intelligence Agency did not react to my Memoranda, I decided to publish them and asked the CIA to declassify them for the purpose. The Agency agreed. Several considerations forced me to take my decision.

First, the democracies of the United States and Western Europe are facing a dangerous situation and are vulnerable because their governments, the Vatican, the élite, the media, the industrialists, the financiers, the trade unions and, most important, the general public are blind to the dangers of the strategy of *'perestroika'* and have failed to perceive the deployment of the Communist political potential of the renewed 'democratic' régimes against the West. The democracies could perish unless they are informed about the aggressive design of *'perestroika'* against them.

Secondly, I could not imagine that American policymakers, and particularly the conservatives in both the Republican and Democratic parties, despite their long experience with Communist treachery, would not be able to grasp the new manoeuvres of the Communist strategists and would rush to commit the West to helping *'perestroika'* which is so contrary to their interests.

It has been sad to observe the jubilation of American and West European conservatives who have been cheering *'perestroika'* without realising that it is intended to bring about their own political and physical demise. Liberal support for *'perestroika'* is understandable, but conservative support came as a surprise to me.

Thirdly, I was appalled that *'perestroika'* was embraced and supported by the United States without any serious debate on the subject.

In the fourth place, I am appalled by the failure of American scholars to point out the relevance of Lenin's New Economic Policy to understanding the aggressive, anti-Western design of *'perestroika'* or to provide appropriate warning to policymakers, and their failure to distinguish between America's true friends and its Leninist foes precisely because these foes are wearing the new 'democratic' uniform. Given the pressures they face, policymakers have no time to study the history of the period of Lenin's New Economic Policy, or to remind themselves of Marxist-Leninist dialectics.

But how could such learned and distinguished scholars as **S. Bialer** and **Z. Brzezinski** have failed to warn them about the successes of the New Economic Policy, the mistakes made by the West in accepting it and Gorbachëv's repetition of Lenin's strategy and its dangers for the West? What happened to their credentials as great scholars? Why was it left to Professor Norman Stone of Oxford University to detect and make the parallel in his article in the London *'Daily Telegraph'* of 11th November 1989, and to express concern at the euphoria over Gorbachëv? In his book, *'The Grand Failure'*, Brzezinski limited his description of Lenin's New Econ-

For Brzezinski, the NEP is 'a shorthand term for a period of experimentation, flexibility and moderation' [see 'The Grand Failure', Charles Scribner and Sons, New York, 1989, pages 18-19]. I am appalled by Brzezinski's failure to explain the relevance of Lenin's New Economic Policy to 'perestroika'.

This failure is further illustrated by the following:

(a) S. Bialer, a former defector from the Central Committee apparatus of the Polish Communist Party, wrote a foreword to Gorbachëv's book, 'Perestroika', introducing it to the US public without inserting any warning about the parallel with the New Economic Policy and its dangers for the Western democracies.

(b) During his recent visit to Moscow, Z. Brzezinski, the former National Security Adviser in the Carter Administration, met leading Soviet strategists including Yakovlev, an expert on the manipulation of the Western media, and advised them on how to proceed with 'perestroika'. Furthermore, Brzezinski delivered a lecture on the same subject to the Soviet diplomats at the High Diplomatic Academy!

In the fifth place, I am disappointed that Gordievsky, a recent KGB defector, did not help much to explain 'perestroika' as the final phase of Soviet long-range strategy, to describe its essence or to point out the deceptive nature of the changes and the strategic danger for the West. Gordievsky's articles in 'The Times' of London of 27-28 February and 1 March 1990, contained a rather optimistic, if not laudatory, description of the 'reforms' initiated under Gorbachëv and Yakovlev. I am puzzled that he should write so enthusiastically about them in the London 'Times'. He might as well have published his comments in the Party newspaper 'Pravda' or in Korotich's 'Ogonek'. His assessment of 'perestroika' and its meaning for the West is in complete contradiction to that set out in my Memoranda to the Central Intelligence Agency. Further comment would be superfluous. I leave it to the reader to make his own judgment.

In the sixth place, misguided Western support for 'perestroika' at all levels, and especially among the Western media, is destabilising Western societies, their defence, their political processes and their alliances. It is immensely accelerating the successful execution of the Soviet strategic design against the West. In 1984 I thought that, in the event of Western resistance to Soviet strategy, the scenario of convergence between the two systems might take the next half century to unroll [see 'New Lies for Old', pages 365-6].

Now, however, because the West has committed itself to the support of 'perestroika' and because of the impact of the misguided and euphoric support for it in the Western media, convergence might take less than a decade. The sword of Damocles is hanging over the Western democracies, yet they are oblivious to it. I believe in truth and the power of ideas to convey the truth.

Therefore, I present my Memoranda to the public – convinced that they will help them to see the 'perestroika' changes, and their sequels, in the Communist world and beyond, in a more realistic light, and to recover from their blindness. ∎

ANATOLIY GOLITSYN, UNITED STATES, 1995

FOREWORD BY THE EDITOR

In July 1991, I was asked by the former British Prime Minister, Mrs (now Lady) Thatcher, to see her at her room in the Palace of Westminster. The subject to be discussed was the network of bilateral treaties, declarations and accords which the Soviet Union had been signing with leading Western countries. By then, the list of such signatories already included Germany, France and Italy, while a treaty had been negotiated between the USSR and Spain, and a Political Declaration had been signed *inter alia* by the Soviet Union and Finland. Germany had in fact signed two bilateral treaties with Moscow. I had carried out a preliminary analysis of these treaties and accords, and had published translations of the texts, and some early findings, in several documents issued by my serials publishing firm in London, placing the treaties in the context of the implications of the Joint Declaration of Twenty-Two States and the Charter of Paris which Mrs Thatcher had signed on 19th November 1990 amid the disruption and anxieties surrounding the challenge to her leadership.

At the meeting, the former Prime Minister expressed great interest in the texts of the treaties and in my explanation of their significance. After admitting that her officials had not, during her final weeks in office, informed her about them, our conversation broadened to include my developing assessment of Soviet strategy in general, and the Soviet agenda for Europe, in particular. When I had finished explaining, as best I could, that Soviet behaviour and what I understood of Moscow's strategy bore familiar Leninist dialectical hallmarks, Mrs Thatcher remarked: 'I don't think Gorbachëv is a Leninist any more'. Later in the interview, after she had become aware of my acquaintance with Anatoliy Golitsyn's work 'New Lies for Old', and after hinting that she did not share Golitsyn's analysis, the former Prime Minister pronounced: 'I don't think we have been deceived – *at least, I hope we haven't*'.

These remarks have haunted me ever since. Obviously, the qualifying afterthought had revealed that the Prime Minister whose action in opening the door ajar had enabled the Soviets to thrust it wide open for the purpose of exporting their insidious 'perestroika' deception to the West, had retained a niggling doubt that the West might indeed have fallen victim to Soviet strategic deception. That she was prepared even to admit such a doubt is a tribute to her inherent intellectual integrity and strength of character. It is more than can be said for most of the West's leaders today, who have evidently allowed Gorbachëv and his successors and collaborators to 'restructure' their minds, in accordance with the true meaning of 'perestroika' – the 'restructuring' *not* of the Soviet system, but of the outlook, thinking and mentality of *the West*. For Stalin, 'perestroika' meant 're-shoeing' – as of a horse: that is to say, *not* of the régime itself, but of the system's means to consolidate its power.

Greatly though Lady Thatcher is to be admired, it is unfortunately the case that she was never the best judge of character. Reviewing the former Prime Minister's book 'The Downing Street Years' in 'The New York Times' Book Review section on 14th November 1993, Dr Henry Kissinger drew attention to the passage in which the former Prime Minister described her reaction on meeting Gorbachëv for the first time: 'If at this time I had paid attention only to the content of Mr Gorbachëv's remarks – largely the standard Marxist line – I would have to conclude that he was cast in the usual Communist mould. But his personality could not have been more different from the wooden ventriloquism of the average Soviet *apparatchik*. He smiled, laughed, used his hands for emphasis, modulated his voice, followed an argument through and was a sharp debater... His line was no different from what I would have expected. His style was. As the day wore on I came to understand that it was the style far more than the Marxist rhetoric which expressed the substance of the personality beneath'. In this passage, as Dr Kissinger had evidently realised, Lady Thatcher had admitted that she had been beguiled by Gorbachëv's *style*. As he cast his spell, Gorbachëv unlocked the key to the control of the Western mind – and to the 'restructuring' of the entire world. The West followed Lady Thatcher's prompting, mistaking the style for the substance. The disastrous consequences of this millennial error are now crowding in upon Western civilisation, threatening its very survival.

Ambition to control the Western mind is a long-standing objective of Soviet policy, embracing the ideas of the Italian Communist Antonio Gramsci, who argued that mastery of human consciousness should be a paramount political objective. As Richard Pipes has pointed out [in *'Survival is Not Enough'*, Simon and Schuster, New York, 1984, page 80], 'such mastery is secured, in the first place, by control of the organs of information'. The objective is 'to control thought at the source – that is, in the mind that absorbs and processes the information – and the best way of accomplishing this is by shaping words and phrases in the desired manner'. Moreover control of the Western mind is to be achieved not only by means of the dishonest use of language, but also through operations to demoralise the West – through corrosive attacks on society's institutions, the active promotion of drug abuse, and the spread of agnosticism, nihilism, permissiveness and concerted attacks on the family in order to destabilise society. Religion and the traditional cultural and moral hegemony must first be destroyed, before the revolution can be successful – a message stated unequivocally by the American activist Ellen Willis, who has written that 'feminism is not just an issue or a group of issues; it is the cutting edge of a revolution in cultural or moral values... The objective of every feminist reform, from legal abortion to child-care programs, is to undermine traditional family values' [see *'The Nation'*, New York, 14 November 1981, pages 494-5]. The still unproven assumption of the strategists is that with Western society 'deconstructed', its leaders will meekly accept and cooperate with the Soviet plan for a 'New World Social Order', or World Government.

In this context, it is interesting to recall that the spy George Blake told Kenneth de Courcy in the early 1960s that 'individual choice would eventually be mastered by a central Soviet control of thought process' [*'Traitors: The Labyrinths of Treason'*, by Chapman Pincher, Sidgwick & Jackson, London, 1987, page 157]. The primary objective of *'perestroika'*, then, is to restructure the Western mind using both deceptive language and the ideas of Gramsci so that it becomes more receptive to, and more inclined to collaborate with, the implementation of Soviet global strategic objectives. As one of the leading strategists, Georgi Arbatov, made clear in his book *'The System'* [Random House, New York, 1992, page 211], the ideas of Gramsci and other Marxists, whose work seeks to 'restructure' the Western mentality and to promote decadent lifestyles, had been consciously incorporated into the 'New Thinking': 'I do respect quite a few Marxist works and ideas. I include not only the "founding fathers" of Marxism but also outstanding leaders of the Socialist International, as well as people like Antonio Gramsci, György Lukacs, Ernst Bloch and Herbert Marcuse'. The importance of Gramsci's ideas as an element of Gorbachëv's' 'New [Leninist] Thinking' was further confirmed in the Soviet literature towards the end of the domestic *'perestroika'* period. Thus the June 1990 issue of *'Sputnik'*, published by Novosti in Moscow, stated that 'modern world [*sic*] culture is inconceivable without a consideration of the contributions made by influential Western Marxist philosophers G Lukacs [and] A Gramsci...'.

'The Perestroika Deception' reveals how the largely unseen Soviet collective leadership, borrowing the mind-control ideas of Gramsci, implemented their long-prepared shift from Lenin's 'dictatorship of the proletariat' to his 'state of the whole people', the primary characteristic of which is a theatrical display of 'democratism' designed to convince the West that a decisive 'Break with the Past' has taken place, in order to encourage Western Governments to abandon caution and to embark upon an open-ended programme of collaboration with the 'former' Soviet Bloc. Implicit in such collaboration is the threat of a 'return to the Cold War' – or worse – if the West does not cooperate. The equation can be summed up as 'cooperation-blackmail'.

In the 1960s, the strategists had established specialist Institutes under the control of the USSR Academy of Sciences. These were instructed to study Western attitudes and to inform the leadership of likely Western reactions to given tactical manoeuvres or scenarios. As the strategists had anticipated as a result of these studies, the West was caught off guard and enticed by the 'Break with the Past'. Indeed it was enthusiastic since, as Anatoliy Golitsyn explains, a deception, to be successful, must match the known aspirations of the target as closely as possible. Thus the West interpreted the cosmetic changes as a deepening of the process of Soviet 'reform', offering fresh opportunities for policy and trade. In reality the West faced an 'acceleration in the unfolding of Soviet convergence strategy which is intended to procure the subservience of the West to Moscow under an ultimate Communist World Government'.

Like the works of Sun Tzu, Machiavelli and Clausewitz, this work is devoted to explaining *strategy*. Unlike the works of those classic authors, however, *'The Perestroika Deception'* deals with the contemporary world, explaining how Russia and China adopted the attitudes and ideas of these thinkers and have applied them globally for a generation. They seek the irreversible 'restructuring' of Western thinking, responses and society itself, as their price for 'no war' and for 'changes' which the West has accepted as genuine, and liable to lead to the normalisation of 'post'-Communist society accompanied by the abandonment of revolutionary objectives.

'The Perestroika Deception' is unique in the literature on the Communist and 'former' Communist states in that it addresses the unbroken continuity and implementation of the 'convergence' strategy, a grand overall design – or what the Soviet Leninists call 'the general line' – since it was decided upon in 1958-60. As the Author explains on page 51, 'the general line' – which is flexible as to timing, contains a variety of options and takes full account of risks and possible losses – guides the course of the Party's actions over a period of twenty to thirty years in pursuit of its unchanging Communist objectives. 'The feature of *strategy* which distinguishes it from *policy* is that it *contains within itself a secret, concealed or deceptive manoeuvre*, designed to take the adversary by surprise and thus secure victory for the strategy'. 'One can', as Arbatov

explains in 'The System', 'trace most clearly a direct continuity between the ideas of the Twentieth Party Congress, *détente*, and the New Political Thinking'. Indeed, one can; and for the elimination of all doubt, further confirmation of 'post'-Communist adherence to the strategy of deceptive 'convergence' with the West has been helpfully provided by Viktor Chernomyrdin. Speaking on the *'Russia'* TV Channel [Moscow, 2030 GMT, 15 December 1992], the newly appointed Russian Premier reaffirmed 'the general line', asserting the inherent flexibility of the strategy without, of course, revealing its content: 'My colleagues in the Government who are working today will pursue this line. *The planned line. The one which has been worked out...* Life makes amendments to our programme, additions, perhaps, changes. *But we will keep to the basic line'*.

Behind the impressive smokescreen of pseudo-democracy, pseudo-capitalism and pseudo-reform, this Russian-Chinese 'cooperation-blackmail' strategy is irreconcilably hostile to the West. Again, this is no mere presumption. It was explicitly confirmed in May 1994 to Clark Bowers, a member of an official US Republican delegation to Peking, by Mr Mo Xiusong, Vice Chairman of the Chinese Communist Party, who is believed to be the highest-ranking Chinese Communist official ever to have answered questions put to him by a knowledgeable Western expert on Communism:

BOWERS: *Is the long-term aim of the Chinese Communist Party still world Communism?*

MO XIUSONG: **Yes, of course. That is the reason we exist.**

Illuminating the cooperation-blackmail 'convergence' strategy with his first-hand experience of the origination of the strategy and his knowledge of how Moscow applies the dialectical political method of Marx, Hegel and Lenin in practice, Golitsyn challenges the fashionable, and increasingly laughable, Western assumptions that the West 'won the Cold War', that the enemy 'disappeared', that 'Communism is dead', that the Soviet Union 'collapsed' and that Russia has embarked upon 'progress towards democracy' (never actually reaching it) – patiently showing that because the West fell for the *'perestroika'* deception, it has failed to connect its present malaise to the impact of Soviet-Chinese strategy, and is unable to see the threat arising from the hostile Sino-Russian axis to which countries like North Korea, Iran and Iraq adhere.

In his book *'Wedge: The Secret War between the FBI and CIA'* [Alfred A Knopf, New York, 1994], Mark Riebling pays tribute to the remarkable predictive record of the Author's famous earlier work, *'New Lies for Old'*, crediting Golitsyn with 'an accuracy record of nearly 94%' [page 408]. Because this record validates the 'secret, concealed or deceptive manoeuvre' within the strategy of 'convergence', all manner of attempts have been made to discredit the Author and the late James Jesus Angleton, who understood the significance of his analysis. For instance, Riebling himself observes that 'British journalist Tom Mangold even went so far as to say, in 1990 – *after* Golitsyn's prescience had become clear – that "As a crystal-ball gazer, Golitsyn has been unimpressive". Mangold reached this conclusion by listing six of Golitsyn's apparently incorrect predictions and *ignoring the 139 correct ones'*.

Counting the Author's accurate predictions and awarding him a 94% accuracy rating has certainly been helpful in 'rehabilitating' the Author at a time when the process of achieving control over the Western mindset has reached an advanced stage. But in one sense, this overdue accolade misses the whole point of the Author's work.

For it is not even necessary to enumerate Golitsyn's accurate predictions, to recognise that he is revealing the truth. All that is required is an understanding that the 'general line' provides the necessary dialectical framework without which the otherwise incomprehensible behaviour of the 'post'-Communists cannot be understood. Once the Western observer has grasped the continuity of Leninist strategy, he possesses the key to interpreting and predicting events correctly. Put another way, it will be found that, as a reward for studying the dialectical nature and continuity of the 'general line', the open-minded sceptic becomes potentially capable of achieving a predictive record as impressive as the Author's.

Why, then, is it that, despite Golitsyn's service at the heart of the KGB in Moscow when the strategy was first adopted; despite his proven track record of providing accurate, verifiable information to the West since his arrival at the end of 1961; despite his 94% predictive accuracy rating; and despite his obvious integrity (as I know from my personal experience of editing this work and responding to his patient, constructive and transparently honest criticisms of my own inadequate understanding of the strategy); why is it that his warnings have been overlooked by Western policymakers?

The first main reason for the general (but not in fact complete) rejection of the Author's analysis is that, as the case of Aldrich Hazen Ames has shown, the Russians won the intelligence war through their penetration of Western intelligence services – a message which, naturally, these services do not wish to hear [*see Author's Note 80, page 219*]. In the course of his work with the American, British and French services, the Author found that penetration had destroyed their ability to interpret events in the Communist world correctly. Since 1969, the West has lacked the necessary genuine secret intelligence to expose the deception buried within the strategy, let alone the existence of the long-range Russian-Chinese 'general line' itself; so policymakers have not been provided with the appropriate correctives to fashionable and conventional diplomatic and journalistic perceptions.

A second factor appears to be an extraordinary reluctance among some analysts to study the available documents. Again from personal experience as Editor and Publisher of SOVIET ANALYST, I can confirm that it is possible for even a private student to identify the existence, outline, characteristics, elaborations and continuity of the strategy from sources such as successive issues of the Russian Foreign Ministry's journal *'International Affairs'*, from a study of Soviet and 'post'-Communist official documents and statements in the public domain, and from articles by known agents of influence and implementers of the strategy in the Western press and specialist journals. Is such study too boring or too much like hard work? The strategists are in little doubt that private study can indeed lead to enlightenment. 'The dangers lie', said President Gorbachëv at a press conference with President Mitterrand on 6 May 1991, 'in the fact that someone, analysing at some private moment or other, this or that instance or episode, or even event, including a dramatic event, should not make hasty conclusions and cast doubt on all that has been acquired, and what we have created in putting international relations onto new channels, onto new *rails* [*sic*], entering, as all of us have said, a period of peaceful development'. Note that, in addition to his expression of anxiety that 'someone, analysing at some private moment or other' would indeed succeed in obtaining independent corroboration of the essence of the deception strategy, Gorbachëv *also* predicted here the forthcoming fake 'August coup' ['a dramatic event'] and warned that collaboration with the West meant that only *one* direction was to be permitted in constructing the 'New World Social Order' ['new *rails*']. As a lifelong disciple of Lenin, who taught his followers the creative use of language for deception purposes, Gorbachëv chose his words with characteristic care. He could have said 'new *road*' instead of 'new *rails*'; but a train travelling along a railway line can proceed in only *one* direction – in this context, that intended by the strategists.

A third general reason for the lack of interest in the Author's accurate analysis is the familiar one that the horizons of Western politicians are usually limited to the forthcoming general election. One consequence of this is that they find it hard to understand that Communist and 'former' Communist systems are capable of evolving strategies which remain valid, with *tactical* adjustments, over many decades. Likewise, many Western analysts and observers tend to focus obsessively on the behaviour and fortunes of particular individuals – Gorbachëv, Yeltsin, Kozyrev, Rutskoi, Yavlinski, Shevardnadze, or whoever – as though each was a personally motivated careerist, like Western politicians jockeying for power and influence. This overlooks the fact that all such characters – each of whom emerged from the security services, Komsomol and other controlled structures – are bound together as collaborators in the pursuit of the common strategy. The 'democratism' display is deliberately intended to obscure this.

An exception to the rule was President Pompidou of France. Unlike his towering predecessor, de Gaulle – who was taken in by deception, cancelled France's military commitments to NATO and embraced the Soviet concept of 'Europe from the Atlantic to the Urals' – President Pompidou accepted strategic political disinformation and the influence of Sun Tzu as realities. Unfortunately [*see pages 168, 177 and 181*] he did not survive long enough to make his influence felt in France and elsewhere.

A fourth reason, touched upon earlier, for the shameful neglect of the Author's analysis, is that it is often difficult for an intelligence service to persuade its political masters that they are being deceived. Obviously, it is also contrary to the interests of the services generally to admit that they themselves have been misled.

In the fifth place, it has to be repeated that, over the years, a partially successful diversion campaign has been mounted to discredit both Angleton and Golitsyn. By contrast, no comparable sustained attempt seems to have been made to detract from the work of other prominent defectors – suggesting that the strategists have good reasons for helping the West to continue rejecting Golitsyn's findings, even though he has a predictive record of such distinction that he puts everyone else to shame.

Finally, the Western media routinely publicise the views and interpretations of agents of influence, both journalists and experts, thereby adding successive layers of confusion which blur the perceptions of analysts and especially of politicians – who are usually reluctant to absorb information which does not correspond with their understanding of the current fashion, or of the opinions of their often misinformed colleagues. Politicians confer mainly among themselves, and with officials who feed them the 'accepted line'. It is therefore particularly hard for them to find 'some private moment or other' in which the 'general line' might be revealed and confusion dispelled. This book is intended to assist them, and many others, in that urgent task. ∎

CHRISTOPHER STORY, LONDON, May 1995.

PART ONE

The Perestroika Deception

The world's slide towards
THE 'SECOND OCTOBER REVOLUTION' ['WELTOKTOBER']

ORGANISATION OF THE DOCUMENTS

This book consists, in the main, of Memoranda written by **Anatoliy Golitsyn** and filed with the Central Intelligence Agency [CIA]. The documents are dated, and in order to assist the reader to remain constantly aware of the period when the relevant Memoranda were filed, *the date appears at the top of the right-hand page*. Reference to the date of filing is necessary, from time to time, in order for the context of the Memorandum in question to remain clear in the mind of the reader, and to illuminate the accuracy of the Author's predictions. The Memoranda have been published in the sequence requested by the Author, which is not necessarily the same as the date order. Reasons for this presentation will become apparent as the reader progresses through the work. Notes appear throughout the main text, and on the same page as the note references, rather than at the end of the work. Most notes are labelled according to whether they were added by the Author or by the Editor. ■

ABOUT THE MEMORANDA

Anatoliy Golitsyn's Memoranda to the Central Intelligence Agency reveal that the method he applies in order to interpret and understand Soviet/Russian strategy is impressively reliable. The essence and purpose of intelligence is to provide governments with accurate *advance information* on developments – not to provide *retrospective evaluations* of events which were *not anticipated*. By reference to the date or period when Golitsyn's Memoranda were filed with the CIA, the reader is provided with irrefutable proof of the reliability of the Author's system of analysis, yielding inspired predictions grounded in his familiarity with, and understanding of, the Leninist dialectical political method. The proven accuracy of his forecasts flows precisely from Golitsyn's recognition of the fact that the 'former' Communists continue to apply this method. Thus, in order to comprehend developments in the so-called 'former' Soviet Bloc, in China and concerning the intended 'New World Social Order' which the 'former' Communists are secretly collaborating to establish, Western analysts must follow Gorbachëv's example and 'go back to Lenin'. Re-reading Lenin, or at least taking the trouble to be informed about Lenin's use of the dialectic of Hegel and Marx, is an essential prerequisite for making sense of the world in which we live – not, of course, in order to re-evaluate events through Lenin's evil eyes, but in order to understand that the West is still having to deal with Lenin's successors, who continue to apply his method. The West's continuing failure to recognise this reality, which stems from its acceptance of the false 'Break with the Past' as genuine, threatens the very continuation of Western civilisation. As the Author explained in *'New Lies for Old'* [page 43], 'to be credible and effective, a deception should accord as far as possible with the hopes and expectations of those it is intended to deceive'.

Certain experts and parties in the West will approach this work from the basis of partial knowledge of the Author's involvement with Western intelligence communities. They would find it more illuminating to set aside any preconceived ideas they may hold about Golitsyn, and to allow the Author to speak for himself through this profound work. An essential prerequisite for understanding Soviet strategy is to see it in the context of the fact that 'New Thinking' means 'New *Leninist* Thinking'. ■

Memorandum to the CIA: MARCH 1989

PREDICTING, UNDERSTANDING AND DEALING WITH 'PERESTROIKA'

[Written in the light of President Reagan's switch from denunciation of the 'Evil Empire' to acceptance of 'perestroika' or 'restructuring' and at a time when a reassessment of 'perestroika' was being conducted in the early months of the new administration of President George Bush].

PREDICTIONS OF 'PERESTROIKA' IN 'NEW LIES FOR OLD'

Many aspects of 'perestroika' were predicted in 'New Lies for Old' [1984].
For instance [*page references refer to editions cited on page ii*]:

Pages 327-328: • The Communist strategists are now poised to enter into the final, offensive phase of the long-range policy, entailing a joint struggle for the complete triumph of Communism. Given the multiplicity of parties in power, the close links between them, and the opportunities they have had to broaden their bases and build up experienced cadres, the Communist strategists are equipped, in pursuing their policy, to engage in manoeuvres and stratagems beyond the imagination of Marx or the practical reach of Lenin and unthinkable to Stalin. Among such… stratagems are the introduction of false liberalisation in Eastern Europe and, probably, in the Soviet Union and the exhibition of spurious independence on the part of the régimes in Romania, Czechoslovakia and Poland •.

Pages 224-226: • It would be worthwhile for the West to study the scenario and techniques of the Czechoslovak experiment [of 1968] – so as not to be taken in again. The scenario could well be repeated in essence, although with local variations … The staging of the "quiet revolution" and its reversal served a wide variety of strategic and tactical objectives. [Among them:]
○ To arouse sentiment against military pacts in Europe.
○ To increase pressure in the West for the convening of a conference on security in Europe, the Communist interest in which is to promote the dissolution of military pacts, the creation of a neutral, socialist Europe, and the withdrawal of the American military presence.
○ To rehearse and gain experience for the repetition of "democratisation" in Czechoslovakia, the Soviet Union, or elsewhere in Eastern Europe during the final phase of the long-range policy of the Bloc •.

Pages 241-242: • The creation of a false, controlled opposition movement like the dissident movement serves internal and external strategic purposes.
Internally it provides a vehicle for the eventual false "liberalisation" of a Communist régime; it provokes some would-be opposition elements to expose themselves to counter-action, and others are driven to conformity or despair. Externally, "dissidents" can act as vehicles for a variety of disinformation themes on the subject of the evolution of the Communist system… It sets the scene for an eventual dramatic "liberalisation" of the system by heightening the contrast between neo-Stal-

inism and future "socialism with a human face." It creates a cadre of figures who are well known in the West and who can be used in the future as the leaders and supporters of a "multi-Party system" under Communism. "Dissident" trade unions and intellectuals can be used to promote solidarity with their Western counterparts and engage them in joint campaigns for disarmament and the reform of Western "military-industrial complexes". In the long run the Western individuals and groups involved will face the choice of admitting that their support for dissidents was mistaken or accepting that Communism has undergone a radical change, making "convergence" an acceptable, and perhaps desirable, prospect[9].

Page 262: [6] One of the objectives [of Euro-Communism] was to prepare the ground, in coordination with Bloc policy in general, for an eventual "liberalisation" in the Soviet Union and Eastern Europe and a major drive to promote the dissolution of NATO and the Warsaw Pact and the withdrawal of the American military presence from a neutral, socialist Europe[9].

Page 323: [6] The Western strategy of a mildly activist approach to Eastern Europe, with emphasis on human rights, is doomed to failure because it is based on misconceptions and will lead ultimately into a trap when a further spurious liberalisation takes place in Eastern Europe in the final phase of the long-range Communist policy. Not the least disturbing aspect of the present crisis in Western assessments and policy is that, if it is recognised at all, its causes are misunderstood. As matters stand the West is acutely vulnerable to the coming major shift in Communist tactics in the final phase of their policy[9].

Page 331: [6] The conclusion [is that] the "renewal" in Poland was planned thoroughly, and well in advance, by the Polish Communist Party in cooperation with its Communist allies and with a view to furthering the Communist strategy for Europe. The conclusion is further supported by the evidence of the Polish Communist Party's involvement in the formation and functioning of Solidarity[9].

Page 334: [6] The creation of Solidarity and the initial period of its activity as a trade union may be regarded as the experimental first phase of the Polish "renewal". The appointment of Jaruzelski, the imposition of martial law, and the suspension of Solidarity represent the second phase, intended to bring the movement under firm control and to provide a period of political consolidation. In the third phase it may be expected that a coalition government will be formed, comprising representatives of the Communist Party, of a revived Solidarity movement, and of the church. A few so-called liberals might also be included. A new-style government of this sort in Eastern Europe would be well equipped to promote Communist strategy by campaigning for disarmament, for nuclear-free zones in Europe, perhaps for a revival of the Rapacki Plan, for the simultaneous dissolution of NATO and the Warsaw Pact, and ultimately for the establishment of a neutral, socialist Europe. The revival of other elements of Communist strategy for Europe [such as human rights negotiations] would be timed to coincide with the emergence of such a government[9].

Page 335: ◆ A coalition government in Poland would in fact be totalitarianism under a new, deceptive and more dangerous guise. Accepted as the spontaneous emergence of a new form of multi-Party, semi-democratic régime, it would serve to undermine resistance to Communism inside and outside the Communist Bloc. The need for massive defence expenditure would increasingly be questioned in the West. New possibilities would arise for splitting Western Europe away from the United States, of neutralising Germany, and destroying NATO ◆.

Pages 338-340: ◆ The intensification of hardline policies and methods in the Soviet Union, exemplified by Sakharov's arrest and the occupation of Afghanistan, presages a switch to "democratisation" following, perhaps, Brezhnev's departure from the political scene... Brezhnev's successor may well appear to be a kind of Soviet Alexander Dubcek. The succession will be important only in a presentational sense.

The reality of collective leadership and the leaders' common commitment to the long-range policy will continue unaffected.... The Brezhnev régime and its neo-Stalinist actions against "dissidents" and in Afghanistan would be condemned as Novotny's régime [in Czechoslovakia] was condemned in 1968.

In the economic field reforms might be expected to bring Soviet practice more into line with Yugoslavia, or even seemingly, with Western socialist models... The Party would be less conspicuous, but would continue to control the economy from behind the scenes as before...

Political "liberalisation" and "democratisation" would follow the general lines of the Czechoslovak rehearsal in 1968. This rehearsal might well have been the kind of political experiment Nikolay Mironov [former head of the Party's Administrative Organs Department] had in mind as early as 1960. The "liberalisation" would be spectacular and impressive. Formal pronouncements might be made about a reduction in the Communist Party's rôle; its monopoly would be apparently curtailed. An ostensible separation of powers between the legislative, the executive, and the judiciary might be introduced. The Supreme Soviet would be given greater apparent power and the president and deputies greater apparent independence.

The posts of President of the Soviet Union and First Secretary of the Party might well be separated. The KGB would be "reformed". Dissidents at home would be amnestied; those in exile abroad would be allowed to return, and some would take up positions of leadership in government. Sakharov might be included in some capacity in government or allowed to teach abroad. The creative arts and cultural and scientific organisations, such as the writers' unions and the Academy of Sciences, would become apparently more independent, as would the trade unions. Political clubs would be opened to non-members of the Communist Party.

Leading dissidents might form one or more alternative political parties. Censorship would be relaxed; controversial books, plays, films, and art would be published, performed and exhibited. Many prominent Soviet performing artists now abroad would return to the Soviet Union and resume their professional careers.

Constitutional amendments would be adopted to guarantee fulfilment of the provisions of the Helsinki agreements and a semblance of compliance would be maintained. There would be greater freedom for Soviet citizens to travel. Western and United Nations observers would be invited to the Soviet Union to witness the reforms in action.

But, as in the Czechoslovak case, the "liberalisation" would be calculated and deceptive in that it would be introduced from above. It would be carried out by the Party through its cells and individual members in government, the Supreme Soviet, the courts, and the electoral machinery and by the KGB through its agents among the intellectuals and scientists... [9].

Pages 340-342: [•] The dissident movement is now being prepared for the most important aspect of its strategic rôle, which will be to persuade the West of the authenticity of Soviet "liberalisation" when it comes. Further high-level defectors, or "official émigrés", may well make their appearance in the West before the switch in policy occurs.

The prediction on Soviet compliance with the Helsinki agreements is based on the fact that it was the Warsaw Pact countries and a Soviet [agent of influence] who initiated and pressed for the [negotiations]...

"Liberalisation" in Eastern Europe would probably involve the return to power in Czechoslovakia of Dubcek and his associates. If it should be extended to East Germany, demolition of the Berlin Wall might even be contemplated...

Western acceptance of the new "liberalisation" as genuine would create favourable conditions for the fulfilment of Communist strategy for the United States, Western Europe, and even, perhaps, Japan... Euro-Communism could be revived. The pressure for united fronts between Communist and socialist parties and trade unions at national and international level would be intensified.

This time, the socialists might finally fall into the trap. United front governments under strong Communist influence might well come to power in France, Italy, and possibly other countries. Elsewhere the fortunes and influence of Communist Parties would be much revived. The bulk of Europe might well turn to left-wing socialism, leaving only a few pockets of conservative resistance.

Pressure could well grow for a solution of the German problem in which some form of confederation between East and West Germany would be combined with neutralisation of the whole and a treaty of friendship with the Soviet Union. France and Italy, under united front governments, would throw in their lot with Germany and the Soviet Union. Britain would be confronted with a choice between a neutral Europe and the United States.

NATO could hardly survive this process. The Czechoslovaks, in contrast with their performance in 1968, might well take the initiative, along with the Romanians and Yugoslavs, in proposing (in the Helsinki context) the dissolution of the Warsaw Pact in return for the dissolution of NATO.

The disappearance of the Warsaw Pact would have little effect on the coordination of the Communist Bloc, but the dissolution of NATO could well mean the departure of American forces from the European continent and a closer European alignment with a "liberalised" Soviet Bloc. Perhaps in the long run, a similar process might affect the relationship between the United States and Japan leading to abrogation of the security pact between them.

The EEC on present lines, even if enlarged, would not be a barrier to the neutralisation of Europe and the withdrawal of American troops...

The efforts by the Yugoslavs and Romanians to create stronger links with the EEC should be seen, not as inimical to Soviet interests, but as the first step in laying the foundations for a merger between the EEC and COMECON. The European Parliament might become an all-European socialist parliament with representation from the Soviet Union and Eastern Europe. "Europe from the Atlantic to the Urals" would turn out to be a neutral, socialist Europe.

The United States, betrayed by her former European allies, would tend to withdraw into fortress America or, with the few remaining conservative countries, including perhaps Japan, would seek an alliance with China as the only counterweight to Soviet power *.

Page 348: • The timing of the release of the Solidarity leader and the news of the appointment of Andropov confirm.... that the "liberalisation" will not be limited to the USSR, but will be expanded to Eastern Europe and particularly to Poland. The experiment with "renewal" in Poland will be repeated again.

This time, however, it will be with full strategic initiatives and implications against Western Europe and NATO. The appointment of Andropov, the release of the Solidarity leader, and the invitation to the Pope to visit Poland in June 1983, made by the Polish government, all indicate that the Communist strategists are probably planning the re-emergence of Solidarity and the creation of a quasi-social democratic government in Poland (a coalition of the Communist Party, the trade unions, and the churches) and political and economic reforms in the USSR for 1984 and afterward *.

Pages 349-350: • How will the Western German social democrats respond when the Communist régimes begin their "liberalisation" by making concessions on human rights, such as easing emigration, granting amnesty for the dissidents, or removing the Berlin Wall? One can expect that Soviet agents of influence in Western Europe, drawing on these developments, will become more active.

It is more than likely that these cosmetic steps will be taken as genuine by the West and will trigger a reunification and neutralisation of West Germany and further the collapse of NATO. The pressure on the United States for concessions on disarmament and accommodation with the Soviets will increase.

During this period there might be an extensive display of the fictional struggle for power in the Soviet leadership. One cannot exclude that at the next Party Congress or earlier, Andropov will be replaced by a younger leader with a more liberal image who will continue the so-called "liberalisation" more intensively...

It is not inconceivable that the Soviets will make concessions on Afghanistan in order to gain new strategic advantages *.

dditional predictions on *'perestroika'* in Memoranda to the CIA

, *x*, 1984: **⁶** At this time, the Soviet strategists may replace the old leader, ⋏onstantin Chernenko, who is actually only a figurehead, with a younger Soviet leader who was chosen some time ago as his successor, namely Comrade Gorbachëv. One of his major tasks will be to implement the so-called liberalisation. The strategists may also replace the old 'hardliner' Andrei Gromyko with a younger 'softliner'... The new Soviet leadership may introduce economic reforms and striking political initiatives in order to project a clear message that the changes in the Soviet leadership and in Soviet policy require changes in US leadership, in US military policy and in the US budget. Inasmuch as both conservatives and liberals are confused by strategic disinformation about Soviet strategic intentions, it is possible that these manoeuvres, assisted by Soviet agents of influence, will be successful **⁹**.

July 5, 1985: **⁶** The changes in the Soviet leadership should be seen, not as indicating the consolidation by Gorbachëv of his personal power, but as meeting the requirements of strategy. The appointment of Gromyko as President and of Eduard Shevardnadze as Minister of Foreign Affairs should be viewed as preparation for the coming programme of calculated economic and political reform which has already been described. Shevardnadze was chosen because of his experience as Minister of Internal Affairs in Georgia during the 1970s. His rôle will be to link the strategy of so-called "liberalisation" with the strategies of Europe and disarmament. In all probability, the model for his appointment was Janos Kadar in Hungary. It was Kadar, the Minister of the Interior under the old régime, who launched the so-called liberalisation in Hungary. Gromyko's image as an old Stalinist would have made him unsuitable for the rôle of Minister of Foreign Affairs during "liberalisation". But his promotion to the Presidency is very important. It is a mistake to regard the position of President of the Soviet Union as purely ceremonial. Since the adoption of the present long-range policy in 1960, the Soviet President, then Brezhnev, later Podgorniy, has played an important rôle in the execution of that policy. As a member of the Politburo, Gromyko will provide Gorbachëv with important advice on strategy. As President, he will use his exalted position to give guidance to *Soviet agents of influence among heads of state in Europe and the Third World* **⁹**.

August 1985: **⁶** There are no valid grounds for favourable illusions or for the euphoria in the West over the Gorbachëv appointment and the coming 'liberalisation'. In fact, these developments may present a major challenge and a serious test for the United States' leadership and for the West. The liberalisation will not be spontaneous nor will it be genuine. It will be a calculated liberalisation patterned along the lines of the Czechoslovak 'democratisation' which was rehearsed in 1968. It will be initiated from above and will be guided and controlled by the KGB and the Party apparatus. The 'liberalisation' will include the following elements:

(a) Economic reforms to decentralise the Soviet economy and to introduce profit incentives on the lines of those in Hungary and China. Since Gorbachëv is a Soviet agricultural expert, one can expect a reorganisation of the *kolkhozy* or collective farms into *sovkhozy* or state farms. In fact, Lavrentiy Beria was already planning the liquidation of the *kolkhozy* in 1953.

(b) Religious relaxation along the lines of Iosif Stalin's relaxation during the Second World War. The recent sensational Soviet invitation to the Reverend Billy Graham to preach in Soviet churches indicates that the Soviet strategists have already introduced this element and have not waited for the formal installation of Gorbachëv as Party leader.

(c) Permission for a group of Jewish émigrés to leave the USSR.

(d) Relaxation of travel restrictions to allow Soviet citizens to make visits abroad. This will be done to impress the West with the Soviet government's compliance with the Helsinki agreements.

(e) Some relaxation for Soviet intellectuals and cultural defectors. Soviet writers and producers will be permitted to write books and produce plays on controversial subjects. Cultural defectors, musicians and dancers will be allowed to perform in the USSR and to travel and perform abroad, thus getting the best of both worlds. One can expect that an amnesty will be declared for the so-called dissidents.

(f) Some reduction in the military budget and the transfer of some military funds to improve the state of the economy [•].

[•] If presented and advertised by the innocent and uninitiated media as a major radical change in the Communist system, the "liberalisation" will allow the Communist leaders immediately to regain the political initiative and to revive the political and diplomatic *détente* which was so disastrous for the West and so beneficial to the Communists in the past. The charismatic personality of Gorbachëv may play an important rôle in the over-reaction of the Western media [•].

[•] The Soviet "liberalisation" is a major part of the strategy of the whole Communist Bloc, and particularly of Poland and East Germany, against the West. The main objective is to launch a political offensive against the United States and NATO and to develop a military *détente* in Europe by changing the political and military situation. This strategy is designed to accomplish the following:

(a) To bring about a "German Confederation" of East and West Germany and withdrawal from both the Warsaw Pact and NATO.

(b) To break up NATO and force a United States withdrawal from Europe [•].

[•] One can expect that, in order to accomplish their objectives, a similar "liberalisation" will be introduced in Poland and East Germany.

Presented and advertised as a new reality in Europe, the Soviet, Polish and East German "liberalisation" will have a stunning and mesmerising effect on both West Europeans and Americans. The resulting confusion will be exploited by the Soviet, Polish and East German leaders through their activist diplomacy especially towards West Germany. Czechoslovak, Hungarian and Romanian leaders may actively contribute to this strategy… [•].

• The "liberalisation" in the USSR, Poland and East Germany may set off a chain reaction in the West and inflict irreparable damage particularly on the NATO countries and the US military posture unless its true nature and rôle in Communist strategy are realised.

The "liberalisation" and its strategic manipulations, combined with overt and covert Communist operations, will also present problems for the leadership of the West. It will be aimed at confusing the Western leaders, splitting the West European allies from the United States and then splitting the people from their elected leaders. The leaders who are taken in by the "liberalisation" can be expected to make erroneous and costly decisions, albeit unwittingly, in the interests of the Communists •.

Winter 1986: • The essence of the strategy is to introduce a calculated and controlled false democratisation and to revive a discredited régime by giving it an attractive aspect and a "human face". Its strategic objective is to generate support, good will and sympathy in the West and to exploit this sympathy in order to shape new attitudes and new political realities which will favour Soviet interests. Another objective is to undercut and isolate traditional political parties and their leaders, particularly the conservatives and the realists in the West. A further objective is to shape new attitudes towards the Strategic Defence Initiative, the budget and the US military and to disarm the United States, basing these new attitudes on the premise that "the new régime which has emerged in the USSR is liberal and no longer poses any threat to the United States". Given the surprise aspect of the Soviet strategy, it may succeed. The possible implications of a failure to understand the essence of this strategy would be damaging to both the United States and Western Europe. The Americans, the West Europeans, their leaders and their military strategists would be influenced and misled by these developments all to the detriment of the national interests of the democracies. The probable impact on the West of such a Soviet revival would be equal to or greater than that of the October Revolution.

The impact would in fact be greater and deeper because it would not be alarming but disarming for the West. The revival would become a significant influence in the political life of the United States and Western Europe. The revival might have a disproportionate influence on the attitudes of the democracies towards their military strategy, the NATO alliance and the Strategic Defence Initiative, all to the detriment of their national interests. It might eventually lead to the realisation of **the final goal of Soviet strategy, namely the convergence of the capitalist West with the Communist East on Soviet terms and the creation of a World Government as a solution to the arms race and nuclear confrontation** •.

March 1987: • The USSR, China, Poland and probably East Germany are now in a position to launch a political and diplomatic offensive against the West to shatter its structure and its foundation... The next strategic moves will include: **(a)** Mass Jewish emigration intended to swing Western public opinion towards acceptance of "democratisation" as genuine; **(b)** The revival of "liberalisation" in Poland and the introduction of economic reforms there; **(c)** New initiatives around the time of the Pope's visit to the USSR; **(d)** *An initiative leading towards German federation* •.

CORRECT PREDICTIONS BASED ON THE NEW METHOD OF ANALYSIS

The great majority of the predictions both in *'New Lies for Old'* and in my subsequent Memoranda to the CIA have proved accurate both in substance and in detail. The question arises: **why were these predictions correct and why did Western experts fail to predict these developments?** The answer lies in the different methods of analysis. The new method takes into account the adoption by the leaders of the Communist Bloc in the period 1958 to 1960 of **a long-range strategy** of which *'perestroika'* is the logical culmination.

The new method incorporates the following elements:

(a) The Author's inside information on the adoption of the strategy, the essence of which was the revitalisation of Communism through the economic and political reform of the earlier repressive Stalinist system.

(b) The Author's inside information on Shelepin's 1959 report allotting the KGB a crucial rôle in the new strategy, in particular the task of **creating a controlled political opposition** which would give the Soviet and other Communist régimes a more liberal image.

(c) The Author's inside information that the Party and the KGB launched a programme of strategic disinformation to support their strategy.

(d) The Author's twenty-eight years of experience in interpreting developments in the Communist world in the light of this knowledge.

(e) Study of the official documents of the 1958-60 period in which the long-range policy was openly expressed and approved.

In addition to predictions on forthcoming 'liberalisation' in the Soviet Union, *'New Lies for Old'* contained a critique of Western methods of analysis and an account of the new method. It is worth mentioning that the late Sir John Rennie, at that time head of the British Secret Service, read the whole of the chapter on this subject in New York in 1968 and expressed the opinion that it should be published. He offered to help in arranging this through his friendship with Mr Armstrong, then editor of *'Foreign Affairs'*. The Author acknowledges that he mistakenly declined this offer. When *'New Lies for Old'* was published in 1984, its message did not attract the attention of the American media and public.

Only the late Mr James Angleton and his colleagues in the 'Intelligence and Security Foundation' realised the importance of the book as the basis for understanding *'perestroika'* and devoted three special reports to a review of the main ideas in the book on long-range strategy. In subsequent Memoranda to the CIA, the Author emphasised that *'perestroika'* is not Gorbachëv's invention but the logical culmination of the long-range strategy of 1958-60.

The new method applies 'creative Leninist thinking' to the analysis of Soviet strategy. Leninist thinking, freed from Stalinist dogma and stereotypes, continues to be a principal source of inspiration in the Soviet strategic approach to national and international problems. The new method augments Leninist thinking by taking three further factors into account in its analysis: Vladimir Lenin's introduction of a limited form of capitalism into the Soviet system in the 1920s in order to strengthen the drive for world Communist revolution; Felix Dzerzhinskiy's creation of GPU[1]-controlled 'political opposition' in the USSR in the same period and its introduction to Western intelligence services and general staffs for strategic political deception purposes; and the thirty years of Soviet experience in applying the strategy culminating in *'perestroika'*.

THE ADOPTION OF THE LONG-RANGE STRATEGY OF *'PERESTROIKA'*

It was not in 1985 but in *1958* that the Communist leaders recognised, after the Hungarian and Polish revolts, that the Stalinist practice of mass repression had severely damaged the system and that radical measures were necessary to restore it. It was *then* that they decided to transform the Stalinist system into a more attractive form of 'Communist democracy'.

It was not in 1985 but in *1958* that the Communist leaders accepted that their economic system was ineffective and lagging behind the West in productivity. It was *then* that they decided that it would have to be revived through the introduction of market incentives.

It was *then* that the Communist leaders realised that Communism could not be spread abroad against a background of fear and mass repression and that world Communist victory could only be achieved by transforming the Soviet and other Communist régimes into a form more attractive to the West.

It was during 1958-60 that the Communist leaders envisaged the convergence of restructured and transformed capitalist systems leading ultimately to one system of World Government. Taking account of the military strength of NATO, the Communist leaders decided to build up their military strength as a guarantee of the success of their programme of domestic 'reform' and as a pressure weapon for disarmament negotiations with the West and the execution of their strategy of convergence.

Accepting the necessity for stability in the political leadership of the USSR for the execution of the long-range strategy, the Soviet leaders rejected Stalin's practice of eliminating his rivals and reverted to Lenin's style of leadership. They solved the problem through the selection by the Central Committee of Nikita Khrushchev's successor in advance of Khrushchev's own retirement. Leonid Brezhnev had already been chosen in this way in July 1960 when he was made President and was given a special briefing by the Chairman of the KGB in preparation for the new responsibilities he would be assuming when Khrushchev stepped down.

A common commitment to the long-range strategy itself became a factor in the prevention of further power struggles. Western experts failed to understand this because Khrushchev's retirement was deliberately misrepresented by the Soviet leaders to the West as his dismissal.

In this and in other ways, the origin of the long-range deception strategy of *'perestroika'* was successfully concealed.

---

1 *Editor's Note:* GPU = State Political Directorate – the first 'label change' of the 'Cheka', which was given this new identity with the reorganisation of February 1922.

SOVIET RESEARCH AND PREPARATION FOR THE STRATEGY

Under the guidance of the Party apparatus, special research studies were initiated and carried out from September 1957 onwards by the Soviet Academy of Sciences in preparation for the strategy. The Party apparatus and its 'think-tanks' – the Higher Party School and the Academy of Social Sciences – employed the results of this research in seeking scientific and theoretical solutions to the primary domestic problems associated with the strategy. It was these 'think-tanks' which developed the scenarios for Soviet reforms and trained Soviet and Bloc Party leaders, such as Dubcek, in the spirit and demands of the strategy.

The KGB Institute and its Research Department conducted a number of special studies for the Central Committee. Among them were studies on 'new methods of neutralising political opposition in the USSR', and 'disclosure of state secrets in the interest of strategy' which has an obvious connection with the present 'openness' or *'glasnost'* – one feature of which is the disclosure of quantities of accurate information together with disinformation.

Special studies of the economies and international relations of the leading capitalist countries were conducted by the Institute of World Economy and International Relations. The Institute paid close attention to the European Common Market and to clashes of economic interest between the United States, Western Europe and Japan. The appointment of the Director of this Institute as a chief economic adviser to Gorbachëv can be explained by the contribution made by the Institute to the strategy.

A special research organ, the Institute for the Study of the USA and Canada, was set up in 1960 in Moscow to meet the demands of the strategy. For almost the whole period of the strategy, the Institute, led by Academician Georgiy Arbatov, has studied in depth every major political, social, cultural and racial problem in the United States. The Institute keeps a close watch on the workings of the Executive, Congress, the press, political parties and the more important religious organisations.

Arbatov and his subordinates have established close relations with the American élite, cultivating many leading politicians, scientists, religious leaders, experts in Soviet affairs, journalists and cultural figures through meetings in Washington and invitations to visit the Soviet Union.

Soviet-American student exchanges have been used to study the workings of American institutions and to train Soviet experts in areas which have a bearing on the execution of the strategy. For instance, Aleksandr Yakovlev, Gorbachëv's key adviser on international policy and the promotion of *'perestroika'* in the American media, studied the media at Columbia University on an exchange programme.

The Soviet Embassy in Washington has played a special rôle in studying the inner workings of American policy formulation and providing advice to Soviet strategists. A significant novelty was introduced into the work of the Soviet ambassador to the United States. In the interests of the strategy, Ambassador Anatoliy Dobrynin was made Chief KGB *Rezident* in Washington in order that the diplomatic work of the Embassy could be fully coordinated with the exploitation of the assets of the KGB *Rezidentura*, especially its important agents of influence among politicians, businessmen, scientists and Western journalists.

The Author prepared a special Memorandum on Anatoliy Dobrynin for the

CIA which confirmed Dobrynin's use of KGB agents along strategic lines. The late Mr James Angleton concluded that the Memorandum should be published in declassified form in order to neutralise Dobrynin's political influence in Washington and have him expelled for interference in the internal affairs of the United States. **The findings of the Memorandum were, however, disregarded after the Watergate hearings which destabilised the American intelligence and counter-intelligence services.**

THE KGB'S ROLE IN THE PREPARATION OF 'PERESTROIKA'

In accordance with a Party decision, the KGB was assigned a key rôle in the execution of the strategy. In 1959 the KGB under Aleksandr Shelepin was instructed to employ its intelligence and security assets, not for mass repression, but in the interests of strategy against the main enemy. Its main task became the neutralisation and dissolution of *genuine* political opposition by nationalists and anti-Soviet intellectuals. The KGB was ordered to create controlled political opposition and to introduce it to Western intelligence services along the lines of Dzerzhinskiy's 'Trust'. As this Author revealed in the early 1960s, the KGB began the creation of a controlled 'dissident movement' with a skilful, controlled dispute between 'liberal' writers, like Aleksandr Tvardovskiy, Yevgeniy Yevtushenko and Nikolay Voznesenskiy, and 'conservatives' like Vsevolod Kochetov. The KGB recruited and developed important agents of influence 'allied' with the 'dissidents' among leading Soviet scientists like Andrei Sakharov and Petr Kapitsa. It was no accident that modern 'dissident' prisoners at this time were allowed by the KGB to become visible and famous and to be monitored by human rights groups in the West unlike the totally isolated and unheard of inmates of Stalin's prisons who simply perished without trace. It is important to note that famous 'dissidents' achieved a high public profile *before* the advent of '*glasnost*', or 'openness'. The task of agents of influence like the late Andrei Sakharov is not a propaganda one; it is to act as assistants in the execution of the strategy of Soviet reform and convergence with the West.

The KGB further recruited a number of theatre and movie directors, writers and journalists and unofficially encouraged them to experiment with formerly taboo and controversial subjects like repression, prison life, rehabilitation and questions of conscience and religion. The object of these experiments was to prepare these chosen individuals for the rôle of initiators and catalysts in the forthcoming controlled 'liberalisation' of the régime.

The KGB reoriented its old agents among Soviet religious leaders – the KGB's Gapons[2] – and used their influence to help convergence with the Western churches. The KGB benefited from the experience of exploiting religious leaders under Stalin in the Second World War, and in the 1960s they employed that experience on a larger scale and with greater sophistication.

The KGB, the Party, the press and even the courts have been used for the calculated public exposure of 'dissidents' and their activities in the West as 'examples' for the education and re-education of Western anti-Soviet intellectuals.

On the initiative of the KGB, an army of Soviet vigilantes five million strong,

2 *Author's Note:* Father Gapon was a senior priest in Tsarist Russia. He operated as a police agent and was used by the police against the workers' movement.

the so-called *'druzhiny'*, was recruited from among the Komsomol activists. Their units were led by retired Chekists[3]. They have been patrolling and policing the streets of all the Soviet cities. Their primary task has been to prepare the Soviet people to 'behave' during the forthcoming 'liberalisation'.

Soviet psychiatry and the incarceration of active anti-Communists in psychiatric hospitals have been used to 'educate' and intimidate the population into further submission to the régime by 'demonstrating' that only the mentally abnormal protest against it. The Party has also used *détente* with the West as a weapon against Soviet anti-Communists, arguing that anti-Communism in the USSR is hopeless because even the West accepts the Soviet system.

The Communist press obtained maximum mileage from the American failure to help the Czechoslovaks when their Party-controlled 'democratisation' in fact ran out of control in 1968. This had a sobering effect on genuine anti-Communists in the USSR and Eastern Europe. Furthermore, for the purpose of dissolving genuine opposition, the KGB facilitated the selective emigration of individuals who were hostile to the system or who wished to join relatives abroad.

All these KGB and Party methods, together with the natural ageing and death of Stalin's former victims, resulted in the disappearance of active anti-Communists and the general acceptance of the régime by the Soviet population. *By the 1980s, there were no social democrats or politically active nationalists left alive in the USSR.* By then, the KGB and the Party apparatus had succeeded in creating conditions in which *only they could form strong grassroots organisations.*

The KGB and the Party conducted their preparations for *'perestroika'* in close cooperation with the parties and security services of the other Communist countries. The successful preparation for *'perestroika'* by the KGB and the Ministries of the Interior of the Georgian and other national Republics of the USSR explains the promotion of their heads – Aleksandr Shelepin, Yuriy Andropov, Gaidar Aliyev, Eduard Shevardnadze, Viktor Chebrikov and Andrei Vlasov – to the Politburo and other key strategic positions.

EXPERIMENTS AND REHEARSALS FOR *'PERESTROIKA'*

Since 1959 the Communist Bloc Parties and governments have been involved in practical experiments and rehearsals for separate elements of *'perestroika'* in different countries in preparation for its introduction overall.

The most important of these experiments and rehearsals were:

○ An attempt at 'liberalisation' in the early 1960s under Khrushchev.

○ Publication of an article about market economics by Professor Yevsei Liberman and experiments with firms and 'trusts' in 1962.

○ Alexei Kosygin's economic reforms in 1965.

○ Alleged 'Romanian independence' from the early 1960s onwards.

○ The 'Cultural Revolution' in China – in fact a campaign of ideological and political re-education and a preparation of the inexperienced and inept Chinese Party bureaucracy for *détente* with the capitalist West.

○ 'Democratisation' in Czechoslovakia in 1968.

3 *Author's Note:* Named after the 'Cheka', the original, infamous Soviet security service.

○ Legalisation by the Polish Communist Party of Solidarity in 1980.

○ The introduction of capitalist incentives in China and Hungary during the 1970s and the 1980s.

The Soviet strategists studied the performance, outcome, lessons and mistakes of these experiments and rehearsals. No doubt, they drew proper, practical conclusions from the excesses of the 'Cultural Revolution' in China and the loss of control over the experiments with 'democratisation' in Czechoslovakia and Solidarity in Poland. They probably also drew conclusions from the painful experiences of Yugoslavia. The experience gained was of enormous benefit for influencing the introduction of *'perestroika'* in all its elements in their totality in the USSR.

The development and execution of the strategy over a thirty-year period has strengthened Soviet power militarily, politically and, with Western help, economically. The Author strongly disagrees with Brzezinski's[4] assessment that the USSR is collapsing. The execution of the strategy has broadened the political base of the Communist Party in the Russian and the other national Republics.

Careful preparation has created the conditions for overall *'perestroika'* and the transition of the régime in the most powerful and experienced of the socialist countries to a phase of 'Communist democracy'.

Naturally, the Soviet leaders seek to avoid alerting the West to what is happening by describing the process in these terms.

From the time the strategy was adopted, *the Party leadership made it clear to its technocrats, bureaucrats, military and intellectuals that the requirements of the strategy are paramount for their activities and the assessment of their performance.* Because of these demands and Party discipline, there can be no genuine opposition among conservatives in the Party, the military or the technocracy.

Bold experiments and successful execution of the strategy in the USSR, Eastern Europe and Communist China have given Party leaders, KGB officials, generals, technocrats and leading intellectuals a political maturity and sophistication which they have revealed in *'perestroika'*.

Because of their longer historical experience, their greater political, economic and military potential and their *thorough preparation*, the Communist strategists and the ruling élite are confident that they can guide and lead their people without the loss of control which occurred in Czechoslovakia in 1968 and in Poland (1981). However, in the event of control nonetheless being endangered in given contexts, the situation will be retrieved in the usual manner – by means of military repression.

---

4 *Author's Note:* Zbigniew Brzezinski, a leading American expert on Communism and National Security Adviser during the Carter Administration.

'*PERESTROIKA*', THE FINAL PHASE: ITS MAIN OBJECTIVES

The new method sees '*perestroika*', not as a surprising and spontaneous change, but as the logical result of thirty years of preparation and as the next and final phase of the strategy: it sees it in a broader context than Soviet 'openness' has revealed.

It sees it, not only as a renewal of Soviet society, but as a global strategic design for 'restructuring' the entire capitalist world.

The following strategic objectives of '*perestroika*' may be distinguished:

For the USSR

(a) 'Restructuring' and revitalisation of the Soviet socialist economy through the incorporation of some elements of the market economy.

(b) 'Restructuring' of the Stalinist régime into a form of 'Communist democracy' with an *appearance* of political pluralism [= 'democratism'[5]].

(c) 'Reconstructing' a repressive régime with a brutal face into an attractive socialist model with a human façade and a seeming similarity to the Swedish social democratic system.

For Eastern Europe

Economic and political 'restructuring' of the existing régimes into pseudo-social democratic models while preserving specific national historical features such as the strong Catholic Socialist tradition in Poland and the pre-war democratic tradition in Czechoslovakia.

For Western Europe

(a) Bringing about a new political alliance between the pseudo-social democratic régimes in the USSR and Eastern Europe and the Euro-Communist parties and genuine social democratic parties in Western Europe.

(b) 'Restructuring' political and military Blocs – NATO and the Warsaw Pact – and the creation of a single 'Europe from the Atlantic to the Urals' incorporating a reunited, neutral Germany[6].

For the main US alliances

(a) Splitting the United States, Western Europe and Japan.

(b) Dissolution of NATO and the US-Japan security pact, and the withdrawal of US troops from Western Europe and Japan.

For Third World countries

The introduction and promotion of a new Soviet model with a mixed economy and a human face in Latin America, Africa and Asia through a joint campaign by the pseudo-social democrat régimes of the USSR and Eastern Europe and the genuine social democrats of Western Europe led by the Socialist International.

5 *Editor's Note:* The Soviets characterise their false democracy as 'democratism' – which can be defined as the creation and maintenance of the illusion of Western-style democracy.
6 *Editor's Note:* In the course of his Nobel Peace Prize Lecture [given in Oslo, June 1992], Gorbachëv

[Note 6 continued on page 18:]

For the United States

(a) To neutralise the influence of the anti-Communist political right in the American political parties and to create favourable conditions for a victory of the radical left in the 1992 US presidential elections.

(b) To 'restructure' the American military, political, economic and social *status quo* to accommodate greater **convergence** between the Soviet and American systems and the eventual creation of a single World Government'.

The paramount global objective

The paramount global objective of the strategy of '*perestroika*' is to weaken and neutralise anti-Communist ideology and the influence of anti-Communists in political life in the United States, Western Europe and elsewhere – presenting them as anachronistic survivors of the Cold War, reactionaries and obstacles to 'restructuring' and peace. Anyone who warns about Moscow's true objectives is automatically branded a 'Cold Warrior', even by people who have doubts about Moscow's motives.

THE ESSENCE OF '*PERESTROIKA*': AN APPLICATION OF 1920S' LENINISM

The new method penetrates the facade, tears the verbal mask off '*perestroika*' and reveals its true meaning– which Gorbachëv and '*glasnost*' have failed to do. Lenin's teaching and the experience of the New Economic Policy [NEP] are keys to understanding the essence of '*perestroika*' and the reasons for Gorbachëv's downgrading and renunciation of elements of ideological orthodoxy like the class struggle and his emphasis on common interests and the benefits of close cooperation.

[**Note 6:** *Continued from page 17*]: explained: 'I dare say that the European process has already acquired elements of irreversibility... Should it now gain the necessary momentum, every nation and every country will have at their disposal in the foreseeable future the potential of a community of unprecedented strength, encompassing the entire upper tier of the globe, provided they make their own contribution. In such a context, in the process of creating a new Europe, in which erstwhile curtains and walls will be forever relegated to the past and borders between states will lose their "divisive" purpose, **self-determination of sovereign nations will be realised in a completely different manner**' [which is to say, in translation from Gorbachëv's Aesopian Lenin-speak, in accordance with the "architecture of control" drawn up in Moscow. Moreover, for the elimination of all doubt about what he meant by the 'enlarged' Europe, Gorbachëv added that 'our [*sic*] vision of the European space from the Atlantic to the Urals is not that of a closed system. **Since it includes the Soviet Union, which reaches to the shores of the Pacific, it goes beyond nominal geographical boundaries**'. Thus the eastern boundary of 'the new Europe' is not in fact to be the Urals, but the Pacific – since the Soviet Union is 'European'. Note, too, that national boundaries are considered by this long-range strategy implementer to be purely 'nominal'.
        Likewise, interviewed on Moscow Television on 19 November 1991, Eduard Shevardnadze explained: 'I think that the idea of a Common European Home, the building of a united Europe, and I would like to underline today, of great Europe, the building of Great Europe, great, united Europe, from the Atlantic to the Urals, from the Atlantic to Vladivostok, including all our territory, most probably a European-Asian space, a united humanitarian space, this project is *inevitable* [*sic*]. I am sure that we will come to building a united military space as well. To say more precisely: we will build a united Europe, whose security will be based on the principles of collective security. Precisely, collective security'. Note both the Leninist note of 'inevitability', and the interchangeability of 'from the Atlantic to the Urals' and 'from the Atlantic to Vladivostok'. Often, 'the Atlantic' becomes 'Vancouver'.
        7 *Editor's Note:* 'Convergence' [*sblizhenie*, a term, meaning 'closing in for contact'] exploits globalist tendencies among Western élites. Their members collaborate with 'ex'-Communists in the common endeavour to establish 'One World', a.k.a. the 'New World Social Order ['World Government'].

Lenin advised the Communists that they must be prepared to **'resort to all sorts of stratagems, manoeuvres, illegal methods, evasions and subterfuge'** to achieve their objectives. This advice was given on the eve of his reintroduction of limited capitalism in Russia in his work *'Left Wing Communism, an Infantile Disorder'.*

The new method sees *'perestroika'* as an application of Lenin's advice in new conditions. Another speech of Lenin's in the NEP period at the Comintern Congress in July 1921 is again highly relevant to understanding *'perestroika'.* 'Our only strategy at present', wrote Lenin, 'is to become stronger and, therefore, wiser, more reasonable, more opportunistic. The more opportunistic, the sooner will you again assemble the masses around you. When we have won over the masses by our reasonable approach, **we shall then apply offensive tactics in the strictest sense of the word'.**

It is obvious that Gorbachëv's opportunistic speeches and his presentation of *'perestroika'* to the West are clever applications of Lenin's thinking. Gorbachëv's reasonableness and moderation are aimed at assembling and winning over the masses throughout the world. And yet another of Lenin's speeches is relevant here. Instructing the Soviet delegation to the Genoa Conference in 1921, he advised them to use moderate language in negotiations in order 'not to frighten the capitalists' and particularly to avoid reference to the class struggle, the violence and the terrorist aspects of Communist doctrine. Gorbachëv's speech to the United Nations and Shevardnadze's pronouncements about a downgrading of the class struggle are classic applications of Lenin's thinking. The new method views the ostensible arguments about the class struggle in the Soviet Union as no more than a calculated device to win over Western policymakers and influence public opinion in favour of Gorbachëv's policies.

The new method also sees a close parallel between Western expectations arising out of the NEP and those arising out of *'perestroika'.* In view of this parallel, the outcome of the NEP can be instructive now. The New Economic Policy was presented by the Soviets and accepted by the West as a retreat from Communist ideology and a decline in the power of the Soviet régime. In fact, the NEP revived the Soviet economy, stabilised Soviet power and facilitated the creation of the Soviet Federation. Because of the NEP, the Soviets were able to broaden their ideological and political assault on the capitalist world.

To sum up, the essence of *'perestroika'* is the creative application of Lenin's thinking and the experience gained through the NEP to the final battle with the capitalist world. It is a step backwards to take two steps forward. *'Perestroika'* is a Leninist strategy involving the calculated renunciation of ideological orthodoxy in order to win over the masses and to achieve strategic objectives in Europe, the United States and the Third World.

The experience of the NEP teaches us that contemporary Soviet pragmatism and opportunism are not lasting, because they are tactical. *Gorbachëv is a committed Leninist who is carrying out the strategy of Communist renewal as a means towards the ultimate conquest of the Western democracies.*

THE CHOICE OF PARTY AND GOVERNMENT LEADERS FOR '*PERESTROIKA*'
The new method and understanding of Soviet strategy provide explanations for the choice of Gorbachëv and other important appointments in the Soviet hierarchy.

Gorbachëv as Party Leader and President

How did it come about that an obscure provincial Party bureaucrat like Gorbachëv[8], who had no political base in the Party other than in Stavropol, and who was not known before his selection as a visionary leader, philosopher or intellect, could emerge suddenly and from nowhere under a totalitarian régime?

Even Mr Kennan (the former US diplomat and leading expert on the Soviet Union) could not provide an answer to this question. The explanation is provided by the long-range strategy and its requirements. The Communist apparatus planned the strategy: they also chose the leaders for its execution.

Since the Party strategists planned '*perestroika*', they realised that it could succeed only if it were carried out by a leader of the new generation, apparently untainted by the stigma of Stalinism and who had undergone proper training. Gorbachëv's appointment did not result from a power struggle: it was a planned selection after deliberate training for the leadership.

There is a parallel between the sudden rise of Gorbachëv and that of Dubcek. Both came from obscurity and both were chosen as Party leaders by co-called 'conservatives'. The rôle of 'conservatives' in the choice shows that the old concept of power struggle is not applicable. The new explanation is that both Dubcek and Gorbachëv were chosen by the Party apparatus to meet the demands of strategy.

There are indications that the selection and training of Gorbachëv were favoured by the late Mikhail Suslov and Yuriy Andropov. Mikhail Gorbachëv received training in law, agriculture and in foreign affairs, which included a visit to England. All these three areas of training corresponded to the requirements of the strategy. Brezhnev's reluctance to vacate his position may have delayed Gorbachëv's installation as the new leader. Mikhail Shatrov, a Soviet writer and an insider in the Party establishment, made an indirect admission that the Central Committee had had difficulty in installing Andropov and Gorbachëv because of opposition from Brezhnev's entourage. Gorbachëv's assumption of the post of President was also required for the execution of the strategy. This explains the swiftness of his confirmation. The notion that an individual leader like Gorbachëv is in sole charge of Soviet strategy is erroneous. The Politburo, the Central Committee, the Party apparatus and the KGB are all charged with its execution: Gorbachëv is only a very able tool of the whole apparatus. The deliberate, advance selection of the Party leader is the apparatus' way of solving the succession problem. The demands of the strategy are *paramount*.

Its requirements have included licensed criticism of Party leaders – including Khrushchev, Brezhnev and now Gorbachëv himself.

8 *Editor's Note:* Gorbachëv was connected with the KGB from his early youth [see Gail Sheehy, '*Gorbatschow*', Munich, 1991; Hans Graf Huyn, '*Die deutsche Karte*', Munich, 1991]. He was never a 'reformer' but rather, always faithful to the Party line, a Stalinist under Stalin and a Brezhnevite under Brezhnev. Selected by Andropov, he rose to become chairman of the Administrative Party Organs, the most powerful position in the system – exercising control over the KGB and the GRU for the Politburo and the CPSU Central Committee [Hans Graf Huyn, privately circulated paper, 1992].

The choice of Ligachev and Yeltsin as critics from right and left

The new method regards the sudden rise of the alleged conservative Ligachev and of the alleged liberal Yeltsin – critics of Gorbachëv and 'perestroika' from right and left – as further deliberate selections by the Party apparatus in the interests of the strategy. Both emerged from political obscurity. Furthermore, Ligachev has no qualifications to be in charge of ideology. He is not another Suslov. The calculated character of their selection is revealed in their public positions on 'perestroika'. One wishes it to be slowed down; the other speeded up. The purpose of their selection, of their alleged disagreements with Gorbachëv and of their dramatic demotion is to give a display of apparent disunity in the Party over 'perestroika', to build up the credibility of 'perestroika' in the West and to support the fiction that there is opposition to Gorbachëv among the conservatives and even among some liberals.

This disinformation is designed to persuade the West of the spontaneity of 'perestroika' in the Soviet Union and to generate Western support for it and for Gorbachëv. The calculated designation of 'conservatives' and 'liberals' in the Party and the alleged disputes between them provide the Party apparatus with opportunities to teach Communists how to introduce and practice 'Communist democracy'.

Shevardnadze as Foreign Minister

Shevardnadze's appointment as Foreign Minister is another instance of a choice of candidate dictated by the needs of the final phase of the strategy. It came as a surprise. A former Minister of the Interior and Party leader of the Georgian Republic suddenly became the successor to Gromyko. What qualification did he have for his new post in charge of Soviet diplomacy? According to the old rationale, none.

The new method, however, sees Shevardnadze's appointment as a key to understanding the strategy behind the current nationalist unrest in Azerbaijan, Georgia, Armenia and the Baltic Republics. The problems of the national Republics, particularly in the Transcaucasian region where Shevardnadze was running internal affairs for more than a decade, are precisely the field wherein lies his expertise.

This made him the candidate best qualified to exploit factors like alleged nationalist unrest in the interests of the strategy of 'perestroika' to influence and provoke genuine nationalism outside the borders of the Soviet Union. The fact that Shevardnadze's appointment was made *before* the nationalist outbursts in the Soviet national Republics supports the view that these outbursts were planned and controlled by the Party apparatus and the KGB for strategic purposes.

Yakovlev as Head of the Foreign Policy Commission

According to the new method, Yakovlev was chosen to be head of the Foreign Policy Commission because of his expertise on the Western and especially the American media acquired during his studies at Columbia University and during a recent tour as Ambassador to Canada. His selection shows that the Soviet strategists realise that Western acceptance of and support for 'perestroika' depend to a large extent on the Western media. Yakovlev's main task is to present, project and sell 'perestroika' to the West as a novel, pragmatic, opportunistic, non-ideological policy which harbours no aggressive, strategic design against the West [see Note 9 page 22].

Chebrikov as Head of the Judicial Commission

Chebrikov's selection as head of the Judicial Commission was logical since the KGB played a crucial rôle in the execution of strategy under the late Andropov and his successor. The Judicial Commission may be expected to review all aspects of the judiciary system under *'perestroika'*. This will include a review and reorganisation of the KGB to help it play its active part in carrying out the strategy of 'restructuring' in the USSR, Eastern Europe, Western Europe and the United States. Chebrikov was well qualified as a Chekist to carry out this reorganisation. His recent removal should further be seen as intended to support the authenticity of the national unrest in Georgia and differences between Gorbachëv and the 'conservatives'.

Kryuchkov as head of the KGB

Kryuchkov's appointment as the new head of the KGB is logical in the light of his closeness to the late Andropov and the depth of his experience in preparing and executing the strategy of *'perestroika'*. Andropov, as Soviet ambassador to Hungary during the 1956 revolt and then as head of the Central Committee's Department for the Communist Bloc Countries, was one of the architects of the long-range strategy.

As head of this department and as head of the KGB from 1967 to 1984, Andropov played a key rôle in the experiments with 'democratisation' in Czechoslovakia in 1968 and with Solidarity in Poland in 1980 and in the preparation of *'perestroika'* in the USSR and Eastern Europe. Kryuchkov was a member of the Andropov circle from the start. He worked as an important assistant to Andropov in the Department for the Communist Bloc Countries from the time of the adoption of the long-range strategy in 1960 until 1967. It was Andropov who took him into the KGB.

As a leading KGB official, he supervised the experiments with 'democratisation' in Czechoslovakia and Poland. His KGB advisers worked closely with the Czechoslovak and Polish security services. As deputy head of the KGB since 1978, Kryuchkov has been intimately engaged in the preparation of *'perestroika'*.

Because of his experience, he is very well qualified to lead the KGB during the final phase of the strategy. His experience of close collaboration with the East European security services and as head of the Soviet intelligence service will be important in the carrying through of *'perestroika'* not only in the USSR but also in Eastern Europe and in the West. Because of his experience with Czechoslovakia and Poland, he will be helpful to the Party apparatus in avoiding similar mistakes and loss of control during *'perestroika'*. He will use his expertise in the active exploitation for strategic purposes of the KGB's security and intelligence assets, particularly its agents of influence among leading Soviet scientists, intellectuals and church leaders and among Western scientists and experts on Soviet affairs and in the Western media.

These KGB assets will be used to generate Western support for *'perestroika'* in the USSR and Eastern Europe and also to prepare a favourable climate for 'restructuring' in, and convergence with, the United States, Europe and the Third World.

9 *Author's Note [see page 21]*: Yakovlev was chosen as Gorbachëv's adviser on the media during the Communist phase of *'perestroika'*. His subsequent re-emergence as head of the national television network and in fact Yeltsin's adviser on the media during the 'democratic' phase of *'perestroika'* illustrates the continuity of the strategy.

Dubinin as Soviet ambassador in Washington

Dubinin's appointment as ambassador in Washington looks strange. He has neither the experience nor the stature of Dobrynin, the previous diplomatic giant of Washington. But it seems that three main considerations determined his selection for this crucial posting:

(a) His experience with the human rights issue as a previous Soviet negotiator in this field. This will have prepared him to exploit the Soviet version of the issue, as against the American version, in order to influence American public opinion in favour of 'perestroika'.

(b) His experience as Ambassador to Spain during the transition from Franco's anti-Communist régime to the present socialist régime which is well-disposed towards the Soviet Union. It may shock some Western experts, but the Soviets see some political similarity between the Spanish and American situations making due allowance for differences of scale. Soviet strategists regard the United States as a reactionary country in which the anti-Communist political and religious right exercises profound influence over the population. Strategists like Arbatov are convinced that removing fear from American minds by projecting the Soviet Union as a peaceful, non-aggressive state can neutralise the influence of anti-Communism and convert the United States into a non-ideological society friendly to the USSR. This in turn will create favourable conditions for 'restructuring' in the context of US and Soviet-American convergence. That makes Dubinin the right man for Washington.

(c) No doubt, Dubinin studied the American élite at Arbatov's Institute in Moscow. The Author concluded from Dubinin's skilful performance during Gorbachëv's visits to the United States and from his meetings with leading Americans that he knows the subject well. He should prove a good salesman for 'perestroika'.

PRESIDENT REAGAN HUGS THE BEAR

President Reagan responded in two ways to the Soviet threat. At first, he revived the American economy and restored American military strength: he described the Soviet Union quite correctly as 'the Evil Empire'. Although unaware of the long-range strategy, he hurt the Soviets with his rhetoric, which threatened their strategic objectives. For his accomplishments in this period, history will treat Mr Reagan kindly.

But subsequently, President Reagan became involved in a new détente with Gorbachëv and went over to support for 'perestroika' without realising its essence and its dangers for the West. In the light of this analysis, President Reagan's embrace of Gorbachëv and his proclaimed closeness to the Soviets was a grave strategic blunder which will have far-reaching and dangerous consequences for the security of America and her allies. It has imparted a misguided direction to the foreign policies of the United States, the European allies and Japan.

It has in fact invited the Soviets to begin their strategy of 'restructuring' in Europe, and especially in Germany. It has given them the opportunity to begin the execution of their strategy in the United States and to engage the American and West European élite, in particular the European social democrats, in close cooperation over 'restructuring'. It has generated enormous euphoria in the West and an eager

24 THE PERESTROIKA DECEPTION

willingness to provide the USSR with credits and technology. West European and Japanese bankers are in frenzied competition with each other, to finance 'restructuring'. West European bankers with encouragement from Hans Dietrich Genscher, the West German Foreign Minister, are already talking of a new Marshall Plan to finance the failing economies of Eastern Europe.

New opportunities have been opened up for the Soviets to undermine and neutralise rational and healthy anti-Communism and the influence of the right in the political life of the Western democracies. President Reagan's closeness to the Soviets has also sent a misleading signal to their adversaries. It allows the Soviet leaders and their Communist Party to strengthen their hold over the Soviet people and to involve them in practical *'perestroika'* in the USSR. Furthermore, it allows them to achieve their main strategic objective of winning over the masses in both the Communist and the capitalist worlds. President Reagan's embrace of Gorbachëv and *'perestroika'* has made it difficult for the new Administration to develop its own policies towards the Soviets by stoking up public expectations and popular pressure for continuing *rapprochement* with the Soviets.

THE SOVIET CAMPAIGN TO ENGAGE THE AMERICAN ÉLITE
The new method detects an active Soviet offensive to reach the American élite and to engage it in close cooperation and 'restructuring' in the United States. This operation is evident, *inter alia*, from the following developments:

1. The meeting between Gorbachëv, his chief American experts (Dobrynin, Ambassador Dubinin, Yakovlev, Arbatov, Pozner[10] and others) and selected members of the American élite present at the Soviet Embassy, during Gorbachëv's first visit to Washington.

2. The consistent and persistent campaign by the Soviet Embassy in Washington to widen its contacts with American businessmen, academics, political, religious and cultural figures in order to exploit the political changes and even the disasters in the Soviet Union, for the purpose of promoting the appearance of irreversible change.

3. The active use by the KGB *Rezidentura* in Washington of known agents of influence in the United States in the interests of the strategy of *'perestroika'*.

4. An increase in the number of Soviet invitations to members of the American élite to visit the USSR and to become involved in some kind of cooperation. The recent joint Soviet-American meeting on missiles in Cuba, was a case in point.

5. The active rôle of Sakharov, the main KGB agent of influence in introducing *'perestroika'* to the United States. Sakharov began these activities in the 1960s. In 1967, he despatched his well known manifesto to the West in which he predicted:

10 *Editor's Note:* Vladimir Pozner is a leading member of a new 'jet-set' of Russian officials who commute between Moscow and the United States. Born in France, he speaks perfect American English having grown up in New York. He returned with his parents to the USSR in 1952, and later became a commentator on Soviet Television. He acquired a reputation as a strong supporter of *'perestroika'* in the early Gorbachëv period. He reappeared in the United States ahead of the 'August coup', and became co-host of the *'Pozner-Donahue Show'*, on which he has offered his comments and interpretations on *'perestroika'*, developments in Russia, socialism, capitalism, and 'life'. According to his own remarks on US television, he commutes regularly between Russia and the United States. Pozner, in short, is a good example of 'convergence' in practice.

(a) The victory of the 'realists', economic reforms and expanding 'democracy' in the USSR [1960-80].

(b) The victory of the left-wing reformers, their attack on the 'forces of racism and militarism' and changes in the structure of ownership in the United States and other capitalist countries [1972-85].

(c) Soviet-American cooperation over disarmament and 'saving' the poorer half of the world (1972-90).

(d) *The restructuring of society and convergence of the Communist and capitalist systems leading to the creation of a (socialist) World Government* [1980-2000].

The predictions disseminated by Sakharov, made when the strategy of *'perestroika'* was already in preparation, represented a deliberate projection of the essence of the strategy to members of the radical Left in the West in order to orientate them on, and prepare them for, forthcoming developments in the USSR. This was a strategic signal by the Soviet strategists to their potential political allies in the West – particularly to their agents of influence and Euro-Communists. In the event, the time-frames laid down by Sakharov proved to have been only marginally 'out'.

Sakharov's predictions *concealed* the fact that restructuring and convergence form the essence of the Soviet long-range strategy with its aggressive intent against Western democracy. What is in fact the development of Soviet strategy in action, is described by Sakharov as a spontaneous process and, in his own typically Leninist words, **'the most optimistic unrolling of events'**. From the mid-1960s to 1980, the KGB under Brezhnev's neo-Stalinist rule allowed Sakharov to conduct his 'criticism' and other activities as leader of, and spokesman for, the 'dissident movement'. It was Sakharov who injected the Soviet view of the human rights issue into the debate by writing to President Carter on the subject. This raises an interesting question. Why was the unreformed KGB so tolerant of Sakharov despite his apparent criticism of Soviet actions? That tolerance is explained in terms of Sakharov's active rôle in the execution of Soviet strategy, operating under cover as a controlled 'dissident'. In 1980, a few years before the advent of Gorbachëv's *'perestroika'*, Sakharov was 'exiled' to Gorky. The 'exile' of Sakharov was a typical KGB device to build up his reputation and influence as a *'dissident'* (as opposed to an *'enemy of the people'*) in the West.

When the unbelievable duly happened and Gorbachëv began the economic 'reforms' and expansion of 'democracy' which Sakharov had predicted, Sakharov was made *chief adviser to Gorbachëv* and a spokesman on *'perestroika'*. He actively promoted it to Western leaders, the media, the élite and the general public. He gave briefings on Gorbachëv and *'perestroika'* to the British Prime Minister, Mrs Thatcher, and to other Western policymakers – advising them to trust and support *'perestroika'*. He extended similar advice to President Mitterrand during his visit to France. And Sakharov acted almost as a national security adviser to President Reagan – *advising him to abandon the Strategic Defense Initiative and also the NATO doctrine of reserving the right to make first use of nuclear weapons.* [In November 1993, the Russian military specifically asserted precisely this 'right'].

Significantly, Sakharov tried to conceal the existence of the Soviet strategy when he stated before an audience of American specialists on Soviet affairs that 'Gorbachëv does not have a unified plan for change. More likely, what he does have is an improvisation'. **This statement was a deliberate misrepresentation of the strategic challenge which the West is facing.**

An especially important element in the present Soviet drive to inject their strategic influence into the United States is the recent creation of 'The International Foundation for the Survival and Development of Humanity', set up during Sakharov's visit to the United States. Sakharov, a leading Soviet agent of influence, is its head. Other members include Velikhov (President of the Soviet Academy of Sciences), and the economist Tatyana Zaslavskaya, who is credited with the reintroduction of the term *'perestroika'*. The Foundation is a joint Soviet-American venture for collaboration in research on the environment, pollution, human rights, arms control and economic development, all of which are relevant to the Soviet strategy of convergence. Zaslavskaya was particularly revealing about the 'restructuring' objectives of the research. She suggested undertaking a study of bureaucracies which, in her words, 'come in different forms in different countries but are like a social cancer'. Such a study would have provided Moscow with valuable detailed information about the US bureaucracy.

Several influential Americans, including the well known industrialist Mr Armand Hammer, the associate of Lenin, and the President of the Carnegie Foundation of New York, Hymburg, joined the Foundation as board members or advisers. The Foundation is envisaged as a global one. It has opened offices in Washington and Stockholm and, with a donation from Hammer, has bought a headquarters building in New York. Sakharov's inaugural message was that the West should interact with the USSR not only because this would reduce the risk of war but because it would have a civilising effect on the domestic behaviour of the Soviets. This is an obvious scenario for convergence. Prominent Americans with philanthropic interests who join the Foundation are open to manipulation by Sakharov and other Soviet agents of influence because they have complete faith in Sakharov and have no notion of the anti-American designs of Soviet strategy.

DIALECTICS OF THE STRATEGY AND THE PREDICTIVE POWER OF THE NEW METHOD
Correct understanding of the strategy and the application of that understanding to the analysis of events enables one to predict otherwise surprising Soviet actions. Since the strategy is long-range, it has several phases. The strategists plan their actions in the early phases in preparation for the final phase. They conceive Soviet reforms in the initial phase, they rehearse them in the preparatory phase and they introduce them in the final phase. Because of this planning framework, the strategy has its own dialectic. It has its **thesis** – the Stalinist régime: its **antithesis** – criticism and rejection of the Stalinist régime: and its **synthesis** – a new, reformed model which *'perestroika'* is designed to create, and which will be the product of 'convergence' (the joining of the two opposites). **Understanding the dialectic and logic of the strategy is crucial for prediction:** *it enables one to see how the situation in one phase will develop in the next phase.*

For instance, it enables one to predict the change in the rôle and status of Soviet 'dissidents'. In the initial phase, they were recruited and trained by the KGB. In the preparatory phase, they were 'criticised' and 'persecuted' by the KGB. In the final phase, they are accepted and even incorporated into *'perestroika'*. It was through understanding this dialectic that the Author was able to predict the simple fact that Sakharov 'might be included in some capacity in government'. In the event, he became one of Gorbachëv's chief advisers.

Likewise, the dialectic enables one to understand that Euro-Communist criticism in the 1960s and 1970s of repressive practices and violations of human rights in the USSR was undertaken and tolerated with official foreknowledge of the impending 'reform' of the Soviet system. The fact that the Berlin Wall was built at the time when the strategy was adopted was a sufficient basis for the prediction that it would be pulled down again in the strategy's final phase. The dialectic enables one to see through the calculated publication of anti-Soviet manuscripts abroad, Soviet condemnation of them at the time and the present lifting of the ban on much of the 'dissident' writing of the 1960s and 1970s. Understanding of the dialectic enables one to provide further predictions and warnings about political and social issues which the Soviet strategists will seek to exploit in Western Europe, the United States and elsewhere.

PREDICTIONS ON THE EXECUTION OF THE STRATEGY'S FINAL PHASE

EXPANDED ROLE OF THE COMMUNIST PARTY

During *'perestroika'*, the political rôle of the Communist Party in Communist countries will increase, not decrease. The Party will continue to exercise overall supervision and control over the mixed economy through Party members among the managers and technocrats. The Party, operating 'underground' and 'working by other means', will provide political guidance to the Congress of Peoples' Deputies and other 'reformed' and successor parliaments and to the new 'political parties' and 'grassroots democratic associations' through Party cells and individual Party members in the leaderships of these organisations. Guidance to Party members will be given through confidential briefings. Freed from day-to-day supervision over the economy, the Party will devote itself to guiding and implementing *'perestroika'* in the USSR and Eastern Europe and to implementing the strategy in the West. **The Soviet Party apparatus will become a true general staff of world revolution to be carried out through the strategy of** *'perestroika'*[11].

STRONGER, MATURER IDEOLOGY

Despite the *apparent renunciation* of ideological orthodoxy, Communist ideology will grow *stronger and more mature*. As *'perestroika'* proceeds, ideology in the Communist countries will be reasserted[12]. Each success for *'perestroika'* will reinforce the belief of Party members and young Communists in the correctness of their ideology and their cause. Communists will continue to analyse international relations and the situation in the capitalist countries in terms of class analysis. Their 'humanism' will continue

11 *Editor's Note:* 'Where do the old Soviet structures hide?... The Gorbachëv Foundation... has somehow taken over the tasks – and the personnel – of the International Department of the Central Committee of the CPSU' [Hans Graf Huyn, private paper circulated in November 1994].
12 *Author's Note:* This prediction has been confirmed by the reappearance of open Communists in control of the national Republics and in Eastern Europe [*see Note 30, page 89*].

to see love and hate in class terms. Capitalists, home-grown and foreign, will be hated, never loved; and they will invariably be deceived and taken for a ride.

The Party will continue with ideological education and training to prevent contamination by foreign ideologies. Attempts to reform and replace capitalism in the West will be accelerated, not through ideological propaganda, but through the strategy of *'perestroika'*, leading to 'convergence'.

AN IMPROVED, REORGANISED KGB

One can expect that the KGB will be converted into a new organisation with a Western-style name[13]. The reorganisation will be presented as a reduction of the rôle of the service in Soviet society. But, because of the KGB's crucial rôle in promoting *'perestroika'* internally and abroad, the reorganisation should not be seen as a downgrading. Just as Dzerzhinskiy's hated Cheka was converted into the more powerful GPU, so will the successor organisation to the KGB be *more powerful than its predecessor*.

The new service will work with kid gloves and more sophisticated methods. Internally, its resources will be devoted to the creation of controlled political plurality ('democratism'). It will create a pseudo-social democratic Party and Estonian, Latvian, Lithuanian and Muslim national parties: it will even set up Stalinist and anti-Semitic groups, to give a convincing impression of plurality. Naturally, the service will be behind these groups and parties – controlling and managing them in the interests of the strategy and its objectives. The service will use its intelligence and security assets, particularly its agents of influence in the newly created national fronts, political groups and parties, to carry out the strategy of 'restructuring' attitudes and policies in the West.

THE NEW MODEL SOVIET RÉGIME

The Soviets will proceed with *'perestroika'* on the following lines:

❐ A mixed socialist-market economy comparable to the Swedish economy will be established with one crucial difference. Soviet 'capitalists' will in fact be secret Party members and Party political tools. Their influence will be used in the interests of the strategy abroad. This is what Soviet maturity means.

❐ The Party will create controlled plurality and a semblance of social democracy in the USSR. It will not be difficult to do. Even the Stalinist régime in Poland had nominally 'non-Communist' 'independent' parties. In fact, they were puppet parties.

❐ As a mature body, the Soviet parliament will play an active rôle in the execution of the strategy abroad.

❐ The new parliament will be closer to the Swedish model – again, with one difference. It will use its contacts with Western colleagues to influence them towards cooperation and 'restructuring' in the West.

13 *Editor's Note:* The Soviet security services have been repeatedly 'relabelled' since 20 December 1917, when the Cheka was established. Following the fake 'August coup' in 1991, foreign intelligence was placed under Yevgeniy Primakov's 'Russian Foreign Intelligence Service', while the KGB was incorporated within the Ministry of State Security, at first under Vadim Bakatin, and subsequently under Nikolai Golushko, a veteran security official from Ukraine. On 20 December 1993, President Yeltsin published a decree on the abolition of the Security Ministry of the Russian Federation and the simultaneous creation of the Federal Service of Counter-Intelligence of the Russian Federation, also known as the Counter Intelligence Agency, or 'C.I.A.'. This title and acronym has been used subliminally by Moscow to imply 'equivalence' between the CIA and Russian Counter-Intelligence, and to create the impression that there is nothing to chose between the two communities. The German expert on Soviet deception, Hans Graf Huyn, has identified no less than 14 Russian agencies with intelligence functions [privately circulated paper, November 1994]. *See also Note 35, page 98.*

❒ The Soviet Empire will not crumble as a result of nationalist unrest. The Party will create a stronger federation which will be in full control of foreign policy, defence and security but which will provide autonomy to the national Republics to run their own local affairs.

❒ As the Party proceeds with successful *'perestroika'* in the USSR, both Russians and non-Russians will be increasingly inclined to accept it and take part in the process. In the final analysis, their attitude will depend on Western support for Soviet *'perestroika'* and the improvement in their way of life.

❒ Successful Soviet *'perestroika'* will result in a Soviet régime of pseudo-social democracy with a human face.

❒ At this juncture, the Party and the successor to the KGB will do their utmost to exploit the image of their new model, their prestige and the contacts and influence of the new parliament, the national fronts, the political groups and parties and the Soviet capitalists, to carry out the intended strategy of 'restructuring' in the West.

'RESTRUCTURING' IN EASTERN EUROPE AND CHINA

A consistent effort will be made to expand and deepen 'restructuring' in Eastern Europe and China. The new models will be like Soviet *'perestroika'* in essence but will reflect the specific national and historical features of each country.

For instance, in Poland the model will include Communist power-sharing with Solidarity and the Catholic hierarchy. In Czechoslovakia, the model will include the experience of 1968; in Hungary the rehabilitation of the revolt of 1956; in East Germany, the desire for reunion with West Germany; and in China, it will reflect the Asian character of socialism, the desire for reunion with Taiwan and the present close relations with the United States. Polish and East German 'restructuring' should be particularly closely watched because of their relevance to the 'restructuring' of Western Europe.

'RESTRUCTURING' IN WESTERN EUROPE

'Perestroika' in the USSR and Eastern Europe will be accompanied by a determined Soviet political and diplomatic offensive to introduce 'restructuring' in Western Europe. Gorbachëv and East European leaders will try to develop the present *détente* into close economic, military, political, cultural and scientific cooperation to create 'one Europe' without NATO and the Warsaw Pact. A particular effort will be made to develop close relations and cooperation with East European social democrats and the Labour Party in Britain – exploiting the new Soviet pseudo-social democratic, mixed economy image. Attracted by this image and convinced of its authenticity, the social democrats may well respond favourably to this courting.

East Germany will play a crucial rôle in the 'restructuring' of Western Europe and of West Germany in particular. The appointment of Valentin Falin, a leading Soviet expert on Germany, as head of the Central Committee's Department of International Relations, indicates that the Soviets are preparing and counting on an East German initiative. Such an initiative will probably be supported by a Polish *démarche* such as revival of the Rapacki plan for a nuclear-free zone in Central Europe. This time, one can expect the Soviets to remove the Berlin Wall. There is no doubt that their strategists realise that they will be unable to proceed with the strategy of 'restructuring' in Europe without removal of the Berlin Wall – just as they were unable to proceed without a Soviet withdrawal from Afghanistan. Through removal of the Berlin Wall, the Soviets may be able to strike a new, Rapallo-style deal with the West Germans, particularly with a Social Democratic government, entailing their departure from NATO and acceptance of neutrality. Given that Soviet *'perestroika'* incorporates by design many Euro-Communist positions (criticism of Soviet repressive practices, condemnation of the intervention in Czechoslovakia in 1968, broadening Soviet democracy), Euro-Communist parties will join and support the movement for 'restructuring' in Europe which will give them new opportunities for revitalising themselves. They will attempt to establish unity of action with social democrats to bring about 'restructuring' in their own countries. Dubcek's re-emergence from obscurity and his recent visit to Italy at the invitation of the Italian Communist Party supports the notion that the Euro-Communists will seek to exploit Soviet and East European *'perestroika'* to regain political influence in their own countries. Support for Soviet and East European *'perestroika'* by the Italian and French governments renders the socialist parties of these countries vulnerable to approaches from the Communists.

'RESTRUCTURING' IN THE THIRD WORLD
An active Soviet and East European offensive to carry out 'restructuring' in the Third World can be expected. The present Soviet readiness to contemplate and even encourage the settlement of armed conflicts by their proxies does not mean the abandonment of their objective of Communist penetration of the region concerned. It represents no more than a change of tactics. The strategy of 'restructuring' broadens Soviet opportunities for gaining influence through the achievement of political solutions. The reformed régimes in the Soviet Union and Eastern Europe will engage with the West European social democratic parties and the Socialist International in introducing and carrying out 'restructuring' in the Third World and particularly in Latin America. Exploiting the debt problem and the example of Soviet *'perestroika'*, they will seek unity of action with labour, religious, student, human rights and ecological movements. The impact of Soviet *'perestroika'* on these countries may be expected to grow. The Mexican press is already drawing parallels between Soviet *'perestroika'* and political change in Mexico described as 'Salinastroika'. The former Mexican Communist leader made the same comparison. Fuentes, the left-wing Mexican novelist, wrote recently that Salinas must become a Mexican Gorbachëv if he wishes to change the state of affairs in Mexico. Another example is the recent offer of the Salvadorean guerrilla leaders to disarm themselves if the Salvadorean army is restructured.

These examples indicate the beginning of a trend towards 'restructuring' in Latin America. The trend will accelerate if the United States begins to help it without taking into account the Soviet strategic design that lies behind it.

Given the fragility of democracy, the desperate economic situation and the debt problem, particularly in Latin America, one can expect an active, joint operation by the Soviets, the East Europeans and European social democrats (with their money) to bring to power Allende- or Sandinista-type régimes and 'restructuring' in these countries along the lines of the new, reformed Soviet model.

'RESTRUCTURING' AMERICAN MILITARY-POLITICAL ALLIANCES

The Soviets will exploit the image of the reformed and peaceful Soviet systems to shatter the Western consensus about the Soviet threat and the need for political and military alliances. In Europe, the Soviets will probably attempt to create a serious rift in NATO or break it up altogether by removing the Berlin Wall and reaching a Rapallo-style deal with West Germany involving West Germany withdrawing from NATO and following Austria into neutrality[14]. In Asia, the Soviets may attempt to break up the US-Japan security pact by returning the Kurile Islands to Japan and offering Japan economic concessions to promote the development of Siberia.

As the Soviets carry out 'restructuring' in the Third World, they will use their influence to reduce the American presence in the region.

'RESTRUCTURING' IN THE UNITED STATES

The Soviets will do their utmost to persuade the new Administration to follow Reagan's policy of embracing 'perestroika' and rapprochement with the Soviet Union. They will intensify the efforts of Gorbachëv and Sakharov to engage the American élite in cooperation over the environment, space, disarmament and the joint 'solution' of social, political, economic, environmental, military and international problems[15].

Visits by Soviet scientists, politicians, intellectuals and cultural delegations will be stepped up in order to put across to the Americans the ideas of 'restructuring' and convergence. Likewise, more American scientists, intellectuals, opinion-formers, politicians and religious groups will be invited to the USSR where they will be subjected to persuasion on the advantages of 'restructuring' and convergence.

Soviet agents of influence in the United States will redouble their attempts to act as catalysts in promoting 'restructuring' and convergence. They will initiate public debates on security aimed at shattering the American consensus on the Soviet threat and destabilising and 'restructuring' the US military-industrial complex. KGB agents among Soviet 'dissidents' and cultural defectors will travel back and forth between the United States and the USSR acting as bridge-builders in cultural and political convergence. The whole political potential of the *KGB-controlled* political parties and so-called 'grassroots organisations' will be used to establish links with their *genuine* counterparts in the United States and influence them towards 'restructuring'.

During their visits to the United States they will try to impress the Americans

14 *Author's Note:* So far, NATO has not followed the example set by the Warsaw Pact, and wound itself up. However its effectiveness has been reduced and, in its confusion, it has been considering acceptance of 'former' adversaries as members. [*See also Note 33, page 92*].

15 *Editor's Note:* Since the beginning of 1992, Gorbachëv has accelerated this dimension of the strategy through the **'Gorbachëv Foundation/USA'**, which operates from an address in the Presidio, a disused US military base in San Francisco. This entity started life on 10 April 1991, *four months ahead of the 'August 1991 coup'*, as the Tamalpais Institute. On 10 April 1992, its name was changed to 'Gorbachëv Foundation/USA', which is fronting a vigorous menu of conferences and 'initiatives' including a 'Global Security Project', in accordance with the influence-building agenda predicted by the Author. In May 1992, the Gorbachëv Foundation/USA organised a fund-raising tour of the United States, featuring Gorbachëv, who raised millions of dollars to 'finance' the Foundation. However the Gorbachëv Foundation/Moscow already employed a large staff in the first quarter of 1992 – a fact which does not appear to have impeded the flow of American funds in favour of the Gorbachëv Foundation in the slightest. The reason for the large continuing payroll is given in *Note 11 [page 27]*.

with the growing similarity of their system to the American system and to convince them of **the soundness of convergence as a means of avoiding nuclear war.**

As 'restructuring' proceeds in Eastern Europe, the East Europeans will join the Soviet offensive to gain a foothold in the United States and to secure their share of political influence over the American ethnic minorities.

THE SOVIET CAMPAIGN AGAINST ANTI-COMMUNISTS IN THE WEST

The Soviets, their allies and KGB agents of influence will conduct a campaign of political and ideological warfare against anti-Communism and the political influence of anti-Communists in the West. It will project Soviet *'perestroika'* as a fundamental change in the Soviet system, as a dissolution of Communist ideology, as a reduction in the Soviet threat and as an end of the Cold War.

Georgiy Arbatov described the process as the 'removal of the Soviet enemy from the minds of the Americans'[16]. The Soviet media, the Soviets' allies and agents of influence will attack and seek to *isolate anti-Communism and anti-Communists as obstacles to 'restructuring', 'cold warriors' and enemies of peace.*

The targets of the assault will be the political leaders and government officials who have a realistic understanding of the Soviet threat; anti-Communists in the Republican and Democratic parties, especially those on the political and religious right; anti-Communists in the socialist, social democratic and conservative parties in Western Europe; American and European experts on Soviet affairs and members of the American and European media who are trying to be objective in presenting *'perestroika'* and its meaning for the democracies.

They will be attacked as reactionaries, bureaucrats with outworn ideas, political or religious Cold War warriors, spoilers or just fascists. The attack will aim to neutralise them by ridicule and to turn them into an endangered species.

An article in *The New York Times* of 19 September 1988 by Stephen Cohen, an American expert on Soviet affairs and *'perestroika'* in particular, gives one an idea of what may be expected. Mr Cohen writes that the centrists lack the guts to respond to Gorbachëv. For this reason, he gives the new President disturbing advice, 'to appoint to all relevant foreign policy positions only people deeply committed to the anti-Cold War effort'. **The Soviet Yakovlevs and Arbatovs can be expected to accelerate the neutralisation and removal from Western political life of anti-Communists through new, calculated projections of Soviet and East European developments.**

For example, they may attack in the press and remove from office their own

---

16 *Editor's Note:* Writing in the June 1988 issue of *'Kommunist'*, journal of the Communist Party of the Soviet Union [CPSU], on page 18, Georgiy Arbatov explained that in fact it was merely the *'image'* of the enemy that was being removed. He chose his words with Leninist care: **'The "image of the enemy" that is being eroded has been... absolutely vital for the foreign and military policy of the United States and its allies. The destruction of this stereotype... is Gorbachëv's weapon... Nei-ther the arms race, nor power blocs in the third World, nor the military blocs, are thinkable without "the enemy", and without the "Soviet threat"... Of course, this weapon is not secret, but it does have enormous power'.** And on 11 June 1989, in the course of a press conference held in Bonn at the height of Gorbachëv's triumphant sales visit to West Germany, Arbatov summed up succinctly what was happening as follows: **'A great turn-round is going on in international affairs and yet some people are not prepared to embrace it... the most horrible thing we have done at the moment is that we are depriving them of the enemy image...'.**

'conservatives' as 'enemies of *'perestroika'*. The recent demotion of Ligachev may be seen in this light. The Soviets may use the creation of Party-controlled 'independent' national organisations in the Baltic States to influence American anti-Communists from the captive nations towards the acceptance of *'perestroika'* and a reversal of their anti-Communist attitudes.

The KGB and its **Department of Political Assassinations** may be expected to take part in this final battle and to carry out assassinations of prominent anti-Communists who are regarded as serious obstacles to the strategy of 'restructuring' in the West. **These assassinations will be conducted skilfully and will be unattributable to the KGB as was the assassination of Stepan Bandera, the anti-Communist Ukrainian nationalist leader, in 1959, until the defection of his assassin.**

In the Author's opinion the assassination of South Korean leaders in Burma, though carried out by the North Koreans, would not have been decided upon by the North Korean leaders on their own but would have had the blessing of both Moscow and Peking. The recent deaths of the Pakistani President, General Zia, and of a leading West German banker and anti-Communist, should be re-examined in this light as possible components of the KGB's destabilisation programme.

The Soviets' strategic interest in the assassination of their serious political enemies will render unrealistic American expectations of genuine, whole-hearted Soviet-American cooperation against international terrorism[17,18].

SOVIET INTENTIONS TOWARDS THE NEXT ELECTION IN THE UNITED STATES AND WESTERN EUROPE: THE RADICAL LEFT

The principal objective of the attack on anti-Communists is to influence the outcome of the forthcoming national elections in the United States and Western Europe. The Soviet strategists relate their chances of successful execution of their strategy of 'restructuring' to victories of the left in these elections. They believe that the conditions are favourable. In their assessment, the intelligence services of the United States, Britain, France and West Germany have been weakened.

They have lost their capabilities through public exposure or through deep KGB penetration. They have been misinformed about Soviet strategic intentions towards the West. Their ignorance about Soviet strategy has reached such depths that some of the services, the British for example, unofficially support and promote Gorbachëv and Soviet *'perestroika'*. For these reasons, the Soviet strategists regard the Western services as 'paper tigers' and discount them as a serious obstacle to their strategy in the West. In their view, serious resistance to their strategy of 'restructuring' can come only from their ideological enemies, the anti-Communist conservatives in the United States and Western Europe. They see that conservative leaders (ex-President Reagan, British Prime Minister Thatcher and West German Chancellor Kohl) have failed to understand the essence of *'perestroika'*, have led their supporters in the wrong direction and have led them into a crisis by their support for Gor-

17 *Author's Note:* Up to early 1995, when this text was finalised, terrorist operations against conservatives were unnecessary because they had become ardent supporters of *'perestroika'*.
18 *Editor's Note:* The Author's reasoned explanation of the circumstances in which the KGB would resort to the political assassination of a Western leader is to be found on page 352 of *'New Lies for Old'*, and is reproduced and discussed in *Note 64* [*see page 168 of the present work*].

bachëv. Conservatives are confused about Gorbachëv and *'perestroika'*. The old assumptions have been upset. They are out of ideas. They have lost perspective. The Soviet strategists, however, are concerned that the conservative crisis and confusion are temporary affairs. They believe the conservatives may recover and resist 'restructuring'. For this reason, strategic objectives of Soviet political warfare include:

○ *First of all*, the neutralisation of anti-Communist influence, especially the conservative parties, as an important factor in the political life of the United States, West Germany, France and Britain.

○ *Secondly*, securing the victory of the radical Left in the next presidential elections in 1992 in the United States and the victory of the Socialist and Labour parties in the national elections in West Germany, France and Britain in the 1990s. The Soviets plan to hold the International Conference on Human Rights in Moscow in 1991; and their keen interest in American participation in it is due to their desire to influence the outcome of the elections in favour of the radical Left. In their assessment, the Left will be prepared to carry out and accelerate 'restructuring' in the United States.

The Soviet strategists believe that an economic depression in the United States would provide even more favourable conditions for the execution of their strategy. In that event, the Soviets and their allies would shift to the doctrine of class struggle and try to divide the Western nations along crude class lines.

The final period of 'restructuring' in the United States and Western Europe would be accompanied, not only by the physical extermination of active anti-Communists, but also by the extermination of the political, military, financial and religious élites. Blood would be spilled and political re-education camps would be introduced. The Communists would not hesitate to repeat the mass repressions of their revolution in 1917, of the Soviet occupation of Eastern Europe in the Second World War or of the Chinese Communist victory of 1949.

This time, they would resort to mass repressions in order to prevent any possibility of revolt by the defeated, and to make their victory final. The Author bases this conclusion in part on the following information. While the long-range strategy was being formulated in the late 1950s, the Soviet strategists asked for a KGB estimate of the number of West Germans who would need to be isolated in order to turn West Germany into a neutral country. The KGB estimate was 150,000 Germans.

THE POSSIBLE REPLACEMENT OF GORBACHEV

The Soviet strategy of 'restructuring' the world is not reversible but Gorbachëv is replaceable. Because Gorbachëv was chosen for the execution of the final phase of the strategy, *one should not exclude the possibility of his being replaced by another leader*. His replacement might take place if the requirements of the strategy were to demand a shift towards a 'harder line' or confrontation with the United States, or if he were to fail in his job. He might be replaced by a 'conservative' of Ligachev's type or by a 'liberal' of Yeltsin's type. Another purpose of the display of alleged differences between Gorbachëv and the 'conservative' Ligachev on the one hand and the 'liberal' Yeltsin on the other hand is to prepare the world public for such a change if it should come about. *Gorbachëv's replacement or 'fall' could well be a calculated move. If circumstances changed, he might be returned to power again.*

CHINA: A STRATEGIC ENEMY OF THE UNITED STATES

Communist China is not a strategic partner but *a concealed strategic enemy* of the United States. China will join in the Soviet offensive to bring about 'restructuring' in the United States and worldwide.

Through penetration, Chinese Communist intelligence destroyed the CIA's sources in China during the 1950s, 1960s and 1970s and prevented the Agency developing reliable sources on the strategic intentions of the Chinese leaders. The National Security Agency cannot help because information on secret Sino-Soviet strategic coordination is not carried on accessible communications channels.

This situation leaves American policymakers poorly informed on the subject. American policymakers from the time of Nixon and Kissinger to the present day have become known for their excessive reliance on the verbal assurances of Mao, Chou En-Lai and Deng. Reliance on their word is no substitute for good intelligence.

Because of this intelligence gap, America's policymakers have not distinguished between China's tactics and her strategy. This failure is not new: it was evident as early as the Second World War when the Americans failed to realise that the Chinese Communists' cooperation with the Nationalists against the Japanese was a tactic adopted in order to achieve their strategic objective – their victory over the Nationalists. Some of the statements of the Chinese leaders to their own followers are unflattering about American policymakers and are, in fact, disturbing. In the late 1960s, Mao advised the Party not to take the Americans seriously in a strategic, but only in a tactical sense. *Deng's well known statement about a cat catching a mouse*, made when China was introducing capitalism and receiving American technology, can be interpreted as meaning that the Chinese Communist leader is the cat that caught the American mouse.

Because of their confusion, American policymakers believe that Communist China is an important strategic partner and a strategic rival and enemy of the Soviet Union. In this they are wrong. China is a *tactical*, not a strategic partner of the United States and a *tactical*, but not a *strategic* 'enemy' of the Soviet Union[19].

The grounds for this conclusion are to be found by analysing the long-range Communist strategy which illuminates the strategic rôle of China.

Communist China was one of the principal architects of the Communists' long-range strategy. The Sino-Soviet 'split' was a common strategic disinformation operation to secure the successful preparation of their common strategy of 'restructuring'. The Soviet and Chinese leaders have continued their secret strategic coordination through a division of labour.

Gorbachëv's *'perestroika'* and Deng's 'Four Modernisations' (a Chinese euphemism for 'restructuring', or *'perestroika'*) are two similar elements in the final phase of the common strategy.

In the light of the new method of analysis, the purpose of Shevardnadze's hastily arranged trip to China *on the eve of President Bush's visit* was to give advice to Deng on his talks with the American President. Gorbachëv and Deng will use their meeting to discuss coordination and new initiatives to be taken during the final

19 *Author's Note:* It remains to be seen whether the late President Nixon's policy towards China and Russia was the epitome of wisdom.

phase of the strategy. The new analysis sees the Soviet withdrawal from Afghanistan as a tactical move *en route* to the principal strategic objective – 'restructuring' by engaging the United States in support of *'perestroika'*.

China's close relations with the United States and even Chinese helpfulness to the United States over the Pakistan-Afghanistan situation are tactics intended to secure China's primary strategic objective of becoming a modern superpower with the help of American technology.

According to this analysis, the Chinese leaders are using their own Party apparatus and security services to try to repeat Soviet successes in creating controlled political opposition and introducing its members to the United States in order to shape American policy in the interests of a common Communist strategy.

In fact the Chinese have been so impressed by Sakharov's success in gaining influence in the United States that they are developing their own Sakharovs – agents of influence among leading Chinese 'dissident' scientists. Thus it can be predicted that the Chinese will establish their own foothold of influence in the United States and will eventually join the Soviet offensive to procure American 'restructuring'.

For China is destined to become a primary Soviet partner in the future World Government towards which Moscow and Peking are jointly proceeding.

DEFECTIVE WESTERN METHODS OF ANALYSIS
Current Western methods of analysis have failed to yield a correct interpretation of the changes in the Soviet Union and of the meaning of *'perestroika'* for the West. They have failed to provide accurate predictions for the future. The reasons for their failure are to be found in the severe defects of the obsolete methods being used.

The main reason that they are obsolete is that they failed to detect and follow the adoption of the long-range Communist strategy of *'perestroika'* in 1958-60 and its execution during the subsequent thirty years. Mr John McCone, the former Director of Central Intelligence, was right when he told the Author in 1964 that 'the American Government works on a four-year basis. It will be very difficult to accept or deal with the long-range aspect of the [Communist] strategy'. Another defect has been the failure to take into account and appreciate the effect on analysis of thirty years of Communist strategic disinformation concerning the alleged decay and disintegration of the Communist Bloc, its ideology and its strategic coordination.

The crucial period, when the gap in Western strategic intelligence opened up, was between 1958 and 1960. At that time, Western intelligence services were unable to acquire reliable information on the adoption of the long-range strategy and the programme of strategic disinformation because they were deeply penetrated by the KGB and their main sources in the USSR and China were compromised.

KGB penetration in the United States did not begin with the Walker ring. As early as 1958, the CIA was penetrated by both the KGB and by Chinese intelligence. In 1958 the Agency lost its most important source, Colonel Popov[20] of Soviet Military Intelligence (GRU), who could have provided strategic information had he not been compromised by KGB penetration and arrested by the KGB.

20 *See Note 57 on page 156.*

Both *British* services were deeply penetrated over a prolonged period.

Both *West German* services were deeply penetrated with effect from their foundation after the end of the Second World War.

Both *French* intelligence services were also deeply penetrated. The KGB had seven sources in the services. This is important in the present context because it was the penetrated French services which provided the bulk of the 'information' on Soviet-Romanian and Sino-Soviet differences. Ironically, in their analysis of the East-West strategic balance, the Soviet strategists used the *French* assessment which was prepared for President de Gaulle in 1958. It was provided to the KGB by their sources in the French Government. The KGB was now confident that the Western services were unable to obtain **strategic** information from the USSR. And in order to exclude any such eventuality, the KGB misinformed the British and American services about Soviet strategy through their 'plant' – another GRU Colonel, namely Penkovskiy, who was accepted by the British and the Americans as genuine, becoming their most important source in the USSR. In his work with one of the Western services the Author found clear evidence that Penkovskiy was KGB-controlled.

Having failed to detect the adoption of the long-range strategy, Western experts were accordingly unable to develop appropriate strategic criteria for interpreting developments in the Soviet Union. Another defect inherent in Western methodology was the failure to observe and understand *the political rôle of the KGB* in preparing and carrying out the strategy of *'perestroika'* over the past thirty years. In the West, intelligence services do not operate within a strategic framework but within the narrow confines of their speciality.

Yet another defect has been the failure to appreciate the KGB's use of its assets and their *entire potential*, particularly their penetration in the Western countries and their agents of influence both in the USSR and the West, in the interests of the strategy. A growing awareness of this problem in American and British counter-intelligence was interrupted by Watergate and the ensuing *débacle* which destabilised American counter-intelligence. As a result of all these failures, the KGB was successful in achieving its objective of presenting a KGB-controlled political opposition in the USSR to the West as a genuine opposition movement.

The KGB also succeeded in introducing to the West *their version* of human rights which is based on KGB manipulation of their controlled opposition. This has resulted in an American fixation with the Soviet human rights issue, without any understanding of the Soviet *strategic interest* in it or of the differences between the Soviet and the Western attitudes to the subject. For the West, human rights are a sacred principle. For the Soviets, the issue provides an opening to shape, influence, manipulate and exploit Western, and especially American, policy in the interests of the strategy of *'perestroika'* both in the USSR and in the Western world. The Soviets see human rights in the context of their dormant but undying doctrine of class struggle. For them, anti-Communist, capitalist 'exploiters' and their supporters have no right to existence. The Soviets are carrying out their political reforms, *not* out of respect for human rights, but in the context of their development of 'Communist democracy' (the application of 'democratism'), in which the formation of *genuine* political opposition can be neutralised and prevented.

Their understanding of the human rights issue envisages a shift to the revival of the class struggle and pressure to replace or 'restructure' the capitalist system in the event of a severe economic recession and mass unemployment in the United States or Europe. For them, the human rights issue provides an opportunity to promote 'restructuring' in the United States and elsewhere, and the replacement of genuine by false democracy. **Their vision includes the extermination of the American and European capitalists and élites.** Through skilful manipulation of the human rights issue and the KGB-controlled political opposition, the Soviets have succeeded in distracting the West from the study and understanding of Soviet strategy. They have succeeded in shaping Western policies and perceptions of the changes in the USSR in their own interest. In pursuing the human rights issue, the West and its intelligence services have lost sight of the KGB's real activities in the preparation of 'perestroika' and the underlying and relentless hostility of the strategy towards the West.

A key rôle in the shaping of Western misconceptions about human rights and 'perestroika' in the USSR has been played by Sakharov, a long-standing Soviet agent of influence. As these misconceptions have accumulated in Western foreign ministries, intelligence services and 'think-tanks', they have created a vicious circle of bureaucratic vested interests which makes the correction of the misconceptions difficult if not impossible. The confusion caused by Soviet strategic disinformation, *the vested interests of bureaucracies in long-accepted misconceptions* and the lack of proper strategic criteria have done serious damage to the assessment of Communist developments by the West. **Most critically of all, Western experts fail to perceive the strategic continuity behind them. They accumulate facts but are unable to see their strategic interaction and cannot build them into a strategic picture. They lack vision and insight, which is why they are floundering in the face of the onslaught which they fail to understand. For instance, they continue to analyse events in terms of outdated, inapplicable Stalinist concepts such as continuing power struggles.**

This was notably the case in connection with the fashionable interpretation of Gorbachëv's rise to power, the removal of his alleged rivals and his assumption of the presidency. 'Perestroika' was and is seen as a purely domestic campaign to overcome the economic and political deficiencies of the Soviet Union – overlooking its broader, anti-Western strategic design. Alternatively, Western experts have gone to the opposite extreme of interpreting the advent of Gorbachëv and 'perestroika' in Western terms as spontaneous, positive developments – pushing the Soviet régime towards capitalism and Western-style democracy. Typically, they see Gorbachëv as an independent innovator facing resistance from the Party bureaucracy and the military.

Ignorant of the Leninist roots and origins of 'perestroika', they fail to see that it is the logical final phase of Communist strategy: they cannot understand its essence, its objectives or its dangers as part of the design for world Communist victory. They are impressed by the drama of 'perestroika' but cannot appreciate its dialectical logic and dynamics, or its revolutionary potential. Faulty in their assessments of the situation, Western experts appear to have failed to warn policymakers, President Reagan and Prime Minister Margaret Thatcher in particular, about the implications and dangers of Western support for Gorbachëv and 'perestroika'. If attempts were made to do so, they were overruled.

THE DEFECTS OF WESTERN COUNTER-INTELLIGENCE
The defective, obsolete methods of analysis outlined above have damaged the quality
of the performance of Western counter-intelligence services against the KGB. Having
failed to understand Soviet strategy and the KGB's rôle in its execution, they have
failed to spot many agents of influence either in the USSR or in their own countries.

The American and British services failed to detect and expose Sakharov as a
Soviet agent of influence. They failed to understand his strategic rôle when he predicted 'liberalisation' in 1967, and began to shape Western attitudes towards it. They
failed to appreciate that his exile by Andropov in 1980 was a characteristic KGB
device aimed at building up his prestige and influence in the West.

They failed to understand Sakharov's rôle when he became an unofficial
adviser to Gorbachëv and began promoting 'perestroika' to the West, or even when he
started advising President Reagan on abandoning the Strategic Defense Initiative
and the first use of nuclear weapons.

They therefore failed to warn their policymakers, including President Reagan
and Prime Minister Thatcher. As a result, a long-standing Soviet agent of influence,
accepted as a genuine democrat and 'the conscience of the world', was allowed to
emerge as a serious political influence in the execution of the Soviet strategy of 'perestroika' and as an adviser to Western leaders on how they should respond.

Failure to understand this new offensive by the Soviets and the KGB has
opened the way for the planting of fresh KGB-controlled sources on the American
and British services and for the despatch of KGB-controlled defectors to their countries. Lacking strategic criteria by which to judge the authenticity of their sources,
these services are no longer able to distinguish true sources from KGB plants, or true
defectors from false defectors. It may well be that an uncritical acceptance of information from intelligence sources favourable to Gorbachëv and 'perestroika' has influenced the attitude of Western leaders towards them. The primary fallacies follow.

FALLACIES ABOUT GORBACHEV AND 'PERESTROIKA'
Confusion and euphoria about changes in the Soviet Union have given birth to many
misconceptions and fallacies about Gorbachëv and 'perestroika'. Even if bankrupt
Western methods of analysis cannot be held responsible for all these fallacies, they
still fail to provide serious correctives to them.

THE FIRST FALLACY: The origin of 'perestroika'
This is the belief that 'perestroika' was a consequence of President Reagan's
military pressure on the USSR and the potency of the American capitalist example.
Believers in this fallacy, who insist that the West 'won the Cold War', do not suspect
that 'perestroika' and its timing are the product of a long-range strategy, planning and
long-term preparation. [In Sun Tzu's terms, they have become arrogant].

THE SECOND FALLACY: The domestic character of 'perestroika'
This is the belief that 'perestroika' is a purely domestic attempt to correct
repressive practices, to revitalise the flagging Soviet economy and to adapt the Soviet
Union to the necessities and norms of the modern world. Believers do not suspect the

Soviet intent to expand *'perestroika'* beyond the borders of the Communist world and to achieve the world victory of Communism through 'restructuring'.

THE THIRD FALLACY: Western-style democracy in the Soviet Union

Believers think that Gorbachëv is trying to introduce Western-style democracy. They do not realise that he is extending 'Communist democracy' – that is to say, a new, more mature phase of socialism in which only the *appearance* of Western-style democracy is created and maintained.

THE FOURTH FALLACY: The decline of ideology

Believers think ideology is dying or already dead and that Gorbachëv has abandoned the class struggle and taken the 'capitalist road'. They do not realise that *'perestroika'* is an expression of ideological strategy and a practical means of reviving ideology. It is not the abandonment of class struggle but a finesse to secure the defeat of the capitalist democracies by the use of capitalist weapons.

The class struggle will yet have its bloody feasts.

The Western élite believe they are helping the cause of democracy. In fact they are financing their own demise and digging their own graves. The tragedy is that they will probably not see it until it is too late.

THE FIFTH FALLACY: The ideological victory of capitalism

Believers think that the West has won the war of ideologies. The irony is that, through *'perestroika'*, the Soviets have captured the strategic and political initiative on the global stage and have begun to carry out their long-nurtured designs against the West which threaten its survival.

THE SIXTH FALLACY: That the Cold War is over

Believers think the Soviet Union is no longer dangerous and that the Cold War is over[21]. They take the deadly flirtation for the romantic marriage. The West perceives the Cold War to be over, and Communism to be dead; but from the Soviet side *the Cold War will accelerate and become more deadly*, especially for the political right which is being targeted as never before with the intention that it should suffer total obliteration.

THE SEVENTH FALLACY: *'Perestroika'* is a blessing for the West

Believers think that *'perestroika'* serves Western interests and that Gorbachëv should be helped. In the United States, even a learned man like Jeremy J. Stone, President of the Federation of American Scientists, has fallen for this fallacy. In a recent article in *The New York Times* entitled 'Let's Do All We Can for Gorbachëv', he called on the Americans to help the Soviets because 'Mr Gorbachëv is, from our viewpoint, the best General Secretary we could dream of seeing'.

---

21 *Editor's Note:* **Sun Tzu**, *'The Art of War'*, c. 500 BC: 'Pretend inferiority and encourage his [the enemy's] arrogance'. This instruction, part of the ancient Chinese tradition of conscious deviousness, is found in Sun Tzu under the heading 'Preliminary Calculations', or 'Estimates' (or Appreciation) of the situation, implying advance 'reckoning' or 'calculations' ahead of conflict.

Believers in Western Europe go even further, advocating a new Marshall Plan to restore the economies of the Soviet Union and Eastern Europe. It was one thing to restore the war-ravaged economies of Western Europe, West Germany and Japan, to shield them from Stalin's armies and to nurture their democratic systems. It is quite another to provide massive economic aid to the ideological enemies and gravediggers of the Western democracies at the very time when they are launching and consolidating their strategic, political offensive against the West.

EIGHTH FALLACY: Fear of *'perestroika's'* failure and the fall of Gorbachëv
Those who lionise Gorbachëv express exaggerated concern for his survival and for the success of *'perestroika'*, which they see as the best hope for the West. They fear that Gorbachëv's departure would lead to a crackdown on 'reformers', rebellion and possible anarchy in the Soviet Union. They would do better to focus on solving their own problems and preserving their societies from Gorbachëv's 'restructuring'.

**NINTH FALLACY: A declining need
for American military-political alliances**
Believers think that the Soviet Union is becoming more peaceful, that Gorbachëv can be trusted and that America's political and military alliances are superfluous. They need to be awakened to the dangers of the Soviet strategy of *'perestroika'* which demand as never before the maintenance and strengthening of these alliances.

THE NEED FOR AN AMERICAN COUNTER-STRATEGY
The Western response to *'perestroika'* has been no less faulty than Western analysis of it. The over-hasty acceptance of and support for *'perestroika'*, overlooking its aggressive anti-Western design, has led the West into a crisis.

Western policymakers have failed to grasp that Soviet reformed 'socialism with a human face' is a more formidable threat than grotesque Stalinist brutality. They do not see that it is part of the drive for world Communist victory and that it will make that victory easier. Western policymakers are trying to seek short-term insignificant gains while Gorbachëv has seized the political initiative and is laying the groundwork for victory over the longer term. Western support for Soviet *'perestroika'* does not provide a sound basis for a better and more durable relationship with the Soviet Union: it merely provides the Soviets with wider opportunities to carry out their strategy. That is the motive behind their willingness to negotiate new agreements on nuclear, conventional and chemical weapons.

In short, the American embrace of Gorbachëv and *'perestroika'* which President Reagan and Prime Minister Thatcher have initiated is a grave strategic blunder, akin to the blunder of President Nixon's embrace with Communist China. The main difference between the two blunders is that time is now running out. In his predictions made in 1967, Sakharov said that 'restructuring', disarmament, socialist convergence and the creation of a World Government could be compiete by the year 2,000. His timetable may have slipped a bit but, given Western ignorance of Soviet strategy and the West's erroneous response to Gorbachëv, the worst may happen.

To ensure that it does not, the West needs new policies which do not assist

Soviet aggressive and revolutionary designs but which counter them. The West learned how to deal with and counteract the repressive but politically passive totalitarianism of Stalin. Now it must learn to counteract the reformed but politically active totalitarianism of Gorbachëv. **It is a new challenge, a new form of undeclared Cold War which the West is facing**. President Reagan's policy of 'trust, but check' is not enough – lacking as it does any appreciation of the essence, objectives, deceptiveness, dangers, strengths and weaknesses of Soviet strategy. It is of paramount importance for the United States to remain strong, not only militarily, but economically and politically. American political, economic and military cooperation with her allies must be reinforced to meet the new form of Soviet threat.

Two forms of response to aggressive Communist strategy are possible. One is that adopted by Alexander Kerensky and Vice-President Wallace which is to ignore it and court disaster: the other is that of Churchill and Truman which is to recognise it and face it down. Reagan and Thatcher have displayed the naïveté of Wallace and Kerensky. It is vital that their strategic blunder is corrected. The new American leader who fails to change course and correct this error will face responsibility for the loss of Western Europe to the Communists and, ultimately, for the end of the great American experiment with democracy.

The moral grounds for a reversal of the American response and for a rejection of the Soviet strategy of *'perestroika'* are very simple. A system which has killed 20 million of its people (50 million if those killed under Communism in China are included), has raped its intellectuals and brought suffering and misery to the peoples of the Soviet Empire, does not deserve to be renewed. The American people are under no moral obligation to help with the reconstruction of such a system.

The pragmatic ground for a new American response to *'perestroika'* is the need to protect and preserve the American system from 'restructuring' and convergence with the Soviet system and to save the American people from the blood baths and re-education camps which such convergence will ultimately bring.

THE CRISIS OF ANALYSIS AND MEASURES TO IMPROVE IT

The continuing use of obsolete methods of analysis breeds fallacies and confusion about *'perestroika'*. The essence of the present crisis lies in the Western inability to detect the aggressive, anti-Western, strategic intent behind *'perestroika'* and Western underestimation of the ability of the whole of the Soviet political machine, including the KGB, to carry that intent into practice.

Western intelligence failures and failures of analysis have not been uncommon in the past. It is time to recognise the fact that the West is facing such a situation now. It is time to break the vicious circle of bureaucratic vested interests in received opinions and conventional wisdom and to clear away the erroneous assumptions and perceptions which have accumulated in Western intelligence services, foreign ministries (especially the State Department and the Foreign Office) and 'think-tanks'.

It is time to examine Soviet *strategic thinking*, not in Western or Stalinist terms, but *in terms of creative Leninism and newly developed Soviet concepts*: to see *'perestroika'* through the prism of the relevant Leninist strategic criteria, to see the Soviet system, not as a passive, but as a politically active form of totalitarianism.

It is time to reassess the capacity of the Soviet political system and the KGB, not as forces for domestic repression, but as executants of anti-Western strategy. It is time to penetrate the dialectical logic of the strategy in order to be able to predict and anticipate further Soviet initiatives and provocations.

DR BRZEZINSKI'S STRATEGY FOR THE WEST IN EASTERN EUROPE

Dr Zbigniew Brzezinski set out his scenario for Eastern Europe and his suggestions for Western strategy there in his Seton-Watson memorial lecture in London in January 1988. The Author feels it necessary to comment on Dr Brzezinski's lecture because it is relevant to the American response to Soviet 'perestroika' and may have an impact on American policymakers[22]. Dr Brzezinski's assessment was that the situation in Eastern Europe was potentially revolutionary. He thought there was genuine political opposition in the region and that the Communist élite there had adopted nationalistic values. He foresaw the possible transformation of East European régimes into pluralist systems. He thought there was a growing desire in Eastern Europe to become part of a European whole. In his view, the Soviet Union and the Communist Parties in Western Europe had ceased to be a potent force and had lost their popular appeal.

Dr Brzezinski was pessimistic about the chances of success for Soviet 'perestroika'. He felt that the Soviet Union was on the defensive and that, in military terms, it was a one-dimensional rival. He considered that Soviet use of the German card to exploit German neutralisation might lead to the dismantling of the Soviet Empire and the neutrality of the East European countries. In Dr Brzezinski's opinion, this situation created an historical setting for 'enlightened policies'. He did not think that a massive revolutionary outbreak in Eastern Europe was in Western interests. He thought the West should not foment, expect or welcome such an outbreak. He suggested that only gradual change in Eastern Europe was desirable. According to him, 'it should be encouraged. It should be facilitated and it is feasible'.

The Western objective should be the transformation of Eastern Europe into a neutral Central Europe, neutral in substance but not in form. He saw the emergence of such a Central Europe in the context of the continued existence of the system of alliances and the promotion of a wider political dialogue within the East. In order to promote this gradual change, Dr Brzezinski advocated the promotion of human rights and the negotiation of extensive East-West economic contacts. He expected that the Soviets would try to achieve through negotiation their long-standing objective of denuclearising Western Europe by promoting a nuclear-free zone in Europe. 'Why not anticipate this', asked Dr Brzezinski, and meet this long-standing objective 'by proposals in the area of conventional arms, aiming at the thin-out and eventual removal from Central Europe of main battlefield tanks?' According to his assessment, the creation of nuclear-free and tank-free zones would lead to the emergence of three parts of Europe – Western Europe, Central Europe and Eastern Europe.

22 *Editor's Note:* Zbigniew Brzezinski was a member of the 'Committee to Support Democracy in Georgia' sponsored by E. Shevardnadze's 'International Foreign Policy Association', which is managed by Dr Jim Garrison in parallel with the Gorbachëv Foundation/USA. The International Foreign Policy Association, like the Gorbachëv Foundation/USA, is an instrument for the mobilisation of the unsuspecting American liberal and policymaking élite in the furtherance of the long-range deception strategy of 'convergence' between East and West on Communist terms [see Note 70, page 191].

Dr Brzezinski's scenario is defective because he does not regard 'perestroika' as Soviet strategy in action and overlooks Soviet strategic designs on Western Europe. He does not take into account the fact that the Soviets have already launched their political offensive and that their strategic objective is not only a reformed Communist system in Eastern Europe but also *the introduction of new 'restructured' systems into Western Europe, using the European Community as a vehicle.*

Dr Brzezinski underestimates the political potential of Soviet power in Western Europe and, in particular, disregards the Soviet intention to use Soviet 'perestroika' to revive the political influence and vitality of the Euro-Communist parties. Dr Brzezinski overlooks the impact of Soviet 'perestroika' on the social democrats in Western Europe which will serve the interests of Soviet strategy.

The 'perestroika' offensive is more likely, in fact, to create favourable conditions for turning Western Europe into a Soviet ally and, eventually, placing it under Soviet hegemony. Dr Brzezinski's scenario also underrates the use of the 'German card' in Soviet strategy. He sees it as 'dismantling the Soviet Empire'. It should be seen instead as part of the Soviet political offensive to increase Moscow's influence in Western Europe. In its essence, Dr Brzezinski's scenario is a wider version of the Polish Government's idea of introducing 'non-confrontational elections' in Poland. It would help the Soviets to avoid political upheavals in Eastern Europe: it would accommodate the Communist régimes there by providing them with Western credits. It might help the Soviets to turn Germany into another Austria. It would serve the purpose of the Soviet strategy of 'restructuring' both Eastern and Western Europe.

If the United States were to adopt this scenario, it would help the Soviets towards their primary objective of achieving a 'common European homeland from the Atlantic to the Urals' – naturally, without any US presence. The Brzezinski scenario, in its approach, comes close to advocating a West European 'Marshall Plan' for Eastern Europe. In underestimating Soviet political potential and the strength of military-security organisations in Eastern Europe, Dr Brzezinski may be making much the same mistake as he made in underestimating the capabilities of the Nicaraguan Sandinistas – with disastrous consequences for the Nicaraguan people and for the United States. The difference lies mainly in the grander scale of the mistake.

For all the reasons given, the Brzezinski scenario should be rejected as defective and dangerous. It is true that Eastern Europe is the Achilles Heel of the Soviet Empire. It should be left to the peoples of Eastern Europe to make their own decisions on revolution. The Author firmly believes that American interests and the interests of people living under Communist domination would be better served by revolution in Eastern Europe and the failure of 'perestroika' in the USSR. If a revolutionary situation develops in Eastern Europe, the West should encourage, not a gradual change through political dialogue there, but a radical change through revolution if the East European peoples choose it.

After all, if a revolutionary situation occurred in Western Europe or the United States, the Soviets would not hesitate to encourage and facilitate it. Why should the West be timid? Political upheaval in Eastern Europe will probably be the only chance of putting a stop to the strategy of 'restructuring' and of getting rid of Soviet domination of the area once and for all.

THE NEED TO IMPROVE WESTERN INTELLIGENCE AND COUNTER-INTELLIGENCE

American intelligence, and in particular the experts on the USSR and China, should adopt a longer term approach in dealing with the Soviet and Chinese challenge to the United States. Coverage and the countering of hostile Soviet strategy should become important priorities for the American intelligence and counter-intelligence communities. Coverage and counter-strategy should be conducted on a global scale but particularly in the United States and Western Europe.

The capability of American intelligence and counter-intelligence should be rebuilt to meet the new challenge and the new threat. American cooperation with the allied services on this threat should be greatly improved.

In particular, Western counter-intelligence services should study the clear pattern of agents of influence working in favour of *'perestroika'* both in Communist and in Western countries. Because of Sakharov's active rôle in promoting the strategy of *'perestroika'* and his excessive influence in the United States, US policymakers should be warned that the emperor of *'perestroika'* has no clothes. The main Western sources in the Soviet political establishment like the FBI's 'TOPHAT' in military intelligence and the FBI's 'FEDORA' and the French DST's 'FAREWELL' in technical intelligence should be reassessed in the light of their information on Soviet strategy. *Sources who have failed to report on significant aspects of Soviet strategy should be regarded as under KGB control.* Application of this new counter-intelligence criterion would provide fresh openings for uncovering the KGB's past and more recent penetrations of Western special services.

THE PRESSING NEED FOR PUBLIC EXPOSURE OF THE STRATEGY OF *'PERESTROIKA'*

The Soviet strategy of *'perestroika'* must be exposed because it is deceptive, aggressive and dangerous. Gorbachëv and *'glasnost'* have failed to reveal that *'perestroika'* is a world-wide political assault against the Western democracies. It has been presented as a purely domestic, spontaneous improvisation by Gorbachëv. *This deliberate misrepresentation must be exposed.*

It must be revealed that *'perestroika'* is the result of thirty years of preparation by the Communist Party, the Soviet Government and the KGB under the guidance of the Party apparatus, that it is not just Soviet domestic renewal but *a strategy for 'restructuring' the whole world*[23]. The KGB's sinister rôle as a vehicle for implementation of the strategy must be explained. Gorbachëv's renunciation of ideological orthodoxy is not sincere or lasting, but a tactical manoeuvre in the cause of the strategy. The Soviets are not striving for genuine, lasting accommodation with the Western democracies but for the final world victory of Communism: they are not

---

23 *Editor's Note:* The accuracy of this prediction is confirmed, *inter alia*, by the hyperactive agenda of the Gorbachëv Foundation/USA, which has sponsored schemes focusing on transnational issues ostensibly requiring supranational cooperation, including a so-called 'Global Security Project'. Coordinated from Moscow by Gorbachëv's close associate, **Georgiy Shaknazarov**, Director of the 'Center for Global Programs' at the Gorbachëv Foundation/Moscow, the project has addressed such 'global control' issues as 'cooperative security arrangements', 'global conventional arms control', and 'enhancing the strength of international institutions'. It has brought together many members of the Russian and American élites. According to *'Argumenty i Fakti'* [Moscow, Number 33, August 1991], Shaknazarov, when asked for his opinion of Yeltsin's performance during the 'August coup' period, responded: **'He has been marvellous. He has done everything that we expected him to do'**. *The Author writes:* Prior to the introduction of *'perestroika'*, Shaknazarov contributed articles to Soviet journals on the future of Soviet society. *See also Note 97, page 231.*

introducing true capitalism or real Western-style democracy but creating an illusion to tempt West European social democrats into new forms of popular front and eventual alliance with the Soviet Union. They intend to exploit the same illusion to induce the Americans to adopt their own 'restructuring' and convergence of the Soviet and American systems using to this end *the fear of nuclear conflict*.

Arbatov was lying when he said that the USSR had ceased to be an enemy of the United States: the USSR is becoming more formidable, more sophisticated and more dangerous because the new design for Communist world victory is more realistic than the old. The new design can be described most succinctly as 'cooperation-blackmail'[24].

Convergence will be accompanied by blood baths and political re-education camps in Western Europe and the United States. The Soviet strategists are counting on an economic depression in the United States and intend to introduce their reformed model of socialism with a human face as an alternative to the American system during the depression. All these points must be publicly revealed.

The urgent necessity for exposing the strategy of *'perestroika'* is dictated *inter alia* by the following factors:

1. The anti-Western character of *'perestroika'* is not understood by Western policymakers, élites or the general public.

2. The Americans, and to an even greater extent, the Europeans, are euphoric about Gorbachëv and Soviet *'perestroika'* as a result of the dramatic changes in the USSR and the support for Gorbachëv by Western leaders.

3. Gorbachëv has captured the political initiative and is actively pursuing an offensive to implement the strategy in Eastern and Western Europe and the USA.

4. The Soviet intelligence and security services and their agents of influence in the USSR and the West are exploiting Western euphoria to shape and influence Western policies and Western public opinion in the interests of their strategy.

---

24 *Author's Note:* i.e., 'cooperate with us or face the prospect of nuclear chaos and conflict'. The developing situation over North Korea should be carefully watched with this in mind. The late Kim Il Sung was a Soviet Korean. The North Koreans would not have acted in a provocative manner without the concealed support of the Russians and of their Chinese comrades-in-arms from the 1950s.

In a different context, the Russians may be expected to provoke an incident unattributable to themselves involving the explosion of a nuclear device somewhere in the West not excluding the United States. The purpose would be to reassert or re-emphasise the necessity for the American-Russian partnership now, and to create pressure for eventual World Government.

US policy for dealing with the North Korean crisis is inadequate because it focuses on North Korea in isolation as a rogue state, and naïvely seeks help from the Russians and Chinese to solve the problem. The North Korean situation and any future nuclear incident, wherever it occurs, must be seen against the background of Sino-Soviet 'convergence' strategy: the interaction of Russian and Chinese policy and the moves they make to derive strategic gains from critical situations should be closely studied.

THE ADVANTAGES OF EXPOSURE

Exposure would strip the glamour away from Gorbachëv and 'perestroika' and reveal them in their true red colour. It would call a halt to the Soviet political offensive and dampen down euphoria in the West. It would prevent Gorbachëv from gaining his important strategic objective of winning the masses over from their Western leaders. It would put Gorbachëv and his strategists on the defensive and reveal Soviet weaknesses and falsehoods. It would force Gorbachëv and Shevardnadze to deny that they have a global strategy or that they are trying to lure the United States into convergence and World Government. It would test 'glasnost' and show whether the cessation of the jamming of American radio broadcasts is permanent or a temporary expedient and a consequence of the loss of anti-Communist sting in the broadcasts and their praise for Gorbachëv and 'perestroika'.

It would help to break Party control over the flow of information which 'glasnost' was not intended to change and has not changed. It would help to dispose of Western fallacies, misconceptions and exaggerated expectations of Soviet 'perestroika'. It would help to preserve the integrity of the election process and reduce Soviet influence over the next presidential and national elections in the United States and Western Europe. It might help to stem the present haemorrhage of West European and Japanese technology and credits to the USSR and Eastern Europe. Finally, exposure would allow the new US administration to correct the mistakes of two former Presidents, to regroup its political forces and capabilities, to develop a sound counter-strategy and to recover the political initiative.

Consideration should be given to implementing the exposure of 'perestroika':

1. By publication of the essence of the Author's Memoranda in 'Foreign Affairs' over the signature of "X' – a KGB defector'.

2. By publication of the essence of the Memoranda in all West European countries and Japan; and:

3. By broadcasting the essence of the Memoranda in American foreign broadcasts for the USSR and Eastern Europe.

It is appropriate to mention that, as long ago as 1962, the Author attempted an exposure of Soviet strategy, the precedent of the New Economic Policy and the new political rôle of the KGB. At a meeting with the late Mr Robert Kennedy, the US Attorney General, the Author put forward general proposals on this matter. Mr Kennedy arranged a meeting with the late Mr Edward Murrow, then head of the United States Information Agency [USIA]. Probably the idea of KGB-controlled 'liberalisation' appeared to the great American broadcaster as too unreal, too remote and unintelligible, because nothing resulted from the meeting.

Now the new Soviet design is clear and close at hand. It is a realistic design. The situation is critical. There is no other choice but to expose the Soviet strategy and its dangers for the United States and its allies. Things are so far advanced that little can be lost in the prevailing chaos and confusion – and it is still surely possible that the West can finally be brought to understand the perils it faces due to this historically unprecedented global strategic 'cooperation-blackmail' offensive. ■

PART TWO

COMMUNIST GRAND STRATEGIES AND WESTERN ILLUSIONS

Memorandum to the CIA: 4 JANUARY 1988

COMMUNIST GRAND STRATEGIES AND WESTERN ILLUSIONS

AN ASSESSMENT OF GORBACHEV'S VISIT TO THE UNITED STATES IN THE LIGHT OF THE GRAND SOVIET DECEPTION STRATEGY

The main purpose of General Secretary Gorbachëv's visit to the United States in December, 1987 was not to prepare for a summit meeting or to reach an agreement on a reduction of nuclear missiles but to engage the American élite in the execution of Soviet strategy and to influence it in directions favourable to that strategy.

Since the strategy presents a threat to the long-term survival of the United States, there is an acute and pressing need for a new American counter-strategy and for a new concept of counter-intelligence.

The following conventional arguments have all been used against renewed *détente* with the USSR and against new agreements on strategic weapons:

1. The risk that the Soviets will succeed in undermining the US nuclear deterrent which, for four decades, has prevented war between the United States and the Soviet Union and has provided a measure of stability for North America and Western Europe.

2. The risk that the Soviets will succeed in destabilising NATO and opening up new possibilities for Soviet adventures.

3. The risk that the Soviet strategists will succeed in killing off the US Strategic Defence Initiative [SDI].

4. The risk that the retention by the Soviets of superiority in conventional weapons and troop strengths will *increase* the danger of war.

5. The risk that the Soviets will violate new agreements and exploit *détente* as before, to swing the military balance in their favour.

All these arguments are cogent and should not be forgotten. But they do not take into account either past Soviet political designs against the West or present Soviet political strategy.

Current euphoria about summit meetings is blinding Western policymakers to Gorbachëv's real strategic designs against the West and is paving the way for further US miscalculations and for the successful execution of Soviet strategy.

The failure of American and other Western leaders to recognise or comprehend Soviet strategic intentions and the dangers for the West of so-called *'perestroika'* and *'glasnost'* is leading towards a new and profound crisis.

The situation demands that we should look beyond the conventional arguments outlined above and review the historical experience of the Soviets in developing their political strategy and the contribution which, wittingly or unwittingly, the West has made to the successful execution of that strategy.

THE THREE GRAND STRATEGIES

The Soviets regard strategy as a grand overall design, often referred to as 'the general line', which guides the course of the Party's actions over a period of twenty to thirty years in the pursuit of its unchanging Communist objectives.

As in military strategy, Soviet political strategy is flexible, elastic as to timing, contains a variety of options and takes full account of risks and possible losses. The feature of *strategy* which distinguishes it from *policy* is that *it contains within itself a secret, concealed or deceptive manoeuvre* designed to take the adversary by surprise and thus secure victory for the strategy.

Since the turn of the century, the Russian Communists have developed three grand strategies. The common essence of these strategies has been the messianic obsession with seizing power in Russia, achieving the world-wide victory of Communism and building a totalitarian, egalitarian society.

THE FIRST GRAND STRATEGY

The first grand strategy was developed by Lenin. Its objective was the overthrow of the Tsarist régime by a workers' revolution and the establishment of the dictatorship of the Communist Party in Russia. It took roughly twenty years to accomplish its objective through the revolution of October 1917. In achieving victory, Lenin took advantage of three main factors in the situation:

1. *The Russian defeat in the First World War against Germany and the consequent hunger and discontent prevalent among the Russian peasants and soldiers.*

2. *The financial help given by the German General Staff to the opposition political parties in Russia including the Communist Party.* The German generals reasoned that these parties would overthrow the Tsar and that Russia would then leave the war. They went so far as to facilitate the return to Russia via Germany of Lenin and his colleagues from their exile in Switzerland.

Lenin, however, did not sell out to the Germans. Once his Party had assumed power, he did everything possible to promote revolution in Germany and came close to success in 1918-19. The help the Germans gave Lenin showed how little they understood his strategic intentions: they paid dearly for their miscalculations.

3. *The weakness and misconceptions of Alexander Kerensky, the last Prime Minister of the democratic Provisional Government of Russia.* The Russian generals, concerned about the disintegration of the Russian army and the increasing influence of the Communist Party, began to prepare for a military-backed régime in order to forestall a Communist coup. Kerensky, himself a socialist, turned against the generals and made common cause with the Left in which the Communists were becoming dominant. This opened the way to the Communist takeover in October 1917.

Asked about this subject in a conversation with the Author in 1962, Kerensky admitted that his move was a grave miscalculation. He said that he had viewed the Communists as just another Party and had underestimated their organisation and strength. He conceded that he had failed to grasp their strategy.

The essence of the special manoeuvre in this first Communist grand strategy for seizing power in Russia was the organisation of an army uprising or *coup d'état* by the minority Communist Party led by Lenin.

THE SECOND GRAND STRATEGY

The two main objectives of the second grand strategy, developed by Lenin after taking power, were:

1. To promote socialism (Communism) in Russia.

2. To foment world-wide Communist revolution.

The execution of this strategy can be considered to have been implemented in five distinct periods or phases:

In the first period, Lenin attempted to implement the strategy through the tactic of rigorous 'war Communism' in Russia combined with a frontal attack on the capitalist world abroad. Early in 1919 he set up the Communist International or Comintern to act as the parent body for Communist Parties in the capitalist countries. These tactics failed both at home and abroad.

In the second period, Lenin implemented tactical readjustments within the strategy. In an effort to revive the Soviet economy, he introduced a limited form of *Party-controlled* capitalism under the 'New Economic Policy' or NEP which offered new incentives for production. Through the NEP he succeeded in obtaining economic aid and increased trade, credits and technology from Western industrialists. In practice, the NEP served to strengthen the socialist base in Russia.

Exploiting the contradictions between defeated Germany and the victorious Western allies, Lenin succeeded in negotiating the Rapallo Treaty with Germany. Secret military collaboration ensued between the Soviets and the Germans under General von Seeckt. Thus the German generals made another grave miscalculation through their failure to appreciate Lenin's ideology and anti-Western strategy.

The help they gave the Soviets in laying the foundations of their military industry worked to Germany's detriment in the Second World War. In addition, Lenin planned a number of political reforms to make the Communist model more attractive to other countries, but his efforts were negated by his illness and his death.

The third period was associated with the continuation of Lenin's strategy by Stalin. But, in place of the New Economic Policy, Stalin applied ruthless industrialisation and collectivisation. To cope with mounting discontent, he introduced mass repression – establishing in the process his own personal dictatorship and a grossly oppressive form of Russian police socialism.

Preoccupied with the internal problems of collectivising the Russian peasantry, Stalin failed to exploit the depression in the United States and the world economic crisis. His repressions discredited Communist ideas and impeded the strategy of Communist expansion in the 1930s.

The fourth period was characterised by Stalin's skilful exploitation along Leninist lines of the contradictions between the Great Powers. By signing the Nazi-Soviet Pacts with Germany, he gained control of the Baltic States. After the German invasion of the Soviet Union, he entered into military collaboration with the United States and Britain. US military aid proved a significant factor in the defeat of Germany and, subsequently, Japan.

But even while this collaboration continued, Stalin engaged in the deception of both President Franklin Roosevelt and Winston Churchill, the British Prime Minister, by successfully concealing from them the expansionist nature of his strategy. He achieved this by playing down Communist ideology, by presenting himself as a nationalist leader, by making minor but highly visible, deceptive concessions to the Russian Orthodox Church, and by his dissolution of the Comintern.

Stalin went on to exploit the victory over Germany and Japan in order to expand the Communist world both in Eastern Europe and in Asia. His secret military aid to the Chinese Communists contributed significantly to their takeover in China. 'Socialism in one country' was converted into a Communist Bloc of 13 states.

With the benefit of hindsight, it is reasonable to say that President Roosevelt underrated Stalin's strategic designs, trusted him too readily and was too naïve in his belief that Stalin's appetite could be controlled. The underestimation of Stalin's strategy proved very costly to the West.

The essence of the special manoeuvre in this period of the second Communist grand strategy, a manoeuvre which contributed greatly both to the victory over Germany and Japan and to the post-war spread of Communism, was Stalin's calculated emphasis on traditional Russian nationalism and patriotism at the apparent expense of Communist ideology, his calculated toleration of the Russian Orthodox Church and his deceptive dissolution of the Comintern.

The fifth and final period of the second grand strategy involved the ruthless Sovietisation of the 'Peoples' Democracies' of Eastern Europe. Here, however, the inefficiency of industry and agriculture led to hunger and discontent among the peoples of the Soviet Empire. Stalin's attempts at mass repression proved ineffective. Disaffection spread even to the Communist leaders themselves. As a consequence, Communist Yugoslavia broke with Stalin and left the Communist Bloc. By 1952 Stalin had abandoned the strategy. He was by now a frightened man preoccupied with preserving his personal power through the elimination of all potential rivals.

The whole Communist system was in the depths of crisis. A revolutionary situation pervaded the Soviet Empire, threatening an explosion at any moment. The Party's revelations of Stalin's crimes added fuel to the flames. Open revolts broke out in Poland and Hungary.

Had the United States and its allies intervened in Hungary, the divided and paralysed Soviet leadership would have been unable to respond effectively. Such was the estimate of the then Chairman of the KGB, General Ivan Serov.

Given US and allied intervention, the revolt would have spread in all probability to the USSR and other Communist states. A golden opportunity to rid the world of Communism once and for all was lost.

Khrushchev, Mao Tse-Tung, Shelepin and other Communist leaders all recognised the damage inflicted on the Communist cause by Stalin's despotism and use of mass repression. They condemned his domination over the leaders of other Communist Parties and his interference in their affairs. They were painfully aware of the deficiencies of their industry and agriculture and of the crisis in the system as a whole. They accepted the need for radical changes in Communist practice and the urgent necessity of formulating a new grand strategy for Communism.

According to the chief of the KGB Institute at the time, Mao Tse-Tung gave up all but one of his leading positions in China in 1959 in order to concentrate on the development of this strategy.

Thoroughgoing research was conducted into the historical experience of the Communist Parties. Consultations took place between the Soviet and Chinese leaders. Khrushchev and Shelepin visited China, where Khrushchev met Mao and Deng Xiao-ping. Shelepin studied the experience of the Chinese Ministry of Public Security in dealing with political opposition.

Following these consultations and research, the new, third grand strategy for the Bloc was adopted and launched in the period between 1958 and 1960. Its principal architects were Mao and Khrushchev. **The strategy was long-range in character and covered the whole Communist Bloc. It took into account not only the political, economic and military potential of the Bloc countries but also, for the first time in their history, the political potential of their intelligence and security services including the KGB.**

In 1959 Shelepin delivered his famous secret report on the active use of the KGB's potential, and in particular *the use of controlled political opposition*, in the execution of the strategy. The KGB was reorganised for the purpose, and its long-term political rôle was approved by the Party Congress.

Ever since, the new strategy has governed the internal and foreign policies of the Communist countries and the activities of the international Communist movement with a view to the further development and strengthening of the Communist system. As with the previous two grand strategies, the third was designed to last for a generation. A generation's delay was needed for Stalin's victims and their jailers to pass away before the final phase of the strategy could safely be introduced.

Internally, the main constituents of the long-range strategy have been:

(a) To abolish Stalinist practices, in particular the use of mass repression, and to introduce other changes needed for recovery from the crisis of the mid-1950s.

(b) To restore Lenin's style of collegial leadership within the Communist Parties and genuine fraternal relations between them.

(c) To prepare for and introduce in the final phase of the strategy economic and political restructuring and democratisation of the USSR and other Communist countries. This is the origin of the current economic reform in Hungary and China and of 'perestroika' in the USSR. Similar innovations to those introduced in Hungary and China may be expected throughout the Communist Bloc.

Externally, **the main constituents of the strategy have been:**

(a) The build-up of the military potential of the Communist Bloc as a whole.

(b) The adoption of a Leninist style of activist diplomacy directed against the 'main enemy' countries (i.e. the United States, Britain, France, West Germany and Japan) and the use of deceptive negotiations, alliances and other agreements along the lines of the Treaty of Rapallo.

(c) The use of the intelligence potential of the Communist countries and especially the KGB to undermine and destabilise the capitalist world and its institutions through *permanent political and psychological warfare.*

(d) The use against the West of the political potential of the Communist countries, the Communist Parties of the non-Communist world and national liberation and anti-war movements.

These elements have been used in the pursuit of the principal objectives of the strategy in foreign affairs, in order:

(a) To reduce the influence of Western countries in the world.

(c) To shift the balance of power in favour of the Communist world by breaking up Western regional alliances including NATO, CENTO and SEATO and by paralysing Western military programmes and commitments, especially by supporting national liberation movements as, for example, in Vietnam.

(c) To exploit the resulting shift in the balance of power to move towards the final conquest of capitalism through the convergence on Communist terms of the capitalist and Communist systems.

There is no doubt that this third grand strategy aims to procure total Communist victory. Khrushchev's notorious remark, reported as 'we shall bury you' (although in fact he said: 'We shall be present at your funeral'), was a slip of the tongue; but it was made at the time when the strategy was adopted *and it expressed the true aim of the strategy.*

Acceptance of this aim was accompanied by a 'joke' popular in bureaucratic circles at the time and attributed to Suslov, one of the top Communist strategists: 'Comrades, should we really take over the whole capitalist world? Wouldn't it be better to leave at least one capitalist state like the United States so that it could feed us?'

To sum up, the central purpose of the third grand strategy and its final phase of *'perestroika'* is to renew the régimes in the USSR and other Communist countries and to convert them into states of 'mature socialism with a human face'. But the strategy goes beyond domestic restructuring and is aimed at the peaceful *and non-peaceful* conquest of the United States and Western Europe *from within.*

The essence of the special manoeuvre within this strategy is the creation of secretly controlled opposition movements (the secret within the strategy, which distinguishes it from a mere policy) and the use of them in the course of transition to new deceptive 'democratic', 'non-Communist' and 'nationalist' power structures which will remain in essence Communist controlled.

It is these renewed régimes which are intended to achieve the world victory of Communism through the convergence on Communist terms of the Communist and non-Communist systems.

'CONVERGENCE' THROUGH TACTICAL CHANGES AND DISINFORMATION

In working out their new strategy, the Communist strategists took due note of the contribution that unwitting Western support had made to the successful execution of the first and second grand strategies. **They concluded that unwitting Western support would be essential for the fulfilment of their strategy of convergence.** They set about procuring it through a long-range programme of deceptive tactical readjustments in the ideological, political and economic spheres and through disinformation calculated to create the grand illusion that the Communist countries were moving closer to the Western model. Their disinformation themes were that Communist ideology was dying if not already dead, that the Communist Bloc was disintegrating into a collection of disparate national régimes and that the European Communist Parties were evolving from Leninist into conventional political parties under the device of Euro-Communism.

The purpose of the disinformation was to conceal from Western governments the degree of coordination between the Communist governments and Parties in the pursuit of their long-term objectives and, by suggesting that the demise of ideology provided a basis for more constructive relations with the West, to engage the West in unwitting support for Communist strategy.

In addition to the disinformation campaign, some Communist states, notably Hungary, China and the Soviet Union, have been experimenting for the past twenty-five years with the introduction of economic reforms. Hungary introduced capitalist incentives both for its internal economy and in respect of its foreign trade. Communist China has also introduced incentives and a limited form of capitalism, inviting foreign industrialists to do business and to invest in its economy.

The Soviet Union is *apparently* reforming its economy. All these economic 'reforms' are part of the Communist strategy. Their purpose is not only to improve economic performance but to serve as a deceptive device for creating and promoting the illusion that both China and the USSR are moving in the direction of a Western style of capitalism and that the growing apparent (but illusory) similarity of the systems provides a basis for convergence. At the same time, the Communist states have been preparing and rehearsing deceptive political reforms for the past twenty-five years, especially in Czechoslovakia, China, Poland and the USSR, all within the framework of the long-range strategy. In the USSR, the KGB under Shelepin and then Andropov created a controlled political opposition movement among Soviet intellectuals to act as a leading element in the programme of political reform.

In China, the Cultural Revolution formed part of the strategic preparation for *détente* and active engagement with the capitalist world, and for the introduction of domestic political and economic reform. Its purpose was to re-educate the discontented Chinese intellectuals and the remnants of the former capitalist classes, and to prepare them and the stagnant Chinese Communist bureaucracy for the active rôle which all of them would be called upon to play.

Now, in the final phase of the strategy, the Soviets have begun to launch their own programme of political reform or 'democratisation' of the Soviet Union. A principal purpose of this programme is to provide a further, political argument in favour of convergence between East and West.

Lastly, the Communist strategists have developed disinformation concerning the alleged existence in both the USSR and China of groups of liberals and conservatives and about conservative resistance to 'democratisation'. There is nothing new about this disinformation, which has been used consistently since the adoption of the strategy. To begin with, there was disinformation about 'revisionists' led by Khrushchev and 'Stalinists' led by Mao.

Then there was disinformation about 'compromisers' and 'hardliners' under Brezhnev in the USSR and about 'pragmatists' and 'dogmatists' in China under Mao and Deng. Under Khrushchev and Brezhnev, the purpose was to promote the first *détente* with the United States and Western Europe and to extract concessions in the course of the SALT negotiations. In the Chinese case, the objects include *détente* with the United States and procuring Western technology for China.

Now, the purpose of the intensified disinformation on 'conservative' resistance to Gorbachëv's reforms and on the Yeltsin affair is to win Western support for further arguments in favour of convergence and to widen the gap between genuine conservatives and liberals in the United States.

The rationale of this disinformation is that that there are two sorts of people: those who recognise change and seek to promote it, and those who oppose it – the implication being that those who oppose it are 'enemies of progress and peace', 'cold warriors', etc. This was the explanation given by Gorbachëv to the prominent Soviet expert Marshall Shulman at a White House reception.

Gorbachëv added that 'we have both kinds of people in both our countries'. In this way Gorbachëv gave evidence of his intention to project and promote Soviet strategy through influential American intellectuals. There are indications that the dismissal of Yeltsin as head of the Moscow Party organisation was prearranged, timed and publicised by giving Mr Dan Rather permission to interview him on the subject, on the Central Broadcasting System one month in advance of Gorbachëv's visit to the United States. The purpose of that specific disinformation was further to exaggerate the alleged pressure being brought to bear on Gorbachëv by Soviet 'conservatives' (to whom Gorbachëv was under latent pressure to defer), to highlight the rôle of both *Soviet and American conservatives* as obstacles to reform and 'progress' and to create favourable conditions for an alliance between Soviet and American liberals for the intended purpose of the 'restructuring' of both societies.

AMERICAN OFFICIAL TACTICS VERSUS SOVIET OFFICIAL STRATEGY

In the time of Presidents Truman and Eisenhower when the Communist system was in crisis and the United States had unquestionable military superiority, the Soviet bureaucracy regarded the United States with apprehension. Now they see it as a confused, disunited and demoralised country fragmented by minority interests. They perceive it as the weaker nation and as an easy prey for their strategic manipulation. They are encouraged by the divisive effects of the Vietnam war and the American defeat. They are heartened by the American decision in 1967 to opt out of the Cold War and to dissolve the American political potential among intellectuals, students and international organisations at the very time when the Soviets were intensifying their political and psychological warfare against the United States.

To this end, the Soviet strategists mobilised their security and intelligence potential among the intellectuals and the entire political potential of their Party, the Komsomol and even Young Pioneer members. The Soviets are further encouraged by the weakening of the Central Intelligence Agency, and in particular of its counter-intelligence capability following the Watergate scandal.

They are gratified by the overall success of their disinformation operations.

Since Western intelligence services recognise the existence only of *tactical* disinformation – for example in the form of forged official Western documents – and overlook the existence of *strategic* disinformation, the Communist strategists have succeeded in confusing Western governments and enlisting their unwitting support for the execution of their strategy. In consequence, the West has made serious mistakes in its dealings with the Communists. The Americans entered into *détente* with China and the USSR and invited Khrushchev, Brezhnev and Deng to visit the United States. The Americans and West Europeans made trade agreements with both countries and provided massive credits and some transfers of technology.

The United States signed political, diplomatic and military agreements which are detrimental to long-term Western interests in the light of Communist designs on world domination. China and the USSR have both recovered from their crises, have consolidated their régimes and have emerged as serious rivals to the United States. The United States has slipped into military parity with the USSR while the USSR has developed into a superpower threatening the United States and Western Europe.

China is emerging as another potential superpower which, together with the USSR, will swing the world balance of military power, particularly in respect of conventional forces, in favour of the Communists.

The Communist strategists perceive the American situation as favourable to the furtherance of their strategy and they are confident of success. Their confidence is based on the past successes of their first and second grand strategies and on the partial success of their third and current strategy. **They take particular heart from the fact that American and West European policymakers have no understanding of their strategy and its dialectic nor any means of countering it.**

They take comfort from the way in which American (and other Western) counter-intelligence plies its traditional trade focused on the exposure of conventional spies, oblivious of the problems raised by Soviet *strategic disinformation* and the use of agents of influence. Involvement in the execution of the strategy for world conquest and in the practice of strategic disinformation dominates the attitudes, thinking and behaviour of the Communist bureaucracy and its diplomats. This involvement has revived their ideological commitment. All their moves and negotiations are guided by the considerations of strategy.

As Mao put it, they take the United States seriously as a tactical adversary but discount it in a strategic sense.

Despite the advent of *'glasnost'*, the Soviet credo – **'whenever required, lie for the Party line'** – is unchanged. Diplomacy and negotiations with the United States are still viewed as elements of an acute class struggle in the international arena. The Soviets' attitude to treaties with the capitalist countries is still that of Lenin, namely that **they are just scraps of paper to be torn up when the balance of power has**

changed[25]. This is why they have violated so many of the agreements they have made with the United States. This mentality further helps to explain the surprise moves at the Reykjavik summit, also dictated by strategic considerations.

Gorbachëv is neither the originator of the strategy nor the father of Soviet democracy. He was chosen and trained by the Party bureaucracy to implement the final phase of the strategy. Originally, Shelepin was a candidate for this rôle; but he ➧

25 *Editor's Note:* Yet while Leninist contempt for the sanctity of accords remains the norm, treaties originating in Moscow are nevertheless actively used in the furtherance of strategy. Gorbachëv spearheaded a bilateral friendship treaty offensive, elaborating a traditional instrument of Soviet foreign policy which continued without respite into the Yeltsin era. Addressing the USSR Supreme Soviet on 26 November 1990, Gorbachëv outlined this element of the Soviet agenda for Europe with Leninist precision: 'For the first time, political trust has acquired the form of documented mutual pledges. The new type of bilateral declarations and treaties which the USSR has recently concluded with the unified Germany, France, Italy, Spain and Finland – and there are others on the way, too – and, of course, the documents signed... at the Paris meeting itself – create the political-legal foundation of the new Europe with which it has decided to proceed into the 21st century'. By 9 November 1992, when President Yeltsin and the British Prime Minister, John Major, signed the Treaty on the Principles of Relations between the United Kingdom of Great Britain and Northern Ireland and the Russian Federation in London, Moscow had signed up most of the key West European countries, including Greece and Turkey. Such treaties are initially drafted in Moscow and presented to the Western countries for their consideration. This is clear *inter alia* from the following information: **(1)** On 28 October 1991, Mr John McGregor (then Leader of the British House of Commons) wrote to Mr Michael Spicer MP [letter reference: ADS/AG] *inter alia* as follows: '... you asked me for details of treaty overtures to the British Government from the Soviet Union. In September 1990, *the Soviet Union proposed a bilateral document...*'. **(2)** Section III ['Organisation of the Ministry's Activity'] of a document entitled 'Temporary Provisions of the Ministry of Security of the Russian Federation', approved by the former Supreme Soviet on 5 March 1992, laid down that the Security Ministry 'participates in *the preparation of international treaties* and organises their implementation within the limits of the Ministry's competence'.

The importance attached by Moscow to the new bilateral treaty network, whereby the European Union Member States are treaty-bound to implement their resulting obligations towards Russia, was reiterated in *'International Affairs'*, the official journal of the Russian Foreign Ministry [March-April 1994] by Andrei Kozyrev, the Russian Foreign Minister: 'First of all, it is time to carry out existing bilateral accords'. Not only are EU member countries burdened with new bilateral obligations towards Moscow, but their Common Foreign and Security Policy, introduced with the Maastricht Treaty, is liable to be directly influenced as a consequence of these obligations – providing Moscow with powerful scope for exercising indirect control over Western foreign and security policy formulation. This little recognised dimension of Russian influence over Western Europe is buttressed by formal 'collective security' arrangements built up *in response to* Soviet diplomacy, of which the Conference on Security and Cooperation in Europe [CSCE], partly financed through the European Community budget, is the most conspicuous component.

The strategy of promoting 'collective security', which is underpinned by the bilateral treaty network, grew out of Soviet initiatives, as Golitsyn explained on page 266 of *'New Lies for Old'*: **'A significant rôle in such coordination, specifically for the realization of the strategy in Western Europe, rests with the Soviet Committee for European Security, headed by Party official V. Shytikov. This committee was created in June 1971 for better coordination between the Soviet mass organizations in the struggle for the realization of a collective European security'**. On page 334 of *'New Lies for Old'*, the Author predicted that the Communists would attempt, as indeed they did at the end of the 1980s, to procure 'the simultaneous dissolution of NATO and the Warsaw Pact' as a step towards 'the establishment of a neutral, socialist Europe'. In 1980, 'the Soviet and East European Committee for European Security was reactivated', with Shytikov 'much in evidence' at 'a meeting of parliamentarians from Communist states held in Moscow in March 1981'.

The CSCE model is also being promoted by Moscow for application in the Middle East, having originally been 'put forward back in 1972, in the opening stages of the all-European process' [*source:* Fidel Bundyukov, of the Russian Academy of Sciences, *'International Affairs'*, June 1993, pages 79-82]. Bundyukov makes it plain that while the 'CSCM' was initially presented as a proposal for a regional bloc covering the *Mediterranean*, its targeted region in reality focused on the Middle East.

was sent into oblivion after his return from Britain in 1975 because he had been discredited internationally. Gorbachëv is no more than the executor of Soviet strategy. Since the strategy was developed by the bureaucracy and a whole generation of Party leaders, Gorbachëv poses no threat to the so-called Party conservatives, the technocrats or the military.

But because the American Administration and its State Department negotiators are oblivious of Soviet strategy and strategic disinformation, they operate on a different level. The Americans adhere to the rules of formal, conventional diplomacy, counting and reporting on the number of rockets and other weapons systems. Their primary concern is with the fine print of negotiations, agreements and means of verification. By contrast, the Soviets' concern is with the success of their long-range strategy of convergence, with drawing the teeth of American nuclear power and with turning the United States, in Mao's words, into a 'paper tiger'. The Soviets secretly despise their American counterparts. Their practice of activist diplomacy makes a sham of all their negotiations and agreements with the West, especially given their adherence to Lenin's view of the sanctity of treaties and accords.

GORBACHEV'S US VISIT A TROJAN HORSE TO ENGAGE THE AMERICAN ÉLITE IN THE STRATEGY OF CONVERGENCE

The visit of General Secretary Mikhail Gorbachëv to the United States, like those of Khrushchev and Brezhnev before him, is a good illustration of Soviet strategic duplicity and American naïveté. The President, the Administration and US counter-intelligence all failed to comprehend that the main purpose of the visit was not to sign a treaty but to introduce the Americans to the strategy of restructuring Soviet and American societies towards convergence, and to engage the American élite in the acceptance and promotion of this concept.

Prior to the visit, the Soviet offensive had met with scant success: only a few leaders had been impressed – notably the British Prime Minister, Mrs Thatcher who set a precedent by seeing in Gorbachëv a man with whom she could 'do business'.

Earlier meetings of representatives of the American élite with Gorbachëv and Sakharov in Moscow had left the Americans sceptical of the sincerity and depth of Gorbachëv and his reforms. Now, with Gorbachëv's visit, the Soviets have stepped up their campaign to influence the American élite – exploiting its fear of nuclear war, its confusion over the true 'convergence' meaning inherent in 'perestroika' and its naïve euphoria over the signing of a treaty.

It is for this reason that the Soviets sent over their top advisers specialising in strategy, diplomacy (Dobrynin), propaganda and public relations (Yakovlev and Arbatov), science (Velikhov) and a group of economic advisers. They also sent their leading experts on the American and European media (Pozner and Falin, also an expert on Germany) and controllers of agents of influence like Bessmertnykh[26]. It is for this reason that they arranged gatherings at the Soviet Embassy for leading American politicians, businessmen, publishers, academics, cultural figures and so forth, for briefings and discussions with Gorbachëv and Soviet strategists.

26 *See text of Note 26 opposite.*

These events, *not* the treaty signing, were the *main events*. Their purpose was to influence the American élite and to seek its cooperation in restructuring Soviet and American thinking and society in accordance with Soviet strategy. According to '*The New York Times*', Gorbachëv addressed American intellectuals as the 'yeast of events'.

The Soviet operation was apparently successful. It was not exposed, challenged or counteracted. **It appears that its strategic political significance went unnoticed even though it took place under the noses of the President, the Administration and US counter-intelligence.**

The gatherings were not fully covered by the media. For example, meetings with executives of leading American newspapers, television networks, news magazines and publishing houses were not televised.

The Cable News Network [CNN] showed only a few minutes of one meeting and explained that transmissions from the Soviet Embassy were cut off before guests had had a chance to question Gorbachëv. According to CNN, once Gorbachëv had finished his address to US legislators, the Soviet television camera was deflected to show a curtain. CNN therefore terminated their broadcast. **Typical Soviet ploys like this, despite so-called *'glasnost'*, only lend credence to this assessment.**

THE NEED FOR COUNTERACTION BY THE UNITED STATES

Because Soviet strategy breeds confusion and is aimed at the peaceful conquest of the United States from within, it is detrimental to American interests and to American security and must be counteracted. President Reagan's earlier rhetoric about the 'Evil Empire', though it took no account of current Soviet strategy, was healthy and effective in that it prevented the Soviets from entering the United States with their political offensive. The United States' sudden switch from confrontation to acceptance of Gorbachëv's 'process', and ignorance of the strategy behind it, will divide the American nation. **In Sun Tzu's terms, the pinnacle of strategy is to be invited into the fortress of the enemy.** Khrushchev used disinformation about Sino-Soviet differences to gain his invitation to visit the United States. Brezhnev and Deng used disinformation about Sino-Soviet hostilities to gain their invitations.

Gorbachëv, in turn, has used disinformation about Soviet democratisation to obtain his invitation. President Reagan's embrace of Gorbachëv's initiatives as positive developments has provided the Soviets and the KGB with an opportunity for

26 [*page 60*] *Editor's Note:* In 1991, **Aleksandr Bessmertnykh**, serving as Soviet Foreign Minister following the resignation in December 1990 of Shevardnadze, commented on the dense network of new bilateral and multilateral accords Moscow was negotiating and signing with countries in both Eastern and Western Europe. He said that **'the groundwork has been laid for *joint action* in every sphere, including political, economic and security areas…'**. Concerning the network of new Soviet bilateral treaties with the East European countries, Bessmertnykh said that they represented an 'effort by the USSR to update the legal basis of relations with East European countries. From multilateral agreements [applied] within the framework of the Warsaw Pact, the Soviet Union is proceeding to mostly bilateral accords and contacts'. It should be noted that Golitsyn predicted this regional bilateral 'treaty offensive' in Central and Eastern Europe on page 265 of *'New Lies for Old'*. Specifically, the Author anticipated 'the development of an effective political, economic, diplomatic, and military substructure under which the Communists can continue to coordinate their policies and actions on a bilateral basis through a system of friendship treaties. This substructure would not be affected by the formal dissolution of the Warsaw Pact'. For the elimination of doubt, the Author has emphasised to the Editor that this prediction 'refers to friendship treaties with the Bloc countries'.

active interference in American politics. It gives them the chance to activate and use for their strategic purposes the friends and agents of influence they have acquired within the American élite over the past twenty-five years. During the confrontational period, these agents were afraid to act because of the danger of exposure.

Now, following Gorbachëv's visit, *they can be activated*. Gorbachëv's Leninist ideas on restructuring will become much better known and every effort will be made to identify and isolate those conservative American anti-Communists who do not embrace Gorbachëv and *'perestroika'* as obstacles in the path of progress. Disinformation concerning the presence of so-called 'conservatives' in the Soviet Union and their 'resistance' to *'perestroika'* will underline this point and will help to present fictitious Soviet 'liberals' and genuine American liberals as natural allies in the restructuring and convergence of their two societies.

The KGB can be expected to try to plant its agents among American experts on the Soviet Union as official or unofficial advisers on national security affairs. Aside from a future visit to the Soviet Union by the Pope, one may expect publication in the Soviet Union of Aleksandr Solzhenitsyn's works and his return to his home country. The so-called cultural defectors will also pay return visits to the USSR. Fresh strategic negotiations may lead to the destabilisation of the existing nuclear deterrent at a time when the Strategic Defence Initiative is not yet ready and the Soviet political offensive has yet to reach its peak. The primary issues between the Americans and the Soviets are not over human rights or regional conflicts like Afghanistan or even over negotiations on strategic weapons in which the Soviets, with their long-term aims in view, may make deceptive and, ultimately, meaningless concessions. **The root of the conflict between the powers is the Soviet grand strategy for world conquest, and the willingness of the American élite to accommodate it.**

In the long run, American acceptance of *'perestroika'* as a genuine, spontaneous process entailing the abandonment of that strategic objective will divide the American nation. The United States might well slide into a political morass comparable to the Weimar Republic in Germany in the 1920s. That would make Soviet victory through convergence coupled with war blackmail a realistic prospect. The risk of war might in any case increase. **The current joke among Soviet bureaucrats in Moscow is said to be that *'perestroika'* will be followed by *'perestrelka'* – that is to say, a 'shoot-out', ending in a bloodbath in the Lenin-Stalin style.**

To prevent these disastrous consequences, the United States must see through Soviet strategy and disinformation. President Reagan's scheduled visit to Moscow should be cancelled and Soviet plans should be exposed to the American people and their allies as part of an American political counter-strategy. An American President who fails to see through Soviet strategy and who fails to warn the American people of the dangers it entails will go down in history, not as a great peace-maker, but as a bankrupt politician – an American Kerensky, who was tricked by Communist strategies and unwittingly paved the way for their success. The legacy he should leave to his successors should be one of countering *'perestroika'*, not embracing it. The miscalculations of Kerensky sealed the fate of Russia. The miscalculations of President Roosevelt sealed the fate of China and Eastern Europe. The present actions of President Reagan will decide the fate of the United States.

THE AUTHOR'S SUGGESTIONS

Given the extent of the confusion about *'perestroika'* and the failure of the American experts on Communism to comprehend Soviet long-range strategy, it is suggested that the Central Intelligence Agency should:

1. Present this Author's assessment to the President of the United States and to the National Security Council.

2. Present this assessment to Congressional leaders and members of the intelligence Committees who supervise US intelligence and counter-intelligence activities.

3. Disseminate this assessment to the Chiefs of allied intelligence and counter-intelligence services in Britain, France, West Germany and Japan.

4. Recommend the issue of an Executive Order directing the US counter-intelligence organs to look into the security and counter-intelligence implications arising from Soviet *strategic* use of the KGB and its agents of influence both in the USSR and in the United States.

5. Upgrade the US counter-intelligence function from its narrow conventional basis to a higher-level politico-strategic function as warranted by the dangers stemming from long-range Soviet strategy.

6. Take immediate steps to develop an American counter-strategy to meet the crisis situation arising out of Gorbachëv's political offensive.

7. Consult urgently with the allies of the United States on the subject.

8. Invite the National Security Council to consider having this assessment published in *'Foreign Affairs'* through its editor, Mr William Hyland, under the anonymous cover of 'a KGB defector' along the same lines as the article by Ambassador Kennan which was published in 1947 and attributed to 'X'. ■

PART THREE

WESTERN COUNTER-STRATEGY AGAINST 'PERESTROIKA'

Memorandum to the CIA: SEPTEMBER 1988

WESTERN COUNTER-STRATEGY AGAINST *'PERESTROIKA'*

PAST AMERICAN STRATEGIC MISTAKES IN DEALING WITH THE COMMUNIST WORLD

After the Second World War the United States made a strategic mistake in adopting the defensive policy of containment of Communism as advocated by Ambassador Kennan. This policy failed to take into account the depth of the crisis in the Communist system at that time, the prevailing revolutionary situation in the Communist countries and the overall strength of the American nation.

At that time, the United States enjoyed a position of superiority. An offensive strategy of support and liberation for the Communist satellites in revolt would have been more appropriate.

The bankruptcy of the strategy of containment was exposed by the uprisings in Hungary and Poland, when the United States missed an historic opportunity to free Eastern Europe from Soviet tyranny once and for all.

THE MISTAKES OF THE VIETNAM PERIOD

During and after the Vietnam war the United States made a further strategic blunder by treating the Communist régimes as separate nationalistic entities operating independently of a common Communist strategy.

Having failed to recognise or understand the new long-range Communist strategy and the disinformation about splits between the Communist countries, the United States adopted a contradictory policy of fighting the Communists in Vietnam while providing trade and credits to the East European satellite régimes and moving into active *détente* with both the Soviet Union and Communist China.

This **contradictory policy of simultaneously fighting and having dealings with the Communists** confused the American people and was the primary factor leading to the American defeat in Vietnam.

The provision of trade and credit to the states of Eastern Europe and China helped to prolong the existence of their Communist régimes.

The SALT agreements and the transfer of Western technology helped the USSR to achieve success in its policy of attaining military superiority.

Strict enforcement by the United States of trade restrictions with all Communist countries during the Vietnam war period would have brought the war speedily to a halt and would have aggravated the economic crisis in Eastern Europe, the Soviet Union and China.

A sound strategic response by the United States along these lines would have jeopardised the implementation of Communist long-range strategy and would have discredited the Soviet strategists in the eyes of the leaders of the other Communist countries. Furthermore, it would have led to real splits between the Communist countries in place of the fictitious splits created by Communist disinformation.

EX-PRESIDENT NIXON'S SCENARIO FOR DEALING WITH GORBACHEV

'Perestroika', the final phase in the execution of Communist long-range strategy, **took American officials and experts by surprise despite the Author's ample and timely warnings of its advent.** The lack of preparedness of the American leadership was illustrated by the contrast between the improvisation of President Reagan and the calculated and polished performance of Gorbachëv during his visit to Washington DC. On the eve of President Reagan's visit to Moscow, ex-President Nixon publicised his scenario for dealing with Gorbachëv in the Sunday magazine section of 'The New York Times'. Nixon's scenario was an improvement on Reagan's performance, which amounted to virtual acceptance of Gorbachëv's position on *'perestroika'*.

No doubt bearing in mind that he and Kissinger had burned their fingers by accepting *détente* with Brezhnev which had resulted in the loss of American military superiority and Soviet expansion in the Third World, Nixon advocated a very strong bargaining position in dealing with Gorbachëv. He reasoned that this would work for Reagan as it had worked for Nixon in his dealings with the Chinese and that the Soviets would give up their expansionist policies in exchange for economic benefits from the United States. The flaw in Nixon's scenario lay in his *conventional approach* to the situation in the Communist world.

He is obviously ignorant of the long-range Communist strategy for world conquest based on the modernisation with American help of the backward Communist economies, the achievement of a decisive shift in the balance of world power and the convergence on Communist terms of the capitalist and Communist societies. In typically Western fashion, Nixon regards the tenures of Khrushchev, Brezhnev, Andropov and Gorbachëv as unconnected periods in Soviet strategy.

He does not realise that the present long-range strategy was initiated under Khrushchev, was continued under Brezhnev and Andropov and is now entering its culmination phase under Gorbachëv. The restoration of Khrushchev to prominence by Gorbachëv is the logical recognition of Khrushchev's rôle as the originator of the present long-range strategy.

Further confirmation of the continuity of that strategy is to be found in the fact that the former Foreign Minister, Gromyko, and the former Ambassador in Washington, Dobrynin, have not only retained exalted positions under Gorbachëv but have been promoted by him. Both of them have played important parts in carrying out the strategy for twenty-five years and more.

The elevation of the ageing Gromyko to the Presidency is a recognition of the value of his contribution, and a symbol of the continuity of the strategy. The elevation of Dobrynin to the post of Chief Foreign Affairs Adviser to Gorbachëv was logical since his long experience as Ambassador to the United States made him the best qualified man for the job. Both he and Gromyko are now engaged in executing the final phase of the same strategy against the 'main enemy', the United States.

Since Nixon fails to see that the long-range strategy is a joint Sino-Soviet venture aimed at duping and defeating the United States strategically, he now erroneously advises the present US leaders to repeat the same strategic error with Gorbachëv which he and Kissinger made in their dealings with the Chinese leaders. He advises Reagan to offer economic assistance to Gorbachëv provided the Soviets abandon their expansionist policies. With due respect, that is the advice of a lawyer, not a strategist. It leads to the same confusion in policy and thinking as in the period of the Vietnam war. Furthermore, it reflects a naïve belief that the Communists can be bribed into giving up their strategy and their ultimate objective, the defeat of 'American imperialism' and free market capitalism.

The Chinese leaders have not given up their world ambitions, they have only lengthened the time-scale for their achievement. When they have become much stronger with Japanese and American help, they will rejoin the Soviets in an offensive against the United States. Asked by students at Oxford University whether China would be hostile to the United States when it achieved world power status, Nixon replied: 'I don't know, only time will show'.

Gorbachëv, like Deng, will promise many things like the abandonment of Communist expansion; but he will only strive the harder to carry through the final phase of the strategy because this is what he was chosen and trained by the Soviet strategists to do. Once strengthened economically with Western help, China and the USSR will join together in an offensive to exploit any severe economic depression which might afflict the American economy. They will exert all kinds of pressure including interference in American affairs, blackmail, economic manipulations, the threat of sabotage, for example, of nuclear power stations, and assassinations.

Stalin missed his opportunity in the 1930s because he lacked an adequate strategy at the time, and was preoccupied with collectivisation and the consolidation of his own power. The Soviet and Chinese leaders will not repeat Stalin's error because they have a strategy, they are stronger politically than Western experts realise and, most important of all, the USSR now enjoys military superiority.

WESTERN COUNTER-STRATEGY AGAINST 'PERESTROIKA'
Improvisation should be replaced by an effective American counter-strategy against 'perestroika'. How effective it will be depends upon how accurately the United States can assess the new situation in the USSR. Because Washington overestimated the strength and aggressiveness of the Communist camp in the immediate post-war period, the United States adopted an inadequate defensive strategy of containment. Now the risk is that the United States will underestimate the political strength and aggressiveness of the Communist camp and engage itself actively with Gorbachëv and 'perestroika'.

Meanwhile, American leaders and experts on the Soviet Union remain as confused as ever by Communist disinformation on internal Soviet developments. Soviet criticism of Brezhnev (under whom the Soviets achieved military superiority), the dismissal of Yeltsin on the eve of Gorbachëv's visit to Washington, the Ligachev affair, the enlistment of Soviet religious leaders for 'perestroika' and the demonstration by national minorities on the eve of President Reagan's visit to Moscow, are all part of the deliberate stage-setting planned and organised by the Soviet strategists to encourage active American involvement in 'perestroika'.

Provoking the national minorities into agitation represents a new category of Soviet covert operations in support of the strategy, with the provocations conducted jointly by the Party apparatus, the Komsomol, the KGB, the mass organisations, religious activists and others. Occasionally, evidence of forward planning is forthcoming from the Soviets themselves. For example, an Armenian economic adviser to Gorbachëv on 'perestroika' recently let slip in talks with American Armenians in California that 'the measures for solving the Armenian conflict were already in preparation in 1987 and I myself supported them'. These operations demonstrated that the USSR, far from falling apart, is using its totalitarian resources more actively and imaginatively for strategic purposes.

The sophistication of these operations contrasts sharply with the primitive 'rent-a-crowd' operations of the stagnant, repressive, Stalinist régime. By emphasising the alleged instability of Gorbachëv's position and the fragility of 'perestroika', the operations are designed to induce an American underestimate of Soviet political strength, to create a favourable climate for Gorbachëv's negotiations with American leaders and to entice them into adopting an ultimately suicidal policy of support for and engagement in 'perestroika'.

Any US strategy of active engagement would be perilous folly. It should never be forgotten that the ultimate objective of Soviet strategy is not 'perestroika' in the USSR but the 'restructuring' of the American political and economic systems including the 'military-industrial complex'. It is this aggressive angle of Gorbachëv's 'perestroika' which American counter-strategy should address. US interests would be far better protected by a cautious defensive strategy. A second argument against active engagement with Gorbachëv and 'perestroika' is that, in the field of political warfare, the United States is presently no match for the Soviet Union.

The Soviets have retained their mass political organisations, their intelligence and counter-intelligence services and an effective political police force unweakened by any hearings. All these can be mobilised for the final phase of strategy. By contrast, the American potential for overt and covert political operations has been severely damaged by Watergate and the Iran-Nicaraguan Contra hearings. In Panama, the US attempt to remove Manuel Noriega has been unsuccessful[27]. A further factor is that the state of American society is not altogether good. The nation has a huge budget deficit. AIDS, drugs, crime and educational problems, exploited by agents of influence, have affected national morale especially among the young. The Vietnam wound has yet to heal. There is no bipartisan foreign policy and no consensus on defence needs, on meeting the threat of Communism in Central America or on rebuilding American intelligence and counter-intelligence. The nation lacks a sense of common purpose.

Confusion over the new developments in the USSR and the embrace with Gorbachëv and 'perestroika', regardless of the dangers it entails, means that the United States is leading its allies in the wrong direction. This will result in the erosion of the influence of the United States as leader of the Western world. The anti-nuclear views of the British Labour leader, Kinnock, the New Zealand Prime Minister Lange and certain Danish leaders could prove contagious to young American leaders who discount Communist ideology and are ignorant of Communist strategy.

There is a risk that, in their haste to engage in 'perestroika', they will seek to solve American problems at the expense of national defence. The risk would be com-

27 Manuel Noriega was removed two years later.

pounded in the event of an unfortunate economic slump. The greater the involvement of the United States and other Western nations in joint ventures with the Soviets, the more vulnerable will they be to Soviet pressure and interference at a time of economic crisis. Brian Crozier, a British conservative expert on Communism, raised the important question of whether the United States or the Soviet Union would be the first to crumble. The answer provided by the analysis is that, given a depression and continuing American support for 'perestroika', the United States would crumble first when faced with Communism's organising power and joint Sino-Soviet strategy.

The United States should disengage from Gorbachëv and 'perestroika'. There should be no summit meetings, no credit and no Western technology for either the Soviet Union or for other Communist countries. The American élite should be discouraged from travelling to the Soviet Union and members of the Soviet élite should not be invited to visit the united States.

The Communist régime should be left to stew in their own juice and to solve their problems without Western help since they claim that their system is the best model for the whole world to adopt. The best way of countering the strategy of 'perestroika' in the Soviet Union and 'restructuring' in the United States is to deny Gorbachëv and his friends everything that they seek to obtain from the West. Naturally, such a counter-strategy can only work if it is applied by the United States and its allies acting together in full agreement.

President Reagan would go down in history as a true American statesman if, after his Moscow visit, he were to issue a frank warning to his successor, to the American people and to their allies concerning the dangers inherent in 'perestroika' and the need to adopt the foregoing counter-strategy.

Under Lenin's New Economic Policy in the 1920s, a wise old Russian grandmother opened a store and made some money. Mistrusting the Soviet authorities, she hid her profits in a stocking. Later, Lenin's secret police, the GPU, came to confiscate her savings and demanded to be led to the place where they were hidden. She refused. They arrested her and threatened her. She remained firm in her refusal; so the GPU men changed their tactics. With great friendliness, they explained to her that they were planning to build a great society called socialism and needed the money of small capitalists like herself. They asked her to go back to her cell and think the matter over carefully. Later they called her back and asked whether she had reached a decision. 'Yes', she replied, 'I've thought it over; if you don't have money, don't build socialism'.

That is the advice which Reagan should give Gorbachëv. 'If you don't have the money, don't build Communism and don't ask us for American help: we are not going to finance our own funeral'. ∎

PART FOUR

THE EXECUTION OF THE STRATEGY OF 'PERESTROIKA' AND THE BLIND WESTERN RESPONSE

The Seven Keys to Understanding *'Perestroika'*

The need to reconsider our response

Memorandum to the CIA: MARCH 1990

THE EXECUTION OF THE STRATEGY OF 'PERESTROIKA'
THE BLIND WESTERN RESPONSE TO IT
THE SEVEN KEYS TO UNDERSTANDING 'PERESTROIKA'
THE NEED TO RECONSIDER OUR RESPONSE

THE BUSH ADMINISTRATION'S ERRONEOUS ASSESSMENT OF 'PERESTROIKA'
AND ITS BLIND RESPONSE HAVE LED THE WEST ASTRAY

The active engagement of the Administration of President Bush in the support of Gorbachëv and 'perestroika' shows that the Administration has failed to comprehend the strategy behind 'perestroika' and is blind to hostile Communist intentions and the dangers they entail. The Administration's reassessment of 'perestroika' has achieved nothing: if anything, the fog of misapprehension has increased. Instead of correcting the errors inherent in former President Reagan's naïve, euphoric embrace of Gorbachëv and 'perestroika', the Bush Administration has compounded its predecessor's error and has gone further by fully adopting the scenario of Brzezinski and Genscher for the Western response to the changes in the USSR and Eastern Europe. By so doing, it has pointed the West – disastrously – in the wrong direction. It is a case of the 'blind leading the blind'. The main consequences of this blindness are obvious:

1. **The meaning of developments in the Communist world is misunderstood and the intentions behind Communist actions are misinterpreted.** Enemies are accepted and treated as though they are allies of the West. The West responds euphorically without realising the potential damage to its democratic system. Western blindness allows the Soviet strategists to turn everything in the West on its head. This blindness becomes a critically destabilising factor in international relations, in Western diplomacy, trade, economics, military strategy and budgets, ideology, election processes, the media and in Western societies in general. The destabilisation and confusion to which this blindness leads can be illustrated by the following examples:

(a) Some American generals express their uncertainties about Soviet intentions and seem to think that the new Soviet military thinking is based on a defensive doctrine. Yet this appears to be contradicted by the continuing Soviet programme to improve their strategic weapons systems.

(b) There are reports of disagreements between the defence and intelligence establishments over their assessments of the Soviet military threat.

(c) There is continuing Congressional pressure for further cuts in the military budget and troop reductions in Western Europe, and serious talk about division of the 'peace dividend'.

(d) Proposals are aired recommending the redirection to Eastern Europe of US aid for Israel, Egypt, Pakistan and other friendly countries, as though this were simple common sense, given the 'changes' which have taken place.

(e) There is increasing acceptance of the ill-advised and hazardous idea of integrating the USSR and its allies into the international economic and financial institutions of the free world, including the European Community.

(f) While a Soviet Foreign Minister is received at NATO headquarters, a leading American expert on Soviet affairs goes to Moscow to advise the Soviet strategists on how to proceed with *'perestroika'*.

(g) Ill-treatment of the Turkish minority in Bulgaria has reportedly led to military cooperation between Bulgaria and Greece against Turkey, Greece's ally on the southern flank of NATO.

(h) In its confusion over *'perestroika'* and *'glasnost'*, American intelligence is said to be shifting from reliance on human intelligence sources to reliance on (tainted) open Soviet sources.

(i) There is confusion among the émigrés from the Baltic Republics and Eastern Europe, some of whom accept the changes as genuine.

(j) In general, *'perestroika'* has had an inflammatory effect on the situation in South Africa, and in Israel *vis-à-vis* the Palestinian issue, and on nationalist movements like those of the Basques and Catalans in Spain. In Nicaragua, *'perestroika'* has had a temporarily positive effect in the shape of the electoral defeat of the Sandinista government; but it remains to be seen whether the Sandinistas will give up power to the elected President or follow the example of Lenin who rejected the verdict of the ballot box and dissolved by force the Russian Constituent Assembly in January 1918[28].

(k) It is a sign of blindness and confusion when the West regards a convinced Leninist like Gorbachëv as a good bet for the future.

2. The blind American response to *'perestroika'* is diverting the United States away from its own priorities, such as the critical situation in Latin America where fragile democracies are in need of close American attention.

3. Because of this same blindness, the US and Western Europe, instead of addressing their own problems, are committing their resources to solving the problems of their adversaries in the Communist world without understanding the true nature of the process taking place there. This blindness enables the Soviets to shift the financial burden of restoring the economies of Eastern Europe from their own onto Western shoulders – thus ensuring a successful transition to 'socialism with a human face'. In its blindness, the West is becoming an active assistant in the successful execution of the Soviet strategy of Communist renewal at the expense of Western interests. The West is becoming a blind catalyst in its own long-term destabilisation.

4. American blindness is diminishing the rôle of the United States as the leader of the Western world and is offering the Soviets new openings to manipulate erroneous Western perceptions of *'perestroika'* to the detriment of the Western alliances. The distinction between the American vision of an enlarged Europe based upon Western values and **the Soviet 'vision' of neutral socialist Europe from the Atlantic to the Urals built upon an expanded socialist European Community under Moscow's effective hegemony, is being lost from sight.**

5. Blindness deprives the United States of opportunities to shape events and trends in Eastern Europe, and in East Germany in particular, towards genuine democracy and in favour of Western strategic interests.

6. Blindness is preventing the United States from appreciating the destabil-

---

28 *Editor's Note:* The Author's scepticism has been proved more than justified. In the event, the Sandinistas have been 'ruling from below' – retaining control of the military and the instruments of repression, rigging the legislature and manipulating the policies of the Chamorro Government.

ising effects on the West German economy of the premature decision to unify the currency and bail out the floundering East German economy. In its blindness, the United States fails to foresee the political destabilisation liable to arise from the West's willingness to contemplate East German participation in federal elections without taking account of the likely impact on them of the 2.4 million past and present members of the German Communist Party. The Communist strategists intend to procure the removal of Chancellor Kohl after he has signed the bilateral documents being prepared for his signature, and his 'conservative' Christian Democrats. They seek to bring to power the Social Democrats (or a Red-Green coalition) who will accept the Soviet concept of a neutral socialist Germany and its destabilising effect on NATO.

7. **Blindness to the Soviet interest in destabilisation and neutralisation prevents the United States from setting in their proper context the assassination over the past few years by the KGB-surrogate Red Army Faction of Dr Herrhausen, Chairman of Deutsche Bank, and** *a dozen or so other members of the German 'military-industrial complex' and members of the US armed forces in Europe.* No doubt, the German names will have been deleted from the KGB's 'hit-list' of 150,000 Germans regarded as potential obstacles to Soviet strategy. Intimidation by assassination of the German élite will be accompanied by a whole range of other practices similar to those in which the KGB engaged in Finland for many years. The reported departure for Moscow of Marcus Wolf, the head of the East German security service, suggests that the control of this service's more important agents in West Germany will be transferred to the KGB. The KGB will use these agents, together with their existing German assets, to intervene in national elections by bribing or blackmailing German politicians and by penetrating, splitting or dominating political parties.

Deep penetration of West Germany's special services by the KGB and by the East German services has compromised members of the West German élite, rendering them vulnerable to KGB pressure and blackmail which may well be used during the reunification process. Blindness to all these activities is partly due to the fact that the West is more concerned about the threat from a reunited Germany than the Soviet threat – a fact which Moscow has been able to exploit to its negotiating advantage.

8. **Western blindness gives rise to grand illusions about the prospects of future cooperation with the renewed Communist régimes.** These illusions inspire ill-founded confidence: they generate their own momentum, making it impossible for the West to regain a clearer, more objective vision of the changes in the Communist world, and of their significance.

9. **Blindness leads to the ideological, political and military disarmament of the West and renders these consequences inevitable.**

10. **Western blindness and confusion enable Moscow to accelerate the pace of Communist renewal, to exploit contradictions between the United States, Western Europe and Japan, to destabilise the West and to advance Soviet strategic designs against the United States.** Blind US support for *'perestroika'* in the USSR and Eastern Europe shows that the Bush Administration does not appreciate the strategic and political implications of such a policy for the West. *This blindness will end in disillusionment with the collapse of false US long-term expectations and may secure the final victory of the Soviet strategy of convergence through political means.*

SEVEN KEYS TO UNDERSTANDING THE STRATEGY OF *'PERESTROIKA'*

The strategy of *'perestroika'* rests on seven pillars which at the same time serve as keys to the understanding of the strategy.

They are as follows:

1. The innovative application of Lenin's experience with the New Economic Policy to the whole Communist Bloc.

2. Preparation for the use of the Bloc's political and security potential.

3. The creation of controlled 'political opposition' by the KGB and the security services of the other Communist countries, along the lines proposed by Shelepin.

4. Lenin's ideas on the forging of new and old forms for the development of socialism and the achievement of Communist victory.

Georgiy Chicherin's ideas on the creation of false 'representative institutions' by the admission of non-Communist members.

5. The development of controlled 'political opposition' in the creation of new 'democratic' and 'non-Communist' structures.

6. Lenin's experience with giving fictitious 'independence' to the Far Eastern and Georgian Republics.

7. The new design for anti-Western strategy and the use of the Bloc's political potential in its execution.

Western blindness to the strategy behind *'perestroika'* is rooted in Western ignorance, ignorance and *ignorance* about these seven keys.

This blindness can be cured, therefore, by *knowledge*. The West does not know what *'perestroika'* is, how it originated, what forces are involved in its execution, what its objectives are or what designs it has against the West.

Dr Henry Kissinger was right when he admitted frankly that the West knows nothing about the new generation of Soviet leaders who are involved in *'perestroika'*. The West regards *'perestroika'* as Gorbachëv's improvisation. The Soviets have succeeded in concealing from the West that *'perestroika'* is a strategy based on Lenin.

THE FIRST KEY: LENIN'S NEP AS A PRECEDENT FOR *'PERESTROIKA'*

To explain how the strategy of *'perestroika'* developed and how Lenin's New Economic Policy [NEP] came to be used as a precedent, an historical summary is helpful. In the next few pages, therefore, the necessary background to the decision to adopt a long-range deception strategy is outlined.

The decision reflected a determined attempt by the Communists to learn lessons from the crisis which overwhelmed the Soviet Empire during the final years of Stalin's life.

Various attempts were made to cure the crisis prior to the adoption of the long-range strategy – by Andrei Zhdanov, who saw Lenin's NEP experience as a way out, by Beria who was planning far-reaching liberalisation including the unification of the Germanys, by Georgiy Malenkov, who was ready to go even further and to embark upon a *genuine* break with the past, and by Khrushchev, whose condemnation of Stalin's crimes hastened the day of reckoning.

The crisis of the Soviet Empire

In Stalin's last years the Soviet Empire was beset by a series of crises which struck at every facet of government, the Party and its policies and ideology, and the international Communist movement. The Soviet economy and agriculture were a shambles. The secret police, fed by an army of informants, arrested countless thousands of Soviet citizens deemed to hold anti-Soviet views.

Intellectuals were harried, intimidated and banished. National minorities were mistreated and suppressed. Anti-Semitism became for a while official Party and government policy. Underground nationalist guerrilla movements were ruthlessly suppressed only to reappear again. Across Siberia was strung a network of prison camps in which millions of Soviet citizens languished. The satellite countries, their economies shattered and their national pride drained away, shared the ills of their Soviet masters. The Party leaders in Eastern Europe became puppets and their people vassals. Yugoslavia was driven into breaking away from the Bloc and seeking Western aid – thereby giving rise to a new heresy, Titoism. Leading Party officials in the other satellite states were arrested and tried as Titoists.

Relations with newly-founded Communist China, staunch before the take-over, deteriorated as the Chinese leaders came to realise how uneasy was the atmosphere throughout the Soviet Bloc. In the non-Communist world, the Communist movement, inflexible in its revolutionary tactics, tainted by Soviet espionage and universally regarded as an instrument of Soviet policy, had lost what sympathy it had won during the war against Germany and had become demoralised, isolated and ineffectual. Stalin's only response to the crisis was more terror and mass repression.

OUTLINE OF VARIOUS ATTEMPTS TO CURE THE CRISIS IN THE SOVIET BLOC
PRIOR TO THE ADOPTION OF THE STRATEGY OF 'PERESTROIKA'

Zhdanov's policy scenario

Stalin's close associates in the Soviet leadership, aware of the irrationality of the policies they were called upon to enforce, lacked the courage to curb Stalin's excesses or to criticise his policies. Only Zhdanov, Secretary of the Party's Central Committee and a possible successor to Stalin, with a small group of fellow Leningrad associates, dared to discuss alternative policies among themselves. Zhdanov and his group recognised the explosive nature of the situation in the USSR and its satellites. They saw a solution to the crisis in the application of Lenin's New Economic Policy experience. The prominent economist, Nikolay Voznesenskiy, a member of that group, wanted more flexibility in planning, reduced investment in heavy industry, the development of light industry and relief for the collective farmers. He even defended the encouragement of private initiative. Aleksey Kuznetsov, who supervised the activities of the secret police, was critical of the emphasis on mass repressions. He suggested an improvement in the treatment of the national minorities and greater freedom for intellectuals (paradoxical, perhaps, in view of Zhdanov's past treatment of intellectuals). As is well known, Zhdanov died suddenly in mysterious circumstances, and his associates were shot. Ironically, Zhdanov's secret plans to apply the experience with the New Economic Policy were to be adopted by Khrushchev's strategists when they formulated their long-range strategy of 'perestroika'.

Beria's policies: Personal dictatorship with liberalisation

Stalin's liquidation of Zhdanov's group left the Party without an obvious successor to the leadership and triggered off a power struggle. Undeterred by the fate of Zhdanov, Beria planned a *coup d'état* to enable him to implement his own programme. He intended to abolish the system of collective farms.

He recognised the crisis in agriculture, which collective farming had failed to solve, and the hostility of the peasants which had discredited the régime politically. He considered that highly mechanised private farming would provide a quicker solution to the agricultural crisis. He based his belief on the example of Lenin's New Economic Policy. Beria intended to replace the repression of national minorities in the USSR with a policy of liberal patronage. He planned to encourage the preservation of national cultures among the Baltic peoples, the Jews and the Ukrainians.

Furthermore, he planned an amnesty for political prisoners, especially for the nationalists who had supported underground nationalist movements.

He saw this as the surest way of putting an end to those movements. For writers and other creative workers, he envisaged greater freedom of expression. He planned to allow mass emigration of Soviet Jews to Israel or elsewhere abroad. In this, his motives were not entirely humanitarian: he intended to exploit émigrés who had left relatives in the USSR, in order to strengthen Soviet influence in Israel. He planned to remedy instability in the satellite countries by introducing economic and political reforms similar to those he contemplated for the Soviet Union.

He hoped to give them more independence in their internal affairs and to encourage changes in their leaderships, bringing back into government men who had been imprisoned or removed by Stalin. He regarded the East German régime as completely discredited and the East Germans as ripe for revolt.

He saw this prospective upheaval spreading to other satellite countries and thence to the Baltic Republics in the USSR. For this reason, he was ready to sacrifice the Communist régime in East Germany. He was in fact ready to make substantial concessions to improve relations with the West. Soviet withdrawal from East Germany, a compromise settlement of the German problem, the dissolution of the Cominform and a 'low profile' in respect of intelligence activities against the West would form the basis for a summit meeting with the Western leaders and a reduction in tension between the two Blocs[29].

Underlying all this, though, Beria's principal aim was to establish a personal dictatorship. His programme was both radical and flexible, owing little to Marxist-Leninist theory. Not entirely without reason, he was exposed as an 'agent of imperialism', arrested and shot.

29 *Editor's Note:* The Author filed these observations on Beria with the CIA before the recent disclosures about Beria were made and before the appearance of a book by Amy Knight, a senior research analyst with the Library of Congress, entitled *'Beria: Stalin's First Lieutenant'* in which she writes that Beria inaugurated a policy of liberal reform after Stalin's death which was far more radical and far-reaching than anything Khrushchev ever attempted. For instance he drafted a secret document entitled 'Measures to Improve the Political Situation in the GDR', directing the East German leadership to abandon the attempt to force socialism on their country, to allow free enterprise, and to foster the unification of Germany [*source: 'The New York Times'*, 3 November 1993].

Malenkov's policy: a brief but genuine attempt to 'Break with the Past'

There were three main areas in which Malenkov sought to make important policy changes: the economy, the rôle of the security service, and relations with the West. Like Beria, Malenkov recognised the crisis in agriculture and the low standard of living of the Soviet people, particularly the farmers. He did not intend to tamper with the system of collective farming, but instead to realign industry.

It was with this in mind that he made his speech to the Supreme Soviet in August 1953 about adopting 'a new course'. His policy was to abandon the preferential development of heavy industry by transferring capital investment to light industry and to divert resources from military production to the production of consumer goods. He increased investment in light industry, in agriculture and in house-building while reducing military expenditure. At the same time, he announced the postponement of Stalin's 'Great Communist Constructions' – a large power station and a canal in Central Asia.

He increased imports of textiles and footwear, paying for them with gold currency from the special state reserves. He planned to reduce the size of the army in order to free more capital and labour for light industry. He provided the peasants with some incentives: collective farms were excused some debts to the state; and prices of farm products were allowed to be increased while taxes were reduced. Furthermore, Malenkov instructed Beria to declare a general amnesty for prisoners.

On Malenkov's initiative, a secret decision was taken to close down 80 percent of Soviet prisons within two to three years of the amnesty taking effect. Greater freedom of expression was allowed for writers and artists: 'critical socialist realism' was encouraged in place of Stalin's 'socialist realism'. This period became known as the 'literary thaw'. After the removal of Beria, Malenkov publicly condemned the whole security system and its techniques. He set in train reforms aimed at reorganising the service and at reducing its rôle in the government of the country.

The Special Board of the Ministry of the Interior which exercised extrajudicial powers in deciding the fate of absent defendants was abolished. Malenkov gave instructions that 'Chekists' (secret policemen) of the 'old school' should be retired. This reduced the total number of security police and opened the way for the entry of better educated men. He ordered the service to comb out imaginary suspects and to concentrate on the selective surveillance and suppression of real 'enemies of the state', foreign spies and anti-Soviet émigré organisations abroad. Since these measures were taken spontaneously and without preparation in response to the crisis, they *might* have led to genuine political liberalisation.

Malenkov initiated a *genuine détente* with the West. In July 1953 the Korean armistice was signed. Diplomatic relations with Israel and Yugoslavia were reopened. Malenkov supported Beria's decision to reduce the number of Soviet security personnel in Germany – which was put into effect before the revolt in East Germany in June 1953. After the revolt, Malenkov decided that, in order to create a basis for *détente* with the West, he too was prepared to sacrifice the Communist régime in East Germany and to accept reunification, provided that a reunited Germany was neutralised. He thought that this would lead to the dissolution of NATO and that East-West *détente* would then become a reality.

In his 'new course' speech, he called for negotiations to improve relations with the United States. Most important of all, in a public statement on 12 March 1954 he admitted that 'in the Third World War there would be no victors'.

Malenkov's policy was defined by Khrushchev as 'reformist deviation in the internal policy and capitulation to international imperialism abroad'. Malenkov was criticised for his 'adventurist, unrealistic approach' to the problem of improving the people's living conditions. He was also criticised for encouraging the leaders of the 'people's democracies', particularly Imre Nagy in Hungary, to adopt his 'adventurous course, thus endangering the situation in those countries'.

Khrushchev claimed that Malenkov's 'capitulation to the Western imperialists' in foreign affairs was exemplified by his willingness to give up the Communist East German Republic to the West and by his politically erroneous statement that there would be no victors after a Third World War.

In Khrushchev's opinion, Malenkov should have said that the capitalist system would perish but that Communism would survive even an atomic war. For these political mistakes, Malenkov was removed from his position as Prime Minister.

Khrushchev's policies before the adoption of the strategy in 1958-60

Before 1959 Khrushchev's policies were amateurish and inconsistent. He played a key rôle in the condemnation of Stalin's practices and crimes. His revelations about Stalin's crimes hastened the culmination of the crisis. The entire Soviet Bloc became engulfed in a wave of profound unrest. Disturbances in Georgia, in the Soviet Baltic Republics and in some of the larger cities of the USSR were accompanied by open revolts in Poland and Hungary and highly explosive situations in Romania, Czechoslovakia and East Germany.

The Soviet leaders were paralysed with indecision. Khrushchev's fate hung in the balance. But prompted by the Chinese leaders and fortified by Western disunity over the Suez operation, Khrushchev moved Soviet troops into Hungary and crushed the insurrection. For a while thereafter, Khrushchev reverted to the Stalinist policy of harsh suppression of political opposition throughout the Bloc.

The Chinese leaders did likewise, with their campaign of 'a thousand weeds', removing all 'revisionists' and 'critics' from positions of influence.

In June 1957 the final battle in the struggle for power took place. The 'anti-Party group', led by Nikolay Bulganin and Vyacheslav Molotov, tried to unseat Khrushchev, exploiting his return to Stalinism and the cult of his own personality. Their attempt was abortive. Khrushchev and his supporters gained the upper hand, and the struggle for power finally came to an end. The way was now clear for long-term planning.

Khrushchev proceeded to normalise relations with the Yugoslav, Hungarian, Polish and Chinese leaders on the basis of condemnation of Stalin's distortions of Marxism-Leninism. *A secret agreement was reached on the need to formulate a long-range policy and strategy for the Bloc and for the international Communist movement.* Soviet strategists embarked upon a trawl of the archives for theoretical and practical ideas, drawn from Soviet experience in the past.

The principal elements of Lenin's 'New Economic Policy' [NEP]

In the course of this high-level investigation, the strategists found striking similarities between the position of the Communist Bloc in 1958 and the position of Soviet Russia in 1921. The similarities were: between the crisis of the Soviet régime in 1921 and the crisis of the Soviet Bloc in 1958; between the separatist tendencies of the national Republics of Soviet Russia in 1921 and the separatist tendencies of the Bloc countries in 1958; and between the unfavourable balance of power facing Soviet Russia *vis-à-vis* Western Europe in 1921 and that facing the Soviet Bloc *vis-à-vis* NATO in 1958 when the United States possessed unquestioned military superiority over the USSR, and the political cohesion among Western countries was greater than that of the Soviet Bloc.

Lenin's solution to the problems of 1921 was to launch a long-range policy embracing the Government, the Party and the Comintern which became known as the New Economic Policy, or NEP. Over the following eight years it yielded spectacular success. At the heart of Lenin's thinking lay the need to induce his Western opponents to adopt policies contrary to their own best interests, by means of subtle deception and misrepresentation. His purpose was to inspire Western attitudes which would favour the success of his policy.

He accepted that, in order to strengthen the régime and its ideology, the Party had to retreat from rigid 'war Communism'. It had to take one step backwards in order to take two steps forward. It had to make temporary concessions.

Lenin's New Economic Policy offered commercial concessions to foreign industrialists and invited them to open businesses in Soviet Russia and, notably, in Georgia. Under the NEP, Soviet industrial enterprises were recognised as trusts which operated on a profit basis. The NEP permitted Soviet nationals to open and to operate their own capitalist enterprises.

Under the NEP, the Soviets emphasised their ideological moderation and their businesslike approach to dealings with the West. Abundant information became available about economic conditions in Soviet Russia. Restrictions on travel were relaxed. Emigrés living abroad were encouraged to return under amnesty, while other Soviet citizens were allowed to emigrate. Soviet diplomats began to stress the importance of peaceful coexistence with the West. The old repressive Soviet security police were reorganised at Lenin's instigation into what was initially a less obtrusive force – the GPU [State Political Directorate].

Despite this facade of apparently opportunistic concessions, which gave the impression that the Soviets' ideological régime was evolving towards capitalism, the essence of the NEP, according to Lenin, was to build socialism: in his words, 'it [the NEP] will be carried out seriously and for a long time – five to ten years'.

During the NEP period, industries remained under Party control. The Party took steps to eliminate separatism by creating a federation of national Republics under a centralised government. National economic planning was introduced, initially in the construction of an electric power system binding the country together.

The GPU played an active rôle in the implementation of the NEP. It watched foreign and domestic capitalists. It took steps to eliminate or neutralise genuine opposition groups among the members of the former political parties and the Church, by creating spurious controlled groups. The State Political Directorate introduced one of these groups consisting of former Tsarist generals and nobility, and known as 'The Trust', to Western intelligence services which accepted it as a genuine underground organisation.

In the Far East, Lenin set up an ostensibly independent non-Communist Far Eastern Republic as a buffer state between Soviet Russia and Japan. But its independence and non-Communism were only a façade. In reality, it coordinated its actions with the Soviets and, after two years, applied for and was 'granted' membership of the Soviet Union.

Capitalist concessions in Georgia and the use of Georgian facilities for trade with Europe and the United States were used to convey an impression of Georgian independence despite the country's occupation by Soviet troops.

Lenin introduced and successfully practised an activist style of diplomacy – exploiting the contradictions and conflicts of interest between the leading Western powers, especially those between the defeated Germans and the victorious allies. Taking full advantage of the concessions and apparent ideological moderation of the Soviet régime, Lenin concluded the Rapallo Treaty with Germany. The treaty extended most favoured nation treatment to Soviet Russia covering all spheres of economic relations. Germany subsequently provided credit and military technology.

Lenin committed the Soviet state and its resources to the support of the international revolutionary movement. The Comintern became active. Using calculated moderation, the Soviet and foreign Communist Parties sought to make temporary alliances with socialists and nationalist parties, particularly in China.

The main question to be answered is: why was this highly ideological policy not understood in the West and why was it accepted as a spontaneous, opportunistic retreat towards capitalism? The answer is that **Lenin and the Soviet press emphasised the opportunistic form of the policy but succeeded in hiding and suppressing indications of its ideological content.**

During the NEP period, Lenin established that the Party's information policy should be based on a double standard concerning what should be revealed about the NEP to the Party membership and what should be revealed to the public. According to Lenin's rules, Party members could be told about real policy and its objectives, *but this information could not be revealed to the public or to foreign capitalists.*

As he put it, when one wants to lure foreign capitalists, one cannot talk as at a Party meeting [see *Lenin's Collected Works*, Fifth Edition, Volume 42, pages 55-78]. Lenin's statement to the Party that the existence of capitalism in Russia would be limited in time and space was suppressed as far as the public was concerned, and was revealed only in 1965 [*Lenin's Collected Works*, Volume 54, page 131].

It is important to note that Lenin recognised the limited opportunities a single Soviet state could have, to exercise influence over Western policy.

As he put it, 'the task of transforming a national dictatorship of the proletariat (existing in only one country and unable to exercise influence on international policy) into an international dictatorship (covering at least several developed countries and capable of exercising decisive influence on the whole of international policy) is becoming very actual and real', [*Lenin's Collected Works*, Volume 41, page 165].

Lenin found a partial, short-term solution to this problem through the expedient of setting up a Communist-controlled Far Eastern Republic behind a façade of political independence [as noted above].

It is important to note also that Lenin understood the need to limit concessions to *economic* matters, given the political weakness of the Soviet régime in the 1920s. In this connection, Lenin rejected a proposal from his Foreign Minister, Chicherin, who had suggested that 'for solid compensation', the Soviets should deceive the Americans by making a small ideological concession and including a few non-Communists in the ruling organisation – thereby passing it off as a representation institution. In their hunt through the archives, the strategists under Khrushchev rediscovered this device – and resolved to implement it on a far larger scale.

The consequences of Lenin's 'New Economic Policy'

The New Economic Policy was a great success. The predictions of Western experts concerning the evolution of the régime and the demise of Communism, were shown to have been wrong. The Soviet Communist régime did not perish but gained in strength. The Soviet conglomeration did not fall apart into its national components, but developed into a federation. The West was confounded.

Through the NEP, *Lenin succeeded in influencing Western policy in the Soviet interest.* The Soviet régime received widespread diplomatic recognition, increased its foreign trade and obtained Western credits and technology. Scope for the emergence of a Western anti-Soviet coalition was reduced. Divisions in Europe and Asia became sharper. The Comintern and foreign Communist Parties were revitalised.

SECRET RESEARCH ON THE LESSONS OF THE 'NEW ECONOMIC POLICY'
Towards the end of 1957, special studies of the New Economic Policy and related subjects were commissioned by the Central Committee of the CPSU as 'most urgent and important tasks'. The Committee of Information, the Research Department of the KGB Institute, the Research Department of the High Intelligence School, the information department of the political intelligence service and specialised institutes of the Academy of Sciences such as the Institute of Law and the Historical Institute, all contributed. For example, in December 1957, on Serov's orders, the KGB Institute assigned numerous tasks to its research and scientific staff, in order to meet the Central Committee's requirement for a special study of security service work.

Among the aspects to be covered were the potential of the security service in the political and ideological struggle between the two systems; the potential for exerting influence on the West through the use of agents among Soviet scientists and intellectuals; the potential for furthering both domestic and foreign policy through the use of agents among priests of various denominations; the promotion of new methods of dealing with nationalists; the problems of state secrecy, including the use of calculated disclosures; and suggestions for new forms of cooperation between the security services of the 'socialist states'.

Some studies were devoted entirely to Lenin's New Economic Policy, its objectives, tactics, 'reforms', the nature of its concessions to capitalism, the means of implementing the policy, the rôle of the security service and the function of disinformation. One study was based on secret documents from NATO countries: it compared the effects of summit conferences on Western democracies with their effects on Communist régimes.

The study concluded that, given public pressure for concessions and the concerns of Western politicians over forthcoming election campaigns, it was difficult for a democratic government to respond rationally at a summit conference and that this provided opportunities for Soviet exploitation. Another study came to the conclusion that the democratic system was at a disadvantage in the field of foreign policy since its accountability to public opinion gave it little space in which to manoeuvre and little chance of making radical shifts in policy.

Special attention was paid to the rôle of the security and intelligence services in connection with disinformation and political action. Past operations of this nature against capitalist countries were researched and their effect on foreign relations was explored. The experience of the Soviet services in implementing the NEP was analysed to see how **the creation of artificial crises** and **the practice of political provocation and disinformation** had influenced international relations to the Soviets' advantage, and how Soviet security service operations like 'The Trust' had been exploited to 'good' effect.

Three special studies were undertaken, entitled:

'State secrets and how they can be disclosed in the interests of policy';
'The content of policy and how it can be presented in different forms'; and:
'Experience in the creation of the Far Eastern Republic'.

Another set of studies centred on ways of strengthening intelligence and security collaboration between the Communist countries so as to use their combined resources for joint political operations. As a result of all this research, it was decided to recommend to the other countries of the Bloc that the new strategy should be modelled on the precedent of the New Economic Policy.

Intensive consultation ensued on the formulation of the new Communist strategy. The consultation was bilateral and multilateral, Bloc-wide and world-wide at both government and Party levels. There is abundant evidence from official sources that, before the adoption of the strategy at the end of 1960, there were active exchanges and consultations concerning the experiences of the NEP between the Communist Parties of the Bloc [see the annual supplements to the '*Great Soviet Encyclopedia*' for the years 1957, 1958 and 1959].

Mao decided to devote his time exclusively to the problems of the new strategy, relinquishing all his posts in government but retaining his chairmanship of the Chinese Party. Even Tito made an important contribution. The culmination of all the studies and consultations occurred at the end of 1960 when the new strategy based on the NEP and other relevant experience was endorsed.

Though based on the NEP model, the new strategy made fundamental adjustments to Communist theory, practice and tactics necessitated by the existence of the Communist Bloc, the NATO alliance and other changes in international relations which had come about since the 1920s. Though using many elements which had been tried out under the New Economic Policy, the new strategy also introduced significant new ones arising, on the one hand, from the lessons of the tragic tyranny of Stalin and his mass repression and, on the other, from the creation of the Communist Bloc. Under Lenin, the New Economic Policy was adopted and carried out by a single Communist Party in a single Communist state, Soviet Russia. The new strategy was adopted and carried out by a Bloc of thirteen ruling Communist Parties in thirteen Communist states including Communist China, all using their *full potential*.

GORBACHEV ON 'PERESTROIKA'

In his book '*Perestroika*' [Harper and Row, New York, 1987)], Gorbachëv fails to explain that '*perestroika*' is the logical continuation and, indeed, the final phase of, the long-range strategy established in 1958-60. Gorbachëv presents '*perestroika*' as a recent product and as a programme or **general line** of the Party adopted by the Central Committee of the CPSU at its meeting in April 1985. Gorbachëv admits that Lenin is an 'ideological source' of '*perestroika*' but his admission is very general. He writes [on pages 11-12, in the new, updated, PERENNIAL LIBRARY edition, 1988]:

' The works of Lenin and his ideals of socialism remained for us an inexhaustible source of dialectical creative thought, theoretical wealth and political sagacity... Turning to Lenin has greatly stimulated the Party and society in their search to find explanations and answers to the questions that have arisen... The Leninist period is indeed very important. It is instructive in that it proved the strength of Marxist-Leninist dialectics, the conclusions of which are based on an analysis of the actual historical situation. Many of us realised even long before the April [1985] Plenary Meeting that everything pertaining to the economy, culture, democracy, foreign policy – all spheres – had to be reappraised '.

It is revealing that, in a footnote to page 96, Gorbachëv refers to the New Economic Policy, describing its content *in one small paragraph* as chiefly the replacement of the requisitioning of food from the peasants with a 'tax in kind'. He also mentions that concessions were to be given to foreign firms and that private enterprise was permitted in small-scale production and retail sales.

Since Gorbachëv misrepresented '*perestroika*' by omitting to state that *it is the final phase of the long-range strategy of 1958-60 based on the precedent of Lenin's New Economic Policy*, this Author was obliged to prepare the foregoing historical background note on the subject, to put the record straight. Given that Lenin's NEP experience is **the first key** to understanding '*perestroika*' it will be shown below in concrete terms, unlike those used by Gorbachëv, how this experience has been developed and applied by the Soviet strategists.

THE SECOND KEY: PREPARATION FOR THE USE OF THE COMMUNIST BLOC'S FULL POLITICAL AND SECURITY POTENTIAL

In 1921 Lenin's régime was weak politically and militarily. Nevertheless, the New Economic Policy strategy was adopted after only one year's preparation. The present Communist strategists have had no less than twenty-five years in which to prepare the final phase of their strategy, namely '*perestroika*'.

During these twenty-five years, the USSR has become a military superpower. The régime has broadened its political base at home and has *neutralised and dissolved genuine political opposition*. More significantly still, the USSR and other Communist states have at their disposal, as former KGB Chairman Shelepin put it, *a political and security potential equal to, or more important than, their military potential.*

The *political* potential includes 19 million dedicated Soviet Communists, millions of young Communist members of the Komsomol, millions of trade union members and millions of scientists and other intellectuals who have been brought up in the Marxist-Leninist Soviet system.

The *security* potential includes, on the one hand, the armies of secret agents of the KGB and the other Communist countries among the Communist Bloc's intellectuals, church leaders and political élite and, on the other hand, the Bloc's intelligence services and their stock of agents including high-level agents of influence. All these assets have been developed and trained over twenty-five years for use in the final phase of the long-range strategy.

THE THIRD KEY: THE CREATION OF CONTROLLED 'POLITICAL OPPOSITION' IN THE COMMUNIST COUNTRIES

The West has failed to understand the deceptive, controlled nature of the new 'democratic' and 'non-Communist' structures which have been introduced in the USSR and Eastern Europe.

The West is jubilant that former 'dissidents', the members of the 'persecuted political opposition', are now becoming presidents, prime ministers, members of government and parliament and ambassadors in these new structures. **The Communists have succeeded in concealing from the West that this so-called 'political opposition' of 'dissidents' has been created, brought up and guided by the Bloc's parties and security services during the long period of preparation for** *'perestroika'*. This phenomenon represents, in part, the deployment of the Bloc's political and security potential in the interests of the strategy.

To this end, the KGB and the security services of the other Communist states were directed to create controlled 'political opposition' on the basis of the NEP experience. During the NEP period, the GPU – Lenin's political police – created a false 'political opposition' called 'The Trust' [*see page 81*]. Its members were drawn from former Tsarist generals and members of the upper classes.

The GPU introduced this 'opposition movement' to Western intelligence services, which accepted it as genuine, put their faith in it and were deceived. Drawing on the GPU's experience with 'The Trust', the Communist security services have created their own versions of 'political opposition' – the 'dissident movement'. The members of these movements have been drawn from the intellectual élite brought up by the Communist régimes.

In the USSR and China, nuclear scientists have logically been included because of their potential impact on the disarmament debate. The KGB and the other services have succeeded in introducing these movements to Western intelligence services and to the West at large. The West has accepted them as genuine and has staked its future on them.

THE FOURTH KEY: LENIN'S 'FORGING OF NEW AND OLD FORMS' FOR
DEVELOPING SOCIALISM, AND CHICHERIN'S IDEA OF FALSE REPRESENTATIVE
INSTITUTIONS THROUGH THE ADMISSION OF NON-COMMUNISTS

The West has failed to understand another aspect of the introduction of false, controlled 'democratic' and 'non-Communist' structures in the USSR and Eastern
Europe which the Communists have succeeded in concealing. This is that the basis of
these structures rests on ideas expressed by Lenin and his able Commissar for Foreign Affairs, Chicherin, during the NEP period.

One key to understanding this basis lies in Lenin's advice to Communist Parties 'to study, to search for, to find and to grasp the one particular powerful, specifically national tactic which will solve our international task... until the final victory of
Communism'. All parties, advised Lenin, must rid themselves of the radical phraseology of the Left Wing. They must be ready to use a variety of tactics, old and new,
legal and illegal. 'International Communism', he went on, 'must subordinate to itself
not only new, but old forms too – not simply to reconcile the new with the old, but to
forge all forms, new and old, into a single weapon which will bring full, complete
and decisive victory for Communism'. Following Lenin's advice, the Soviet strategists and Arbatov's Institute for the Study of the USA and Canada have studied
Western democracy, its political processes and its media.

It is particularly revealing that Aleksandr Yakovlev, a leading strategist of
'perestroika', Yevgeniy Primakov, another leading strategist, Tatyana Zaslavskaya [see
page 26], an economist and public opinion institute director, and Nikolay Shmelev, a
leading economist behind 'perestroika', all studied in the United States. Drawing on
Lenin's advice, these strategists have borrowed the forms of Western democracy,
filled them with new Communist content and introduced them in the USSR and
Eastern Europe as means for laying down the basis for convergence and as powerful
new weapons to bring about the world victory of Communism.

It is also likely that prominent agents of influence in the West with knowledge of American conditions will have suggested that, to conquer the United States,
Communism would have to be Americanised and dressed in 'democratic' garb. The
introduction of deceptive 'democratic' forms in the Communist world is a further
instance of the use for the purposes of strategy of the Bloc's political and security
potential, and particularly of controlled 'political opposition'.

Another key to understanding these 'democratic' forms is the well known
advice given by Chicherin to Lenin. On 20 January 1922, shortly before the Genoa
Conference, Chicherin wrote to Lenin:

'In case the Americans insist on representative institutions, don't you think
that, for solid compensation, we can deceive them by making a small ideological concession which would not have any practical meaning? For example, we can allow the
presence of three representatives of the non-working class in the body of 2,000 members. Such a step can be presented to the Americans as a representative institution'
[Questions of History of the CPSU, Number 4, 1962, page 152].

Because of the crisis in Soviet Russia at the time and the narrow political base
of the régime, Lenin rejected Chicherin's rather modest deception proposal. But the
idea has been taken up on a massive scale by Lenin's successors.

THE FIFTH KEY: THE DEPLOYMENT OF CONTROLLED 'POLITICAL OPPOSITION'
IN 'DEMOCRATIC' AND 'NON-COMMUNIST' STRUCTURES

Given the maturity of the present Communist régimes, the strength of their political and security potential and the long period of preparation of controlled 'political opposition', these régimes are in a position to give representatives of 'non-Communist' parties a third, a half or even more of the seats in their governments and parliaments so as to present these institutions as 'representative' and 'democratic'. It should be noted that Chicherin's letter to Lenin was held as a state secret until its publication in 1962, *after* the adoption of the strategy. The timing of its publication shows the letter's relevance to that strategy.

The deployment of controlled 'political opposition' has rendered possible the introduction of deceptive 'non-Communist' and 'democratic' structures. **Even so-called free elections do not present a problem for the Communist Parties. Because of their secret partnership with the 'opposition', the Communist Parties are always in a winning situation. It is *their* candidates – Communist or 'non-Communist' – who *always win*.** No other truly independent candidates exist.

This is the new statecraft of the Communist Parties and their security services: it is a new form for developing socialism. Its introduction allows the Communist Parties to broaden their political base and, in accordance with a decision of the 22nd Party Congress in October 1961, to replace the outlived concept of the 'dictatorship of the proletariat' with the new concept of 'the state of the whole people' while maintaining their power and strengthening their actual leading rôle.

The Communists have succeeded in concealing from the West that the 'non-Communist' parties are secret partners of the Communists, not alternatives or rivals to them, and that the new power structures, though they have democratic form, are in reality more viable and effective structures introduced and guided by Communist Parties with a broader base. Because of this Communist control, the Bloc countries are not true democracies and cannot become so in the future. The earlier acceptance of false 'political opposition' by the West as genuine has led logically to the present uncritical acceptance of deceptive 'democracy' as true democracy. Marx said that when an event occurs once, it is genuine. When it repeats itself a second time, it is a farce. The abortive attempts to establish democracy in Hungary and Poland in 1956 were genuine. The present introduction of democracy in the USSR and Eastern Europe is a farce: it is pseudo-democracy ('democratism'). The Communists have left us plenty of clues; but Western officials and policymakers have overlooked them.

THE SIXTH KEY: LENIN'S USE OF FORMAL POLITICAL 'INDEPENDENCE'
FOR THE FAR EASTERN AND GEORGIAN REPUBLICS

The West fails to understand the controlled nature of the emergence of 'independent' Republics in Eastern Europe and in the Baltic and Transcaucasian regions of the Soviet Empire. The West fears that the growing 'independence' of these Republics will lead to the dissolution of the Empire, and to anarchy and chaos. But a key to the understanding of this emergent 'independence' lies in Lenin's experience with the creation of formally 'independent' Far Eastern and Georgian Republics, which secretly coordinated their policies with Lenin's government in Moscow.

According to certain disclosures by A S Stepanov in an article which appeared in 'History of the USSR', Moscow, Number 5, 1979, published significantly during the preparations for the final phase of the strategy, the formal 'independence' of the Far Eastern Republic (DVR) was proclaimed in April 1920 in accordance with Lenin's strategic plan for securing peace in the Far East.

The plan, wrote Stepanov, had a number of objectives: to prevent a further Japanese advance into the region and to create favourable conditions for the withdrawal of all foreign troops from it; to establish friendly trading relations with foreign powers and at the same time to exploit contradictions between American and Japanese business interests through offers of concessions; to break out of the economic blockade and diplomatic isolation to which Soviet Russia was then subjected; to win time for the strengthening of the army in the DVR; to create conditions for the defeat of both the internal opposition and the external counter-revolutionary threat from the Russian emigration in China and Mongolia; and to provide favourable operating conditions for a branch of the Comintern in the DVR.

When the DVR was proclaimed, the Politburo of the Russian Republic issued a secret directive on the secret coordination of Soviet and DVR foreign policy. The Party and administration of the new Republic, including its Ministry of Foreign Affairs, were instructed in advance to implement Lenin's plan while concealing the ideological basis of it.

In July 1920 the Japanese concluded an agreement with the DVR on the 'creation of a buffer state which would not include Communism in the foundations of its social system' and in which foreign states would not interfere.

The new 'independent' Republic became a trading partner of the Russian Republic in the Far East at the same time as it expanded its trade with the United States and Japan. Although the promised concessions did not materialise, rivalries between these two powers were sharpened.

Soundings were taken by the DVR (acting secretly on behalf of Soviet Russia) for the establishment of diplomatic relations with China. An unsuccessful attempt was made to take part in the Washington conference and gain recognition for the Soviet régime. At the same time, the Far Eastern branch of the Comintern was established on DVR territory and set about the formation of Communist Parties in the Far East. As the army was built up in the 'independent' Republic, it first pacified the territory of the DVR and then tackled the White Russian émigré movement in Mongolia led by Baron Ungern-Sternberg. In July 1921, the resistance of the émigrés was used as the pretext for mounting a coup d'état in Mongolia backed by Soviet troops. After the coup, Soviet troops stayed on in Mongolia 'at the request of' the new Communist government. By the autumn of 1922, the Soviet régime and the Far Eastern army were strong enough for the next move. The Japanese were told that 'Russia had returned to the Pacific': and military, diplomatic and political pressures were used to secure the withdrawal of the Japanese from the DVR.

On 13 November, a 'people's meeting' of the DVR decided to seek the Soviet government's approval for its union with the Russian Republic. On 16 November, the request was granted. The DVR was liquidated and its territory was incorporated into the Soviet Union as its Far Eastern region (kray).

Stepanov's article gave credit for this exemplary instance of activist diplomacy to Lenin and Chicherin and also to the premier of the DVR, Krasnoshchekov, the old Bolshevik who had been the Minister of Internal Affairs, F. Petrov, the Foreign Minister, Y. Yanson, and many other Party workers. The main reason for the success of the operation and for the failure of foreign diplomacy to split the Far Eastern region away from Soviet Russia was explained by Stepanov as 'the coordination of the foreign policy of the Soviet state and the DVR which was secured by Lenin and the Party leadership'.

Another example of Lenin's use of the political 'independence' form can be taken from the history of the crisis in Georgia in 1921. The Georgians had been very hostile to Communism, as the majority of them are to this day, and Lenin advised the Communists there to be less harsh towards the bourgeois elements than would have been the case in the Russian Republic.

He based his advice on the belief that this would prove a more effective way to pacify the Georgians. But, at the same time, he used the 'independence' of Georgia as a cover for promoting Soviet trade with Italy, Germany and the United States. He effectively employed a liberal, national form and an opportunistic tactic to achieve an ideological objective.

The present Communist strategists are concealing that it is *they* who are now creating 'independent' Republics, repeating on a broader scale Lenin's experience with the Far Eastern and Georgian Republics and also Stalin's deceptive dissolution of the Comintern in 1943. The strategists are concealing the secret coordination that exists and will continue between Moscow and the 'nationalist' leaders of these 'independent' Republics. There has been ample time and every opportunity to prepare this coordination in advance. Because of its existence, the fragmentation of the Soviet Empire will not be real but only fictional. **This is not true self-determination but the use of 'national' forms in the execution of a common Communist strategy**[30]. ➡

30 *Editor's Note:* By 1994, it should have dawned on US policymakers that the Author's warning and advice that 'the fragmentation of the Soviet Empire will not be real, but only fictional', had been sound. Throughout the 'former' USSR, key Communist strategists and implementers were in open control. Specifically, **Azerbaijan** was under the thumb of KGB General Gaidar Aliyev, formerly a member of Brezhnev's Politburo; **Georgia** was controlled by MVD General Eduard Shevardnadze, former Communist Party Secretary in Georgia and Foreign Minister under Gorbachëv; **Kazakhstan** was ruled by Nursultan Nazarbayev, former member of Gorbachëv's Politburo; **Latvia** was ruled by Anatolijis Gorbunovs, former Communist ideology chief; **Lithuania** was managed by Algirdas Brazauskas, with a long Communist pedigree; **Moldova** was controlled by Mircea Snegur, a Communist who had retained power, and it had 'voted' in a Communist Government; the **Dniestr Republic** openly proclaimed itself to be a state using the methods of 1945-47; **Russia** was under the presidency of the former Secretary of the Central Committee of the CPSU; **Tajikistan** was controlled by Rakhmon Nabiyev, the Tajik Communist Party leader; **Turkmenistan** was run by Saparmurat Miyazov, a member of Gorbachëv's Politburo; the President of **Ukraine**, Leonid Kravchuk, former Communist Party ideology chief, was succeeded by Leonid Kuchma, formerly the Communist Director of a Soviet missile plant; **Uzbekistan**, under Islam Karimov, operated an unaltered Communist state; **Belarus** was a 'neo'-Communist ally of Moscow; **Armenia** was under the control of Lev Ter-Petrosyan, born in Syria, and known to cooperate with the strategists; **Kyrgyzstan** was under the thumb of Askar Akayev, a scientist who was a Communist Party member; and **Estonia**, 'succeeding' under Lennart Meri's 'miracle' reforms, was under threat from Moscow, jealous of its economic achievements. On 20th March 1994, the British journalist Matthew Campbell wrote from Moscow in *'The Sunday Times'*, London, that 'many of the former Republics are meekly resigned to the historic, economic and political reality of dependence on the Kremlin for survival... Russia has set a dilemma for the West by insisting that the now-independent former states of the USSR are its own fiefdom. *The Russian Ambassador in Kiev, the Ukrainian capital, has told foreign colleagues not to bother expanding their embassies since they will eventually have to be downgraded to consulates again'* [Editor's italics]. The same message has been conveyed by the leading strategist and National Security Council member **Yevgeniy Primakov** [*see Note 62, page 166*].

At first sight, it is remarkable that the Communist Parties of the Baltic Republics should have been converted almost overnight into 'national democratic' parties. But it all makes sense when one sees that these Communist Parties form the core of the new organisations, just as the Polish Communist Party formed the original core of Solidarity. All members of the old Lithuanian Communist Party automatically become members of the new 'independent' Lithuanian Party. Sajudis, the Lithuanian popular movement, contains many Communists as well as non-Communists. In Latvia, the Communist Party claims 180,000 members and the Popular Front 220,000. About 40,000 people are reported to be members of both organisations.

The objectives of the adoption by the Baltic Communist Parties of a 'nationalist democracy' form, agreed to in advance by the Soviet Communist Party, are:

(a) To repudiate, at least in form, Stalin's historic legacy of the forcible occupation of the Baltic States in 1940;

(b) To broaden the popular base of these Communist Parties and make them more active and effective participants in the common strategy;

(c) To undermine the strong anti-Communist stance of the Baltic émigré movements;

(d) In the future, to increase Communist representation and influence in the United Nations, the European Parliament, other international organisations such as the International Monetary Fund, the World Bank and the future 'Common European Home'.

The West has shown particular concern over the situation in Azerbaijan. Fears of the disintegration of the Soviet Empire have led to a Western commitment not to take advantage of unrest in the USSR and to approve the use of Soviet force if necessary to maintain order. This has created favourable conditions for the introduction of new 'non-Communist', 'nationalist' forms and structures in Azerbaijan as well as in the Baltic Republics. The most revealing evidence that this has been done is that a former Politburo member, Gaidar Aliyev, has expressed his support for the new 'political opposition' in Azerbaijan. This is logical since, as the former head of the KGB and Party leader in that Republic, he played a crucial rôle in the creation and preparation of this 'political opposition' and new 'nationalist' structure.

There has been great confusion in both the Soviet and Western media about what actually happened in Azerbaijan in January 1990 when Soviet troops allegedly intervened to quell the violence there. The real facts may indeed never be known. However, Bill Keller's article from Baku headlined 'Did Moscow Incite Azerbaijanis? Some See a Plot', published in 'The New York Times' of 19 February 1990, cited evidence that the violence in Azerbaijan was deliberately provoked by the régime and was organised by Polyanichko[31], Second Secretary of the Azerbaijani Communist Party. There may well be solid grounds for the conclusion. Keller's article offered three possible explanations for the Soviet provocation: that Gorbachëv inspired the incidents to bolster his claims for greater presidential power; that hardliners out to discredit Gorbachëv were behind the provocation; or that the Kremlin was sowing division as an excuse to hold the Republic together by force.

---

31 According to unconfirmed reports, Viktor Polyanichko was killed on 1 August 1993 near Vladikavkaz.

But the real explanation, according to this analysis, is that the incidents formed part of the preparation and mobilisation by the Soviet strategists of the political potential of the Azerbaijani Communist Party and its associated mass organisations operating in 'nationalist' and even 'anti-Soviet' guise.

Bearing in mind that a conventional Iranian Communist Party stands little chance of making headway under the present Iranian régime, the immediate target for the deployment of the disguised Soviet Azerbaijani political potential is Iranian Azerbaijan which twice before in history, in 1920-21 and in 1945, has suffered under a Soviet régime.

Already, the largest 'national democratic' faction in the Azerbaijani Popular Front has called for a Greater Azerbaijan that would unite 23 million Azeris on both sides of the Iranian-Soviet border.

The 'nationalist' potential of the other Soviet Republics may well be deployed on similar lines in future against Turkey or the Arab states[32].

THE SEVENTH KEY: THE DEPLOYMENT OF THE BLOC'S POLITICAL AND SECURITY POTENTIAL IN THE EXECUTION OF ANTI-WESTERN STRATEGY

The West is eagerly looking forward to cooperation with the Soviet Union in solving the major problems of the world. This optimism is unfounded because, although the West is ignorant of the fact, the Soviet intention is to use the political and security potential of the Bloc aggressively in its strategy against the West.

In the past, under Lenin and Stalin, the use of political and security potential had only one dimension: the Soviet security services used their political and security potential repressively against their own population. Now the employment of this potential has two dimensions: domestic and international.

The *domestic* aspect involves the use of this potential to broaden the political base of Communist Parties and to create new 'non-Communist', 'democratic' and 'nationalist' structures, replacing the 'dictatorship of the proletariat' with the 'state of the whole people'. With the wholesale introduction of deceptive, controlled 'democracy', this process is virtually complete.

The *international* aspect involves the aggressive use of the political and security potential of the whole Bloc in the execution of the Communists' anti-Western strategy. Given the growth of this potential and their military power, the design of the strategy is broader, more comprehensive, more aggressive and more realistic than was Lenin's anti-Western strategy under the NEP. Lenin's strategy was based on creating united fronts between Communist and socialist parties.

The design of *'perestroika'* is based on the deployment of the Bloc's political and security potential for the practical promotion of convergence on Communist terms of the Communist and non-Communist systems.

---

32 *Editor's Note:* Among evidence of the accuracy of the Author's assessment that 'nationalist' potential is being exploited in order to achieve intended responses from Turkey and/or Arab states, the following example may be cited. A document dated 2 August 1994 issued *from Moscow* by the Supreme Council of the Republic of Georgia, asserting support for the murdered President Zviad Gamsakhurdia, noted that 'the presence and activity of Russian forces in Georgia and in the whole Trans-Caucasus, and the annexation of Georgia... destabilises the situation and can become dangerous for Turkey and the whole Near East. We would hope that the USA will give further impulses to the prospect of drawing Azerbaijan and Turkey closer'.

The main objective of Lenin's strategy under the New Economic Policy was to induce the West to create favourable conditions for building socialism in Soviet Russia and for strengthening it as the base for world revolution by granting recognition to the Soviet régime and reviving its economy through trade, credits, technology and the help of Western specialists.

The main objectives of the strategy of 'perestroika' are:

(a) To induce Western responses which will accelerate the process of Communist renewal and the transformation of Communist régimes into attractive models of 'socialism with a human face';

(b) To create favourable conditions for Communist world victory through convergence of the two systems.

Lenin's NEP offered concessions to foreign and home-grown capitalists. The strategists of 'perestroika' emphasise joint ventures. This is understandable. Joint ventures can become bridges for the promotion of political convergence.

Because of the narrow political base of his régime, Lenin's NEP was limited to *economic* reform. The strategists of 'perestroika', drawing on their political and security potential, have incorporated and developed *political* as well as *economic* reforms which assist in the execution of their anti-Western strategy.

Lenin used activist diplomacy to swing the unfavourable balance of power in his favour and to prevent the establishment of a European anti-Soviet coalition. Exploiting the contradiction between the victorious Western allies and the defeated Germans, he concluded the Rapallo Treaty with Germany.

The strategists of 'perestroika' have also resorted to activist diplomacy, exploiting the contradictions between the United States, West Germany and other European countries. They are exploiting the changes in Eastern Europe, the removal of the Berlin Wall and the reunification issue with a view to neutralising West Germany and dissolving NATO[33]. They are concealing their intention to exploit the new 'democratic' image and the political potential of their renewed régimes in the USSR, Eastern Europe and China to promote 'restructuring' in Western Europe and especially in the United States.

33 *Editor's Note:* The dissolution of NATO would have been Moscow's preferred solution, but the West did not reciprocate when the Soviets wound up the Warsaw Pact. Despite its confusion, NATO had not severed links with reality. However the Soviets had more elaborate plans, given the improbability of NATO packing its bags just because Moscow was insisting that 'the Cold War was over'. Writing in *'The Future Belongs to Freedom'* [Sinclair-Stevenson Ltd, London, 1991], MVD General Eduard Shevardnadze outlined the detailed preparations Moscow had made to link the prospective political unification of Germany, which only the Soviets could deliver, with a 'restructuring' of NATO – the alliance's own *'perestroika'* – within the framework of a bilateral treaty network. 'From the outset, we linked the German unity issue with the problem of forming new structures of European security... When the news came out about the NATO session in London [July 1990], I knew there had been a response. The declaration passed in London indicated that NATO too was embarking on the path of transformation, decreasing its purely military emphasis, and changing its strategy. Most importantly, the declaration expressed a readiness to announce that the two alliances were no longer enemies... The two sides came to a mutual understanding, which opened up the possibility now of accelerating a draft agreement... for international legal settlement of the external aspects of German unification. In addition, we discussed... the signing of important bilateral agreements. Their basis was to become the so-called Great Treaty, the idea for which had originated in 1987 but in the conditions of that time could not be implemented'. However, with the signing of the INF Treaty in December 1987, under which US Pershing and Cruise missiles would not threaten the USSR, the risks inherent in implementing the planned Leninist strategic retreat from Eastern Europe could now safely be undertaken.

FUKUYAMA AND 'THE END OF IDEOLOGY'

In his article 'The End of History?' published in '*The National Interest*' magazine [summer 1989], Francis Fukuyama[34] refers to Hegel's concept of history as 'a dialectical process with a beginning, a middle and an end'. He mentions in particular Hegel's proclamation that history was at an end in 1806 when he 'saw in Napoleon's defeat of the Prussian monarchy at the battle of Jena the victory of the ideals of the French Revolution'. Fukuyama sees the present changes in the world as the triumph of the West and 'an unabashed victory of economic and political liberalism' over Communism.

He states that the fundamental class contradiction between capital and labour has been successfully resolved in the West and that, consequently, the appeal of Communism in the developed world is lower today that at any time since the end of the First World War. Fukuyama believes that the changes in the Soviet Union 'have put the final nail in the coffin of the Marxist-Leninist alternative to liberal democracy' and that nobody in that country, particularly in the Soviet élite, truly believes in Marxism-Leninism any longer.

Fukuyama regards liberalism as 'the only connecting thread' in the principles of Gorbachëv and the Soviet reform economists around him.

He implies that Gorbachëv's 'claim that he is seeking to return to the true Lenin' should not be taken seriously. He believes that 'Marxism and ideological principle have become virtually irrelevant as guides to policy' in China, and sees a prospect that 'Marxism-Leninism will cease to be a factor driving the foreign policies' of either China or Russia.

Fukuyama says that the 'real question for the future is the degree to which the Soviet élites have assimilated the consciousness of the universal homogeneous state that is post-Hitler Europe'. On the basis of Soviet writings and his own personal contacts with the Soviets, Fukuyama's belief is that 'the new political thinking' of the 'liberal Soviet intelligentsia round Gorbachëv has arrived at the end-of-history view in a remarkably short time' as a result of their contacts 'since the Brezhnev era with the larger European civilisation around them'.

Fukuyama implies that Shevardnadze was sincere in his statement that 'the struggle between two opposing systems is no longer a determining tendency' and that the effort to build up material wealth and the protection of the environment have acquired 'decisive importance'.

In Fukuyama's opinion, the Soviet Union has a choice 'to start down the path that was staked out by Western Europe forty-five years ago, a path that most of Asia followed, or to realise its own uniqueness and remain stuck in history' as a nationalistic, Slavophile and possibly even fascist state. Fukuyama concludes that 'the passing of Marxism-Leninism first from China and then from the Soviet Union will mean its death as a living ideology of world historical significance' and will undermine its 'pretensions to being in the vanguard of human history'.

34 *Joint Note:* Fukuyama has connections with the Rand Corporation, which conducts research for the Central Intelligence Agency among other US Government Departments. That Fukuyama's arguments caused such a stir in the United States at the time is remarkable, in view of the paucity of the relevant material's factual content. In fact Fukuyama constructed a theory based on little more substantial than opinions reinforced by an array of curious misconceptions.

The death of this ideology 'means the growing "Common Marketisation" of international relations and the diminution of the likelihood of large-scale conflicts between states'. He feels nostalgia for the time when history existed with its ideological struggle calling forth 'daring, courage and imagination', and deplores the prospect of 'centuries of boredom'.

Clearly, Fukuyama has misread the true nature of the changes in the Communist countries. More importantly, he has totally ignored Communist grand strategy and its anti-Western angle. This makes his analysis superficial and his 'dialectics' absurd. Lenin himself was a great dialectician. He valued skill in dialectics most highly among the qualities of other Communist leaders.

In his 'testament', he expressed concern that the 'Party's darling', Nikolay Nikolay Bukharin, had not fully mastered the use of dialectics.

Fukuyama has no inside knowledge of the real 'new political thinking' of the Soviet élite. This thinking is not the result of contact with the 'European civilisation around them'; *it is the product of their own creative development of Lenin's dialectics and strategy.* **Current Soviet strategists like Yakovlev are skilful dialecticians who are creatively developing and applying Leninist ideas derived from the period of the New Economic Policy.**

As indicated earlier, the present grand strategy, adopted in 1958-60, is based upon a classic realisation of the Hegelian dialectical triad:

Thesis: Stalinism [or Stalinist Communism].
Antithesis: Rejection of Stalinist Communism.
Synthesis: Converging, merging and marriage of Communist (socialist) substance (content) with democratic format, or 'democratism' [= 'convergence'].

This use of 'democratic' form is *deceptive*: it is the *essence* of the strategic manoeuvre which is intended to secure the final world victory of Communism. Here, in addition to Hegelian dialectics, the Communist strategists took Sun Tzu's advice.

Sun Tzu wrote: 'I base my plans for victory on form, but this is not understood by the common man. Although each has the ability to behold things as they appear, none understands how I have forged victory'.

Sun Tzu, not Fukuyama, provides the key to understanding the use of 'democratic, non-Communist, nationalist' forms by the Communist strategists in their *'perestroika'*. Fukuyama detects no echoes, in Shevardnadze's statement, of the classic Stalinist deception which pulled the wool over the eyes of Roosevelt and Churchill in 1943-44. Fukuyama is misinformed about the ideological dedication of the Soviet élite. **The élite consists basically of Communist Party and Komsomol members and intellectuals who are fulfilling Party and KGB political assignments.**

The fact that the Soviet élite has been actively involved in many years of preparation for *'perestroika'* and is playing an active part in it now, means that its members remain firmly dedicated believers in the Communist cause.

The Soviet strategists and their élite remain persuaded that the contradictions between capital and labour are not fully resolved in the West. They still view the United States and Western Europe as class societies.

They believe that class conflicts and contradictions in the West, while subdued during periods of prosperity, will re-emerge in periods of recession or depression. They remain determined that these contradictions can and should be resolved, not in a truly democratic context, but in the context of socialism and the complete elimination of capitalists and capitalism.

They still regard themselves as the vanguard which will bring about the higher form of society free of capitalism, which they purport to see as the ultimate cause of wars and human exploitation.

Fukuyama sees 'perestroika' as the final nail in the coffin of the Marxist-Leninist alternative to democracy. Communist strategists see 'perestroika' as the final nail in the coffin of Western capitalism.

Fukuyama overlooks the fact that a massive operation to establish and develop contacts with Western Europe to promote the CSCE (the Helsinki process) was launched under Brezhnev in July 1971 when a Soviet Committee for European Security was set up under Viktor Shytikov.

Shytikov, together with Arbatov and Zamyatin (later ambassador in London) and other Soviet 'parliamentarians', *started* this process. These representatives of the Soviet élite did not go to Europe to 'assimilate the consciousness of the universal homogeneous state of Europe': they went to *change* it.

By developing contacts, they were contributing to the strategic aim of converting Europe into a neutral, socialist Europe stretching from the Atlantic to the Urals, free of NATO and the American military presence.

Now, owing to the strategy of 'perestroika', this aim is beginning to look more realistic than it has appeared for forty years.

Fukuyama is mistaken when he writes of the death of Communist ideology and the end of the struggle between two systems. For Communists, ideology is not dead. It is embodied in Soviet and Chinese strategy.

The new challenge and threat arises, not from old-fashioned appeals to Marxism-Leninism by conventional Communist Parties, but from **the political mobilisation of powerful Communist states seeking to secure the world victory of Communism through the strategy of convergence**.

Convergence is not, as Fukuyama claims, a thing of the past, but a Communist blue-print for the future.

The Soviet Union and China are not going to follow a path that most of Asia has followed, nor is the Soviet Union going to revert to Slavophile nationalism. The Soviet and Chinese leaders have made their choice.

They believe they are in the vanguard and they believe in victory. They have a comprehensive agenda for new social, political and economic structures for Communism and the West as was clearly revealed in Sakharov's essay, '*Sakharov Speaks*'.

The struggle is not over: *it has entered a new and sharper phase.* The next decade will not be a decade of boredom. History will continue and the possibility of large-scale conflict with the Communist system may well increase.

There will be an acute and lively resistance to Communist execution of the strategy of convergence. There will be a place for daring, courage, imagination and sacrifice in the defence of the Western democracies and their values.

If the Communist strategists win the battle, it will not be because their system is superior but because the West has failed to understand their deception strategy and their new political weapons.

To understand the strategy, the West must first discard erroneous concepts, such as those advanced by Fukuyama. Fukuyama's conclusion that 'international life... is far more preoccupied with economics than with politics or strategy' is dangerously misleading since it diverts attention from reality.

The observed interest of Arbatov's Institute for the Study of the USA and Canada in promoting the wider publication in Europe of Fukuyama's article is not difficult to explain. The Soviets see a parallel between Napoleon, who embodied the ideas of the French Revolution and defeated the Prussian monarchy, and themselves. They consider that they embody the ideals of the October Revolution and that, through *'perestroika'*, they are destined to achieve victory over Western capitalism.

They also see the irony in the fact that they can skilfully and dialectically present Fukuyama's analysis to the Party audience in the USSR as an endorsement of their strategy. Recycling Western analyses and television reports which reinforce disinformation themes for the benefit of domestic audiences is a standard procedure.

THE PROCESS OF *'PERESTROIKA'* IN THE COMMUNIST COUNTRIES:
COMMON PATTERN AND SPECIFICS

The deceptive introduction of 'democratic' and 'non-Communist' structures in the Communist world has been accepted by the West as *genuine democracy* in the making. This uncritical acceptance of the authenticity of the process of *'perestroika'* demands a new analysis of it through the prism of the long-range strategy.

Analysis reveals the existence of a common pattern as well as the specifics of the process as applied in different target countries.

The main indicators of the common pattern are as follows:

○ The introduction of economic and political reforms and the appearance of democracy ('democratism') in the majority of Communist countries;

○ The resignation or removal of the old Communist leaders and the deletion from the constitutions of the leading rôle of the Communist Party;

○ Legalisation of the (controlled) 'political opposition' – the former 'dissidents' – and their emergence as a new political factor in forming new governments and new political parties;

○ The introduction of new 'democratic' and 'non-Communist' structures which include both Communists and members of the 'political opposition';

○ The Communist Parties hold their Party Congresses, change their names from Communist to socialist and elect new Party leaders who are not tarnished by association with Stalinist practices and who support Gorbachёv and *'perestroika'*;

○ The power of the military establishments remains unaffected by the changes: in fact, they support *'perestroika'* and act as guarantors of its success;

○ The security services are 'criticised' and respond by changing their names;

○ The reforming régimes remain loyal to the USSR, support Gorbachёv and maintain their allegiances and international commitments.

PARTNERSHIP BETWEEN THE OLD AND NEW GENERATIONS OF LEADERS

The turnover from one generation of leaders to another has followed a logical pattern. In general, the old leaders have resigned without a struggle. Those who have been arrested have usually been spared trial because of old age or ill health. It was of course under the old generation of leaders that the reforms were prepared – under Brezhnev and Andropov in the USSR, under Kadar in Hungary, under Honecker in East Germany, and so forth.

It was this generation which created and developed the controlled 'political opposition' and allegedly persecuted it.

For the reforms to be credible, the old generation had to make way for the new, including non-Communist members of the former 'opposition' who had allegedly been persecuted. **Since these new, 'non'-Communist leaders are the secret partners of the Communists, there is no hostility between them.**

It is therefore logical for the new President of Czechoslovakia to advise the United States to support Gorbachëv and finance *'perestroika'* or to accept a Communist as his Defence Minister or, when asked whether his country would remain in the Communist alliance, to reply 'if a totalitarian system is dismantled some peculiarities remain. Some things I cannot discuss with *"The New York Times"* before I discuss them with President Gorbachëv in Moscow'. It is logical that the new Czechoslovak Foreign Minister should favour the revision of 'obsolete strategic conceptions' and suggest the withdrawal of both Soviet and American troops in Europe.

It is logical for the new Polish non-Communist Prime Minister to suggest that Soviet troops should remain in Poland to protect Soviet communications with their troops in Germany. **It is logical that Lech Walesa should have declared that he wanted a Communist as Poland's President or, as a potential candidate himself to that high office, should have said 'we want to cooperate constructively with the Communist authorities'.**

It was logical that he should have urged Solidarity voters to support 'liberal' Communist leaders like General Kiszczak who, together with General Jaruzelski, imposed martial law in December 1981, placing Walesa under house arrest and forcing Solidarity underground. It was logical that it should have been General Kiszczak who 'negotiated' the agreement providing for the free elections which enabled the 'anti-Communist' Solidarity organisation to enter parliament as the 'opposition'.

Furthermore, it is logical that, despite the dramatic changes in the leadership, there should have been no significant revelations about the secret agents of the security services among the former 'dissidents' who have become leading figures in the 'democratic', 'non-Communist' and 'nationalist' structures.

The explanation is that the new leaders have a common interest with the Communist strategists and their security services, in keeping the files secret. So long as these secrets are not revealed, and they will not be, the Communist Parties will retain their monopoly of real power.

As John Lenczowski put it in the *'Los Angeles Times'* of 11 January 1989:

'For all the increased openness in these countries, a great deal remains secret. And where there is secrecy, there is, perforce, uncertainty'.

THE MEANING OF THE REORGANISATION OF THE KGB
AND THE EAST EUROPEAN SECURITY AND INTELLIGENCE SERVICES

The Communist Parties are adapting the KGB and the East European security and intelligence services for their work within the new 'democratic' structures. Past and present heads of the KGB – Vladimir Semichastniy (under Khrushchev and Brezhnev), Chebrikov and Kryuchkov – have been giving 'interviews' to the Soviet press. A number of less senior 'retired' officials have done the same.

The articles have contained criticism of KGB practices and abuses in the past under Brezhnev, and discussion of the service's rôle under *'perestroika'*. For example, a retired KGB Colonel, Karpovich, deplored the fact that the KGB had been engaged in systematically suppressing dissent and regretted his own personal involvement in the persecution of Sakharov, Solzhenitsyn and others. The publication of his article in *'Ogonek'* gave rise to a series of letters in response, some defending the KGB and some attacking the Colonel as an opportunist seeking cheap popularity.

Some deputies, including Sakharov and Yeltsin, have attacked the KGB in the Congress of Peoples' Deputies for its secret police rôle or for its incompetence. It appears that changes are under consideration in the structure and functions of the KGB and the arrangements for its supervision. For example, senior KGB officials have said that some of its Directorates are being reorganised[35] and their staff reduced, implying that the KGB is shifting away from monitoring the churches, the intellectuals, the 'dissidents' and the army, to conventional and legitimate intelligence and counter-intelligence tasks such as the fight against foreign spies, terrorism, sabotage, smuggling, embezzlement and organised crime.

The Chairman of the KGB, Vladimir Kryuchkov, declared the KGB's loyalty only to the Supreme Soviet, implying that the Supreme Soviet and not the Party's Politburo was the country's main decision-making body. The Minister of the Interior, Bakatin, hinted that control over the security organs may in future be exercised by a National Security Council attached to the office of the President.

These criticisms and reflections on the KGB in the Congress of Peoples' Deputies and the Soviet press have given the impression that a genuine, ongoing debate is taking place in the evolving Soviet system over the past, present and future rôle of the KGB. Radio Liberty even held a Round Table on the subject [see *'Report on the USSR'* for 22 December 1989], to discuss Aleksandr Rahr's article 'Gorbachëv and the Post-Chebrikov KGB'. The reaction of the participants in the Round Table showed that they had been taken in by this controlled 'debate'.

35 *Editor's Note:* The KGB was 'reorganised' (as well as being 'relabelled') after the 'August 1991 coup' into four divisions: Civil Intelligence [SWR], Counter-Intelligence [MB], Internal Security [MWD] and Centre Section [GRU]. The last-mentioned section was an entirely separate unit within the thus 'reorganised' KGB, and as its title implies, all decisions of substance were to be routed through Centre Section for approval. In a decree issued by President Yeltsin on 21 December 1993, the merged KGB with the Security Ministry of the Russian Federation was relabelled the Federal Service of Counter-Intelligence of the Russian Federation under Nikolai Golushko. Golushko was dismissed in a one-line Presidential decree dated 28 February 1994. News of the 'relabelling' of 21 December 1993 was disseminated in the West with emphasis on the 'fact' that Yeltsin had abolished the Ministry of Security, but without reference to the parallel fact that the Ministry had been replaced by 'new' entities, including one subsequently referred to in reports from Moscow as the 'Counter-Intelligence Agency', or 'CIA'. In February 1995, the Russian Duma gave a second reading to a proposed law (approved in March) under which the Federal Counter-Intelligence Service [FSK], as it was by now known, was to be renamed the Federal Security Service [FSS] and granted extended responsibilities, with the identity of its agents a state secret and surveillance operations against suspects no longer accountable to the Public Prosecutor's Office. This development was reported in *'The Times'* of London [17 February 1995] as though the 'strengthening' of the domestic intelligence service was a new development, without reference to any of the preceding 'post'-KGB 'relabelling' and 'reorganisation' operations implemented under Yeltsin. *See also Note 13, page 28.*

For the 'debate' is not spontaneous, but rather organised and conducted by the Soviet strategists and the KGB itself. The main purpose of the 'debate' is to misinform the West about the KGB's rôle in the past by concealing the crucial part it played in the preparation of controlled 'political opposition' for eventual deployment during *'perestroika'*.

To do this, the Soviet strategists and the KGB have attributed to the KGB in the Brezhnev period old Stalinist practices of monitoring and suppressing the churches, intellectuals and 'dissidents', which had in fact been abandoned many years earlier. Since 1959 the essence of the KGB's rôle has been, not the suppression of these elements, but *their development and use in Soviet strategy against the West.*

In sum, the alleged 'debate' is controlled disinformation intended to conceal that the KGB has been the Party's main political weapon in the preparation and execution of the strategy of *'perestroika'* since its adoption in 1958-60.

The power of the KGB remains as great as ever. It is not affected by calculated, inaccurate and irrelevant criticism of some of its old practices. Talk of cosmetic changes in the KGB and its supervision is deliberately publicised to support the myth of the 'democratisation' of the Soviet political system.

Furthermore, calls for 'parliamentary oversight' over the KGB imply that it is becoming another CIA or FBI. To some extent, the present 'reform' of the KGB repeats Lenin's ploy of reorganising the old repressive Cheka into the GPU.

This time, however, a new element has been added. The Soviet strategists are deliberately conveying a false impression of 'equivalence' between their service and the American services in order to lay down a basis for deceptive cooperation with them. Such cooperation would broaden their opportunities for furthering their strategy of convergence, and of course for even deeper penetration of the US intelligence and policymaking communities. The security services in Eastern Europe are also adapting themselves to the new conditions and, following Lenin's precedent, are being reorganised and given less provocative names. The East German service is considering a name similar to its West German counterpart. In Hungary, the security forces are being preserved through their dispersal among the uniformed police.

In Romania, the army has been put in charge of the security services. Bulgaria is retaining its services as is 'democratic' Czechoslovakia. The new Czechoslovak President concluded a new treaty on cooperation between his country's service and the KGB, limited ostensibly to anti-criminal matters. Asked if Czechoslovakia was ready to dismantle its foreign intelligence services, a Czechoslovak Foreign Ministry spokesman said: 'As soon as the United States dismantles its espionage services, we will do the same'. All these countries will retain strong counter-intelligence services operating against Western countries and their embassies in Eastern Europe. No doubt their intelligence services will scale down their operations to steal Western technology, which will become legally available. They will keep a lower profile and concentrate on targets which directly affect their own national interests such as the Polish, Czechoslovak and other national departments or sections dealing with the Central Intelligence Agency and the State Department.

The fact that there have been no significant disclosures by the new 'democratic' governments about the important secret agents of the security services operating among their respective leading 'dissidents', intellectuals, scientists, cultural and religious leaders or cultural defectors, confirms that continuing use will be made of the political, intelligence and security potential of these countries to further the strategy of convergence. Though seemingly conducted on a national basis, East European political and intelligence operations will still be coordinated with the Soviet strategists and the KGB. The East European services will continue to establish and develop contacts with American and West European political, cultural, scientific, sporting, media and labour figures, Members of Congress and parliaments, and their apparent counterparts in Western political parties. Particular attention will be paid to organisations in the United States of émigrés from their respective countries.

The rôle of KGB advisers to the East European services will become obsolete, and they will be withdrawn. Coordination between the Soviets and the governments and their special services will be carried out at a political and KGB level through Soviet embassies which will contain representatives of the Central Committee and the KGB, however 'relabelled'.

THE MEANING OF THE COMMUNIST PARTIES' SURRENDER OF THEIR MONOPOLY AND OF PARTY AND GOVERNMENT REORGANISATION

Gorbachëv and his strategists are not true democrats and never will be. They remain committed to socialism and Communism. They are a new generation of revolutionaries who are using 'democratic' reform as a new way to achieve final victory. The Communist strategists appreciated that they could not implement their strategy of convergence using the old, obsolete, Stalinist, Communist Party structure and dormant institutions like the old Soviet parliament. But they do believe that they can carry it out using new, revitalised, 'democratic' structures.

They are therefore reorganising the Party system, the Presidency and the legislature to give them more power and prestige and at the same time greater likeness to their American equivalents. Meanwhile, the Communist Party is *apparently* relegated to the shadows. The Communist Party, however, has not surrendered its real monopoly of power. In fact, it has broadened it by giving power to its members in the Presidency and Congress to execute the strategy of *'perestroika'* and convergence. Greater Presidential powers are needed to carry out the strategy throughout the world. This is not a transfer of power from the Party to the President. The President remains a member and an instrument of the Party, the executor of its strategy.

He is not the Pope or Luther. He does not impose his will on the Party; he is fulfilling the Party's will. The ultimate decision-making power rests with the Politburo, the Party apparatus and their strategists. Although the end of the Party's monopoly is proclaimed, the Party apparatus remains in being and is still being run by the same old-timers. For example, Yakovlev, who is now a leading strategist of the *'perestroika'* reforms, is a typical, old-style Party bureaucrat who, apart from his spell as Ambassador in Canada, served for fifteen years in the Central Committee apparatus in Moscow before the reforms began.

As a Party *apparatchik* and head of Party propaganda under Brezhnev in the 1960s, Yakovlev published vicious ideological books about the United States with such titles as [*see top of page 101*]:

'*The Call to Slaughter: American Falsifiers of the Problems of War and Peace*' [**1965**],
'*Ideology of the American 'Empire*' [**1967**];
'*Pax Americana – the American Ideology*' [**1969**] and:
'*The USA: From 'Great' to 'Sick*'' [**1969**].

**These books expressed the true views of Yakovlev the *apparatchik* – not
the reformist posture he has subsequently adopted for the purposes of assisting
the implementation of the deception strategy.**
 The Party apparatus, though less visible, will continue to provide guidance to
Party members in the reformed institutions. The Party not only has a vast organisation but also has long experience including periods of illegal operation under the
Tsarist régime and in those territories which fell under German occupation in the
Second World War. It will have no difficulty in adjusting to the environment of a fictional 'multi-Party system' which in practice it will control. The Party itself may well
be split in two – into reform and orthodox Communist Parties, as is already happening in Hungary. **The ultimate control will stay the same.**
 What has changed is the system of appointments. The old, fossilised *nomen-
klatura* system has given way to selection for Party and government appointments
made in accordance with the requirements of the strategy. Examples are the appointments of Vadim Medvedev, a former professor of social sciences, as head of ideology;
of Falin, former ambassador to Germany and former head of the Novosti news
agency, as head of the Central Committee's Department for International Affairs; and
of Dobrynin, former ambassador in Washington, as foreign policy adviser to Gorbachëv. The appointments illustrate the new creative style of the Party apparatus.
 All the reforms – the strong Presidency, the new and livelier Congress, the
talk of a National Security Council and 'oversight' of the KGB, and the creation of a
'loyal opposition' – are being carried out with emphasis on their similarity to the
American system. They should all be seen in the context of the strategy of convergence. This explains the introduction of the pretence of 'opposition', the calculated
arguments between old-style conformists and 'Western-style' members of Congress
like Yeltsin on the subject of the KGB and the nationalist and other issues.
 It also explains the emergence of groups of Russian nationalists, inheritors of
the Slavophile tradition, Stalinists and even anti-Semites represented by '*Pamyat*'
(memory): all are controlled by the Party and are being used in the interests of the
strategy to play on Western hopes and fears. The Party will continue to exercise its
leading strategic rôle through its members in the Presidency, the government, Congress, the new political groups and the new parties and national fronts. Even those
'reform Communists' who are seemingly calling for a reduction in the Party's rôle
and the introduction of a 'multi-Party system' are in fact fulfilling the instructions of
the Party strategists. This is the essence of the 'surrender' of its monopoly by the
Party and of the associated 'reforms'. It is no accident that these innovations have
been worked out by the Party's 'think-tank', the Higher Party School, under its rec-
tor, Shostakovskiy, who is also a leader of the Party's 'reform group'. The main con-
tributor to the design of the new Presidency, based on the American and French
models, was Vladimir Kudryavtsev, a member of the Congress.

He was also made Director of the Institute of the State and Law in place of another Soviet legal affairs strategist and former Professor at the KGB Institute, Viktor Chikvadze. The execution of the strategy of *'perestroika'* and convergence is not governed by any laws or rules[36]. It is a skilful application of the Soviet political potential in its absolute totality. The strategists no doubt realise that they cannot march to victory under Lenin's banner or even use the word 'convergence' while Lenin remains unburied. They may have toyed with the idea of finally burying him with full honours while in practice they follow his ideas in their final assault on the capitalist West. But the fact that they have not actually done so implies that to bury him might send the wrong signal to any waverers among the Communists.

THE COMMON PATTERN INDICATES A 'REVOLUTION FROM ABOVE'

The orderly pattern of transition in Eastern Europe cannot be spontaneous. It is all too good to be true. There has been a general absence of excesses (the Romanian events excepted), bloodshed, upheavals, chaos and disorder. The East Germans called theirs a 'friendly revolution', the Czechoslovaks a 'velvet revolution'. All this is inconsistent with a genuine popular revolution 'from below'. The old leaders have resigned without a struggle (again, with the exception of the top Romanian leadership) – which confirms that the change of leaderships is a calculated novelty of *'perestroika'*. The new Communist and non-Communist leaders are acting in harmony to introduce 'democracy' and are cooperating to prevent unrest.

There have been no serious attempts to break off relations with the USSR, and no convincing expressions of hostility towards the Soviet troops stationed in Eastern Europe. There is no real breakdown in Communist Party control. Even where the Communist Parties apparently share power, as in Poland and Czechoslovakia, they retain control over the armed forces and the Ministries of the Interior. Despite the dramatics of the alleged shifts towards capitalism, the governments' control over key industries and central planning mechanisms remains in general intact. It is often overlooked that it is the central planning organs themselves which have introduced some elements of capitalism. The state monopolies over foreign trade continue. Even COMECON – the coordination mechanism for the economic cooperation of the Communist countries – still functions for the time being with some adjustments to meet the new situation[37]. **Despite the changes, Russian influence over the foreign policies of the East European states persists, though in a new, less conspicuous form[38].**

All these factors indicate that the emergence of the common pattern reflects the planned, guided and coordinated introduction of *'perestroika'* in the framework of the common strategy. This is a revolution 'from above' conducted by the Communist Parties, their apparatus, their security services and their armed forces.

36 *Editor's Note:* 'In the art of war there are no fixed rules. These can only be worked out according to circumstances' – Li Ch'üan, commentator of the T'ang period [618-905] in China, on *'The Art of War'* by Sun Tzu, cited in the edition Oxford University Press, 1963-71,.The work was translated into Russian by N.I. Konrad in 1950, shortly after the Communist victory in China [*'New Lies for Old'*, page 42].
37 *Editor's Note:* COMECON has been re-established as the **International Council of Industrialists and Entrepreneurs**, which held a formal Congress on 20 September 1994 in the huge 'People's Palace' constructed under Ceausescu in Bucharest. The mastermind behind COMECON's revival in this new guise is **Arkady Volsky**, believed to derive his power from his close association with the military-industrial complex.
38 *Author's Note:* Notwithstanding the formal independence of the East European countries, the leverage which continues to be exerted by the provision of oil, gas and electricity via networks established by the 'former' USSR, constructed prior to *'perestroika'*, remains as powerful as under the overt Soviet Bloc system.

THE SUCCESS OF 'PERESTROIKA'

The dynamic but orderly introduction of 'democratic', 'non-Communist' governments and 'independent' Republics shows that a successful transition is being made to new, more viable political structures. Since this process of renewal has been conceived, prepared, initiated, led and implemented by the Communist Parties, the actual rôle and influence of these Parties is growing despite all the manifestations to the contrary. The surrender of the Parties' leading rôle is tactical and deceptive.

Its intention is to make the new 'democracies' and their political parties credible in the West. This is not a manifestation of the decay of the power of the Communist Parties. It simply reflects a rejection of Stalinism and the renewal of the Parties – giving them a more active rôle in their societies without loss of their ideological identity, political objectives or strategic vision.

The introduction of 'perestroika' in Eastern Europe and the USSR has been successful because the Soviet and East European armies act as guarantors of its success and because the United States made an ill-advised commitment not to take advantage of the 'unstable' situation and, indeed, decided to help 'perestroika'. This rendered the so-called 'Brezhnev doctrine' superfluous: the Soviets could now safely withdraw their troops from Eastern Europe except from East Germany and Poland, and Gorbachëv could safely pronounce the doctrine dead.

'Perestroika' is also successful because the Soviet strategists are guiding it and there is close coordination between the Soviet Party apparatus, the Soviet Defence and Foreign Ministries and their counterparts in Eastern Europe. **The Soviets are not even bothering to conceal that they are the determining factor in East European 'perestroika'.** No doubt the Soviet embassies are fulfilling their rôle in this coordination. There is also ample evidence of the visits of the new 'non-Communist' leaders to Moscow to meet Gorbachëv and others, and of the visits of Soviet strategists to Eastern Europe in the middle of the changes. For instance, Yakovlev went to Prague in November 1989 just ahead of the Czechoslovak changes, Gorbachëv went to Berlin on the eve of the changes in East Germany and Shevardnadze went to Bucharest following the overthrow of Ceausescu.

How much do the peoples of these countries know about the strategy, what is their attitude towards the process of 'perestroika' and what capacity do the Communists have to control the crowds? Undoubtedly, Communist Party members, leaders of the 'political opposition' and political activists among the intellectuals know almost everything. The strategy can be implemented only with their knowledge and active participation. They are informed through Party briefings. The Party and Komsomol members, the activists in the trade unions and other mass organisations form a large part of the population of the big cities in which the most spectacular manifestations of 'democracy' are taking place. They are the predominant political force in these cities. They have the capacity to mount controlled 'demonstrations', 'strikes' and such other 'democratic' exhibitions as the strategists may require. They can control the crowds either directly through the Party and its mass organisations as in the USSR, or through their secret partners in the 'non-Communist' organisations in Eastern Europe, using their authority and prestige.

Party and KGB officials excel in handling 'spontaneous crowds'. As a student at the KGB Institute in the 1950s, the Author often took part in briefings and 'spontaneous demonstrations'. For example during Tito's visit to Moscow, tens of thousands were brought out at short notice to form 'spontaneous, friendly crowds' at the airport, in the stadiums and on the streets. The same technique is being used today, the only difference being that the régime then was a passive form of totalitarianism: now it is an active form of totalitarianism, deliberately copying elements of Western democracy. The dominant position of the Party-controlled mass organisations still precludes any genuine opposition or demonstrations against the system.

The common people who have no ties with the Party know nothing of the strategy and its practical execution. Like public opinion in the West, they are deceived by the Communist press. Many such people may suspect what the authorities are up to, but they keep silent. As the great Russian poet Pushkin put it: 'People are speechless, silent, mute'. In the Author's opinion, support for the Communist Party in the USSR is growing because of the success of the Party's policy and the West's ill-advised support for Gorbachëv and 'perestroika'.

SPECIFICS IN INDIVIDUAL COMMUNIST COUNTRIES

Although there is a common pattern in the transition to the insidious, deceptive new structure, there are *also certain national specifics in each individual Communist country* which determine the detailed character of the process and provide opportunities for strategic exploitation.

In this matter, the Communist strategists are following Lenin's advice and are *using these specifics in the common strategy*. According to Lenin: **'All nations will come to socialism. This is unavoidable. But all will not come in the same way. Each of them will bring its own traits into one or another form of democracy, into one or another variety of dictatorship of the proletariat, into one or another rate of socialist transformation in various aspects of social life. But of course, there is no need to exaggerate the significance of these peculiarities'.**

The main specific of **the USSR** is that it is a nuclear superpower. This gives it opportunities to exploit disarmament negotiations with the United States, including the use of surprise tactics as at the meeting with President Reagan at Reykjavik.

Another specific of **the USSR** and of **Yugoslavia** is that both are multinational states. This dictates the exploitation and the search for solutions of their nationalist and ethnic problems.

In **Poland**, the specifics are related to the strength of the Catholic Church and of the trade unions.

In **Czechoslovakia**, they are related to a strong democratic tradition.

In **East Germany**, the specifics lie in the division of Germany into two states and in the Soviet occupation.

In **Hungary**, they are related to the suppression of the revolt in 1956, the strong entrepreneurial spirit of the people, and the former multi-party system.

These specifics determine the degree of economic and political reform and the particular shape that the new 'democratic', 'independent' and 'non-Communist' structures are taking. In some cases, they may dictate a delay in the introduction of 'perestroika'. For example, the specifics in **North Korea** lie in its military conflict with the United States, the division of the country into two states and the presence of American troops in South Korea. In **Cuba**, they lie in the relative youth of the Communist régime and its proximity to the United States.

The specifics of *'perestroika'* in **Romania** and **China** require special examination, so these cases are addressed now.

THE SPECIFICS OF *'PERESTROIKA'* IN ROMANIA

Romania is the only country in which transition to the new structure took place through so-called real or violent revolution. This departure from the common pattern was due to the repressive, Stalinist nature of the Ceausescu régime. To be credible in the West, a variation of the revolution model was required – a scenario of revolution, not in this case 'from above', but 'from below'. Could a Communist régime in a country like Romania prepare and carry out a scenario such as this?

In the Author's opinion, a totalitarian state in which the Party, the security service and the army control all aspects of political life, all means of communication and the media, has the capacity to do so. Moreover the Romanian régime could do it because it was acting in coordination with the USSR, China and the other Communist states which have been working in secret competition to produce the best scenario for *'perestroika'*. And Bucharest could arrange a 'revolution from below' because the framework for a safe transition to the new structure had already been established elsewhere in Eastern Europe and because of the Western commitment not to exploit the 'unstable' situation there. Furthermore, a 'real' revolution 'from below' in at least one country would add credibility, by association, to the preceding, less credible peaceful upheavals 'from above'. The Romanian strategists also knew that the outcome of their 'changes' would be helped by the West's confusion over the changes in Eastern Europe, and its biased interpretation of the process which misreads its real meaning. Several indications that the upheaval in Romania was indeed prepared and carried out by the army and military counter-intelligence are evident.

These are as follows:

(a) Gorbachëv's visit to Romania and his meetings with Ceausescu and other Romanian leaders in 1987. These put the Romanians on notice as to timing.

(b) The timing of the Party Congress in Bucharest – at which Ceausescu rather dramatically stressed the Party's socialist purpose. It looked as if he had some idea of what was coming, and was anxious to preserve his socialist legacy for the future. He was heard out stoically by the assembled Communists.

(c) Access to the region where the alleged unrest and atrocities began was at first denied to Western reporters.

(d) The unrest and atrocities in that region were reported first in the Communist media of Yugoslavia and Hungary.

(e) These reports gave exaggerated figures for the number of victims. This fact was even noticed by Amnesty International. The first reports spoke of over 60,000 victims. Estimates have since been lowered to 100 or even less.

(f) The strange concern of the leaders of the 'revolution' for Ceausescu's life, implying that their original instructions had been that he should be arrested but not killed. One would not expect such instructions in a genuine revolution.

(g) Gorbachëv, who is in charge of *'perestroika'* and the transition to new structures in Eastern Europe, rejected President Mitterrand's call for Soviet troops to be sent to Romania – an invitation, in fact, to restore the 'Brezhnev doctrine'. Gorbachëv's reaction demonstrated his confidence in the strategists' control over the outcome of the Romanian upheaval.

(h) The *sudden* emergence of embryonic 'political opposition' groups in Romania fitted the common pattern of the transition in the rest of Eastern Europe. The 'political opposition' – called the National Salvation Front – consists of small 'dissident' groups and of 'disenchanted Communists' who, significantly, have connections with the Soviet Embassy.

(i) The strange timing of President Ceausescu's visit to Iran during the 'turmoil' in Eastern Europe, and immediately ahead of his overthrow and execution. *Party leaders do not normally travel abroad during periods of genuine crisis.*

(j) The most significant indicator of Communist strategic direction of the events in Romania is that Iliescu and Manescu, the new leaders of Romania, are both Communists. Their emergence as leaders after Ceausescu's 'overthrow' fits the Dubcek pattern. In 1971, Iliescu was demoted for 'bourgeois liberalism' and exiled to Timisoara – the site of the alleged massacre – where he served in a minor Party job. By striking coincidence, Iliescu has an unusual connection with Gorbachëv. In the early 1950s both attended schools in Moscow and became friends. It is interesting that, during Gorbachëv's visit to Bucharest in 1987, Ceausescu prevented them from meeting by sending Iliescu to the Carpathians. Manescu, the Foreign Minister under Ceausescu, is known as a 'reformer'. In March 1989 he joined five other Party veterans in denouncing the Ceausescu régime, and lived under house arrest.

The father of the new Prime Minister Petre Roman, was a pre-war member of the Romanian Communist Party who served in the International Brigade in the Spanish civil war and in the Comintern in Moscow. In the post-war period, he was briefly Chief of Staff of the Romanian Army and a Minister.

After falling into disfavour as a potential Titoist, he was rehabilitated in 1953 and became director of a political publishing house. His son, the new Prime Minister, was a privileged student in Romania and holds an engineering professorship at Bucharest's Polytechnic University. In this capacity, he became an associate of Iliescu. In his youth, he was also a close associate of Ceausescu's daughter; and he is distantly related by marriage to Manescu.

In short, he has been described by a Romanian émigré who knew him, as a member of the Romanian élite.

(k) The visit to Romania of the Soviet Foreign Minister, Shevardnadze, shortly after the removal of Ceausescu from power is a further indicator of Soviet coordination with the new Romanian leaders.

(l) Alleged attempts by the new leaders and the army to get rid of the detested security service look largely phoney because there have been no significant disclosures about the most important agents of the service among prominent Romanian intellectuals, church leaders and the élite, and because the army itself took over responsibility for the security service.

(m) Ceausescu's Ministers of Defence and Internal Affairs remained in office for several weeks after the 'revolution'.

(n) According to an official comment by a spokesman for the Romanian Army, subsequently denied, the army was planning a coup six months in advance.

(o) The transcripts of the Ceausescus' trial revealed that it was a trial of individuals, *not* a trial of the Communist Party.

(p) Only Ceausescu and his wife and a handful of his henchmen have been indicted for unjustified shootings. There has been no general indictment of the Communist Party and of its Stalinist régime.

To sum up, the main *specific characteristic* of the Romanian transition to a new structure was that it was the Communist-controlled army and the military counter-intelligence service, not the secret security police, which played the leading part in the scenario and guaranteed the success of the 'revolution'. This makes sense because the new Romanian régime could not have gained a 'democratic' image without the apparent dissolution of the repressive, Stalinist security police.

The question naturally arises whether Ceausescu himself was a party to the scenario which included his own removal from the leadership, his disgrace and death. The likely answer is that Ceausescu went beyond all reason and control. The army and some Party leaders, with Soviet agreement, decided that he had to go and killed him, even though this may not have been the original intention.

Before the 'revolution' in Romania, the Communist Party comprised 3.5 or 4 million members. Even allowing for the presence of careerists in the membership, this means that the Party comprised the main political force in society, especially in the cities. Neither the basis nor the forces were ever available for the formation of genuine non-Communist opposition.

This explains why the Communists are the dominant force in the National Salvation Front and in the government which it formed. Despite the recent cosmetic reorganisation of the Front, it is inevitable that these 'reformed', controlled Communists will continue to control and run 'democratic' Romania.

THE SPECIFICS OF 'PERESTROIKA' IN CHINA

Western misreading of developments in Communist China calls for a new interpretation of them in terms of the long-range Communist strategy in which China participates, and of China's national specifics for the transition to new structures.

Before the suppression of the student pro-democracy demonstration in Peking, the Chinese Communist Party was basically following the same common pattern of *'perestroika'* as the USSR and Eastern Europe. The Chinese strategists had introduced economic reforms and some elements of 'capitalism'.

There was also beginning to emerge an embryonic form of 'political opposition' – 'dissident movements' – complete with a Chinese version of Sakharov. Then came the demonstration which indicated the emergence of a student pro-democracy movement. The emergence of this movement reflected China's *national specifics*.

These specifics are that China is a predominantly peasant country in which the students have an old revolutionary tradition as the initiators of political movements and political change. The Chinese Communist Party itself started as a student movement. It is logical, therefore, that the Party strategists should have chosen to follow this tradition and should have attempted to introduce 'democracy' in China through the active participation of their students.

The more important arguments which support this analysis are as follows:

(1) The initiators and the core of the student pro-democracy demonstration were the children of Communist Party officials – in fact the generation from which the future leaders of Communist China will be drawn.

(2) According to some reports, the movement was initiated in the Research Institute for Social Change.

(3) The students are said to have had supporters in the ruling Party élite, so-called 'reformers' like Zhao who was allegedly the catalyst of the movement.

(4) The demonstrators were not calling for a rejection of the socialist system or for the overthrow of the Government. Banners were observed which read: 'We firmly support the correct leadership of the Communist Party'.

The demonstrators' demands were rather modest: an end to corrupt practices and 'a meaningful dialogue' with the country's leaders.

(5) During the first period of the demonstration there was toleration of, if not cooperation with, the demonstrators by the Party and its officials. There was no army interference with, or repression of, the students.

(6) The Party's toleration of the demonstration was evident in the shape of its cooperative attitude towards Western television coverage of the events, which were shown in detail on Western TV networks.

(7) The orderliness of the demonstration and the singing of the Party song, the 'Internationale', contrasted sharply with the violent and hostile demonstrations of South Korean students which had been taking place in Seoul.

(8) The uninterrupted stream of rumours about an alleged struggle between 'liberal reformers' and 'hardliners' reflected a familiar disinformation technique designed to confuse the West about the true nature of the developments.

It is a fact that these rumours were fed to Western observers by Communist officials themselves. It appears that both the 'liberals' and the 'hardliners' were using these rumours to manipulate the responses and attitudes of the West, especially the Americans and the Japanese, in the interests of their deception strategy.

Then, suddenly, Western television coverage was cut off and the student pro-democracy demonstration was suppressed. Why did the Chinese leaders 'change' their line, why the retreat? Probably, the most important reason was that the original Party-organised demonstration brought out on to the streets genuine spontaneous elements, and the situation threatened to run out of control as the 'Prague spring' of 1968 had done in Czechoslovakia.

Was there a real massacre in Tienanmen Square? Many Western reporters covered the event from their hotel rooms. They heard the sound of firing and the movement of the tanks. How many actually saw the massacre? Published reports on the subject are conflicting.

On 12 June 1989 'The New York Times' published an account, previously published in Hong Kong and San Francisco, of troops attacking students in Tienanmen Square before dawn on 4 June.

SELECTIVE KILLING OF THE UNORGANISED ELEMENTS IN TIENANMEN SQUARE

On 13 June 1989, 'The New York Times' published a report by Nicholas D. Kristof, its Peking correspondent, disputing the report published on 12 June and asserting that, while troops were shooting and killing victims in the area around the square, there was no firm evidence that students were killed in the middle of the square itself. If Kristof's version is correct, it would support the suggestion that the crackdown was aimed, not at the original pro-democracy demonstrators who, by Kristof's account, left the square together singing the 'Internationale', and who had been carrying placards supporting the Communist Party, but at the unorganised elements who sought to join them or otherwise to take advantage of the demonstration.

Other considerations may well have affected the Chinese suppression of the demonstration. No doubt the decision was coordinated with the Soviets. It almost coincided with Gorbachëv's visit to Peking, which had been preceded a few weeks earlier by a visit by Shevardnadze.

It may be that the Communist strategists sought to avoid too obviously uniform a pattern of transition to new structures in the USSR, China and Eastern Europe, and preferred to emphasise opposite approaches – Soviet support for and Chinese intolerance of 'democracy' and reform[39].

The Chinese crackdown occurred on the eve of the changes in Eastern Europe. It sent (and may have been intended to send) a clear signal to the East Europeans that too much unrest in the course of 'perestroika' could lead to military intervention, and to the Chinese that the forthcoming changes in Eastern Europe could not be agitated for in China. It may be that the Chinese also saw a need to take advance precautions to stabilise their régime politically and to give it a clearer socialist direction after their

---

39 Editor's Note: Furthermore, there is a crucial dialectical difference between Russia and China, connected with the strategists' ruse of fabricating a 'Break with the Past'. In his book 'Soviet Propaganda as a Foreign Policy Tool' [Freedom House, New York, 1991], M. Leighton observed [page 14] that 'the Communist Party of the Soviet Union [CPSU] must posit the existence of an external enemy in order to justify its monopoly of power. If the United States didn't exist as the arch foe, the Kremlin would have to invent it'. This was the standard perception, the accuracy of which was taken for granted for generations – until the 'abolition of the enemy' was formalised in Paris on 19th November 1990 with the signing of the 'Declaration of Twenty-Two States' and the 'Charter of Paris'. Point One of the Declaration asserts that 'the signatories solemnly declare that, in the new era of European relations which is beginning, they are no longer adversaries, will build new relationships and extend to each other the hand of friendship'. But NATO and the West had failed to notice, let alone understand, the meticulous Leninist use of language concerning the 'abolition' of the enemy by the Communist apparatus. For instance, Academician Georgiy Arbatov, one of Gorbachëv's closest advisers, had referred in the June 1988 issue of 'Kommunist' to the forthcoming 'erosion of the image of the enemy' [see Note 16, page 32]. If he had meant that the enemy itself was to be erased, he would have said as much; but he did not. Thus the West mistook the image for the reality – just as this leading strategist had anticipated. If the Communist Party needed, as Leighton says, 'to posit the existence of an external enemy to justify its monopoly of power', it followed that the 'abolition of the image of the enemy' would need logically to be accompanied by the 'disappearance' of the Communist Party itself. Hence the 'August coup' and its aftermath, which represented a 'Break with the Past', opening the way for 'convergence' as intended by the strategists. By contrast, since the West had not, since Nixon's détente with China, regarded China as 'the enemy', the reverse of this logic required no 'vanishing act' by the Chinese Communist Party.

introduction of elements of 'capitalism' – a Chinese tactic of taking one step forward with one foot, then one step forward with the other.

In the not too distant future – and perhaps coinciding with Deng's departure from the scene – the Chinese strategists may re-enact the Polish formula for the transition to the new structure.

The student pro-democracy movement might again be legalised like Solidarity, becoming a leading political force in China. Deng might be criticised for his rôle in the suppression of the student demonstration.

'Liberal' Communist leaders would return to, or new 'liberals' might appear in, the Chinese Communist leadership – working in harmony with the leaders of the pro-'democracy' movement.

On the other hand, the message delivered in Tienanmen Square may prove more than adequate to enable the régime to continue its feat of achieving the 'synthesis' stage of the Hegelian dialectical triad – the supremacy of the Communist Party plus elements of Western capitalism and democracy.

THE DIFFICULTIES FACED BY THE WESTERN MEDIA IN COVERING 'PERESTROIKA'

The Western media are in a difficult and vulnerable situation. They have to cover the process of 'perestroika' in the Communist countries within a frame of reference wrongly defined for them both by the Communist strategists, who naturally do their best to ensure favourable coverage of 'perestroika' by the Western media, and by Western governments which mistakenly accept and support 'perestroika' as a process serving Western interests. Like Western governments and their intelligence services, the Western media lack reliable sources of information on the *strategic intentions* of Communist officials. Like their governments, the Western media have been caught unprepared by the advent of 'perestroika' and have no understanding of its origin, its motivation, its use of political and security potential or its anti-Western strategic design. All these factors contribute to the media's uncritical and inaccurate coverage of the subject.

Simon Leis, a Western observer, made a shrewd observation about the difficulties of covering the Cultural Revolution in Communist China. 'I maintain', he wrote, 'that foreigners who live permanently or temporarily in those conditions in Communist China cannot write anything except superficial trifles. Those who suppose they can write something serious, when they pass on their impressions about China, or those who pretend knowing Chinese reality, are actually describing a spectacle on the stage of the Chinese theatre of shadows which is staged for them by the Maoist authorities. Either they are deceiving the reader or, which is even worse, they are deceiving themselves'. Although Mr Leis wrote his observations during the Cultural Revolution, there is no reason to believe that his remarks have ceased to be valid. On the contrary, his explanation accounts for the present poor quality of the coverage of the introduction of 'democracy' in the Communist countries. By and large, reporters are covering spectacles staged for them by the Communist strategists. They rely too much on official coverage in the Communist media and accept uncritically the information which is fed to them by Communist officials and their agents.

It was disturbing, for example, to watch the coverage on American television of the student demonstration in Peking by Western reporters from their hotels. Ethnic and nationalist tensions in Azerbaijan, Armenia or the Baltic Republics are often covered from Moscow, Leningrad or even London. Such coverage, when the media are ignorant of the strategic and political intentions of the Communist strategists, can be inaccurate, misleading and damaging to Western interests.

Confused about the true process of *'perestroika'*, its forces and its objectives, the Western media apply Western notions to the situation they observe in the Communist countries, and report developments in Western democratic terms. Hence they observe the resignations of old Communist leaders and their replacement by 'non-Communist' leaders of the 'political opposition' and they report on the new 'non-Communist' structures in Eastern Europe and the USSR all in Western terms – failing to see the difference between genuine Western democracy and false, deceptive, controlled, Communist 'democracy' ('democratism'). Their misguided perceptions are accepted, reported and presented as realities. Newspaper editorials, based on this confusion and containing advice to take this or that activist course of action to exploit the situation in the Communist countries, can be especially faulty and counterproductive, while providing further confirmation to the strategists that the 'penny has not dropped' in the West.

Another obstacle for the Western media is the improved quality of the means being employed to manipulate it by the new 'democratic' establishment in the Communist countries, which remain totalitarian in the execution of their strategy. Their totalitarianism differs from the Stalinist version in that it is politically active and has a civilised style. Party and KGB officials and their agents in the new structure have passed through a formidable schooling in the manipulation of Western reporters, under the tutelage of KGB Colonel Norman Borodin, the son of the American-born Comintern official, Michael Borodin (Grusenberg). Norman Borodin spent the whole of his long KGB career engaged in the recruitment and manipulation of American, British, French and German journalists in Moscow.

He accumulated vast experience in this activity, which he passed on to the new generation of Party and KGB officials who are now involved in the execution of the strategy. This new generation of experts in media-manipulation is advised and guided by Yakovlev, Arbatov and Nikolay Shishlin who have studied the Western media, know their workings and have learned how to exploit their craving for sensation, in order to misinform the public both at home and in the West.

Thus the Western media are facing a new situation and a new challenge. The Communist strategists realise that the success of *'perestroika'* and their chance of achieving the world victory of Communism by political means depend upon the manipulation of the media. Regardless of *'glasnost'*, they will stop at nothing to deceive world public opinion. 'Demonstrations', 'strikes', 'nationalist unrest', 'shootings', 'atrocities', 'trials' and 'executions' can all be staged if necessary for Western consumption.

During the war with Hitler, the British used a corpse – 'the man who never was' – to convey military deception material to the Germans. Nowadays the Communists, operating on the far grander scale that their totalitarian system and mentality allow, are inventing many 'corpses' and other alleged 'victims' in order to further their deceptive purposes and attain their strategic objectives.

On the basis of his own studies at the KGB Institute of KGB methods against Western journalists, the Author considers that Robert Woodward and Karl Bernstein's feats of investigative journalism would be impossible in the USSR or other Communist countries. Their security services could and would prevent them.

The Western media remain outside the inner circle of the Communist establishment and have no effective means of finding out the truth about 'perestroika'. Its coverage can therefore be influenced and shaped by the establishment's manipulators, the security services and their agents.

Caught in the straitjacket of their erroneous frame of reference, and confused by Communist manipulation, there is a danger that the Western press and broadcasting media may become, not only channels for, but *generators* of misleading perceptions of 'perestroika'. They may indeed become unwitting instruments for the acceleration of the Soviet strategy of convergence of the two systems.

For example, Mr Dan Rather, the CBS news anchorman, reported the news while *taking part* in the Chinese students' pro-democracy demonstration in Tienanmen Square before it was suppressed. The question is whether this style of reporting leads to true objectivity, or whether it approximates the style of John Reed, the US journalist who participated in and wrote about the events of the October Revolution.

A recovery of Western policy and the adoption of a more realistic response to 'perestroika' cannot take place without a restoration of critical reporting by the Western media and their understanding of the inner process and rationale of 'perestroika' which the Communists are successfully concealing.

The Communists now allow their public to listen to the Voice of America[40] and to the BBC precisely because the Western media have accepted the Communist version of the meaning of 'perestroika'. Would they continue to do so if the Western media became critical of 'perestroika' and exposed the secret partnership of the Communist and 'non-Communist' leaders in Eastern Europe, the secret coordination between 'conservatives' and 'reformers', the hidden links between the Communist strategists and the 'nationalist' leaders of the 'independent' Republics and the anti-Western design of Soviet strategy?

Herein lies the future test of Soviet '*glasnost*'. And here lie fresh opportunities for intelligent Western journalists, provided their proprietors will listen[41].

40 *Editor's Note:* However far-reaching reductions in the volume and coverage of broadcasts to 'former' Soviet Republics and Eastern Europe by Voice of America have been promoted by the Clinton Administration, which has also facilitated a plan to relocate Radio Free Europe from Munich to Prague. By late 1994, it was clear that a sizeable proportion of both services' broadcasts to the 'former' Soviet Bloc were under threat – just when, in the light of developments such as the Russian military operations against Chechnya, a few Western journalists were at last beginning to reassess the nature of the false 'post-Soviet' 'democratist' régime. As **George Soros**, involved with reorganisation of Radio Free Europe, told '*Focus*' [Germany], in August 1994, 'it was a strategic chess move'.

41 *Author's Note:* One such opportunity would be to study on a broad scale a surviving feature of the old régime, namely, the lavish provision for the élite, especially the military and the KGB, of state dachas, hospitals, sanatoria and rest houses. This subject remains unmentionable in the Russian press, indicating that *glasnost* is controlled. Along with mysterious purchases by Russians of expensive property abroad, it could be a fertile field for Western journalists concerned about the possible diversion of Western aid for Russia.

COMMENTS ON AN ARTICLE BY 'Z' IN *'DAEDALUS'*[42]

'Z''s analysis of Gorbachëv's *'perestroika'* is misleading and inaccurate. The analysis disregards the long-range strategy which has been in action since the period 1958 to 1960. Deng's introduction of market forces and the appearance of Solidarity were not spontaneous events but developments within the framework of this strategy. *'Perestroika'* is not a response to a crisis but the final phase of the strategy which the Communist strategists had been preparing for the preceding twenty-five years. **We are not witnessing the disintegration of the system but its renewal, its political offensive and its deployment of the full political potential of the renewed Communist régimes.** On the question of helping or not helping Gorbachëv, 'Z''s suggestions are conflicting. On the one hand, he suggests that Western help is futile and should not be given. On the other, he suggests that Western help could play a constructive rôle since 'events are pressing towards the eventual dwindling away of the system'.

Here 'Z''s scenario for Western help does not differ much from Brzezinski's scenario, discussed on pages 43-44. For 'Z' suggests:

(a) Reducing the mutual burden of armaments with due attention to legitimate Soviet security anxieties ('Z' pointing out that Gorbachëv has indicated that he is willing to engage in such reductions);

(b) That Western help could usefully be applied, on the lines of Western help to Poland, to the piecemeal development of parallel private and market structures and the promotion of political pluralism 'in such places as the Baltic States, Armenia or the Soviet Far East'. In his view, the parallel sector would eventually spread across the Soviet Union.

Again 'Z''s scenario does not differ much from Brzezinski's. In fact, it is an extension of it from Eastern Europe to the emerging so-called 'independent' Republics of the USSR. Like Brzezinski, 'Z' fails to warn the West about the lessons of Lenin's New Economic Policy period. And like Brzezinski, 'Z' exaggerates Soviet difficulties. His statement about the Soviet Union's 'terminal crisis' is erroneous. He underestimates the Soviet Union's political strength and its deployment of its political potential in the execution of its strategic designs against the West.

'Z''s statement that Communism has always been successful in holding on to its monopoly of power is incomplete. Communism has also been successful in expanding from one to thirteen states and is now trying to expand into Western Europe and the United States in a new guise using its full political potential. The timing of the publication of 'Z''s article is puzzling. In January 1988 and in March 1989, this Author suggested in Memoranda to the CIA that his view on Soviet strategy should be published in *'Foreign Affairs'* and attributed to an anonymous KGB defector in the way that Kennan's article was published in 1947 and attributed to 'X'. This suggestion was not adopted.

Since 'Z' and this Author hold opposing views on *'perestroika'*, the publication of 'Z''s article – in the manner suggested by this Author for publication of his own interpretation – is probably coincidental.

42 See '*The New York Times*' Op-Ed article, 4 January 1990.

CONCLUSIONS AND THE NEED FOR RECONSIDERATION
OF THE WEST'S BLIND RESPONSE TO *'PERESTROIKA'*

The blindness of the West, and of its intelligence and policymaking circles, to Soviet **strategy**, its uncritical acceptance of the authenticity of deceptive, controlled pseudo-democracy and its support for *'perestroika'*, have given the Soviets significant advantages and have worsened the position of the Western democracies.

First of all, the Communist strategists have found a new way of controlling society by replacing open Party domination with a new 'non-Communist' structure. They have found a way of reviving their economies with Western credits, technology and joint ventures. They have adopted Lenin's ideas of influencing the West through economic concessions. This does not amount to the introduction of capitalism: it is a sophisticated game involving the use of capitalist trimmings to *destroy* capitalism. The strategists have found a way towards achieving the neutralisation of Germany. They have succeeded in identifying themselves with democracy. Although this identification is tactical and deceptive, they have gained a hearing in and the support of true democracies in the West. *'Perestroika'* may become the model, not only for the Communist countries, but for the West and the Third World. *'Perestroika'* is proving to these countries that, with Western help, it can bring them economic improvements and greatly improved access to Western technology and finance.

Secondly, Western support has immensely accelerated the successful renewal of the Communist régimes and their transition to new, more viable political structures. What could have taken decades without Western support is *already* emerging as a new reality.

Thirdly, Western support has brought about real confusion and paralysis in the Western democracies and has *established the basis for their military, ideological, political and diplomatic destabilisation*. It has confused their people, neutralised anti-Communists and turned American and West European conservatives into active and enthusiastic supporters of *'perestroika'* in the Communist world.

Fourthly, Western support has created favourable conditions for the deployment by the Communists of their full political and security potential. It has immensely accelerated the implementation of their strategy. Had this strategy been understood and exposed by the West, the Soviet design would have had little chance of success. But given the prevailing blindness, confusion and euphoria, it may become reality within a decade or so.

The dramatic impact on the West of the changes in the Communist world has created a situation in which radical changes in the West can be brought about through the media, votes in parliaments and campaigns and demonstrations on the streets. The situation is critical. Capitalism and true democracy in the United States and Western Europe are threatened by spurious, controlled pseudo-democracies.

Ignorant of aggressive Communist intentions, the Western democracies are acutely vulnerable to the entry into their countries of the political and security potential of the renewed Communist régimes. This potential consists of the 'non-Communist' governments, the new political parties, the members of the new parliaments, renewed trade unions, prominent churchmen and intellectuals and the leaders of the new 'non-Communist', 'democratic' structures in the newly 'independent', 'nationalist' states. This potential has been retained, inspired and revitalised by the success of *'perestroika'* and its acceptance by the West.

All these forces are ready to develop contacts with their counterparts in the West, to promote solidarity with them and to engage them in joint campaigns for disarmament and radical reform of the social, political and military structure of the United States and Western Europe. The deployment of this potential has already begun in the shape of visits to the United States and Western Europe by the new 'democrats' from the Communist countries like Walesa, Yeltsin, the late Andrei Sakharov and the new Czechoslovak President. They are the vanguard of the Communist political potential, exploiting Western gullibility which has been so painfully exhibited in the shape of the euphoric Western reception which they have received.

Walesa, for example, lectured his Western hosts on the need to be generous to the new régime in Poland, a régime in which, despite its 'non-Communist' form, the real power – the Presidency, the Ministry of the Interior and the army – remains in Communist hands. Walesa was arrogant and behaved as if the West was indebted to the new Polish régime, overlooking the extent of Polish financial indebtedness to the West. Moreover Walesa demanded his pound of flesh and was successful in extracting it. He demanded help for a régime the security and intelligence services of which, improved under the supervision of Stanislaw Kania, the late Moczar and Kiszczak, have become the next most effective intelligence services after the KGB, which runs the most important agents of influence. The deployment of the political potential of the new 'democracies' to bring about 'restructuring' in the West is a real threat to the true democracies, their values, their freedoms and their free enterprise capitalist systems. **It is time to wake up to it.**

It is not only against the Western democracies that the deployment of the Soviet political and security potential has begun. It is being extended against the anti-Communist Muslim and Arab countries, beginning with the Soviets' neighbours, Iran and Turkey. Here, the offensive is being launched, not through Communist Parties or the Soviet Army, but through Soviet Muslims in the guise of 'independent', 'nationalist', 'anti-Communist' Muslims in the 'anti-Soviet' Republic of Azerbaijan who are deceptively identifying themselves with the Islamic religion and its values. This is the key to understanding the developments in Azerbaijan and the emergence of 'independent fronts' and 'guerrilla groups', and their entry into Iran.

THE MAIN PRIORITIES FOR RE-THINKING
Until the West abandons its simplistic thinking and penetrates into the complexities of the changes in the Communist world, the Communist strategists will retain the upper hand. The critical situation demands urgent Western re-thinking of the response to the strategy of *'perestroika'* and its dangers for the West. That is the main priority. It will take courage and statesmanship of the highest order.

First, Western governments should put an end to the confusion, euphoria and destabilisation of their societies by admitting their mistakes, disengaging from support of *'perestroika'* and exposing its dangers. Regardless of any effect on the polls, they should concede that they have hastened to assist the forces which intend to undermine and destroy Western democracy. Their main concern should be to stabilise their own societies, *not* the Communist societies.

They should concentrate on strengthening their alliances, addressing their domestic problems and developing an effective counter-strategy to *'perestroika'*. Conservative leaders in the United States and Western Europe should wake up to the threat, overcome their confusion and regroup their forces.

Since West Germany is particularly vulnerable and oblivious of the fact, Western leaders should encourage the West Germans to reject Genscher's scenario of active engagement with and massive assistance for *'perestroika'* in the Communist world. The German claim to have a better understanding of the Soviets than other Western countries is unfounded, in the light of the history of the blunders which have bedevilled German policy towards the Soviet Union in the past.

The West showed its maturity in rejecting Euro-Communism. Now it should comprehend and reject the strategy of *'perestroika'* in order to prevent the rape of Western democracy by Communists in 'democratic' dress.

Secondly, the Vatican should reverse its mistaken support for the renewal of the Communist régimes in the USSR and Eastern Europe. The Vatican ignores the anti-Western design of Soviet strategy. It fails to understand that **greater apparent official tolerance of religion in the Soviet Union is accompanied by a secret drive to increase Party and KGB penetration of the Catholic and other churches and to use agents therein for political and strategic purposes inside and outside the Soviet Union**. As part of the programme to destroy religion from within, the KGB, in the late 1950s, started sending dedicated young Communists to ecclesiastical academies and seminaries to train them as future church leaders. These young Communists joined the Church, *not* at the call of their consciences to serve God, but at the call of the Communist Party in order to serve that Party and to implement its **general line** in the struggle against religion[43].

In the present phase, secret agents in the Catholic and other churches are being used to implement Communist strategy[44]. When they achieve their Commu-

43 *Editor's Note:* 'There must be no let-up in the war against religion because as long as religion exists Communism cannot prevail. We must intensify the obliteration of all religions wherever they are being practised or taught': statement by Mikhail Gorbachëv on 15 December 1987 to a group of Communist Party officials, cadres and Soviet military personnel in Uzbekistan. With his wife Raisa, Gorbachëv is a disciple of the late Sardinian Communist **Antonio Gramsci** – the Marxist proponent of a policy of active social demoralisation (attack against morality) and the Marxisation of religion.

44 *Editor's Note:* As Malachi Martin, a close associate of Pope John Paul II, has explained, in *'The Keys of This Blood: The Struggle for World Domination Between Pope John Paul II, Mikhail Gorbachëv and the Capitalist West'* [Simon and Schuster, New York, 1990]: 'Mikhail Gorbachëv burst upon the world scene as the first Soviet leader big-minded enough to appraise, appreciate and fully embrace the Gramscian formula. The only Soviet leader realistic and courageous enough to commit even his own satellite territories to the dead Sardinian's plan for victory in Marxism's constant struggle for total geopolitical predominance among the nations, and for its total acceptance in the newly de-Christianised hearts and minds of the men and women who people those nations... In Gorbachëv's hands... Gramsci has entered into the globalist competition. [The Pope] is certain that Mikhail Gorbachëv will move confidently into the deep waters of the new globalism, with the ghost of Antonio Gramsci as companion and guide'. Gramsci taught that Stalinist repression is an inefficient means of achieving 'irreversible' political control. A more effective method would be to pervert the approach of the Roman Catholic Church, with which Gramsci was familiar – namely, to seek con-

[Continued on page 117 opposite:]

nist world victory, they will use mass withdrawal of their agents to disrupt and destroy the churches. Never in its history since Nero has Christianity faced such a threat of possible destruction. The dictum of the late Pope Pius XII about the incompatibility of Communism and religion is as correct as ever. The Vatican should reaffirm this dictum and should use its influence and its 'divisions' to defend Western values from the new Communist assault.

The Vatican should also re-examine the possible assassination of the predecessor of the present Pope. Recent books have disposed of some conspiracy theories but have not explored the possibility of KGB involvement. The question should still be asked and answered: was the late Pope assassinated? If so, who was behind the assassination? Was it the KGB? If so, what were the KGB's motives?

Thirdly, Western industrialists and financiers should reverse their mistakes in involving themselves in joint ventures with the Communists, financing the revival of their main political adversaries and supplying them with new technology. They are repeating the Rapallo mistake of the German industrialists during the period of the New Economic Policy. They should realise that, while they may make some profits from joint ventures, in the long run they will be exterminated as a class[45]. They should forego their profits and defend Western democracy and the capitalist system.

Fourthly, free Western trade unions, especially the AFL-CIO, should discard their illusions about the new 'non-Communist' unions in the Communist countries, and not walk into their trap. Such marriages would not work. The American

---

trol through *the possession of the minds of the people.* Thus religion must be destroyed, and the worship of God (above Man) replaced by the worship of Man – to 'help Man establish his home on earth'. Malachi Martin elaborates: 'The professional counter-intelligence experts in the Party-State of the Soviet Union [were] the first officially to recognise the truth of Gramsci's prediction that in following the Leninist and Stalinist policy of fomenting violent revolution abroad, they could not create the proletarian revolution in the minds and lives of capitalist populations... And they were the first to understand that, in Gramsci's blueprint, they had stumbled onto the counter-intelligence formula *par excellence.* They knew that he had provided the Soviets [with]... the most far-reaching exercise of deception ever executed by the Party-State, an exercise already perfectly fitted to the international structure Lenin had created'. It is important to underscore the fact that Gorbachëv, as Golitsyn explains, was the executor, not the originator, of the strategy and this key dimension of it.

45 *Editor's Note:* The following authoritative confirmation of the Author's warning to industrialists and businessmen was received by the Editor in February 1994, and was published in SOVIET ANALYST [Volume 22, Numbers 7 & 8, on page 32]. The report was contained in a letter from **Peter Palms II**, head of the **Russian Venture Capital Fund of America**, based in Kirkland, near Seattle, Washington State: 'The Russian Government's policy continues to be to increase taxes on revenues of private enterprise, irrespective of, and unrelated to, whether they are profitable. Subsequent to investment by American entrepreneurs in the Russian oil industry in 1993, the Russian Government suddenly imposed a $5.0 per barrel new tax on oil production. This tax eliminated any possibility of a return on investment. Similar taxes are imposed by auctioning of licenses and export permits and other administrative mechanisms, which assure that all revenues from private enterprise in Russia are transferred back to the State. **Russian 'capitalism' is state-owned capitalism in disguise. Entrepreneurs are tolerated if they operate at a loss and pay tribute to the state for the privilege.** The Russian Government continues to subsidise state-owned industry with ten trillion roubles' worth of annual handouts. Western entrepreneurs are expected to provide similar subsidies by paying the Government for the privilege of losing money. **It seems that in Russia the word "investment" will continue to mean "donation" for the foreseeable future.** Socialism means socialism. The tax decrees, issued daily, rectify any conflicting expectations, and [yet] verbal platitudes continue to lure unsuspecting Western private capitalists into making their donation'.

attempts to deepen contacts with these trade unions and to capitalise on their popularity will result in the penetration of American labour by these Communist unions.

Fifthly, the élite of the United States and Western Europe should re-think their support for *'perestroika'*. The famous appeal of the Soviet writer Gorky 'to the masters of Western culture' during the struggle with Hitler comes to mind, and offers a solution. As before, Western intellectuals have to choose between Western democracy and the new quasi-democracies run by Communists who raped Russian culture and Russian intellectuals in the past and are manipulating them now in their political schemes against the West. Western intellectuals must decide whether they are to become, in Gorbachëv's words, the 'yeast of *'perestroika''* in their countries, or whether they are to become the 'yeast' for defending Western freedoms from their would-be Communist stranglers. The élite should not be blinded by the glitter of Western-style 'democracy' in the Communist countries but should adopt a more critical attitude to developments and their meaning.

In the sixth place, the Western media should cleanse itself of the present biased presentation of *'perestroika'*, penetrate the façade of *'glasnost'* and the new 'non-Communist' structures and provide more realistic and objective accounts of the changes in the Communist countries and their meaning for the West. **The prime task for an objective Western reporter who believes in the truth should be to unmask the true relations between the Communist apparatus and the 'non-Communist' structures.**

Finally, the United States should correct the serious mistake it made when it weakened and degutted its intelligence and counter-intelligence services and took away the CIA's residual rôle in policy formulation before the Cold War was over. Now, Washington should realise that, contrary to the fashionable, self-congratulatory view, the West lost the Cold War when it began to support *'perestroika'* and to regard it as serving Western interests. It should realise that its refusal to learn the lessons of Soviet Communist history and behaviour has been inexcusable.

Even at this late hour, the American intelligence and counter-intelligence services should be radically rebuilt to meet the threat from the strategy of *'perestroika'* and to counter the deployment against the West of the Communist political and security potential. Western counter-intelligence must find effective ways of dealing with Communist agents of influence in the West.

Since the Author's warnings about the strategy of *'perestroika'* have failed to reach or influence American policymakers and since the situation is becoming every day more critical, the Author requests that the Agency clear his Memoranda for publication so that the American people may be informed. ∎

PART FIVE

EXPOSING 'PERESTROIKA' AS THE SOVIET STRATEGY FOR A 'SECOND OCTOBER REVOLUTION' ['WELTOKTOBER']

Non-violent revolution, controlled fake 'democratism' and strategic disinformation

Memorandum to the CIA: SEPTEMBER-NOVEMBER 1990

1 EXPOSING *'PERESTROIKA'* AS THE STRATEGY FOR A SECOND OCTOBER WORLD SOCIALIST REVOLUTION [*'WELTOKTOBER'*]

2 THE NEW PATTERN OF NON-VIOLENT REVOLUTION, NOT BY COMMUNIST PARTIES, DICTATORSHIPS, THE SOVIET ARMY AND VIOLENCE BUT THROUGH FALSE REFORM, INFLUENCE AND THE POLITICAL ACTION OF THE SOVIET FORCES ENGAGED IN PARTY-CONTROLLED 'DEMOCRATISATION' AND THE SO-CALLED MULTI-PARTY SYSTEM IN THE USSR

3 THE PARAMOUNT ROLE OF SOVIET STRATEGIC DISINFORMATION IN THE SUCCESSFUL EXECUTION OF THE *'PERESTROIKA'* STRATEGY

It was not the Author's intention to submit further political Memoranda to the CIA on Soviet affairs. But he found that he could not sit idly by and watch the United States and its political leaders being taken in by Soviet strategic disinformation and overwhelmed by their own wishful thinking about the evolution of the Soviet system. He therefore decided to make a further attempt to explain the real essence of *'perestroika'*, to expose its contradictions, to reveal its strategic design, to give warning of its potentially dangerous impact on the United States and to counteract the present simplistic and over-optimistic Western view of its significance. Sooner or later informed opinion in the Western democracies will comprehend the new dimensions of the Soviet threat and the pendulum of US policy will begin to swing back from its present confusion to a greater sense of reality. The Memorandum is submitted in the hope of accelerating the process.

SOVIET REJECTION OF THE DISCREDITED PATTERN OF
VIOLENT REVOLUTION IN SELECTED PARTS OF THE WORLD
The first attempt at World Socialist Revolution was based on violent action by Communist Parties and the Comintern seeking to establish the dictatorship of the proletariat through uprisings, civil war and terror. The Revolution succeeded only in Russia in 1917 and failed elsewhere with the collapse of the Bela Kun régime in Hungary in 1919 and the suppression of the Communist uprisings in Germany in 1919 and 1923. After the Second World War Stalin succeeded in spreading Revolution into Eastern Europe through occupation of the area by the victorious Soviet Army and successful diplomacy *vis-à-vis* the Western allies. In China, Mao Tse-Tung and the Chinese Communists, with concealed military assistance from the Soviets, took power through civil war.

After the anti-Communist uprisings in Hungary and Poland in 1956 the Soviets strategists realised that Stalin's 'police socialism', which had thoroughly alarmed the Western democracies, was discredited and that violence and terror offered no possibilities for the advance of the Revolution at least in the developed world.

WHY DID THE SOVIET STRATEGISTS OPT FOR A
NON-VIOLENT PATTERN OF WORLD REVOLUTION?
From the late 1950s onwards the Soviets have been developing and pursuing a new long-range strategy for World Socialist Revolution. Its essence has been:

(a) Replacement of the outdated concept of the 'dictatorship of the proletariat' by the concept of the 'state of the whole people':

(b) Development of new political forces under the 'state of the whole people':

(c) The preparation of economic and political reforms and the transition to a planned socialist market economy and a controlled 'multi-Party system':

(d) A shift in the pattern of World Revolution from one of violence to one of non-violence consistent with a parallel elimination of the image of the enemy.

In adopting a non-violent pattern for the time being, the Communist strategists were following Lenin's advice to choose forms of revolutionary action corresponding to the correlation of forces between capitalist and socialist countries. From the late 1950s onwards, in order to weaken their main enemy – the United States – and to strengthen themselves, the socialist countries developed two legs of their strategy, the military and the political. Militarily, the socialist countries, alongside the consistent build-up of their nuclear and conventional arsenals, engaged the United States in an unpopular guerrilla war in far-off Vietnam to which they provided military aid, using their political influence in the West to undermine American morale. With Soviet and Chinese help, the Vietnamese under their able strategist, General Giap, achieved their objective. The victory demoralised and split the American nation, bringing it almost to the verge of civil war.

Politically, the Soviet and other Communist strategists have been building up their political arsenals ever since the late 1950s. While the United States was obsessed with the Vietnam war, the Soviet strategists were developing their political potential, most notably through the creation of controlled political opposition, in preparation for the defeat of the United States in the final phase of Communist strategy, namely 'perestroika', and its aftermath.

The Communist assessment is that their victory in Vietnam weakened the United States militarily, politically and morally. They believe, not necessarily correctly, that, despite US intervention in Grenada, the Americans have not recovered from the Vietnam syndrome and that their will to resist has been sapped. They have also taken into account the fact that the American, British, French and especially, the West German intelligence services have lost their effectiveness through KGB penetration or self-inflicted wounds. Their view is that Western, and particularly American, weakness dictates that the non-violent pattern of revolution is the most appropriate form for the *current* political and social situation. They consider that American hostility to the multinational corporations even among the middle classes can be exploited effectively and that the United States can be vanquished by political means. They are convinced that they can bring about the necessary military, political and economic restructuring of the United States – what they call the 'renewal of American democracy' – and the convergence of the American and Soviet systems through the influence and actions of the political arsenal represented by their controlled 'democratisation' and 'multi-Party system'. It was this conviction that led to the launching by the Soviet strategists in 1985 of the final phase of their non-violent strategy, namely *'perestroika'*.

THE OBJECTIVES, TARGETS AND METHODS
OF THE COMMUNIST STRATEGY AND POLITICAL OFFENSIVE

'Perestroika' is the second round of the October World Socialist Revolution. The principal objectives of the Soviet strategy and political offensive are still world socialist victory and the creation of a World Government. From the outset of *'perestroika'* the main targets of the offensive have been the United States, NATO and Western Europe. At the time, West Germany was regarded as politically the weakest and most vulnerable NATO country.

The most important methods being applied in pursuit of the Soviet strategy of convergence between the Communist and Western systems are:

(a) Economic 'reform' of the state-controlled economy into a planned socialist market economy from which the growth of large-scale native capitalism is excluded and in which certain key industrial and strategic sectors remain under state control:

(b) Party-controlled 'democratisation' including a 'multi-Party system':

(c) Secret policy coordination between the Party and the 'independent' governments, 'nationalist' parties and 'nationalist fronts' in the Soviet Republics.

THE RESOURCES FOR THE SOVIET POLITICAL OFFENSIVE

The resources available to and developed by the Soviet strategists during the thirty years of preparation for *'perestroika'* constitute a veritable army of political activists equipped with a formidable arsenal of political weapons. The core of this army is the Communist Party itself, the Union of Young Communists (Komsomol), the Party's mass organisations, trade unions, the unions of creative workers, the vigilantes (*druzhiny*), the KGB's secret agents in the USSR and its agents of influence in the West and, most important of all, the new 'democratic', 'non-Communist' parties, the 'independent', 'nationalist' governments, fronts and other groups in the Party-controlled 'multi-Party system'.

THE ENHANCED ROLE OF THE PARTY AS THE GUIDING FORCE BEHIND THE STRATEGY

The *'perestroika'* strategy demands a widening of the scope of the Party's political activity and an increase in its effectiveness. The Party has introduced and is practising a greater degree of inner-Party democracy, which is vital to the successful conduct of the strategy. Official and unofficial Soviet statements have referred to resignations from the Party, to an overall loss in its membership and even to the possibility of its long-term disintegration. *The New York Times* of 4 November 1990, quoting the Central Committee paper *'Glasnost'*, gives a decline in membership of from over 19 million to 17.7 million. A more reliable figure can be derived from the representation at the Party's 1990 Congress. This was attended by 4,700 delegates each representing 5,000 Party members – indicating a total membership of 23.5 million, a figure consistent with the increase in the strength of the Central Committee from over 300 to 412 members[46]. The Party remains the best organised force in the USSR. Together with the Presidency and the Government, it guides and controls the process of political and economic reform, the introduction of a 'multi-Party system', the secret policy coordination with the 'independent' governments and 'nationalist' forces in the Republics and the political offensive against the West.

Like the Party, the Komsomol has increased its strength and widened its rôle in the support of the strategy. Its membership probably exceeds 40 million. The Party and Komsomol have close ties with the trade unions, the unions of creative workers and the 6 million vigilantes who assist the Ministry of the Interior and the militia in the policing of the population of the larger Soviet cities. Their existence and their rôle have been important factors rendering possible the introduction and control of Soviet 'democratisation'.

THE 'MULTI-PARTY SYSTEM' IS A FABRICATED INSTRUMENT OF THE KGB

The basic weapon in the Soviet political armoury is the KGB with its 5 or 6 million secret agents inside the USSR. Together, the Party and the KGB have fabricated controlled political opposition in the main cities of the USSR and in the national Republics. Together they have chosen and trained the organisers, leaders and activists of the new 'democratic', 'non-Communist', 'nationalist' and 'independent' organisations which are mushrooming under the Soviet 'multi-Party system'. Even non-democratic groups like the anti-Semitic 'Pamyat' movement are creatures of the régime. Gorbachëv is not the creator of a true multi-Party system: he is not a Soviet Stolypin intent on saving Russia through capitalism.

He is a Leninist, chosen and trained by the Soviet strategists to engineer the defeat of the United States and the West generally through the use of false, controlled democracy and a specious capitalism. The young Communists and KGB secret agents who form the core of the 'multi-Party system' are not genuine, ardent democrats bent on overturning the principles of the Bolshevik Revolution. They are still dedicated, disciplined revolutionaries and committed enemies of Western democracy who, on the instructions of the Party, are acting as 'democrats', 'non-Communists' and 'nationalists' in order to carry out the final assault on the capitalist West in accordance with the non-violent pattern of the Second October Revolution.

Scratch these new, instant Soviet 'democrats', 'anti-Communists' and 'nationalists' who have sprouted out of nowhere, and underneath will be found secret Party members or KGB agents. The West will pay dearly for its failure to understand that 'perestroika' is not a denial of Leninism but a radical, creative and effective application of the tactic described by Lenin in 'Left-wing Communism – an Infantile Disorder'. In this document, Lenin wrote that true revolutionaries should not be afraid to discard revolutionary phraseology and adopt right-wing tactics to carry out a revolutionary policy.

After the Second World War the victorious allies correctly applied a denazification programme to eliminate former Nazis and their influence from the institutions and political life of the new Germany. **No equivalent decommunisation programme**

46 'The New York Times', 15 July 1990.

has been applied in the USSR or Eastern Europe. The Soviet Party, the KGB and the armed forces with their political commissars remain intact[47].

Yet the West is eager to proclaim and believe in the death of Communism and the evaporation of Communist influence virtually overnight. This over-hasty optimism is destined to end in disillusionment.

THE SOVIET MEDIA AS A STRATEGIC WEAPON FOR THE POLITICAL OFFENSIVE
The Party-controlled Soviet media (television, newspapers, magazines, TASS [subsequently ITAR-TASS] and individual spokesmen and commentators) constitute an important and integral part of the weaponry for the Soviet strategy of internal 'democratisation' and external political offensive. The media have been developed from the propagandistic instrument of the past into a principal channel for Soviet strategic disinformation and the exercise of political influence on the West. In secret coordination with Soviet agents of influence in the West, they seek to serve the interests of Soviet strategy through the Western media, political parties, parliaments and governments with a view to establishing the Soviet Union as a major political power in a new united Europe and to achieving a 'restructuring' of the American military, political and economic system through 'convergence'.

THE SUCCESS OF THE SOVIET POLITICAL OFFENSIVE
AGAINST THE UNITED STATES AND NATO
The Soviet strategists and Gorbachëv in particular have displayed remarkable skill in exploiting the 'democratic' changes in the USSR and Eastern Europe to enlist the support of their political enemies – staunch conservatives like Reagan, Thatcher, Kohl and the Bush Administration – for the successful execution of their strategy. Western conservatives, centrists, liberals and socialists have all been competing with one another in making concessions to 'help' *'perestroika'*.

Unaware of the strategy Gorbachëv is implementing, they have unwittingly become his most ardent helpers. In consequence, the West is making far too much haste in giving way to the Soviets. Given continuing development of the Soviet nuclear arsenal, the military disarmament of the United States, the denuclearisation of Western Europe and the weakening of its deterrent are moving ahead too fast. NATO is losing its meaning and its substance.

The global rôle of the United States is being eroded as the partnership with Gorbachëv develops. Germany and Japan are going their own way in offering massive economic aid to and cooperation with the USSR and China. Dr Kissinger was right when he said: 'While the West is celebrating, its underlying cohesion is hollowed out'. Stronger language should be used to describe the situation than the remark of Dr Kissinger[48]. For the American-European alliance is in a critical state of

47 *Editor's Note:* 'Abolition' of political commissars in the armed forces was announced in the first quarter of 1994. *Author's Note:* It is likely that the political commissars have been absorbed into military counter-intelligence which would provide them with the right cover to collect information on morale etc. Their functions would include political briefings of troops, giving guidance to officers who make public statements or talk to journalists and briefing those who take trips abroad, participate in military visits and exchanges, or negotiate with foreign powers.
48 *'The Washington Post'*, 25 July 1990.

confusion and disarray. The Bush Administration committed a grievous error in deciding to encourage contacts with the emerging 'democratic' and 'non-Communist' opposition in the USSR in the persons of Yeltsin, President of the Russian Republic, Popov, the Mayor of Moscow, and others. This policy is dangerous in that it encourages genuine American democrats, Republicans and those of other political persuasions, oblivious of Soviet strategy, to walk into a well-laid Soviet trap.

It is tantamount to an invitation to the Soviets to invade the United States with their political army which, under cover of 'democracy' and 'nationalism', is intent on spreading its radical ideas on political reform of the American system, the redistribution of wealth and changes in US political and military arrangements.

THE SOVIET POLITICAL BREAKTHROUGH IN GERMANY:
THE DEVELOPMENT OF SOVIET-GERMAN PARTNERSHIP

Since West Germany was considered by the Soviets as politically the most vulnerable country in Western Europe, the main weight of the Soviet assault was directed against that country. To ensure success, the Soviets made use of skilled diplomacy, agents of influence, pressure and significant concessions to the Germans on reunification. The result was a breakthrough for the Soviets[49].

The Germans responded with enthusiasm, providing massive financial, economic and technological aid to the Soviets – developing into their principal partners in the execution of their economic strategy. Ironically, Germany is moving towards partnership with the USSR under a conservative chancellor, Kohl. The problem with Kohl is not that he is using the situation to gain his re-election but that he is recklessly disregarding the lessons of the history of Germany's past dealings with the Soviets. He overlooks the fact that it was the German General Staff who financed Lenin and brought him to the Finland Station.

No sooner had Lenin succeeded with his October Revolution than he attempted to re-export it to Germany. Although Kohl dismisses the idea, the comparison between Lenin's negotiation and exploitation of the 1922 Treaty of Rapallo with the Germans and the present Soviet strategy with regard to the economic collaboration offered by Kohl and his Foreign Minister, Genscher, is close and compelling.

What Kohl fails to realise is that the Soviet strategists aim to use Germany's economic and technological might to convert the USSR into the dominant power in a united Europe. Chancellor Kohl has his eyes on the next election. But Gorbachëv and the strategists are thinking further ahead. It was no accident that Gorbachëv referred to reunited Germany's right not only to participate in NATO but *to join whatever alliance Germany preferred*. What he had in mind was the possibility that a future Germany under a Social Democratic Government would switch to political alliance with the USSR. **Domination of a united Europe by a Soviet-German political and economic partnership would be a significant achievement for the second round of the October World Socialist Revolution.**

49 *Editor's Note:* On 9 November 1990, President Gorbachëv and Chancellor Helmut Kohl signed a Treaty on Good-Neighbourliness, Partnership and Co-operation and a Treaty on Co-operation in Economy, Industry, Science and Technology, together with side agreements. The treaties formed key elements of the bilateral treaty network launched by Gorbachëv and expanded under Yeltsin.

AN ASSESSMENT IN STRATEGIC TERMS OF THE IRAQI INVASION
OF KUWAIT AND SOVIET AND CHINESE CONDEMNATION OF IT

The longstanding close political and military relationship between the USSR and Iraq, the continuing presence in Iraq of Soviet military advisers and the arrival in Baghdad of General Makashov in July to act as Saddam Hussein's military 'adviser', the visit of the Iraqi Foreign Minister Tariq Aziz to Moscow on the eve of President Bush's meeting with Gorbachëv in Helsinki, and Primakov's visit to Iraq, all point to the conclusion that the Iraqi occupation of Kuwait was undertaken with the connivance of the Soviets or even at their suggestion. Western enthusiasm for the Soviet and Chinese condemnation of the Iraqi action is thus naïve and misplaced. It demonstrates a superficial understanding of Soviet and Chinese dialectical intentions, which can only be determined through a proper understanding of their strategy.

Soviet condemnation of Iraq was intended to give and has given a new impetus to apparent Soviet-American collaboration in the international arena. If a solution to the crisis is to be sought through non-violent means, it might be through an international conference on the Middle East. At such a conference, Soviet and Iraqi interests would coincide and an attempt would be made to trade-off an Iraqi withdrawal from Kuwait against an Israeli withdrawal from the Occupied Territories[50].

Better still from the point of view of Soviet strategy would be the involvement of the United States in a protracted war in the Middle East while the Soviets continue to pursue their political offensive against the United States and Western Europe. Such a war would intensify the oil crisis and drive the American economy into depression. The Soviets would then be in a strong position to exploit both the depression and the cleavage in American opinion which prolonged warfare would entail, to promote their strategy of 'convergence'. Whether a solution of the crisis is sought through violent or non-violent means, its prolongation serves to distract American attention from the Soviet political offensive.

The nature of Soviet and Chinese coordinated strategic intentions dictates the utmost caution on the part of the United States. The United States and its allies should seek to solve the conflict with Iraq by diplomacy and by all other means short of actual war, which could suit the interests of Soviet long-range strategy.

THE THREAT OF FUTURE DENIABLE SOVIET MILITARY OR NUCLEAR ACTION

Soviet success in persuading Western leaders of the sincerity of the Soviet desire for cooperation with the West has been so great that the idea that the Iraqis acted jointly with the Soviets over Kuwait has been almost universally rejected.

Yet the deliberate and sudden provocation of a crisis to gain specific objectives, including the creation of new openings for specious collaboration with the adversary, is a classic method of deceptive, activist, Leninist diplomacy.

The Gulf crisis is analogous to the Cuban crisis provoked by the Soviet strategists under Khrushchev acting jointly with Fidel Castro. In the Cuban case, the key element was the installation of Soviet missiles on the island. In the Gulf case, it is the

---

50 *Editor's Note:* At the time of writing, the Author could not have been sure, of course, whether the crisis over Kuwait would end in war or not. But what he *was* able to deduce by applying his method of analysis based upon his first-hand knowledge of Communist dialectical strategic practice, was that the Soviets would extract a Middle East conference from the crisis, which they would then proceed to manipulate in furtherance of the strategy.

continuing presence of Soviet advisers in Iraq even *after* Moscow's public condemnation of the Iraqi action. An outcome of the Gulf crisis favourable to Soviet interests would encourage them to resort to similar provocations in the future. For example, a terrorist nuclear attack on a US military installation which was unattributable to the Soviet Government could be used to strengthen the anti-nuclear forces in the United States and to provoke heated demands for still closer Soviet-American collaboration and eventual World Government.

Western belief in the genuine independence of the Soviet national Republics opens the way for future *local military actions by these Republics* – responsibility for which would be denied by the Soviet Federal Government and/or Russia. Such denials would be accepted by the West, which would again show itself susceptible to Soviet requests for help in establishing a New World Order – a phrase already being used by President Bush. Western belief in the existence of serious disaffection among 'ultra-conservatives' in the Soviet armed forces could be exploited by the Soviet strategists to similar effect.

Only if the United States and allied governments understand Soviet strategy and its use of deception and provocation, only if they accept its existence and publicly expose it, can an effective counter-strategy be adopted and an end be put to further provocations of this type. The Cold War may be 'over' for the West. **For the Soviets it has entered a new, active and promising phase.**

THE BASIC DIFFERENCES BETWEEN THE SOVIET AND
WESTERN CONCEPTS OF DEMOCRACY AND THE MARKET ECONOMY

The West fails to appreciate the **irreconcilable differences of principle** between the Western and Soviet versions of democracy and the market economy. In the West, elections actually decide which Party achieves political power. In the USSR *the Communist Party continues to decide the outcome*. It maintains its monopoly of political power through controlled 'reformers' and 'conservatives', and through a controlled 'multi-Party system'.

In the West, genuine political opposition exists. Under the Soviet system of 'democracy' there is no genuine, organised, political opposition and no real possibility of such opposition emerging. True non-Communists among the Soviet people are no doubt saying in private: 'They pretend that they are giving us democracy: we pretend that we are free'. Any attempt to form genuine, uncontrolled, political opposition is crushed as it was by Deng and the Chinese army in Tienanmen Square, by Iliescu and his miners in Romania or by the use of tanks as threatened by Mladenov in Bulgaria. Similar attempts in Poland, Czechoslovakia or the Soviet Union will no doubt be dealt with in comparable fashion by the present 'reformers' again revealing an ugly Leninist and Stalinist face. Soviet 'democracy' will remain dictatorial in its attitude towards genuine political opponents. Those who dare to raise their heads will be branded 'reactionaries', 'counter-revolutionaries', 'fascists' and 'Western hirelings'. Soviet 'democracy' will remain a façade behind which the Communist Party, with its monopoly of power, will pull the strings and manipulate its puppets.

The West has little understanding of the radical difference between a truly capitalist Western economy and a Soviet quasi-market economy. In the West, capitalist classes from tycoons down to small shopkeepers own and run their businesses. The USSR physically eliminated its capitalist classes. The Party and state will continue to own and run key industries. Only calculated elements of the market will be introduced into what will still be basically a planned economy. The West, and the international financial institutions, are being naive in expecting otherwise.

One Soviet objective is to carry out a technological revolution in order to make the socialist economy more efficient with the help of Western capital, expertise and technology. The Communists like Western capital, but hate capitalists. The Soviet Communist Party administered a bloody lesson to the Soviet and East European peoples concerning its attitude to capitalists by exterminating three generations of them. During the period of 'War Communism' after the Revolution, the capitalists of old Russia were eliminated. After Lenin's New Economic Policy, the new generation of home-grown capitalists was eliminated. Finally, after the Second World War, the capitalists of Eastern Europe, China and the Baltic States were eliminated. **The Soviet people have got the message that the Party which has systematically eliminated capitalists as a matter of principle is not about to restore them permanently**.

The Soviets and East Europeans may make their workers shareholders in the factories where they work. What the West fails to appreciate is that the motive for doing so and for introducing controlled 'democracy' is to stimulate changes in the Western system and to facilitate the convergence of the two systems with a view to the eventual absorption of the Western democracies within a World Government.

WHY THE WEST IGNORES THE ESSENCE AND DANGERS OF SOVIET 'DEMOCRATISATION'
Western acceptance of the changes in the USSR and Eastern Europe as a trend towards genuine democracy which serves Western interests and therefore merits Western support shows how little the West comprehends the essence of the changes and the dangers they entail. In part this non-comprehension arises from confusion over terminology. What the West calls 'democratisation', Soviet strategists call the transformation of the 'dictatorship of the proletariat' into the 'state of the whole people'.

For the Soviet strategists, this is a new, politically more broadly-based organisation of society which nevertheless continues to fulfill the function of proletarian dictatorship. The Communist Party can permit the existence of other political parties because there are no capitalist classes to form a basis for them and because it can control them anyway. Faced with an abundance of 'information' on the changes in the East, Western experts fail to discern their meaning or their consequences. They are drowning in a sea of raw facts plus Soviet disinformation. Lacking any means of distinguishing facts from fiction, they are incapable of producing a valid and objective synthesis. The capacity to analyse Communist developments effectively, which existed up to the early 1960s, has been lost. Misunderstood and misinterpreted, the wealth of information available is of no greater value than the volumes of an old encyclopaedia. **The key to the correct interpretation of the facts, which brings them to life and makes them useful, is informed study of the Soviet long-range strategy which has been in operation since the late 1950s. This study reveals what Lenin called the 'algebra' of modern Soviet politics. Without the key, Western studies are confined to conventional, pedestrian arithmetic.**

EVIDENCE OF THE STRATEGY

There is solid, factual evidence of the adoption and practical application of the strategy since the late 1950s. Among the principal items of evidence are the following:

1. The conferences of the ruling parties of the Communist Bloc including the Chinese held in Moscow in November 1957 and November-December 1960 which discussed, formulated and adopted the long-range strategy.

2. The December 1960 manifesto of the 'Eighty-One Party Congress' and Khrushchev's speech of 6 January 1961 which confirmed the adoption of the strategy and outlined its main objectives – consolidation of the socialist states and world Communist victory.

3. Official records indicating that the strategy was based upon the broad application of the experience of Lenin's New Economic Policy in the 1920s.

4. The decisions of the 21st Soviet Party Congress in Moscow in January-February 1959 which laid down the political rôle of the KGB for the period ahead.

5. Shelepin's report on the new political rôle of the KGB in the execution of Party strategy delivered at the KGB conference in Moscow in May 1959.

6. Shelepin's reorganisation of the KGB with a view to developing its intelligence and security resources into a political arsenal and in particular to creating a secretly controlled political opposition along the lines of the GPU's 'Trust' operation in the 1920s, and to prepare for controlled 'liberalisation' in the USSR and other socialist countries.

7. The creation by Shelepin of a strategic disinformation service and the launching of a series of Bloc disinformation operations in support of the strategy.

8. The Party programme adopted by the 22nd Soviet Party Congress in Moscow in November 1961 calling for the transformation of the 'state of dictatorship of the proletariat' into the 'state of the whole people'.

9. Official records of exchanges between the Soviet and East European parties in the 1960s on the experience of the New Economic Policy.

10. Numerous indications from official sources that the Soviet, Hungarian and other Communist Parties have experimented with the introduction and testing of elements of a market economy leading up to the present economic reforms.

11. The international conference of the Communist Parties held in 1969 which discussed progress in the execution of the strategy and outlined future steps.

12. Solid evidence of the continuing co-ordination between the Communist Parties of the Bloc at all levels during the 1960s, 1970s and 1980s. Of particular significance were the annual summit meetings held in the Crimea in the 1970s. According to the 'Annual Supplement of the Great Soviet Encyclopedia' for 1975, page 502, the Crimean meetings had become a forum at which the international situation was assessed, common tasks were discussed and **the strategy of joint action was developed**.

13. Numerous indications that the Soviet Communist Party was preparing for a broadening of 'socialist democracy'.

To enlarge on this last point, a study of back issues of the Soviet magazine 'State and Law' published during the 1960s, 1970s and 1980s reveals a serious and continuing discussion of issues relevant to theoretical preparation for the development of 'socialist democracy' in the USSR and, in particular, to increasing the powers of the Soviet parliament and its members, strengthening the influence of the mass organisations, widening the responsibilities of the national Republics and adopting human rights legislation. Similarly, a review of back issues of the periodical '*Problems of Peace and Socialism*' – the theoretical and informative journal of the Communist Parties – over the same period reveals a similar discussion concerning the development of 'socialist democracy', a revised political organisation of the socialist states and how it might affect the strategy and tactics of Communist Parties, particularly in Europe.

Special attention should be paid to an article published in this journal in July 1974. Its Authors were **Zawadski**, director of the Scientific Institute of State and Law at Warsaw University; **Guliyev**, head of section at the Soviet Institute of State and Law; and officials of the Greek and Argentine Communist Parties. The article was based on a discussion which took place at Warsaw University.

The paper considered the question of the political power of the working class in the development of democracy in the mature socialist countries and how this relates to the strategy of the Communist Parties [Russian edition, pages 44-45]. The article reminded the reader that, according to Lenin, the essence of the dictatorship of the proletariat is the leading rôle of the Communist Party, not the participation of other political parties in the government [page 47]. The article referred to the transition from the 'dictatorship of the proletariat' to the 'state of the whole people' and explained that the 'state of the whole people' continues, in reality, to uphold the cause of proletarian dictatorship under mature socialism, joining other socialist states to wage the class struggle against imperialism in the international arena [page 51]. **The 'state of the whole people' does not need to break the resistance of the exploiting capitalist classes because by now they have been eliminated. However, it remains dictatorial and repressive in its attitude towards capitalists abroad.** The article further emphasised that, under the 'state of the whole people', the leading rôle of the Communist Party is retained and enhanced [page 51]. It explained that new elements have been introduced into Communist strategy against the developed capitalist countries, in order to take into account the changes which the technological revolution has brought about in the social structure of these countries.

The strategy defines the present class enemy as the monopolies which are in opposition to the majority of society. The strategy sees a broad base for the formation of a new, anti-monopoly movement which will embrace the middle class. The strategy defines its main objectives as breaking up the power of the monopolies, carrying out political, economic and social changes and creating an 'anti-monopolistic democracy' or a 'renewed, advanced democracy' [page 49].

This unusually frank article was published at a time when Solidarity was still an illegal, 'underground' organisation in Poland and 'dissidents' in the USSR and Eastern Europe were allegedly being repressed. It constitutes significant evidence of the planned character of the new 'democratic' structure or, more correctly, the 'state of the whole people'. It illuminates the rôle of the new structure as a broader and seemingly less menacing form of proletarian dictatorship which nevertheless retains its aggressive strategic designs against the West.

THE STRANGLEHOLD OF SOVIET STRATEGIC DISINFORMATION

Factual evidence of the adoption and execution of the long-range Soviet strategy has been ignored, discarded or dismissed by the West because of the success of Soviet disinformation. In the past, disinformation had a dual thrust: *first*, to persuade the West that there was no long-range Bloc strategy and no strategic coordination between the ruling Communist Parties, and that the Communist Bloc had disintegrated into individual Communist countries pursuing their own national or superpower interests; and *secondly*, to convince the West that secretly controlled movements in the USSR and Eastern Europe represented the emergence of genuine, embryonic, political opposition which would bring about genuine democratisation of the Stalinist régimes.

In the present advanced phase of the *'perestroika'* strategy, the mass of Soviet strategic political disinformation has been increasing by geometrical progression. Its main thrust now is to convince the West that true democratisation has arrived, that the Communist régimes have abandoned their Communist ideology and their hostility to the capitalist West, and that they are becoming conventional national states like other Western countries.

The growth of disinformation is logical given that it is a paramount factor in securing the success of the Communist political offensive. The West and its intelligence services have never understood strategic political disinformation because they have never fathomed Soviet political strategy. They have recognised only Soviet 'active measures' – that is, *tactical* disinformation – which they have understood only in terms of their own covert operations.

Failure to comprehend the *strategic* variety of disinformation has led to the acceptance of Soviet 'democratisation' as a reality of great political significance – whereas it is in fact an instrument of deception designed to 're-shoe' the West.

It is imperative to realise that this disinformation is conveyed through the speeches and statements of Soviet leaders like Gorbachëv, strategists like Yakovlev, the Foreign Minister, Shevardnadze, official spokesmen like Gennadiy Gerasimov and Shishlin and through the words and actions of the alleged political opposition, the 'liberal' and 'conservative' leaders of the new, so-called political parties, the governments of the 'independent' national Republics, 'nationalists', 'anti-Semites' and individuals such as 'former' KGB officers.

The Soviet media portray Party-controlled strikes, demonstrations and disturbances in different parts of the USSR as real, domestic and nationalist outbreaks pointing to the disintegration and perhaps the collapse of the Soviet Empire. Orchestrated disputes between phoney reformers and phoney conservatives are reported as real struggles within the Party. The Soviet media and Party-controlled activists presented the 1990 Party Congress in Moscow to the West as a real showdown between 'reformers' and 'conservatives'. KGB and Party provocateurs in *'Pamyat'* have conveyed a misleading impression of the growth of nationalistic anti-Semitism and chaos in the USSR.

In their ignorance of Soviet Leninist strategy and strategic disinformation, the Western media have uncritically accepted all these Party-fabricated simulations and passed them on to the Western public as realities. This naïve, uncritical attitude was illustrated by the way in which Western reporters covered the Party Congress almost as if it was a US Presidential Convention. The problem is aggravated by the use of Soviet consultants. CBS, for example, hired a Soviet consultant to help with its coverage of the Party Congress.

The Soviet disinformation campaign has paid off handsomely. The Soviet strategists have gained significant concessions from the West.

In the 1960s, when the CIA was strong and its counter-intelligence staff had begun to recognise Soviet disinformation for what it was, effective action was taken to educate appropriate people. A senior member of the Kennedy Administration visited Moscow at the invitation of Khrushchev's son-in-law. On his return to Washington, he was debriefed about the Soviet officials he had met in Moscow. Among them he listed Vasiliy Sitnikov, whom he described as a senior member of the Party.

He was startled to be informed that Sitnikov was a former KGB Rezident in West Germany who, at the time of his meeting with the American, was a leading member of the KGB's disinformation service with responsibility for NATO.

The question of educating US and allied officials, politicians, diplomats, the media and the public about Soviet disinformation, its new channels and techniques is now acutely urgent. In itself the problem is not insoluble. **Unfortunately, the CIA and allied intelligence and security services which should initiate this overdue process cannot do so because they do not recognise the problem and have themselves been taken in by the disinformation.**

It is imperative that this situation be reversed. Many proposals are being aired for the reorganisation of the American intelligence and counter-espionage services in the light of the changes in the USSR and Eastern Europe, without any awareness that these changes are being dangerously misinterpreted. The main purpose of any reorganisation should be to address this problem.

THE PROBABLE OUTCOME

Since the West does not comprehend the strategic design behind Soviet 'democratisation' and economic reform, it cannot foresee the probable impact of these changes on the West. The question to be addressed is not whether the changes are reversible or irreversible but what their meaning is for the West in the long run. Because of the basic differences between the Western and Soviet-style concepts of democracy and the market economy, Western attempts to educate Soviet and East European 'instant democrats' in true democracy and market economies are naïve and short-sighted.

Optimistic expectations of long-term Western dividends from Western support for 'perestroika' are doomed to disappointment. Present Soviet-Western cooperation is only temporary: the East-West alliance is only tactical. Soviet-style democracy is 'cuckoo-egg democracy'. *When the chick hatches, it will display its true antagonistic nature and seek to dominate the nest.* **Blind to Soviet strategy, the United States will find itself increasingly marginalised in world affairs. To paraphrase an expression used by Marx, the United States will be left stranded in isolation to contemplate its own destruction and demise.**

The Soviet pattern of violent revolution and terror came to be understood and effectively resisted by the West. Unless the West can bring itself to understand the new, temporarily non-violent pattern, it is destined to suffer defeat. Had an improvised form of *'perestroika'* been hastily introduced in the Soviet Union, it would have led to an anti-Communist and nationalist explosion and, conceivably, to true democracy and freedom. But the current *'perestroika'* offensive has been launched by the Soviet strategists after *thirty years of preparation and experiment*: the risks have been calculated, and uncontrolled eruptions have been, and will continue to be, forestalled and suppressed.

Western support for the Communist leaders who are imposing *'perestroika'* from above has extinguished any remaining possibility of it evolving spontaneously towards genuine democracy. When with Western help the Soviet strategists have overcome their deliberately exaggerated economic difficulties and can provide their population with an abundant supply of consumer goods, they will be able to demonstrate to the world the superiority of the Soviet system. They will have successfully rebuilt, restructured and renewed their society.

At that point, they will turn on the 'hated capitalist' and a new holocaust will result. The new holocaust will be based on class, not race. Its principal victims will be the Western political, military, religious and managerial élites. ■

PART SIX

THE FAKE
'AUGUST COUP'
AND ITS CALCULATED
FAILURE

A deliberately engineered
'Break with the Past'

Memorandum to the CIA: APRIL 1991

For the attention of: The Director of Central Intelligence

A TOUCH OF REALISM IN ASSESSING THE STRUGGLE BETWEEN GORBACHEV'S SUPPORTERS, YELTSIN'S SUPPORTERS AND NATIONALISTS IN THE SOVIET REPUBLICS

1. The 'fighting' between Gorbachëv's supporters, Yeltsin's supporters and the nationalist 'independent' Republics' supporters, is a deliberate attempt by the Soviets to create and develop three parallel political structures of power in the USSR. The *first* is the Communist 'democratic' structure; the *second* is the anti-democratic structure; and the *third* is the nationalist 'independent' Republic structure, both Communist and 'anti'-Communist. *All three structures*, however, are controlled, guided and coordinated by the Communist Party and by the Communists in the Republics.

Thus, all three structures have a good chance of succeeding. When they have succeeded, they will not give the credit to the West but will instead congratulate themselves on the formation of their new system which they will then try to introduce to the West as a model which the West should emulate.

2. Their new complex three-tier system will become politically stronger and more truly 'democratic' than the American system. Thus, it could become the foundation for the establishment of a World Government.

3. One can then expect that all the Soviets including the 'democratic' Communists led by Gorbachëv or by another Leninist, the 'democratic' anti-Communists led by Yeltsin and the 'nationalists' of both the Communist and anti-Communist variety, may try to influence confused and naïve American politicians, Members of Congress and the American public to accept the following lines of convergence:

(a) That Soviet society has been renewed and has 'solved' its political and economic problems (without any indication of how this has occurred being evident).

(b) That the Soviet system has evolved into one which should serve as a model for the West, given such attractions as its free education and medical services.

4. The new strategy is designed in part to influence American society to demand similar changes in the American system. It will be argued that the American system is decadent, deeply in debt, ridden with crime, crippled by drugs and heavily burdened with the high cost of education and the higher cost of medical care.

The impact of this old-style propaganda on the American public may well be effective because of the alleged changes in the Soviet system described above. ■

Memorandum to the CIA: **19 AUGUST 1991**

Written as news of the 'hardliners'' coup was announced
and **delivered to the CIA on 20 August 1991.**

BEHIND THE SOVIET COUP –
SOVIET STRATEGY AND ITS DEVELOPMENT:
THE MAIN OBJECTIVES OF THE COUP

Who called the shots in the USSR before the 'coup' and who introduced the 'reforms'? Gorbachëv and his 'liberals'?

NO, the Party and its strategists.

Who is calling the shots now and who proposed the coup to replace Gorbachëv? The 'hardliners', the Minister of Defence and the Chief of the KGB?

NO, the Party and its strategists.

The 'coup' was proposed in accordance with the requirements of the Soviet strategy of convergence leading to eventual World Government. This strategy and its moves, like the present Soviet 'coup', can only be understood in the light of the theories of one of the principal Soviet agents of influence, namely Sakharov, and his timetable for convergence. According to Sakharov, during *the first phase* the Leninist realists (i.e. Gorbachëv and other 'liberals') will expand and strengthen 'democracy' and economic reform in the USSR and other socialist countries.

As we know, this has already happened.

According to Sakharov, **in** *the second phase* **the pressure exerted by the Soviet example and by the internal progressive forces would lead to the victory of the Leftist Reformist Wing (the Soviet term for American liberals) which would begin to implement a programme of collaboration and convergence with the USSR on a worldwide scale, entailing changes in the structure of ownership.** According to Sakharov, this phase would include an expanded rôle for the intelligentsia and an attack on the forces of racism and militarism.

We had reached this phase before the war with Iraq. In the assessment of the Soviet strategists, the US victory over Iraq *adversely* affected the political balance in the United States. In their view, the victory weakened and demoralised the liberals (or Leftist Reformists) and strengthened the centrist and conservative forces and the US military. This disturbed Soviet plans to carry out their strategy of convergence.

They saw that their main political allies in achieving convergence with the United States had been weakened. Accordingly they engineered this strategic 'coup' to reverse and improve the political fortunes of their American allies. Seen in strategic terms, the main purpose of Gorbachëv's 'dismissal' is further to confuse American opinion and to alter the political landscape in the United States so as to accelerate the progress of the Soviet strategy and to put it back on the rails.

This strategy is a deliberate and coordinated walk towards ultimate victory by advancing first the left leg of action by 'liberals', then the right leg of action by 'hardliners' and then once more the left leg of action by 'liberals'. The 'dismissal' of Gorbachëv is temporary. In earlier Memoranda I predicted a calculated 'resignation' by Gorbachëv and his eventual return to power.

The 'coup' confirms this prediction. According to my analysis, the 'coup' is aimed at intensifying American anxieties over the fate of Gorbachëv and the other 'liberals' and 'reformists' in the USSR like Shevardnadze. When these concerns reach their peak, the Soviet strategists' next move can be expected. They will return Gorbachëv and other 'liberals' to power through a campaign of strikes and demonstrations organised by the Party.

As the Soviet strategists see it, Gorbachëv's return and the strengthening of the 'reformists' in the USSR will also strengthen the American liberals, revive their fortunes and help them win future elections – leading eventually to the convergence of the United States and the USSR. In short, Gorbachëv's return will be a repetition of the device of the suppression of Solidarity in Poland, followed by its victory.

The *main* purpose of the 'coup' is to reverse an unfavourable situation for potential Soviet allies in the United States and to create favourable conditions for the implementation of the convergence strategy. The *second* objective is to secure the non-violent creation of the new Soviet Federation of Republics. The *third* objective is to provide any potential adventurers there may be in the Soviet military with a lesson and thereby to eliminate any possibility of a genuine coup in the future. ■

Memorandum to the CIA: 20 AUGUST 1991

Delivered to the CIA on 21 August 1991

A FURTHER ANALYSIS OF THE OBJECTIVES OF THE SOVIET 'COUP'

The point has already been made that Gorbachëv will be returned to power at the moment when it best serves the Soviet strategy of convergence. Depending on the circumstances prevailing at the appropriate time, he could be returned to power through an election, after a period of other activities[51].

His alleged removal from power and house arrest are deliberate devices to build up his popularity before such an election. Meanwhile one can expect that the Soviet strategists intend to replace him or to add to his team another ace card, the 'anti-Communist' (but, like Gorbachëv, protégé of Andropov) Boris Yeltsin, leader of the Russian Republic. As the Soviet strategists see it, Gorbachëv has exhausted the influence he exerted on their behalf in the West. He was unable to extract more economic aid at the London Summit Meeting and his advice concerning a diplomatic solution to the conflict with Iraq was ignored by President Bush. It is the strategists' belief that Boris Yeltsin will give greater credibility in the West to Soviet economic and political 'reform'. He will be in a better position to exploit his influence to extract additional economic aid from the West and, in particular, to obtain from the West a commitment to a new Marshall Plan for Russia.

A Marshall Plan for Russia is one of the primary interim objectives of the Soviet strategists and one that Gorbachëv failed to achieve. The strategists expect that Yeltsin will be able to exert greater influence in diplomatic, economic and political relationships and will receive more cooperation in the international arena particularly in the Middle East and at the United Nations. One can expect that the Soviet strategists will come forward with fresh initiatives combined with deliberate provocations and crises in order to enhance the rôle of the United Nations.

They will do this because **they regard the United Nations as a stepping stone to a future World Government**. The Soviet political game and the Soviets' trickery in 'manipulating' politicians like Gorbachëv and Yeltsin for Western public consumption demand more imagination and a better grasp of these machinations from the Bush Administration. For example, to proceed with the appointment of Mr Robert Strauss as the new Ambassador in Moscow is a great mistake because the appointment is being made at a time when the Soviet strategists are deliberately undermining the credit and prestige President Bush gained from his dealings with

51 *Editor's Note:* Gorbachëv has said on several occasions that 'the time is not yet ripe' for him to return to power, implying that his return to power is an option. Commenting on his 'future plans' in *'Svobodnaya Mysl'*, Number 13, September 1992, Gorbachëv remarked: 'At present, I have no plans for any kind of state position. For some reason we think that if you do not occupy a state position, you are in the *taiga*, in the desert, or somewhere else, I don't know, beyond the Arctic Circle. I have not left politics; as previously, I remain in the sphere of public and political activity'. Interviewed by Larry King on the *'Larry King Live'* TV show in the United States on 6 November 1993, Gorbachëv, asked what his 'plans for the future' were, said: 'I'm not hiding in the woodwork. I'm involved in a different political rôle... I have not abandoned links with the past'. On 7 December 1994, Gorbachëv reiterated that he was 'considering' the possibility of standing as a candidate in the presidential elections. When asked what he would change, he said: 'You will learn that when I am in his [Yeltsin's] shoes'. That the former International Department of the CPSU Central Committee has been relabelled the Gorbachëv Foundation indicates Gorbachëv's continuing importance as an implementer of the strategy.

Gorbachëv. They are undercutting the President in favour of their political allies – namely, the American liberals. Nowadays the situation is more serious than it was after the Second World War. **President Truman woke up to the nature of Stalin's mentality, his deeds and his intentions. The Bush Administration, by contrast, has no understanding of Soviet strategy and its ultimate, aggressive, strategic designs against the United States.**

Given this situation and the Soviet 'game plan', the President, instead of appointing a politician/businessman like Robert Strauss as American Ambassador in Moscow, should consider appointing someone like Richard Helms or General Vernon Walters – that is to say, a professional man and an intelligence expert who might see through the Soviet game plan and help the Administration as General Bedell Smith helped President Truman in 1947. ■

Memorandum to the CIA: 26 AUGUST 1991

THE AUTHOR'S ANALYSIS OF THE OBJECTIVES OF THE CALCULATED SOVIET 'COUP' AND OF ITS CALCULATED 'FAILURE'

According to my assessment, the Soviet 'coup' and its 'failure' constituted a grandiose display of deception – a provocation. The 'ineptitude' of the participants in the 'coup' and the 'failure' of it were skilfully planned and executed. The main argument in support of this assessment is that the Soviet military, the KGB, the Party and leading media figures apparently had neither the skill to launch a successful coup nor the guts to crush resistance to it. This is news indeed!

Facing a real crisis in Hungary in 1956, the same forces displayed exceptional skill, knowhow and determination in crushing a genuine revolt. Knowledge of the Soviet mentality and of Moscow's record of ruthless action has convinced this analyst that the Soviet military, the Party and the leaders of the media all have the skill, the will and the courage to crush genuine resistance and opposition. They did not display them on this occasion because the abortive 'coup' was carried out in accordance with Party instructions; and it was the Party and the Komsomol themselves which organised the alleged resistance to it.

The real participants both in the 'coup' and in the 'failure' were some 20,000 or more chosen Komsomol and Party members in Moscow with two or three tank divisions guided by their political commissars and a handful of dedicated Party officials and generals who sacrificed their prestige in the interests of the Party's strategy and under the guidance of its strategists. The calculated nature of the 'coup' and its timing show that it was staged by the Russian, President Yeltsin, to save the essence of the Union at the time of transition to a new form of federation.

The abortive 'coup' and the 'resistance' to it were carefully calculated displays intended primarily for the West. This explains why Western media contacts with Moscow were not curtailed. On the contrary, the big guns of the Soviet media like Vitaliy Korotich and representatives of the Arbatov Institute were on hand both in Moscow and in the United States to 'help' the Western media with their interpretation of developments in the USSR. The episode shows how well Soviet strategists like Arbatov and his experts on the American media have mastered the art of projecting such displays for consumption *by* the American media, and throughout the West.

The Soviet strategists sought to underline for the West the dramatic ineptitude of the 'coup' and the spectacular courage and resistance displayed by the new 'Russian democrats' and their leader Yeltsin in 'defending' the Soviet Parliament – their symbolic equivalent of 'The White House'. The main external objective of the display was to demonstrate to the West that Soviet democratisation is genuine, that it has the support of the people and that **it is working**. They want to convince the West that Western investment in the USSR will pay dividends.

They expect that the West will now respond with a new Marshall Plan which will bring Western technology flooding in to the Soviet Union, promoting joint ventures and stimulating a restructuring of the Soviet economy along the lines of the revival of the German and Japanese economies after the Second World War.

Internally, one objective is to influence the Soviet population towards acceptance of the new Party-controlled 'democracy' as a real power and to develop the strength and maturity of the new 'democratic' structure and the popularity of its leaders, especially Yeltsin. Another objective is to exploit this staged 'coup' in order to reorganise and 'reform' the Soviet bureaucracy, the military, the intelligence and counter-intelligence organisations and the diplomatic service, and to give them a new 'democratic' image.

The Soviet strategists realise that only with such a new image, implying a 'Break with the Past' and severance from Communism, can these organisations be converted into effective weapons for convergence with their counterparts in the United States. A further internal objective is to emphasise the change in the system by means of the spectacular, televised but calculated removal of old Communist symbols like the monuments to Lenin and Dzerzhinskiy, and the red banners.

These changes do not represent a genuine and sincere repudiation of Soviet design and intentions to secure an eventual world victory. Although very spectacular, the changes are cosmetic. They demonstrate only that Arbatov and others know how to manipulate the American and other Western media through the use of powerful symbols such as the dismantling of the Berlin Wall, the toppling of Lenin and Dzerzhinskiy statues and Yeltsin's staged 'defence' of the Soviet 'White House'.

If the Soviets were truly moving towards genuine democracy, and were intent on a true 'Break with the Past', these symbolic changes would be accompanied by the introduction and implementation of a de-communisation programme, the irrevocable (not cosmetic) prohibition of the Communist Party and Komsomol organisations at all levels throughout the USSR, and the removal of 'former' Party and Komsomol members from all the main seats of power including the KGB, the Soviet army and its political commissar administration, the Ministries, especially those for the Interior and Foreign Affairs, and the trade unions.

Yeltsin has allegedly banned the Communist Party in Russia. But the question should be asked: 'Why did he forget to ban the Komsomol youth organisation?' [*Note:* According to '*The New York Times*' of 29 September 1991, the Komsomol voted to dissolve itself; its regulations were changed '**to allow subordinate youth leagues in the Soviet Republics to succeed it**' – Author's emphasis].

To carry conviction, the necessary purge of former Communists would have to be carried out at all levels, as was the intention with the de-nazification programme in Germany after the war. Without any such programme, present changes, however impressive, will remain cosmetic.

There are at present no means of distinguishing reliably between a genuine democrat and a former Communist in Russia. However one important criterion for judging the sincerity of the abrupt and virtually simultaneous conversion of former Communist leaders into true democrats would be **a frank official statement from them that the Soviet Party and Government adopted a long-range strategy in the years 1958 to 1960, that '*perestroika*' is the advanced phase of this strategy, and that it is to be abandoned forthwith in favour of normal, open, civilised relations. There has been no sign whatsoever of any such admission.**

Further criteria for judging the sincerity of the abrupt conversion of 'former' Communist leaders into believers in true democracy would need to include:

○ An official admission that the 'dissident movement' and its leader, Sakharov, were serving the interests of that strategy under KGB control;

○ Public exposure of the main KGB agents among Soviet scientists, priests, writers and theatre and movie personalities who have been playing an active rôle in the KGB-controlled political 'opposition' – especially those like the 'conservative' Kochetov and the 'liberal' Tvardovskiy who in the 1960s engaged in a Party- and KGB-controlled debate intended to convey the false impression that Soviet society was evolving towards democracy;

○ And finally: a categorical repudiation of any strategic intention on the part of the Soviets of working towards 'convergence' with the United States.

The self-evident absence of any of these criteria indicates that **the symbolic changes mean no more than that the strategists had reached the conclusion that the old symbols had outlived their usefulness – at least, in the Soviet Union and Eastern Europe – and had to be replaced by new, more attractive, popular symbols.** Moreover these cosmetic changes are logical *and were predicted earlier by this analyst*. **The Soviets realised that convergence with the United States cannot be achieved under the old compromised symbols like Lenin, Dzerzhinskiy and others associated in the Western mind with terror, repression, exile and bloodshed. Convergence requires the introduction of new, attractive, national and 'democratic' symbols conveying the impression that Soviet 'democracy' is approaching the Western model.**

No doubt these cosmetic changes, the reorganisation of the Soviet bureaucracy and the new, more enigmatic status of its leaders like Yeltsin will be seen by the West as a deepening of the process of Soviet' reform', offering new opportunities for Western policy. But the West's main weakness remains unchanged: it cannot grasp the fact that it is facing *an acceleration in the unfolding of Soviet convergence strategy which is intended to procure the subservience of the West to Moscow under an ultimate Communist World Government.*

The Machiavellian boldness and imagination displayed by the Soviet strategists through their staged 'coup' and its preordained defeat are alarming. No doubt these manoeuvres will be followed not only by faked suicides, but also by staged trials of the alleged leaders of the 'coup'. These leaders may well be sentenced to *apparent* prison terms. But in fact they will live in comfortable retirement in resort areas like the Crimea and the Caucasus. Russia is a big country and places can be found for them to hide.

The 'coup' and its 'defeat' show that the Soviets will go to *any lengths* in pursuit of their convergence strategy. This reminds me of remarks by Vladimir Zhenikhov, the former KGB *Rezident* in Finland, and Aleksey Novikov, another KGB officer, at the time the strategy was adopted in 1961.

Both of them had recently returned from home leave in Moscow. When I asked for the latest news from headquarters, both replied using different words but to the same effect: **'This time the KGB are going to finish with capitalist America once and for all'.** I believed them then, and I believe that what is happening now is a bad omen for Western democracy.

The other alarming aspect of the situation is **Western euphoria and the uncritical acceptance of present Soviet developments at their face value**. This shows how easily the West can be taken in by staged Soviet spectacles, and how justified the strategists are in believing that their **'era of provocations'** will produce the intended results. Furthermore, Western euphoria and naïveté serve only to encourage the Soviet strategists to *stage new spectacles more convinced than ever that their strategic designs are realistic.* ■

Memorandum to the CIA: 2 SEPTEMBER 1991

AN ASSESSMENT OF THE SOVIET DECISION TO SUSPEND THE ACTIVITIES OF THE COMMUNIST PARTY

The West regards the Soviet Parliament's decision to suspend the activities of the Communist Party as the death of the Communist Party and as a victory for the new democratic forces: it welcomes this development as beneficial to Western interests.

This assessment is erroneous. It reflects the naïveté of Western Soviet experts who, in a deep sleep like Rip van Winkle, have missed out on the thirty years of preparation for '*perestroika*' and the transition from the old Soviet state of 'dictatorship of the proletariat' (meaning the Communist Party) to the new Soviet 'state of the whole people'. Western experts have forgotten that this transition was envisaged and planned in the Communist Party programme adopted by the 22nd Party Congress in October-November 1961. The present Soviet parliament's decision shows that this Party programme has been successfully carried out by the Communist Party itself.

A new political structure in 'democratic' form has been established. It has become possible for the Soviet parliament to suspend the old Communist Party because the old Party and Komsomol members have been merged into the new 'democratic' structure. **This means that the new political structure created by the old Communist Party is broader, more vital and more dangerous to the West.** It also means that the old Party's cause lives on in the new 'state of the whole people'.

This cause is still the essentially aggressive strategic design of achieving convergence with the United States. Western experts overlook the fact that transition to the 'state of the whole people' has taken place while the Party's instruments of real power, the KGB, the Soviet military (including the GRU) and their political commissars, have remained intact. Now that the new political structure has safely replaced the old Communist Party, the KGB and the Soviet military can be reorganised and 'reformed' to suit the new political structure and the requirements of the convergence strategy. 'Reform' of the Soviet bureaucracy including the military and the KGB will now be undertaken, but it will be deceptive.

The main objectives of the 'reforms' will be:

(a) To create the impressions that the Soviet bureaucracy is becoming more democratic and its components more like their Western counterparts;

(b) Through these deceptive 'reforms' to influence the United States Congress towards introducing real reforms in the American bureaucracy, including a weakening of the CIA and the American armed services and a reduction in their budgets;

(c) To create conditions for the active engagement, cooperation and convergence between the 'reformed' Soviet bureaucracy, the KGB under new labels and the Soviet military on the one hand, and their Western counterparts on the other.

A restructuring of the Western political system along these lines was envisaged in Sakharov's agenda and timetable for convergence. In all probability, all these 'reforms' and the process of convergence will take place while the West is in a state of total confusion and misapprehension about the real nature and purpose of the changes and 'reforms' in the Soviet Union.

There is important evidence which shows that leading Soviet 'reformers' cannot be trusted. For example, Bakatin, the new Chairman of the KGB and an alleged 'reformer', began his tenure of office with an outright deception. He promised the Soviet parliament that the KGB would no longer employ secret informers. This was a deception aimed at the West because the term 'informers', i.e. people who inform on their colleagues and friends, was abandoned by the KGB thirty years ago under Shelepin. Secret informers were the KGB's main assets under Stalin. They were the main instruments for the mass repression of the Soviet population up to the late 1950s. But from 1959 onwards, secret informers were replaced by secret KGB *agents*.

Under Shelepin the KGB was reorganised and given a political rôle in the execution of the long-range strategy of which *'perestroika'* is the final phase. Under Shelepin a new concept of using the secret army of KGB agents to carry out this strategy *against the West* was introduced and adopted. This concept replaced the old KGB concept of using its army of informers for the *internal* repression of the Soviet population. For the past thirty years, the KGB has been using, not informers, but its most skilful agents for political tasks to implement the strategy and to conduct strategic disinformation in preparation for *'perestroika'*. Bakatin is thirty years behindhand with his promise, showing quite clearly that he is not to be trusted.

The quality and skills of KGB agents can be illustrated by such cases as those of Colonel Penkovskiy who was planted on the British and American intelligence services, and the Soviet journalist Oleg Bitov who 'defected' to the British and subsequently 'redefected' to Moscow.

They were KGB *agents*, not KGB *informers*. The same is true of the Soviet nuclear scientist Sakharov and the poet Tvardovskiy, editor-in-chief of the magazine *'New World'*, who were leading figures in the KGB-controlled 'dissident movement'.

The KGB's most skilful *agents*, not informers, are playing principal rôles in Soviet 'democratisation': they are the most vital and effective element of the Soviet 'multi-Party system'. Only a public confession by Bakatin of the existence of these KGB concepts and practices, together with the official, public exposure of the thousands of KGB secret agents operating in the new political structures, in the parliament and in the leadership of the national Republics, would provide convincing proof that the 'democratisation' is genuine and not a political manoeuvre to further the Soviet long-range anti-Western strategy of deception.

The Soviet transition to a new political structure shows that the Soviet strategists are thinking, planning and acting in broad terms, way beyond the imagination of Western politicians. For this reason Western politicians cannot grasp the fact that the Soviet intention is to win by 'democratic' means. Through transition to a new system, the Soviets are revitalising their own people and institutions, and they are succeeding. Contrary to Western belief, they are holding their ranks together.

They are committed and resolute because they firmly believe that they have a sound political strategy. They are acting with a clear understanding of their objectives. Their strategy follows the ideas of the great German strategist Clausewitz who wrote that we can only apprehend the mass of events in their unity from *one* stand-point, and it is only keeping to one point of view that guards us from inconsistency.

The question may be asked: 'Where are the Soviet strategists in the new Soviet political structure?' They will be found in the **[National] Security Council**, in the coalition government, in the leadership of the Soviet parliament, in the KGB, in the Institute for the Study of the USA and Canada and other key Institutes such as the Institute of Europe, and in the new political groups and parties.

Despite the alleged coup, the alleged disunity and the alleged death of the Communist Party, there are indications that the strategists are making important appointments in accordance with the requirements of their strategy. For instance the new Minister of Foreign Affairs, Boris Pankin, was for fifteen years editor of the main Komsomol newspaper in Brezhnev's time. Then for eight years he was Soviet Ambassador to Sweden covering the early period of *'perestroika'*.

Since 1990 he has been Soviet Ambassador to Czechoslovakia during the transition to the new democratic structure there[52]. His experience with the Soviet youth movement, with the Swedish socialists and with the new democracy in Czechoslovakia make him the ideal choice to promote unity of action between European social democrats and the new Soviet 'democrats' and to underline the point that the Soviet system is moving towards the Swedish model of socialism. Gorbachëv himself recently confirmed that the Soviets were interested in the experience of European socialist states and governments with regard to democracy, development of the economy and human rights.

The transition to the new political structure means that the new 'democratic' forces are ready to engage in practical contacts with the United States while carrying out their strategic designs against it. Western interests will not be served but threatened. The danger is real because the West is confused and fails to understand that, behind the democratic façade, the Soviet 'democrats' are engaged in a struggle to the death with Western capitalism. Western aid to the new Soviet 'democrats' will only enhance their effectiveness in pursuing their ruthless strategy of 'convergence'.

The American political forces are in total disarray. Their leaders are devoid of understanding of the real processes in the USSR and of the emerging realities there. They are worried about the dissolution of the Soviet Union and the possibility of civil war. They argue amongst themselves whether they should deal with Gorbachëv in the centre, Yeltsin in the Russian Republic or with the other national Republics. They

---

52 *Editor's Note:* Boris Pankin's importance was subsequently further reflected in his appointment as Ambassador to London. Ahead of the televised 'Reichstag Fire' assault on the 'Parliament' Building (previously the headquarters of the CPSU, subsequently in subliminal imitation of the US President's residence, the 'White House', and following the bombardment in October 1993, the 'Black and White House'), Pankin was recalled to Moscow along with Lukin, the Russian Ambassador to the United States, and one other Ambassador to a key Western country, for an 'insider' briefing on the objectives of that provocation. On 4 October 1993, the British Prime Minister, Mr John Major, stepped out of the front door of Number 10 Downing Street more or less arm-in-arm with Boris Pankin, to speak in front of the television cameras. With Pankin at his side, Mr Major expressed his unreserved support for 'what Mr Yeltsin is doing' – i.e. directing tank fire at the so-called 'Parliament building'. By this provocation, the strategists proved, *inter alia*, that the leaders of the West would support the most extreme and barbaric excesses of the strategy unwittingly, even when the cherished symbol of 'democracy' was being attacked by tanks in front of the world's television cameras.

argue whether aid should be given in the form of cash, technical assistance or a new Marshall Plan. Most confused of all are the giants of conservative thinking who are jubilant about the changes in the Soviet Union.

They are inviting Soviet 'democrats' from the centre, from Russia and from the national Republics and welcoming them as their new comrades-in-arms. This gladdens the hearts of the Soviet strategists, for whom such a welcome is a great accomplishment. They have demonstrated that their strategic skill has reached its zenith: *following the advice of Sun Tzu, they can enter the American fortress – the enemy's camp – without opposition.* ■

Memorandum to the CIA: 26 MARCH 1992

GEOPOLITICAL STRATEGIES OF RUSSIA, THE 'COMMONWEALTH OF INDEPENDENT STATES' AND CHINA: A COMMENT ON EX-PRESIDENT NIXON'S ADVICE ON MASSIVE AID TO RUSSIA

In an earlier Memorandum to the CIA this analyst explained **the common Sino-Soviet long range strategy of convergence with the West** and the intended exploitation for the purposes of this strategy of the new openings arising from the 'reformed' political structure of the former USSR and the emergence of the alleged 'democrats', 'non-Communists' and 'independents' who are running it.

The present assessment shows how, because of Western ignorance of and confusion about the strategy underlying *'perestroika'* and because of Western political and economic support for the so-called reform of the Soviet system, the Commonwealth of Independent States (CIS) has been successfully installed and has begun to carry out concrete new geopolitical strategies within the framework of the long-standing overall Communist strategy of convergence.

These strategies are still being guided and coordinated by the same Soviet strategists who have simply shifted away from the use of the old worn-out ideology and the familiar but obsolete patterns, to the exploitation of geopolitical factors and of the new potentialities of the 'reformed' Communist system. The common feature of these geopolitical strategies is the manipulation and use of the 'democratic' and 'independent' images which the change in form from the USSR to the CIS and its individual members has provided so abundantly and the nature of which the West has, so far, failed to comprehend.

The following upgraded strategies may be distinguished:

○ *The first strategy* involves the CIS and Russia in particular dealing directly with longstanding American allies like Germany and Japan and causing their allegiance to be shifted away from the United States towards economic and political alliance with the CIS and especially with Russia.

To this end Russia is exploiting American economic rivalry with Germany and Japan, together with the large-scale involvement of Germany and Japan in economic cooperation with Russia and the offer to them of lucrative market and investment opportunities in Russia. China can be expected to join in this campaign to steal away old American allies by concentrating on offering the Japanese various investment opportunities in China.

○ *A second upgraded strategy* **involves the use of the new 'independent' Muslim states in the CIS to establish and develop economic and political cooperation with the fundamentalists in Iran and elsewhere in the Muslim world.**

According to this assessment the much-advertised feud between the Armenians and the Azerbaijanis of Turkish descent in Nagorno-Karabakh may be a tactical ploy to involve Turkey, Iran and other Muslim countries in support of eventual alliance with Azerbaijan and other Central Asian Muslim states in the CIS. This strategy takes into account the growing power of the fundamentalists and the possibility of their gaining control over substantial oil reserves[53].

A primary objective of the strategy here is to achieve a partnership with the fundamentalists in Iran and Algeria and to replace the present American-oriented rulers of Saudi Arabia with fundamentalists. The opening in Saudi Arabia of a Russian Embassy and the probable opening of Embassies by Muslim states of the CIS should be seen, not only as an attempt to extract a few extra Saudi billions, but as part of an offensive to bring about a political reorientation in that country.

Chinese Muslims can also be expected to play an active rôle in promoting alliances with the fundamentalists. The supply of missiles to Iran by the Chinese should be looked at in the context of this strategy[54].

○ **The third strategy is to facilitate a shift of the emerging régime in South Africa from the Western sphere of influence towards close economic and political cooperation and alliance with the CIS using for this purpose old friendships with leaders of the African National Congress and the South African Communist Party with which it is effectively merged.** One can expect that the offensive to facilitate such a partnership will become more active and more visible than ever, after the 'reforms' in the CIS and South Africa have stabilised.

○ **The fourth strategy is that of using and manipulating the changes in the former Soviet Union to bring about, in the longer run, radical changes in relations between the United States and Israel, in the political power structure in Israel itself, in Israel's position in the Middle East and in world opinion towards Israel.**

The fact that the new leaders in Russia have promised the withdrawal of Soviet troops from Germany, the Baltic countries and Poland, and that they are insisting on a seven-year term for the strategic arms reduction treaty being negoti- ➡

53 *Editor's Note:* As a further dimension of these preparations, Turkey has been targeted and was prevailed upon to sign a bilateral treaty with Moscow in May 1992. This followed the threat of a Third World War by **Marshal Shaposhnikov**, then supreme commander of Commonwealth of Independent States Forces, in the face of a Turkish press report (believed to have been planted) that Turkish forces might have to intervene in neighbouring Nakechivan, which happened to be the hideaway of **KGB General Gaidar Aliyev** as he prepared to take power in Baku. Aliyev was formerly Soviet Premier under **Yuriy Andropov** [*'New Lies for Old'*, page 390, Note 11]. Writing in *'International Affairs'* [official journal of the Russian Foreign Ministry], Volume 10 1994, **Nikolai Kovalsky** stated that 'Turkey has become a major partner of Russia in the [Black Sea] region. Relations with it are based on the Agreement on Friendship and Co-operation signed in 1992. Cooperation covers both the political and economic spheres... In September 1993, the sides reached agreement on delivery of coal and gas from Russia... Turkey has begun purchasing Russian military equipment'.

54 *Editor's Note:* In late 1991, only months after Kazakhstan had become 'independent', and during the period of maximum confusion in the West over the nature of the 'changes' ostensibly taking place in the 'former' USSR, Iran purchased its first operational nuclear weapons, primarily from Kazakhstan. Iranian intelligence agents brought the weapons and related materials via Turkestan, and 'ex'-Soviet experts were brought in as troubleshooters. By the end of January 1992, the operational status of the weapons had been confirmed. At roughly the same time, Iran acquired parts for the Soviet aerial nuclear gravity bomb from 'former' Soviet military depots in the Turkestan Military District and Tajikistan, where key details of the purchase were apparently negotiated. Iran is also believed to possess a nuclear artillery shell of 0.1 kiloton yield, which was offered to Iran by Kazakhstan during negotiations in the region for the other nuclear devices. [*Sources: 'The Grand Strategy of Iran'*, Task Force on Terrorism and Unconventional Warfare, US Congress, Washington DC, in *'Global Affairs'*, Fall issue, 1993; *'Security Affairs'*, published by Jewish Institute for National Security Affairs [JINSA], Washington DC, June 1992, citing a 1992 report by the Task Force]. The deception related to the channelling of this Soviet nuclear weapons technology via newly 'independent' 'ex'-Soviet Republics – leaving Russia, as the continuing signatory of the Non-Proliferation Treaty, with 'clean hands' in the matter. Moreover, while these very transactions were being finalised, the West hastened with enthusiasm to become embroiled in 'collective security' arrangements which were widely justified as being necessary, in part, to *curb* nuclear proliferation.

At a meeting in the House of Commons in on 27 April 1994, the Ukrainian Ambassador to Britain, Sergui Komisarenko, told MPs that Kazakhstan could not have transferred *fully-operational* [sic] nuclear weapons to Iran [*source:* information conveyed to the Editor by Christopher Gill MP (Ludlow), who attended the meeting].

ated with the United States, are indications that the Russian strategists have their own timetable. This is not based on what is going to occur in the CIS according to the optimistic expectations of Western observers, but rather upon the Soviet estimate of the time needed for the strategies described above to take effect. The possibility that the United States will lose valuable allies during this period is not something new. There is nothing permanent in international relations. The Americans experienced this not so long ago when they *suddenly* lost Iran.

The vulnerability of the United States arises from the fact that its basic premises, assumptions and perceptions about the present and future of Russia and the CIS are wrong. Where the United States sees golden opportunities, it is in reality facing traps set for it by the Soviet long-range strategists. The impact on the United States of the successful execution of these strategies would be devastating.

The loss of old allies and the loss of oil reserves, following the equally catastrophic loss of South Africa, would result in the re-emergence of the CIS and China as stronger adversaries, and in an 'irreversible' change in the balance of world power in their favour. The United States would be weakened and divided and the pressure for the impetus towards convergence of the CIS and China with the United States on Sino-Russian terms would be intensified.

THE DANGEROUS ADVICE OF MR RICHARD NIXON

In this context a comment needs to be made on former President Nixon's criticism of President Bush for giving insufficient aid to Russia and his recommendation that massive economic and technological aid comparable in scale to the Marshall Plan should be provided to the CIS. Nixon suggested that the present administration was missing an historic opportunity to help Yeltsin and to transform Russia into a democracy. This analyst believes Mr. Nixon's advice to be erroneous and damaging to the vital interests of the United States for three important reasons:

(1) Mr Nixon has no understanding of the true nature and meaning of the changes in the former Soviet Union. He does not appreciate the calculated origin of the new realities there. He fails to see that *'perestroika'* and the introduction of quasi-democracy and limited capitalism are all being carried out on the lines of Lenin's New Economic Policy within the framework of the long-range strategy adopted by the Soviet and Chinese leaders in 1958-60.

(2) Mr Nixon puts too much trust in the former Communist leaders and in their instant conversion into 'democrats', 'non-Communists' and 'independents'. He does not realise that **this is a tactical conversion along the lines of Lenin's classic advice to Communists to abandon leftist and revolutionary phrases and to adopt a rightist, opportunistic image in order to achieve their strategic objectives.**

(3) Mr Nixon ignores the geopolitical strategic designs of the present leaders of the CIS and China aimed at weakening the United States and at achieving convergence. Even more important, he misinterprets the motive forces at work in the structure of the CIS. Following his advice by extending massive aid to the CIS will have the opposite effect to that which he intends. It will *not* transform Russia into a democracy and it will *not* prevent a new despotism there. But it will finance the transforma-

tion of Russia and the CIS into a more viable, more powerful adversary of the United States which will resume its old ideological hostility towards genuine American democracy and capitalism. It will allow the leaders of the CIS and Communist China to accelerate the pace at which they carry out their aggressive strategies against the United States and its present allies. And it will lubricate slush funds, directing hard currency into offshore bank accounts to finance intelligence activities.

Here in the United States we have a high regard for Mr Nixon's opinions. But it is more important to consider how the leaders of the CIS regard Mr Nixon and his metamorphosis from a fervent anti-Communist into a strong supporter of Gorbachëv, Yeltsin and *'perestroika'*, and an advocate of massive aid to Russia. The question was put somewhat diplomatically to the Russian Ambassador, Lukin, by a Western journalist. Watching Ambassador Lukin on the television screen while he was giving his cunning reply, this analyst was left in no doubt that the CIS leaders regard Mr Nixon's conversion in the light of Lenin's alleged advice on how to assess and deal with Western politicians.

Lenin is supposed to have divided Western politicians into two categories: those who were clever, anti-Communist adversaries who should be taken on, confronted and dealt with seriously; and those who were confused and 'useful idiots', who could be exploited up to the hilt in the Communist interest.

Since the Soviet long-range strategy and its final phase of *'perestroika'* were based upon Lenin's New Economic Policy experience and were imbued with Leninist spirit and thought, it is natural that successive Communist leaders should have seen Mr Nixon through Lenin's eyes. In 1959, when Mr Nixon held strongly anti-Communist views, Khrushchev, who initiated the long range strategy designed to bury capitalism in America, invited him to Moscow through the Soviet ambassador in Washington and took him seriously – that is to say, flattered him – by debating his views on Communism with him. Brezhnev took him equally seriously by simultaneously engaging him in SALT negotiations while fighting him in Vietnam, and then concluding the agreement on Vietnam which led to the American defeat there. During the impeachment process, Soviet officials mocked Mr Nixon. According to an American reporter, Soviet officials and journalists asked him at the time with obvious sarcasm: 'What are you doing to our Nixon?' Now that Mr Nixon is Yeltsin's most ardent supporter and exponent of the case for a Marshall Plan for the CIS, its leaders must be laughing their heads off recalling Lenin's phrase about 'useful idiots' – while harvesting the benefits of Mr Nixon's support for their devious policies.

RETAINING THE CAPACITY TO THINK

US intelligence agencies should be on the lookout for signs of the implementation of the geopolitical strategies of the CIS and its members and should provide policymakers with timely warnings. To be successful, these agencies must first distance themselves from the superficial assessments of ignorant television commentators who accept at face value everything that emanates from CIS officials or TV channels. They should focus on developing reliable human intelligence on the real strategic intentions and actions of the CIS and should analyse developments in terms of the geopolitical strategies described above.

The 'reformed' KGB is active and its intelligence offensive against the West continues as before. In fact, its political and operational capabilities have been broadened. Instead of the familiar unified KGB the West is now faced with fifteen KGBs which have not only changed their names, but have adopted a new *modus operandi* – or, to cite Lenin, a 'new way of working'.

The Central Intelligence Agency's analysts should ask themselves the question why, if Communism is really 'dead', if the USSR has really disintegrated and if the Communist ship of state is really sinking, there has not been a wave of *high-level* defectors comparable to and greater than the wave which occurred after the death of Stalin in 1953.

High-level defectors might have been expected not only from the intelligence and security services but from the armed forces, the Central Committee apparatus, the diplomatic service and Arbatov's Institute for the Study of the USA and Canada. **The absence of high-level defectors of such calibre to date indicates that the former Soviet machinery of state has been successfully transformed into the 'state of the whole people', as envisaged in the Party programme adopted by the 22nd Party Congress in October-November 1961**.

The armed services of the CIS remain a formidable force with nuclear capability as well as political commissars. The United States should be on guard and should conserve its military strength because basic American assumptions about the military strategies of Russia and China will turn out to have been confused, if not totally erroneous. The United States should ignore Mr Nixon's advice and steer clear of deep economic and technological commitments to Russia, the CIS and China. It should warn its allies such as Japan, Germany and France against such commitments. It should concentrate on addressing the immediate problems which beset the country at home and undermine its strength.

Abroad it should pursue an active foreign policy to maintain its position of world leadership, preserving and strengthening its alliances. But, for all this to be possible, it must first shed its naïve illusions about the nature of the changes that have occurred in the 'ex'-Soviet Union (CIS). It must recognise that democratisation there is false and that the fundamental nature of the adversary has not changed: only its strategy and tactics have changed, in that they have become more candid, more realistic and more dangerous.

Only if the United States comprehends the calculated nature of the changes and the Leninist strategy which lies behind them, will it wake up to the realisation that financing the economic revival of the present Russian/CIS system will enable the strategists to pursue more effectively their objectives of engineering an irreversible shift in the world balance of power and eventual convergence with the West.

This 'convergence' is to take place *not* on the West's terms – as élite Western globalists surely imagine – but rather on the terms intended by the Leninist strategic planners. The resulting 'one world' will be Marxist-Leninist-Gramscian-Communist – hardly what unwitting Western collaborators truly want to see established. ∎

Memorandum to the CIA: 28 SEPTEMBER 1992

For the attention of: The Director of Central Intelligence

PROPOSED STUDY OF THE ECONOMIC INTENTIONS OF THE 'NEW' RUSSIA IN THE LIGHT OF THE POLITICAL STRATEGY OF THE 'SECOND OCTOBER REVOLUTION' [*'WELTOKTOBER'*]

In earlier Memoranda to the Central Intelligence Agency, I have usually addressed the strategic and political intentions of the new Russian leaders: I have made assessments and predictions, by which I stand. Now there are suggestions that the CIA should shift its priorities to economic ones.

I agree that the CIA should address economic problems, provided that the strategic economic intentions of the new Russian leaders are kept clearly in view.

In my opinion the CIA should consider making a study of Russian strategic economic intentions and design, taking into account the *political* strategy of 'convergence' as envisaged by the 'Second October Revolution'. The leaders of the new Russia and the other former Soviet Republics strongly believe that the Group of Seven industrialised nations are either exhausting their natural resources like the United States or lack them like Japan. They consider that the natural resources of Russia and the other Republics are largely untapped.

They therefore conclude that, if they can succeed in attracting from the Group of Seven sufficient capital and technological investment to develop their resources, they will be in a position to impose a twenty-first century *'Pax Russiana'* on the rest of the world which will help them to achieve a political victory of the 'Second October Revolution' over the capitalist West[55].

I strongly urge the Central Intelligence Agency to use some of its extensive resources to exploring the validity of this thesis. ■

---

55 *Author's Note:* I want to see prosperity for the Russian people but not under their present system with its deceptive form of democracy and its strategy for the revival of Communism in a new guise.

Memorandum to the CIA: FEBRUARY 1993

For the attention of: Mr James Woolsey, Director of Central Intelligence[56]

THE IMPORTANCE OF THE STRATEGIC FACTOR IN ASSESSING DEVELOPMENTS IN RUSSIA AND COMMUNIST CHINA

I am a KGB defector who came to the United States in 1961 in order to convey to the US Government **a warning about the Soviet long-range political strategy for the defeat of the United States**. In October 1964, I gave Mr McCone, then Director of Central Intelligence, an account of **the report delivered by Shelepin, former Chairman of the KGB, to a KGB conference in 1959. The report included a call for the creation of KGB-controlled 'opposition' in the Soviet Union as an essential part of the strategy leading to a future liberalisation of the régime.**

From 1963 onwards I argued that **the well advertised Sino-Soviet differences were intended to conceal a common Sino-Soviet strategy, in other words that the 'split' was a joint strategic disinformation operation intended to deceive the West. Between 1963 and 1969 my view of the 'split' was debated within the CIA.** *I have good reason to believe that information on the existence of this internal debate in the CIA was leaked to the KGB and through them to the Soviet leadership who took drastic steps to settle the argument within the CIA in their favour.*

In 1969, in collaboration with their Chinese allies, the Soviet leadership staged a show of military hostilities on their Far Eastern border modelled on the genuine hostilities between the Soviets and the Japanese in that area in 1938. On the evidence from US reconnaissance satellites, the CIA experts accepted the hostilities as genuine and thus as conclusive proof that the Sino-Soviet split was also genuine.

I continued to argue that satellite information alone could not throw light on the strategic intentions and considerations behind an apparent military conflict on the ground. Secret intelligence from reliable human sources was also required. At that time, through KGB penetration, the CIA had lost its reliable human sources and was unable to replace them: it was therefore blind. US policymakers also accepted the 'split' as genuine and believed that the United States and the USSR now had a common interest in confronting the growing peril from a nuclear-armed, hardline Communist régime in China. It was against this background that the US Government entered into SALT talks with the USSR in 1969 and then embarked upon *détente* with the Chinese Communist leaders in 1971.

The apparent conflict on the Sino-Soviet border and the attempt at liberalisation in Czechoslovakia in 1968 together delayed completion of my book 'New Lies for Old' which was submitted to the CIA for clearance in 1980 and was published in 1984. The delay did not alter my thesis that the attempt at liberalisation in Czechoslovakia was a rehearsal for a forthcoming political and economic liberalisation of the system in the USSR and the Communist Bloc as a whole. In 'New Lies for Old', I predicted that this liberalisation in the USSR would be accompanied by the introduction

---

56 *Editor's Note:* Mr Woolsey's resignation as Director of Central Intelligence in December 1994, was reported one day after Aldrich Hazen Ames had given an extensive televised interview in which he repeated allegations of further penetration of the CIA by Soviet/Russian intelligence.

156 THE PERESTROIKA DECEPTION

of KGB-controlled political 'opposition', the dismantling of the Berlin Wall and the reunification of Germany. I also said it was more than likely that the West would accept these developments at their face value. **My predictions were correct. More important, however, is the fact that they were correct** *because they were based on my knowledge of Soviet political strategy.*

For many years until recently, I have presented Memoranda to successive Directors of Central Intelligence in which I have sought to follow and explain this strategy, the true meaning of political and economic reform of the Soviet system and the KGB's rôle in the creation of controlled political opposition within the system. I have also tried to explain the part played by disinformation in this strategy. In my Memoranda I have argued that an abundance of information does not automatically confer understanding. **From the late 1950s onwards, Western intelligence lost its comprehension of Communist, and especially Soviet, developments because it was ignorant of their adoption of a long-range political strategy backed by strategic disinformation.** At the time, the CIA was uninformed because it had lost its genuine high level agent in Soviet military intelligence [GRU], Lieutenant-Colonel Popov, who had been replaced by the KGB *provocateur*, Penkovskiy[57].

In the 1960s and 1970s the Western failure to understand Soviet political strategy was masked by the fact that the United States matched the Soviet military build-up and maintained a strong military deterrent. **But the failure of understanding became apparent when the '*perestroika*' reforms, which were the product of over twenty-five years of preparation, took the West by surprise and were blindly accepted by the West as the advent of genuine Western-style democracy and a genuine market system in Russia deserving of Western political support and economic aid.** Two approaches to the study of developments in the former Soviet Union and Communist China are possible. One is that of the man-in-the-street who uncritically absorbs what he sees on television and in the press, in official Russian statements and in symbolic displays like the removal of selected statues of Lenin and Dzerzhinskiy, and photographs of empty shelves in stores. On this unsound basis, he draws far-reaching conclusions that the Russians are starving, that Communism has collapsed, that the USSR has disintegrated, that the Communist Party has been banned, that 'the Cold War is over' and that civil war is around the corner. He interprets the reforms in Russia which he reads about in the newspapers and sees on TV 'news analyses' as the spontaneous outcome of genuine political pressures and therefore develops over-optimistic hopes for the future of democracy in Russia.

57 *Editor's Note:* A standard Western perception, perpetuated by many analysts and lay writers, is that **Oleg Penkovskiy** was an Anglo-American spy within the GRU whose invaluable assistance to the West during the Cuban missile crisis enabled President Kennedy to 'face down' Nikita Khrushchev, and that Penkovskiy was brutally tortured, sentenced to death in a show trial in May 1963, and shot for his pains. But Golitsyn makes it plain that Penkovskiy was a *provocateur* sent to reveal crucial military intelligence to the West, providing a pretext for Khrushchev to 'react' to the United States' acquired knowledge in a manner calculated to avoid a nuclear showdown while enabling the Soviet leadership to extract the *quid pro quo* they really sought – abandonment of the Monroe Doctrine in the form of a US pledge never to intervene in Cuba and thus to tolerate Moscow's control of the island in general, and installation by the Soviets of permanent sophisticated electronic eavesdropping and other aggressive facilities there in particular. Penkovskiy 'replaced' **Lieutenant-Colonel Popov**, a genuine agent, in such a way as to convince the West that his intelligence 'product' was as reliable as that of Popov – which, up to a point, it was. But it was provocatively incomplete because it omitted revelation of the long-range deception strategy.

Unfortunately, it is this man-in-the-street approach which dominates the minds of Western policymakers. The old generation of sceptical Kremlinologists has faded away. Their successors, lacking insight of their own, parrot ideas and disinformation derived from the maelstrom of television interviews, staged tele-spectacles and press clippings. The result is euphoria, unrealistic expectations and unsound responses such as those demonstrated conspicuously by former President Nixon in his call for massive economic aid to Russia.

The alternative approach is to **study the long-range Communist strategy adopted in 1958-60 and to explore the full meaning of the transition from the 'dictatorship of the proletariat' to the 'state of the whole people'** which the Russian 'developed socialist society' has accomplished.

Against this documented background, political and economic reform and 'democratisation' in Russia can be seen to be the planned product of over twenty-five years of preparation and rehearsal in the USSR and Eastern Europe. The 'ex'-Communists' 'reforms' and their style of 'democracy' are peculiar to themselves. The 'state of the whole people' is in fact an adaptation of Lenin's idea of the withering away of the state (which also looks ahead to the time when there is to be a Communist World Government), and its replacement by mass social organisation.

'Glasnost' and 'democratisation' are neither of them genuine. Americans only display their naïveté by expecting a genuine answer from the Russians, for example, to the question whether Alger Hiss was a Soviet agent. Preoccupation with the issue of MIA [US military personnel 'Missing in Action'] in Russia is of burning interest to the American families involved. Investigations into the whereabouts of the missing servicemen are fully justified; but they are not enough.

Before plunging into deeper political and military partnership with Russia and loosening its purse strings further, Congress should demand from the Russian leaders a full and frank official acknowledgement and public explanation of the fact that their predecessors slaughtered 20 million Russians, Ukrainians, Belorussians, Moldavians, Latvians, Lithuanians, Estonians, Jews and others. Congress should also demand to know how many secret agents there are among the so-called 'democrats' in Russia and Eastern Europe.

The lack of frankness and public debate in Russia on these and other *fundamental* issues makes it clear that '*glasnost*', 'democratisation', the removal of statues and the alleged abolition of the Communist Party are nothing more than cosmetic changes. Without free and open debates, genuine opposition cannot emerge and supplant the present pseudo-opposition. Unexposed as the true heirs of Communism which they are, the Soviet strategists remain at the helm and continue to mesmerise the West into supporting them. In fact no long-term good can realistically be expected from the present system. When its economic situation has improved, Russia can be expected to revert to hostility towards the West: Western belief in the collapse of Communism will be shown to be an illusion.

The Soviet strategists have reformed their system, introduced their own type of pseudo-democracy and made changes in their economy. They have replaced the outdated and discredited domination of the Communist Party with a new, controlled mass political structure. In so doing they have retained the same political élite, the same army with its political commissars, basically the same intelligence and security services and other elements of the former Soviet system such as Arbatov's Institute for the Study of the USA and Canada and the other key institutes such as the Institute of Europe, working under the supervision of the Academy of Sciences.

The political élite still consists of the 25 million 'former' Communists and 50 million young Communists who are the most active political element in Russia and the 'independent' states and who retain real power. This élite initiates, permeates and directs the new parties and opposition groups, even the anti-Semitic ones, in accordance with the demands of the strategy. The élite receives guidance through various government and semi-official channels. The 'reformed' KGB and its agents remain active, especially in sensitive areas like anti-Semitic operations where they use the secret police expertise inherited from the Tsarist and Stalinist periods. **The political élite do not regard Communism as defeated. On the contrary, they see reforms and 'democratisation' as the means of carrying forward their longstanding strategy of 'convergence' with and victory over the West.**

US intelligence seems to underestimate the morale of the Russian Army and its generals. My observation of their performance suggests that their morale is high. They have not been defeated militarily or politically. On the contrary, they are winning the strategic battle with the United States and Western Europe by political means with the help of a financial boost from Western sources. This makes the task of their political commissars easy. They will obviously retain more than sufficient nuclear weapons to ensure that the CIS/Russia qualifies for superpower status.

The United States does not understand developments in Russia, but Arbatov and his team at his Institute have a good understanding of developments in the United States. That is why they have survived the so-called collapse of Communism. Arbatov is one of the chief strategic advisers to the Russian leadership. His self-declared aim is to erase the *image* of Russia as a power hostile to the United States. The recent handover by the Russians to the US ambassador in Moscow of microphones taken from the US embassy building was inspired by the same motive.

Yet there is no genuine, broadly based, organised political opposition in Russia and no foundation on which one could be built. The purported opposition exists to deceive and manipulate the perceptions and reactions of genuine democrats in the West. The West fails to comprehend the mentality of the Russian leaders and overestimates their willingness to reform themselves. **They have the same mentality as their predecessors who adopted the still current long-range strategy.** It was these people who not only executed the CIA agent Popov but made a movie of him being burned alive to show to young officers to deter them from following Popov's example.

Behind the mask of diplomatic and political cooperation and partnership with the United States and Europe, the current Russian leaders are following the strategy of their predecessors and working towards a 'New World Order'.

When the right moment comes the mask will be dropped and the Russians with Chinese help will seek to impose their system on the West on their own terms as the culmination of a 'Second October Socialist Revolution'.

In this light it is easy to understand why the Russians have not thrown away either their military power or their political commissars, why Russian troops still remain in East Germany, Poland and the Baltic States, why the Russians have been in no hurry to reach meaningful military agreements with the United States, why the 'reformed' security and intelligence services continue their activities, why the reins of power are still in the hands of 'ex'-Communists, why leading Soviet strategists like Arbatov and Yakovlev retain their influence and why the so-called 'democratic' Russian leaders have close ties with the Communist Chinese.

In the past, when the USSR was perceived to be a monolith and Soviet parliamentary institutions could be seen to be mere rubber-stamps, Soviet negotiating tactics *vis-à-vis* the Western countries were more or less understood. Now they are not. The introduction of a controlled political opposition and the new structure of the CIS with its so-called 'independent' states like Ukraine, Kazakhstan and Belarus, provide many new openings for bolstering Russian negotiating positions through disinformation. Russian negotiators have the edge over their American counterparts because their moves are planned on the basis of a political strategy and deceptive negotiating techniques which the Americans do not understand.

The Bush Administration, with its eye on history, rushed the final stages of the negotiations for the recent nuclear missile treaty which had been deliberately dragged out by the Russians until near the end of the Administration's life. Ignorant of long-term Russian intentions, the Administration put its trust in Yeltsin and, according to 'senior Administration officials', made significant concessions. These concessions were made 'to help Yeltsin defend the treaty against criticism' in the mistaken belief that he was under pressure from 'conservatives', as a Western politician might have been. In fact, since the 'conservative opposition' is coordinated through the political élite with Yeltsin and his strategists, its activities can be stepped up or down to suit the needs of the Russian negotiators. Similarly, alleged difficulties in the Ukrainian or other parliaments can be used to accelerate or delay ratification and wring further concessions out of the Americans. By signing the treaty with the outgoing US Administration, the Russians established a basis for pressing the new Administration to carry the process further and faster.

The United States does not understand the real nature of relations between the Russian and Communist Chinese leaders. Washington believes that a genuine improvement took place in relations in the 1980s between the Chinese and Gorbachëv and Yeltsin. I see these contacts as evidence that '*perestroika*' in Russia did not take the Chinese by surprise, that they have a complete understanding of the realities behind it and that their strategic cooperation with the Russians continues as it has done since the late 1950s though now with open acknowledgement of their good relations. The United States views the Russian sale of complete factories and new weapons systems to the Chinese as dictated by Russian desire to ease their current economic difficulties. To my way of thinking it amounts to the deliberate transfer of advanced technology to an old and trusted ally.

US officials count missile numbers, but there is no comprehension of continuing Sino-Russian strategic cooperation. Insufficient attention has been paid to the fact that Yeltsin signalled his assent to the recent missile reduction treaty *from Peking*. His visit there, like earlier visits by Shevardnadze and Gorbachëv, *pointed to the continuity of this cooperation*. No doubt Yeltsin discussed the new treaty with the Chinese and reached an understanding with them about it. It would be no surprise if some of the Soviet missiles ended up in China. Deception would be used to cover up their transfer. The Russian capacity for deception could well outweigh the American capacity to verify the disposal of all missiles.

My assessment is that, when the long-range strategy was worked out and adopted in the period 1958-60, the Soviets and Chinese agreed to plan and prepare for the eventual reform and liberalisation of their régimes while, in the meantime, following different paths. Liberalisation formed part of the strategic design of procuring the disarmament of the West and the convergence of the Communist and Eastern systems on Communist terms.

The present Russian and Chinese leaders face three centres of nuclear military power with which they have to deal: the United States, Western Europe and Israel. They calculate that they will be able to neutralise American military power through the combination of their new 'democratic' image, their 'partnership' with the United States and nuclear disarmament negotiations and agreements. Western Europe will be neutralised through the concept of common European security and the membership of the East European 'independent' states in West European institutions. Israel's nuclear capability, which will not be reduced on account of changes in the former USSR, will be a matter of continuing concern to the Russians and Chinese. The appointment of Primakov, a Middle East expert, to take charge of the Russian Foreign Intelligence Service indicates the importance attached to this theatre by the leadership. It cannot be ruled out that, behind the screen of cooperation with the West in preventing the spread of nuclear knowhow, the Russians, through their intelligence assets in the area, will prepare a covert operation to sabotage Israeli nuclear installations. The operation might ostensibly be conducted by Arab or Iranian Muslim fundamentalists or perhaps by a renegade Soviet scientist or general in the service of some other terrorist group.

It is true that my assessment of developments in Russia and China in terms of their joint strategy is in sharp conflict with the views of Western governments and their intelligence services. However it is also true that **I predicted liberalisation in the USSR long before 'perestroika' was ever heard of**. At that time I was in a minority of one. But my predictions were proved correct and a conservative expert on Communism, Brian Crozier, drew attention to the fact. The Central Intelligence Agency has recently been criticised for its failure to predict 'liberalisation'. Had it taken greater account of my views it might have escaped this criticism.

I remain convinced that the current view taken by Western politicians and the media of developments in Russia is erroneous and over-optimistic. History has shown the capacity of Communism to deceive its own subjects and its opponents. The October Revolution which promised the Russians bread, peace and freedom, ended up by killing 20 million of them. Wartime Soviet 'partnership' with the Eastern allies against the Nazis, instead of leading to peacetime cooperation, was used to facilitate the Soviet Army's takeover of Eastern Europe. Another wave of slaughter and repression followed. The same thing accompanied the Communist takeover in China. In each case Western hopes and expectations were dashed. The ferocity of Communism came as a most unpleasant surprise.

Because of the failure of Western policymakers to understand Sino-Russian strategy particularly since the launching of *'perestroika'*, I fear that there is a real chance of the Russian and Chinese leaders succeeding in carrying through their strategy of convergence with the West in the next ten years or so.

Experiments with false democracy by so-called former Communists present a critical test for Western intelligence services. If they fail to assess them and their possible consequences correctly, *their mistakes may well result in bloodshed in the United States and Western Europe.*

Western intelligence should not be intimidated either by political pressure or by the weight of conventional wisdom. It should not rely exclusively on technical and overt sources of information. The need for reliable secret intelligence on the strategic intentions of the Russian and Chinese leadership is as acute as ever, as is the need for willingness to think the apparently unthinkable.

Now that you are assuming the responsibility of leading the CIA and adapting it to the so-called 'post-Cold War' situation, I am sending you a collection of Memoranda that I have addressed to your predecessors in which I have tried to follow and explain the Russians' reforms in terms of their long-range strategy. My purpose in sending the Memoranda to you is to try to counter the prevailing inadequate and misleading man-in-the-street perception of events in Russia and China.

I know that you will have a vast amount to read in taking over your new appointment. But I urge you to read my Memoranda because they are unique in taking account of Sino-Russian strategy and disinformation and, I believe, provide some insight into the strategic thinking that underlies the activities of Yeltsin, Gorbachёv, Primakov and their corps of aides and advisers. The Memoranda also provide a corrective to current euphoria and a warning of the challenge which, despite appearances, still faces Western democracy.

In the mid-1960s, when Mr McCone was Director of Central Intelligence [DCI] and Mr Angleton was head of counter-intelligence, the information I provided on the new strategy as evidenced by the Shelepin report of 1959 was taken seriously. In later years the CIA, to an ever increasing extent, ignored the warnings I had given. My hope is that, bearing in mind the correctness of my predictions of *'perestroika'*, **the new leadership of the CIA will not reject out of hand the new warnings I have given of the specious nature of the present system and its anti-Western designs. If once more I am right and the conventional wisdom wrong, the consequences will be serious indeed.** After more than thirty years of association with the Central Intelligence Agency, my political testament to the agency is:

'Ignore Russian and Chinese strategic designs against the United States at your peril'.

Respectfully,

ANATOLIY GOLITSYN

Memoranda to the CIA: 26 March & 12 October 1993

ASSESSMENT OF THE CONFRONTATION BETWEEN PRESIDENT BORIS YELTSIN AND THE CONGRESS OF PEOPLES' DEPUTIES: OBSERVATIONS ON THE 'REICHSTAG FIRE' EPISODE, OCTOBER 1993

The following text is based upon two sources: a Memorandum filed by the Author with the CIA on 26 March 1993 amid the apparent confrontation between President Yeltsin and the Congress of Peoples' Deputies ; and observations by the Author following the televised shelling of the 'White House' in October 1993:

26 March 1993: According to the Author's assessment the present confrontation between President Boris Yeltsin and the Congress of Peoples' Deputies [March 1993] is not spontaneous but actually arranged in accordance with the the requirements of the Russian strategists. One of the main objectives of the confrontation is to commit the new Administration of the United States and the other six leading industrialised countries to an aid programme for Russia and the other Republics on the model of the Marshall Plan. While planning the introduction of *'perestroika'* , the Russian strategists, who form a largely unseen collective leadership, envisaged a range of options for the top leadership (public face) of the Government. The first option which they exercised was *'perestroika'* under a Communist, Gorbachëv, who was sponsored by Andropov. Their next option was the continuation of *'perestroika'* under a 'democratic' leader who had 'renounced' Communism – Boris Yeltsin.

Yeltsin, also sponsored by Andropov, was chosen at the same time as Gorbachëv to be Gorbachëv's eventual replacement and to conduct the transition to the régime of so-called 'democracy', to manage the replacement of the Soviet Union by a new, more flexible dominion and to continue *'perestroika'* under 'non-Communism'. The first phase of the Yeltsin Government up to March 1993 involved cooperation with the Communist element.

At the same time as Yeltsin became President, Aleksandr Rutskoi was selected as Vice-President. Given his background as a military hero, this appointment was an indication that the strategists had in mind the possibility of exercising the option of a military/nationalist government, brought to power, perhaps, by a 'military coup'. Rutskoi had other qualifications for the leadership of such a government. As a Ukrainian, he would serve as a symbol of closer Russian-Ukrainian relations. He would also be a credible figure in fulfilling the rôles of slowing down the pace of 'reform' and bringing stability to Russia and to the other Republics. More important still, he would symbolise the support of the military for the government, would strengthen the Russian army and would overtly maintain the status of the country as a military 'superpower'.

It is possible that, his health permitting, Yeltsin, much like Gorbachëv, might eventually become another 'statesman in reserve', available to play a rôle in future strategic options. Gorbachëv may return to the Presidency in the future, if and when required by strategic considerations. The active involvement of the United States in the affairs of Russia and other Republics, without taking into consideration that they are all participants in their common long-range strategy, will ensure that US policies and policymakers remain captives of the Russian strategists. For these Russian strategists are in the business of exploiting calculated crises and manipulating the promotions and demotions of government leaders in order to shape American and Western responses to suit their strategic interests and purposes.

12 OCTOBER 1993 163

12 October 1993: The possibility that Yeltsin might be replaced in the next prearranged 'crisis' was discussed in my Memorandum dated 26 March 1993. In the event Yeltsin 'survived' and Rutskoi was required by the strategists to play a rôle as one of the leaders and symbols of the 'Communist old guard' in opposition to the 'democratic reformer', Yeltsin. The option of a military or military/nationalist government under a leader chosen by the strategists remains open for future application, as and when they so require.

Meanwhile the Yeltsin Government entered a second phase characterised by 'confrontation with Communists', beginning in March 1993 and reaching a climax with the dissolution of Parliament in September and then the staging of a new type of 'Reichstag Fire' when the 'White House' was bombarded in October. This provocation was carried out in front of the television cameras and with the understanding and support of the Western democracies. Among the more conspicuous indicators that the events were staged were:

○ The non-involvement of the masses on either side in Moscow, let alone anywhere else in Russia.
○ The apparent relaxation of security in Moscow on the day before the attack on the 'White House' which enabled demonstrators to breach the cordon round the 'White House' and launch their attack on the television station. This relaxation was deliberately misrepresented as a consequence of Yeltsin's restraint.
○ The timing of the events so that they coincided with the meetings of the Group of Seven, the World Bank and the International Monetary Fund in Washington.
○ The presence in the United States, at the time, of the Russian Foreign Minister, Andrei Kozyrev, and the Russian Patriarch who was recalled to Moscow to act as 'mediator'[58]. Kozyrev's presence enabled him to influence the US Administration's reaction to the provocation. It followed the pattern set by the presence in the United States during the 'confrontation' in March 1993 of Zorkin, head of the Russian 'equivalent' of the US Supreme Court. Zorkin, too, interpreted developments in Russia for the benefit of the US media and was then 'abruptly recalled' to Moscow.

The 'White House' provocation[59] has provided the strategists with a pretext for reasserting control from the centre, while symbolically destroying some of the 'last vestiges of Communism' and proceeding with elections and constitution-making – through which their influence and that of the Communists will become stronger, though still not visible[60]. Yeltsin, for his part, will appear, for the time being, to be taking steps to improve his tarnished 'democratic' image in order to continue to extract Western aid and expand Moscow's partnership with the United States.

The emergence of Zhirinovskiy was not a spontaneous political development. Solzhenitsyn was right when he said recently that someone created Zhirinovskiy as a deliberate caricature of a Russian nationalist. Solzhenitsyn did not explain who that someone was or what his purposes were. In my view, the strategists created Zhirinovskiy with two aims in mind: to forestall the emergence of uncontrolled ultra-nationalism in Russia, and to use the fear of the so-called 'Zhirinovskiy factor' for strategic purposes. The West is alarmed by Zhirinovskiy but fails to spot the use that is being made of him, for example, by Yeltsin on his recent visit to Germany when he referred obliquely to Zhirinovskiy when demanding a special place for Russia within the forum of the Group of Seven. ∎

58 *Author's Note:* In all probability, the Patriarch travelled to the United States specifically so that he could be recalled, his recall being noticed and publicised by the Western media.
59 *Editor's Note:* The ['Black and] White House' provocation, or new type of 'Reichstag Fire', also served to prove to the strategists that they could even go so far as to stage the televised bombardment of the very symbol of 'democracy', and yet retain the globally publicised and enthusiastically dispensed support of the leaders of the West. As the Author accurately advised the CIA in his Memorandum dated 26 August 1991, following the fake 'August coup' [*see pages 141-144*], **'Western euphoria and naïveté serve only to encourage the Soviet strategists to stage new spectacles more convinced than ever that their strategic designs are realistic'**. This dangerous precedent has again shown that there may scarcely be any lengths to which the strategists can go which the West will not support – a hazardous state of affairs, since both provocateurs and provocatees could overreach themselves.
60 *Editor's Note:* Not long after the 'Reichstag Fire' provocation, the Russian Government was packed with overt ('former') Communists.

Memorandum to the CIA: 30 APRIL 1993

For the attention of : The Director of Central Intelligence

A WARNING OF THE PERILS OF PARTNERSHIP
WITH RUSSIAN 'REFORMERS' AND 'DEMOCRATS'

The Clinton Administration has adopted a policy of partnership with the 'Russian reformers' led by Boris Yeltsin. **Superficially the policy is highly attractive in the short run and the President has argued with conviction that it will serve the interests of the United States. In the longer run, however, it spells disaster.** This is because US policymakers , having taken on trust statements by former Soviet leaders particularly on military matters, ignore certain fundamental realities, namely:

    1. As this analyst has persistently maintained *for thirty years,* the Soviets elaborated and adopted a long-term political strategy during the period 1957 to 1960 which they have pursued consistently to the present day.

    2. The present generation of Russian leaders including Gorbachëv, Yeltsin, Rutskoi and Ruslan Khasbulatov, were all committed to this strategy and were actively involved in pursuing different aspects of it. If any one of them had become a genuine democrat, he would have been regarded as a traitor to the cause and the strategy which serves it, and he would not have survived physically.

    3. Since the Communist Party first came into existence, certain important members of it have concealed their allegiance to it, the better to serve the cause. Early instances include the pre-revolutionary activities of Stalin, Maksim Litvinov and Leonid Krassin who, with Lenin's approval, used clandestine methods to raise funds for the Party.

    4. To a varying extent, contemporary Russian leaders have adopted the guise of 'reformers', 'democrats','non-Communists' and even 'anti-Communists'. This has enabled them to persuade Western governments and public opinion that there has been a genuine revolution in Russia – whereas in fact the same government élite is in power as in 1984. There has been no true discontinuity, no 'Break with the Past'.

    The 65 million or more former Communist Party and Komsomol members did not disappear or change their views overnight. The Party operated underground for *fifteen years* before the October Revolution and *again during the Second World War in German-occupied Soviet territory.*

    For example, Kiril Mazurov, who later became a member of the Politburo, ran a secret wartime Party Committee in Belorussia. For over seventy years the CPSU led the world's Communist Parties both legal *and illegal.* **The Party did not lose its expertise in underground work:** it retains *its capacity to operate effectively behind the scenes in a pseudo-democratic system* as well as openly.

    5. Following advice provided by Lenin in his *'Left-wing Communism: an Infantile Disorder'* that the Communists should project an image of moderation and avoid revolutionary phraseology, *the Russian leaders have assumed different political colours.* This has enabled them to stage spurious disputes and confrontations between themselves in order to suit the needs of their common strategy and tactics and, specifically, to extract significant aid and concessions from the West.

6. The West has failed to perceive how political 'crises' in Russia have been used to drum up Western support for the 'survival' first, of Gorbachëv and later, of Yeltsin ahead of summit meetings or at other moments of decision concerning the provision of Western aid for Russia and ahead of key decisions involving NATO.

7. An essential component in promoting Western misconceptions about Russian realities and long-term ambitions is the successful Russian manipulation of the Western media through Russian experts and agents of influence like Georgiy Arbatov and his cohorts who emerge during Russian political 'crises' and 'confrontations', and interpret them for the Western public.

8. The West has failed to learn the lesson of history that Western aid to Communist Russia has invariably been shortsighted and has consistently disappointed the hopes and expectations of its sponsors. For instance:

○ German financial and logistical help for Lenin during the First World War was gladly accepted and used by Lenin for Party purposes. The October Revolution helped to knock Russia out of the war to the advantage of the Germans; but within two years Lenin was engaged in fomenting revolution in Germany.

○ Food aid delivered to Russia by the American Relief Administration in the 1920s, when Russians were genuinely starving, was diverted on a grand scale to the Party and the GPU State Political Directorate, successor of the Cheka[61].

○ German military aid to the USSR following the Rapallo Treaty of 1922 helped to build up Soviet military industry and the Soviet Army which defeated the Germans in the Second World War.

○ Lend-lease and allied collaboration with the USSR during the Second World War did not alter Stalin's expansionist objectives: *on the contrary the alliance and its victory were exploited by him for the purpose of taking over Eastern Europe after the war.*

Similarly, current and future Western aid for Russia will fail to deflect the Russian leaders from their long-term objectives of world hegemony which they will continue to pursue in concert with the Communist Chinese.

While US policymakers are mobilising massive Western support for Russia and building up optimistic expectations of the future for democracy there, the same Soviet strategists as before are quietly carrying out their strategy. As this analyst has argued in previous Memoranda and publicly in *'New Lies for Old'*, the late Academician Sakharov under the guise of a 'dissident' was used as an unofficial mouthpiece of the former Soviet régime before being officially 'rehabilitated' and lionised under Gorbachëv's *'perestroika'*. In the late 1960s he went some way towards expressing publicly the essence of Soviet strategy, though without revealing that the developments he foresaw were deliberately planned. He predicted that in the period 1968 to

---

61 *Editor's Note:* Diversion of foodstuffs and medical supplies distributed in bulk by the West has been taking place under some of the 'post'-Communist régimes on a routine basis. In Washington, the Editor was told that the attitude adopted by a State Department official when asked about this problem was as follows: 'We know they are corrupt, but they have only just emerged from Communism, so this generation doesn't know any better. Our hope is that the next generation will not be corrupt'.

1980 'a growing ideological struggle in the socialist countries between Stalinist and Maoist forces on the one hand and the realistic forces of leftist Leninist Communist (and leftist Westerners) on the other will lead… in the Soviet Union… first to a multi-Party system and acute ideological struggle and discussions and then to the ideological victory of the [Leninist] realists, affirming the policy of increasing peaceful coexistence, strengthening democracy and expanding economic reforms'.

The period 1972 to 1985 would be characterised by pressure from the progressive forces in the West combining with pressure from the example of the socialist countries to implement a programme of convergence with socialism, **'i.e., social progress, peaceful coexistence and collaboration with socialism on a world scale and changes in the structure of ownership**. This phase includes an expanded rôle for the intelligentsia and an attack on the forces of racism and militarism'. In 1972 to 1990, 'the Soviet Union and the United States, having overcome their alienation, solve the problem of saving the poorer half of the world… At the same time disarmament will proceed'. In 1980 to 2,000, 'socialist convergence will reduce differences in social structure, promote intellectual freedom, science and economic progress, and lead to the creation of a World Government and the smoothing of national contradictions'.

All Sakharov's main predictions have so far been fulfilled with the exception of Russian-American partnership in solving the problem of the poorer half of the world and the creation of a World Government. What Sakharov, like the present Russian leaders, clearly had in mind was *East-West convergence on socialist terms* leading to World Government dominated by the Russians and the Chinese.

But ignoring the long-term strategy behind developments in Russia, US policymakers have plunged into partnership with the so-called 'Russian reformers' without realising where this partnership is intended by them to lead[62].

Sakharov foresaw World Government by the year 2000. The question may indeed be on the agenda within the next seven years. Within that period, if present trends continue, Russia, with Western help, may well be on the road to a technological revolution surpassing the Chinese Communist 'economic miracle' without loss of political control by the present governing élite of 'realistic Leninists'.

A campaign for a new system of World Government will be launched at Summit level and will be accompanied by pressure from below, the active use of agents of influence and secret assassinations of leaders who are seen as obstacles[63]. The campaign will come as a surprise to the US Administration. In the ensuing negotiations, the US President of the day will find himself facing combined pressure from the Russians and the Chinese. The Chinese will by then have adopted a 'reformed', pseudo-democratic system. In the course of the negotiations the Russians and the

---

62 *Editor's Note:* Penetration *en masse* by the 'ex'-Soviet Republics of the international institutions – the United Nations, the World Bank, the International Monetary Fund, prospectively even the European Union – will survive the *de facto* extinguishing of the national Republics' false political 'independence'. The model for this is the UN membership of Byelorussia and Ukraine despite their inclusion within the USSR. On 13 December 1994, *'The Independent'*, London, reminded its readers that 'three months ago, Yevgeniy Primakov, the head of the Russian Foreign Intelligence Service, said in Moscow that, apart from the three Baltic Republics, the other 12 former Republics which belonged to the Soviet Union would largely reunite'.

63 The Author's observations on the KGB's use of assassination are given in *Note 64 on page 168*.

Chinese will begin to reveal their true colours, their fundamental antagonism to the free world and the threat they represent to it. **The US policy of partnership with Russia will be exposed as bankrupt.** Internally in the United States this will lead to divisions, recriminations and a search for scapegoats. Externally, the reputation of the United States as the leader of the free world will be irreparably damaged and its alliances, particularly with countries like Japan which have been pressured into helping the Russians out, will be jeopardised.

The US President will find himself without the finest armed services in the world. Reformed and cut back by budget reductions based on mistaken assessments of long-term threats, the services will be equipped for handling regional conflicts but will be unprepared for global confrontation.

US intelligence and counter-intelligence, if they survive, will have lost any remaining effectiveness from continuing financial pressure and a campaign of revisionist allegations like those that the CIA and the FBI were involved respectively in the assassinations of President Kennedy and Dr Martin Luther King.

Too late it will be realised that there have been no equivalent reductions in the power and effectiveness of the Russian and Chinese armed forces or their intelligence and security services. A real swing in the balance of power in favour of a Sino-Soviet alliance *vis-à-vis* the free world will have taken place giving the Russians and Chinese a preponderant share in setting up the new World Government system and leaving the West with little choice but to compete with them in designing the New World Social Order. If the Russian leaders continue to demonstrate to the Russian people that they can successfully extract Western aid and contribute to signs of economic progress, the Russian people will follow them and, like the Chinese, will end up laughing with their leaders at the folly of the West. ■

Note 64: **GOLITSYN ON POLITICAL ASSASSINATION**

The Author's remarks on the use of political assassination by the KGB were published in *'New Lies for Old'*, pages 352-354, in the context of his analysis of the attempted assassination of Pope John Paul II. Whereas [*see page 117 of the present work*], Golitsyn raises the possibility that Pope John Paul II's predecessor, a great and humble Christian, was murdered, he does not believe that the KGB attempted to murder Pope John Paul. In giving his reasons for this assessment, he also explained the circumstances in which Soviet intelligence would assassinate a leader, and mentioned methods by which they might achieve such an outcome. Assassination might be used...

‘ **A.** ... if a Western leader, who is a recruited Soviet agent, is threatened in office by a political rival. This is based on a statement made by **Vladimir Zhenikhov**, a former KGB *Rezident* in Finland. He stated that if his agent, holding a high office, was threatened by an anticommunist Social Democrat during the elections, the latter would be poisoned by a trusted KGB agent.

B. If a Western leader became a serious obstacle to Communist strategy and to the strategic disinformation program, he would be quietly poisoned at a Summit Meeting during negotiations or while visiting a Communist country, since *détente* provides such opportunities in abundance.

The practical lesson here is that a Western leader who is involved in furthering an effective counterstrategy against the Communists should not visit Communist countries or take part in any Summit Meetings with their leaders.

The technique [used] for a poisoning was described in a statement made by a KGB General, **Zheleznyakov**, at an operational conference of senior officers of Soviet intelligence in 1953 in Moscow. Zheleznyakov stated that the major requirement for success is mere physical contact with the target, as the Soviet service has technical means (special poisons) to bring about death without leaving traces of the poison, so that death will be attributed to natural causes.

[Assassination may also be contemplated] if a leader's assassination provides the opportunity for a controlled Soviet agent to take over the position. According to **Nikolay Levinov**, a KGB adviser in Czechoslovakia, this rationale was used by both the Soviet and the Czech services in the assassination of President Benes, thus vacating a place for a Communist leader, Klement Gottwald ‘.

In addition to these circumstances, assassination of Communist rivals was practiced under Stalin. However given that the struggle for power in the Party leadership ceased with the adoption of the common long-range strategy, the Author explained in *'New Lies for Old'* that he did not think this rationale was now in use. Concerning the attempted assassination of Pope John Paul II, the Author pointed out that, given the arguments addressing Polish developments in *'New Lies for Old'*, especially those revealing Solidarity to be a product of 'mature socialism', it was clear that there was no motive for such an assassination by the KGB and their Communist intelligence partners. The accuracy of this assessment has recently been confirmed by General Volkogonov, who has written that *'perestroika'* would not have been possible without a secret understanding between Gorbachëv, Jaruzelski and the Pope. In any case, the KGB was not a primitive and inefficient service which would resort to the use of the Bulgarian service to recruit a killer for hire, especially since the killer in question had previously murdered a 'progressive' editor in Turkey.

‘ ... The KGB is always apprehensive about using escapees, suspecting the possibility of their being police *provocateurs*. The KGB would not consider such a candidate, unknown to them and over whom they had no control, for an operation of such importance and sensitivity.

If the Soviet strategists had reason for such assassinations, they would not attempt to act through the Bulgarian service. More likely, the KGB would undertake such a mission through their trusted illegals or through opportunities available to the Polish service. It is well known that the Pope maintains a vast staff of secretaries and kitchen help, almost all consisting of Polish nationals. He further receives visitors from Poland. The Polish security service, through its antireligious department, would study the relatives of people on the Pope's staff and would use them as hostages in the preparation of such an operation'. It would all be done quietly and secretly.

In any case, 'there is also a serious contradiction in the actions of the Polish and Soviet Governments regarding this affair. If the Soviet Government perceives the Pope as an anticommunist involved in subversive activities against Poland and other Communist countries, as implied in a TASS statement, it is incongruous that the Polish Government would invite the Pope to visit Poland in June of 1983, since all such matters are coordinated with the Soviets ‘.

Any truly conservative leader who achieves power and seeks to frustrate Russian and Chinese long-range strategy should take appropriate precautions. ■

APPENDIX

EXTRACTS FROM
Anatoliy Golitsyn's

MEMORANDA
TO THE CENTRAL
INTELLIGENCE AGENCY
Between 1973 and 1985

Predicting *'Perestroika'*

Memorandum to the CIA: **1973**

A CRITICAL REVIEW OF THREE RECENT BOOKS

**SOVIET STRATEGY FOR THE SEVENTIES: FROM COLD WAR
TO PEACEFUL COEXISTENCE, *1973***
By Foy D. Kohler, Mose L. Harvey, Leon Goure and Richard Soll

SCIENCE AND TECHNOLOGY AS AN INSTRUMENT OF SOVIET POLICY, *1972*
By Mose L. Harvey, Leon Goure and Vladimir Prokofieff

CONVERGENCE OF COMMUNISM AND CAPITALISM: THE SOVIET VIEW,*1973*
By Leon Goure, Foy D. Kohler, Richard Soll and Annette Stiefbold
[Center for Advanced International Studies, University of Miami].

EXTRACTS FROM THE AUTHOR'S 1973 MEMORANDUM:

' …What is crucial is that conventional Communist methods and tactics have changed and the authors' presentation does not reflect that change. The change is so radical that it may be called a shift in methods and tactics.

The new tactics consist of the introduction of an activist style in the exploitation of existing contradictions and the provocation and exploitation of new conflicts in non-Communist countries; also of the active use of the Bloc's intelligence potential and of disinformation to facilitate the implementation of Bloc policy.

These changes in style and tactics have been determined by Lenin's concept of an active change in the balance between the two systems and by the Bloc's strategy based on this concept.

This determined the two main methods and principles for accomplishing a change in the balance between the two systems:

(a) An active increase in its own capacity to expand its own potentials;

(b) A simultaneous reduction of the adversary's capacity.

Thus, the basic element in Lenin's concept is not peaceful coexistence but the struggle with, and the undermining of, the adversary. Therefore it is viewed by the Communist leaders as an undeclared war between the potentials of the two camps.

And it should be pointed out in this connection that the authors failed to include in their collection on Soviet strategy Khrushchev's statement on the Bloc's potential made in public in January 1958. Khrushchev spoke of the significance of the political, economic and psychological potentials of the Bloc. He emphasised that all these potentials are interlocked in their practical activity. Since the main objective of the strategy is a change in the balance, it has determined and added a new dimension to conventional methods and tactics which have become instruments for undermining the enemy's potentials and strengthening their own… '.

' … In accordance with the main objective of Bloc strategy to change the balance in the Communists' favour, Communist diplomacy has started to reduce Western (and especially US) military potential through a number of diplomatic agreements while at the same time accelerating the Communists' programme to increase their own military potential. Thus, the atomic test ban agreement, the Non-Proliferation Treaty and finally the SALT agreement have been concluded. The West has responded again to promote these agreements and the display of Sino-Soviet differences has acted as a catalyst here too.

In this connection it should be pointed out that there has been a rather strange coincidence in the increase of alleged Sino-Soviet differences on the eve of and during the Soviet-American negotiations of the agreements mentioned above… '.

'… One can also expect a concealed Communist offensive through their agents of influence to exert influence on the American public in order further to undermine the establishment, especially the Pentagon, the so-called "military-industrial complex" and the American Special Services; and further to reduce the authority of the President in the military field and to reduce expenditure on defence using the controversial points in the recent Soviet-American agreements.

One can also expect concealed Communist attempts to intensify their influence in the United States and thus oblige the United States to withdraw from overseas involvements.

At the end of the decade, one can further expect operations through new theories of convergence, from the Western and Communist sides (Academician Sakharov and others) *to justify the West's half-concealed surrender to the Communists.*

Because of these factors, Soviet-American military parity and the Bloc's offensive to gain superiority over the West through secret Sino-Soviet cooperation, the challenge for the West in the military arena looks grim… '.

' … The Soviet and Chinese rocket strike units and strategic bombers will make a surprise raid on Pearl Harbour lines on the main government and military headquarters of the leading Western countries and on their missile sites. The main idea will be to knock out the primary Western sources of retaliation and to paralyse, at least for a short period, their physical ability to take a decision on retaliation.

In their estimate, the Communist leaders may expect that the advantage of surprise, given that they will be in hiding in their secret government headquarters, will provide them with the opportunity to paralyse Western governments and military authorities with a good chance of avoiding any retaliation.

Such an approach was revealed by the KGB authorities in their academic estimate of steps which should be undertaken to change the political situation in West Germany and to prepare it for absorption into a socialist federation with East Germany. When questioned by the Soviet leaders, the KGB strategists answered that 150,000 of the ruling West German élite in the political, military and other spheres should be eliminated or removed. Such a surprise attack may be followed by a simultaneous use of 'hot lines' to confuse and frustrate any Western decision on retaliation and also by Communist radio announcements about the liquidation of "hotbeds of aggression" with their appeal to "the world" and to "the workers" of the main Western countries to commence immediate negotiations for the settlement of the conflict peacefully in order to avoid nuclear confrontation.

Such an attack will probably be accompanied by an intensification in the activity of the Communist countries' intelligence agents designed to increase panic in the West and to operate blackouts and paralyse normal life in the capitals of the Western countries. Such an attack and proposal to settle the conflict will probably also be accompanied by intensive activity by agents of influence in these countries, especially among the proponents of theories of the 'convergence' of the two systems – but this time on Communist terms, to emphasise the wisdom of settlement and by all possible means, in order to avoid nuclear conflict. The main argument of these agents of influence will probably be that in circumstances where the Communists have military superiority, it will be "better to be red than dead". Although, of course, this vision of a surprise attack on the West is the reviewer's speculation, it is his belief that it is definitely in the realm of possibility, given that it has been the subject of study by the KGB, and should in any case be prepared for…'.

' … The authors' conclusions and expectations that the Moscow Summit and the Soviet-American agreements represent "an important step forward in the very long, long process of developing a sounder base for Soviet-American relations, are completely unrealistic. The Communist threat has not diminished.

In fact, the Communist Bloc and its most serious offensive against the West in history present an increased threat and challenge for the West.

The present Communist threat cannot even be compared with the Soviet threat to the United States and NATO in the late forties and fifties for, at that time, the Communist régimes were in serious crisis and the United States had a nuclear near-monopoly. Now, however, the Communist Bloc has recovered from its crisis and has succeeded in switching the crisis to the non-Communist world.

Now the United States has lost military superiority, while the Communist Bloc has reached parity and is heading for military superiority itself…'.

' …A special project should be initiated by the West to study, for future counter-action, Communist disinformation, its political influence in the West, its techniques, its channels and its order of battle '.

' … One or two thousand new scientific and technical intelligence workers were chosen from young scientists and experienced KGB agents of the 'internal line' to become KGB officials in 1958-60. After training, they were placed under cover of the State Committee for Coordination of Technology and other organisations .

Certain factors determined the active rôle of the scientific and technical intelligence potential in Bloc policy:

(a) The Soviet experience in acquiring advanced technology from the West, especially from Germany during the period of the New Economic Policy period in the 1920s, and during the Second World War from American Lend-Lease;

(b) The experience of the Soviet intelligence service in the successful exercise of influence over the West through the participation of prominent Soviet scientists at Pugwash meetings and other international conferences during 1956-58, to ease the effect of American pressure on the socialist countries.

On the basis of this experience the use of Soviet and foreign scientists was intensified and they became active participants in the new strategy.

The Authors [*of the books reviewed: see page 170*] emphasise Soviet pronouncements during the 1967-72 period. This selection is really rather arbitrary. It takes the period out of context and treats it in isolation... Lenin's NEP, which is known for its significant rôle in the early stages of industrialisation and its contribution to military potential, is mentioned casually without showing the reader, on the basis of Lenin's pronouncements, its essence and connection with current Soviet strategy.

The selection does not include, for instance, Lenin's pronouncements on the New Economic Policy and Soviet concessions as the effective way to divide the United States, Germany, Britain, Japan, and France, to make them fight one another, and to exploit the differences between them to Soviet political, diplomatic and military advantage in order to weaken the capitalist system and change the correlation of forces in the Soviets' favour.

The selection does not include official material on Soviet operations to procure advanced technology from American, German and British firms like General Motors, Krupps, Metro-Vickers and others, or official data about the contribution of these firms to Soviet industrialisation and the creation of Soviet military industry.

Nor does the selection include the official Soviet Party assessment of Western businessmen and 'concessionaires' like **Averell Harriman** and **Armand Hammer** who dealt with the Soviet Union during the period of the New Economic Policy as "assistants in the construction of socialism in the USSR" [9].

Memorandum to the CIA: 1974

**A CRITIQUE OF MR JAMES SCHLESINGER'S ASSESSMENT OF THE SOVIET
CHALLENGE AND THE MILITARY POTENTIAL OF *DETENTE* BETWEEN
THE UNITED STATES AND THE SOVIET UNION, AND OF CERTAIN CHANGES
IN US MILITARY STRATEGY – IN THE LIGHT OF INSIDE INFORMATION
ON THE SITUATION IN THE COMMUNIST BLOC**

' In view of the Author's background and knowledge of Soviet realities, he
was asked to make a critique of Mr Schlesinger's statement and speeches on issues
concerning the United States' security and defence. The fundamental issue is how to
assess *détente* between the Soviet Union and the United States. In his assessment of
détente Mr Schlesinger points to its dual nature; while *détente* provides opportunities
for the improvement of relations between the two countries and hope for the future,
it also contains dangers inherent in the Soviet offensive to gain strategic advantages
over the United States and uncertainty over the intentions of Soviet leaders for the
future. Mr Schlesinger believes that *détente* can work if the United States continues to
take advantage of the opportunities which *détente* presents, and matches the Soviet
offensive to gain strategic advantages. It is his understanding that *détente* was undertaken successfully on the American initiative. On the basis of his conclusions about
the threat of growing Soviet military capacity and concerning the dangers of *détente*,
Mr Schlesinger suggests that *détente* can be cautiously continued while at the same
time some changes in US military strategy can be introduced... '.

'... To sum up, it can be said that any analysis which does not take into
account the existence of a long-range Communist strategy, its objectives, its active
employment of the Bloc's intelligence potential, and particularly its use of disinformation, cannot form the basis for rational decisions about *détente*, about Western
diplomacy, about US policies to maintain the Western alliance or about US military
strategy. This leads to the conclusion that a true appreciation of disinformation is the
key to the restoration of rational thinking so that rational changes in Western policy,
diplomacy and military strategy can be made. A true appreciation of disinformation
is also the key for restoring national cohesion and common purpose to the American
nation and for rebuilding the United States' relations with its allies in Western
Europe. The problem of disinformation is real and to ignore it is to permit events and
trends to continue to develop in an irrational direction.
Communist disinformation is important because it permits the Communist
leadership to exploit Western confusion while at the same time distorting the Communist challenge and methods, thereby preventing the West from viewing them
realistically. The rôle of Communist disinformation has not yet been fully recognised
nor has it been dealt with except on a piecemeal basis... The natural inclination of the
West is to see and judge opponents in the context of the Western system – an attitude
strengthened by Communist penetration in the West and by Communist activity to
maintain the disinformation offensive through new operations and deceptions. The
time has come for the United States to investigate and reconsider the situation '.

Memorandum to the CIA: **15 January 1978**

THE LONG-RANGE POLITICAL OBJECTIVES AND INTENTIONS OF THE SOVIET LEADERS: AN ASSESSMENT OF AN OFFICIAL REPORT BY A SOVIET EMIGRE IN THE LIGHT OF THE COMMUNIST BLOC'S LONG-RANGE STRATEGY AND ITS DISINFORMATION OFFENSIVE

⁶ At the time of the adoption of the long-range strategy in the period 1958 to 1960, there was strong internal opposition to the Soviet régime from dissatisfied workers, collective farmers, intellectuals, clergy, Ukrainian, Latvian, Lithuanian and Jewish nationalists etc. These oppositionists did not call themselves "dissidents" and nor did the KGB call them "dissidents".

On the contrary, the KGB and the Party referred to them as "enemies of the régime."... The KGB was instructed to adopt new methods to deal with this opposition, based on the experience of the GPU (the Soviet political police) under Dzerzhinskiy in the 1920s...

This entailed the creation of a false opposition in the USSR and other countries... The current "dissident movement" is just such a false opposition designed and created by the KGB....

The main objectives which the Soviet rulers are trying to achieve through the "dissident movement" are as follows:

(a) To confuse, neutralise and dissolve the *true* internal political opposition in the Union of Soviet Socialist Republics;

(b) To prevent the West from reaching the genuine internal opposition in the USSR, by **introducing to the West a false KGB-controlled opposition**. This explains the easy access of the Western media to the alleged "dissidents";

(c) To influence the foreign policy of the United States through the "dissidents' in the interests of the Communist long-range strategy and exploit this issue in the strategy's final phase ⁹.

⁶ ... Another significant disinformation theme is the alleged existence of "hidden liberals" in the Party establishment. For example, Aleksey Rumyantsev has been described as a liberal. In fact, he is a hardcore Communist who has always worked in the field of ideology. For a number of years after 1958 he was an editor of the international Communist journal *'Problems of Peace and Socialism'*.

Because of his position and experience, he was deeply involved in the development of the new strategy and deceptive tactics.

This explains why he is now being misrepresented as a liberal. A similar case is that of an important official who served as a case officer concerned with the penetration of a leading Western intelligence service before, during and after the Second World War, who is now being misrepresented as a liberal in the Party establishment.

The scale of disinformation on these lines may be expected to increase and new "defectors" may be expected to provide such disinformation ⁹.

'... This analyst has reached the following conclusions about probable developments in the USSR:

(a) One can expect the introduction of economic reforms; which will have similarities to Yugoslav or even Western socialist practice.... .

(b) Liberalisation of the Soviet régime on the lines of the Czechoslovak liberalisation of 1968, including an apparent curtailing of the monopoly of the Communist Party, an apparent separation of the legislative, executive and judicial powers, an increased rôle for the Soviet parliament, 'reform' of the KGB, an amnesty for "dissidents", greater artistic and cultural freedom and freedom to travel, compliance with the Helsinki agreements and the emergence of a younger Party leader to initiate the reforms....

(c) Similar reforms in Eastern Europe including the return of Dubcek in Czechoslovakia and perhaps the demolition of the Berlin Wall...

(d) The liberalisation will, however, be false and will be aimed at breaking up NATO and dismantling the US "military-industrial complex" in the first instance. The new liberal image will be exploited by East Germany politically and diplomatically against West Germany to establish their political confederation...

(e) The deceptive liberalisation will be accepted as genuine and spontaneous and will be blown up out of all proportion by the media...

(f) It may generate pressure for real *détente* and far-reaching changes in Western societies...'.

'... The main objectives of the disinformation which is coming from Brezhnev and his Soviet policymakers are:

(a) To reconfirm for US policymakers the essence of the larger Communist disinformation theme that the Communist Bloc does not exist and that Communist ideology is dead;

(b) To conceal the existing secret coordination between the Communist states and Communist Parties in the non-Communist world in the implementation of their long-range strategy in its final phase;

(c) To reconfirm on this basis to US policymakers the correctness of the US *détente* with the USSR and the correctness of US support for the Soviet "dissidents" as the viable way to bring about the internal liberalisation of the Soviet régime; and, finally:

(d) To prepare US policymakers psychologically for a favourable response to the false liberalisation when it comes.

Since this liberalisation in the USSR will be calculated, false and controlled, the conclusion can be drawn that the main purpose of the disinformation is to influence the US response to the coming false liberalisation in the USSR in the interests of their long-range strategy in the final phase.

The arrival of other high-level Soviet "defectors" or "official émigrés" can be expected, armed with similar disinformation to influence US foreign policy along these lines '.

❛ ... Over the past fifteen years this analyst, in oral and written reports to the CIA and other Western services, has described various aspects of the Communist Bloc's long-range strategy, the new political rôle of the KGB and the rôle of disinformation... The West and its scholars underestimate the gravity of the Communist threat which is more serious than after the Second World War when the United States had a nuclear near-monopoly... Communist ideology is alive again and the Communist world is on the political, economic and diplomatic offensive against the West in the framework of their long-range strategy...

All means are used in the battle, legal and illegal; that is why they have resorted to the use of disinformation on an unusually large scale, which throws a completely new light on their *détente*, on their attempt to change the military balance in their favour and, which is most important of all, on their intentions...❜.

❛ ... A crisis in US foreign policy has been building up since the adoption of the Communist Bloc's long-range strategy because of the West's inability to understand and interpret the true meaning of events in the Communist world. The crisis is hidden, unrecognised... Now the situation is complicated by the activist approach of the Carter Administration to diplomacy towards the USSR, China and Eastern Europe and in seeking solutions to existing conflicts on the basis of misconceptions. An attempt is being made to bring about liberalisation in the USSR without realising the existence of Communist strategy and disinformation and, for example, the falsity of the KGB-controlled "dissident movement"... In this way, a trap is being laid by the Communist policymakers which will be exploited when the USSR carries out a deceptive liberalisation of its régime...❜.

❛ ... The problems associated with the new Communist tactics, of the political use of their intelligence potential, their agents of influence and their disinformation, have not been dealt with properly for the last eighteen years, and their priority has not been recognised.

The US, British and French counter-intelligence services have been impaired by reorganisation and KGB penetration. Counter-intelligence has a key rôle to play in understanding and dealing with the new dimensions of the Communist threat, **since this entails an analysis of US and other sources of information on Communist developments and of how they might have been compromised by penetration or otherwise exploited by the KGB for disinformation purposes...**

A special committee or group of qualified and reliable people should be set up by the US Government to study this problem. The project should be approved by the President and should be directly under him. The heads of the Senate Intelligence and Foreign Relations Committees, the Senate and House leaders of both parties and the Attorney General should be told and consulted about this project in advance...

A confidential project along these lines was in preparation at this analyst's suggestion under the late French President Pompidou. President Pompidou was a scholar who had read Lenin's and Mao's works and Sun Tzu's treatise on 'The Art of War' which dealt with disinformation and its patterns. When President Pompidou died the project was cancelled. **But the point is, if the French could recognise the**

**challenge, why cannot the Americans? No other Western government has the
capability to make such a reassessment.**

This analyst wishes to conclude with the request that, if something happens to
him, this analysis and his suggestions should be treated as his political will and testament... One can ignore the analysis and suggestions for a time but one will be forced
by future developments to come back to them and start rethinking the unthinkable,
though under less favourable conditions. The Communist challenge and threat will be
the major preoccupation of US foreign policy for the years ahead '. ∎

Memorandum to the CIA: 11 FEBRUARY 1982

For the attention of: The Honorable William Casey, Director of Central Intelligence

AN ANALYSIS OF DEVELOPMENTS IN POLAND
IN THE LIGHT OF COMMUNIST STRATEGY

[The Author requested the distribution of this Memorandum to Mr Clark, National Security Adviser, Secretary of State Alexander Haig and Secretary of Defense Weinberger. The Memorandum also requested direct or indirect support for publication of the analysis in *'Foreign Affairs'*, along the lines of Mr Kennan's article published in 1947 and signed by *'X'*].

' … There are strong indications that the formation and functioning of Solidarity during the period 1980-81 took place with the full participation of the Polish Communist Party and under its direction. It was revealed by Kania himself that there are one million Party members in Solidarity. It is also known that 40 of the 200 members of the Central Committee of the Polish Communist Party in 1981 were also members of Solidarity. Party officials were in the leadership of Solidarity right from its formation and continued so throughout 1980 and 1981. In fact one of the officials, Bogdan Lis, a member of the Central Committee of the Polish Communist Party, was number two to Walesa himself. One of the female Solidarity leaders was Zofia Gryzb, a Communist Party Politburo member. The conclusion that **Solidarity is the brainchild of the Communist Party** is supported by the following:

(a) The recognition by Solidarity of *the leading rôle of the Party;*
(b) The Party's recognition of Solidarity;
(c) The pro-Solidarity statements of Kania and Moczar;
(d) The access enjoyed by Solidarity to the *fully controlled* media…'.

' … Walesa's extensive travels and his contacts with Japanese, French, Italian and American trade unions were not objected to by the Polish Communist Party… The Polish ambassador in Tokyo, who recently defected[65], revealed that he had assisted in organising Walesa's visit and contacts with Japanese trade unions… '.

' … As the key figure who guided the security service in the preparation of the false opposition in the 1970s, Kania was made Party leader to conduct the practical introduction of the 'renewal' during its initial phase in 1980-81. It was only logical that the Defence Minister, Jaruzelski, should replace Kania as Party leader during the political consolidation of the 'renewal', in order to keep it under control.

Following the same reasoning and dialectic of the strategy, one can expect

65 *Editor's Note:* Zdzislaw M. Rurarz, the former Polish Ambassador to Japan who defected to the United States in 1981, writes a column in *'The Washington Inquirer'*, published weekly by The Council for the Defense of Freedom, Washington DC.

that during the next period the coalition government which would include the Party, Solidarity and the Church, will display the semblance of a social democratic structure. It is possible that some alleged Party liberals will be appointed as new Party leaders and representatives of the government.

As for the visits of Kania and other Polish leaders to Moscow and the 'surprise visits' of the late Suslov and Gromyko to Poland in April and July 1981, these visits should be viewed not as visits involving the exertion of pressure but as visits for the coordination of the 'renewal' within the broader strategy.

In view of this evidence, the Polish 'renewal' is neither spontaneous nor promising... **It is the product of twenty years of preparation with the purpose of broadening the political base of the Communist Party in the trade unions.** It is an attempt to turn the narrow élitist dictatorship of the Party into *a Leninist dictatorship of the whole working class* and to make the trade unions politically active against the capitalist West. It is not the end of Communism, but a creative development effected in accordance with the teaching of Lenin...'.

'... The primary internal objectives of the 'renewal' are:

(a) To influence the non-Communist workers and the Poles in general in favour of the renewed Party and its direction;

(b) To complete the acceptance of the Communist régime;

(c) To reach and influence the large Polish population abroad, and to reverse its strong anti-Communist position.

The Soviet military manoeuvres around Poland should be viewed as an act of intimidation of the population in Poland and East Germany and also as securing the smooth introduction of the 'renewal' and most importantly preventing the emergence of a genuine anti-Communist movement during the 'renewal'. The primary strategic objectives of the 'renewal' are as follows:

(a) To confuse Western governments and their policymakers as well as the leadership of the political parties, especially the conservatives, and to discredit them as leaders [*by 'revealing' their opposition to Communism to be misplaced*];

(b) To exploit this confusion by depriving the Western leaders of the support they need from free trade unions, social democrats and Catholics, and to manipulate these forces against Western interests. They hope to establish solidarity and unity of action with these groups to achieve the replacement of NATO and the Warsaw Pact by a neutral socialist Europe based on collective security and to further the neutralisation of Germany and the American withdrawal from Europe...

(c) To have the Polish Communist 'renewal' paid for by the West by writing off Polish indebtedness and generating a new 'Marshall Plan' for the renewed Polish régime [*1994: much of Poland's remaining external debt has duly been written off*].

One can expect the Polish 'renewal' to be broadened to Romania, East Germany, Bulgaria and the USSR... The new circumstances will be exploited by the Communists to launch the final offensive for the execution of their strategies...'. ∎

Memorandum to the CIA: **12 December 1983**

For the attention of: The Director of Central Intelligence

THE RISK TO PRESIDENT REAGAN'S LIFE[66]

⁶ This analyst feels obliged to express concern and to warn that President Reagan may be risking his life by planning a visit to Communist China in April 1984.

Any Western leader who becomes a serious obstacle to Communist strategy may be secretly assassinated during an official visit to a Communist country, the USSR or China. His death would be attributed to natural causes such as age or a heart ailment etc. In this analyst's opinion, the President would be perceived by the Communist strategists as the only Western leader who has developed a successful military counter-strategy against the USSR.

They would consider his removal an advantage if it would interrupt that strategy. This analyst therefore requests your assistance in bringing this warning to the attention of the President and his security advisers.

In this connection, this analyst would like to draw attention to the death of the late French President, Georges Pompidou, shortly after his state visit to China, when he acquired, naturally or unnaturally, an unusual form of cancer.

It is this analyst's understanding that, at the time, President Pompidou had begun to take account of Communist strategic disinformation, of the possibility that the Sino-Soviet 'split' was a joint operation, and that there was secret Sino-Soviet collaboration. If so, and if the President's thinking had become known to the Soviets through their sources in Western Europe, they could have perceived him as a threat to their strategy. In that event, his visit to China would have been a grave mistake.

Attention should also be drawn to the sudden death of the late Indian Premier, Lal Bahadur Shastri, allegedly from a heart attack during his visit to Tashkent to negotiate with the Pakistani leaders in 1965. In this analyst's opinion, the physical removal of Shastri might have been considered to be in the interests of the USSR since his only likely successor was **the pro-Soviet Mrs Indira Gandhi.**

Since Western analysts believe that the Sino-Soviet split is genuine and therefore discount the likelihood of secret Sino-Soviet collaboration, the Soviets would assess their chances of getting away with a secret assassination in China as good.

President Reagan's forthcoming visit cannot be compared with President Nixon's visit to China in 1972. The Communist strategic motive then was to involve President Nixon in political *détente* and accommodation simultaneously with China and the USSR, and to induce him, a leading exponent of anti-Communism, to abandon the anti-Communist element in US foreign policy.

The Communist leaders would have regarded him as an unwitting asset in implementing their strategy, since he accepted the Sino-Soviet split as genuine ⁹. ■

---

66 See *Note 64* on political assassination, *page 168.*

Memorandum to the CIA: 4 JULY 1984

SOVIET STRATEGIC INTENTIONS AND THE
FORTHCOMING U.S. PRESIDENTIAL ELECTION

I. This analyst's book ['*New Lies for Old*'][67] contains an analysis of Soviet strategy and its objectives *vis-à-vis* the United States, NATO and the political parties in the United States and Western Europe. **It predicts that the Communist leaders are preparing to introduce false controlled liberalisation and economic 'reform' to achieve their strategic objectives.**

In essence, they expect to further their influence abroad and especially in Western Europe by replacing the discredited Soviet model with a new, more liberal and attractive one along the lines of the Dubcek model. As explained in the book, the Soviet leaders tie the success of their strategy to the support of leftist and reformist circles in the United States.

This analysis leads to the following assessment of Soviet strategic intentions during the Presidential election period:

(a) The Soviet strategists are concerned that the present successful US policy of restoring its military strength may continue during a second Reagan term.

(b) The Soviet strategists are also concerned that their so-called 'liberalisation' may not succeed under the re-elected President in terms of a favourable response from him towards disarmament, the neutralisation of Germany, and economic aid and credits for their 'liberalised' régime.

Thus, they have mobilised a determined attempt to influence the US Presidential election and to undercut and embarrass the present Administration. This intent is evident from their confrontational position, in their refusal to participate in missile negotiations or the Olympic Games, and from their detention of US diplomats in Moscow.

Other indications of the campaign include the visit to the United States by their leading strategist on American affairs, **Georgiy Arbatov**, and a delegation of ten prominent Soviet journalists. Soviet use of Sakharov is part of the operation. In the past, Sakharov's views were injected to influence the outcome of the SALT negotiations and the development of the nuclear freeze movement in the West.

Now they are being used to lure conservative politicians into a trap and to build up the position of Soviet agents of influence in the West.

2. One can expect that the efforts of the Soviet strategists to influence the US Presidential elections may reach their culmination in September or October 1984 when they will attempt to embarrass the President during the negotiations for a summit, depicting him as intransigent. More important, however, they may attempt to influence the outcome by calculated changes in the Soviet leadership.

---

67 *Joint Note:* The Author had completed '*New Lies for Old*', with its remarkable predictions, as early as 1980; but it was not published until 1984. The CIA was fully informed about the book.

The Soviet strategists may replace the old leader, **Konstantin Chernenko**, who is actually only a figurehead, with a younger Soviet leader who was chosen some time ago as his successor – namely, **Comrade Gorbachëv. One of Gorbachëv's primary tasks will be to carry out the so-called liberalisation.** The strategists may also replace the old 'hardliner' **Andrei Gromyko** with a younger 'soft-liner'; and they may also elevate a woman into the Soviet leadership.

The new Soviet leadership may launch economic 'reform' and some striking political initiatives to project a clear message that the changes in the Soviet leadership and Soviet policy require changes in US leadership, US military policy and the US budget. Inasmuch as both conservatives and liberals are confused by strategic disinformation concerning Soviet intentions, these Soviet manoeuvres, assisted by the Communists' agents of influence, could succeed. ■

Memorandum to the CIA: JANUARY 1985

UNDERSTANDING THE NEW ACTIVE METHODS THEY ARE USING

COMMUNIST POLITICAL ACTIVISM AND NEW METHODS

❛ ... The basic change which has taken place involves the introduction of a creative approach combined with intensified political activism. This combination has been introduced throughout all spheres of Communist activity:

○ Within the Communist movement itself, instead of the monolithic Comintern of Stalin's days, the strategists have introduced false splits while at the same time stepping up their secret coordination. Instead of glorifying the USSR as in the past, the Communists now allow calculated criticism of Soviet practices. Instead of isolation as in earlier periods, they are involved in making political alliances with socialist parties and trade unions in the West.

○ In economic affairs, the Communists, and particularly the Chinese, have resorted to the calculated introduction of capitalism to revive their economies and to acquire Western credits and technology using Lenin's New Economic Policy tactic as a model for action.

○ In the diplomatic arena, instead of the passivity and isolation observable under Stalin, the Communists have introduced active diplomacy along the lines of the principles underlying Lenin's Rapallo Treaty which involves visits to and *political and military agreements with the capitalist adversaries concerning military technology and weaponry.* This activism has been displayed by Khrushchev, Brezhnev, Ceausescu and now by the Chinese leaders.

THE ACTIVE METHODS OF THE KGB

Instead of the primitive repression inflicted under Stalin, the KGB and other Communist security services have introduced the active methods which were successfully practiced by the security services under Dzerzhinskiy. These methods included the creation of a false, controlled political opposition, planting it on Western intelligence services and manipulating those services through disinformation. These methods also included, when required by political or operational needs, the staging of faked trials, faked murders etc. For example, the Soviet security service, the GPU, arranged the faked execution of Opperput, one of their best provocateurs and the founder of the 'Trust', on charges of being a British spy and terrorist. The GPU reported his execution at a press conference.

The West has recognised the need for verification of claims by the Communist world concerning nuclear missiles. **Likewise, because of the KGB's active methods, it is necessary and urgent to recognise the need for verification of what we are being told about political developments, before accepting them at face value.**

Given the use of these active methods, it was entirely logical for the KGB to arrange a faked arrest of Sakharov in order to reaffirm his credibility [as a dissident]. This was easy to accomplish through the manipulation of their sources with Western contacts and a calculated campaign of innuendo...

Earlier disinformation about Sakharov remains intact...❜.

FUTURE STRATEGY AND ITS OBJECTIVES

'... Now the Soviets can proceed with the implementation of their New Economic Policy and liberalisation in the USSR under Gorbachëv and can proceed with the next phase of their strategy in Poland – the creation of a coalition government made up of representatives of the Communist Party, priests and Solidarity.

Now they can resume their diplomatic offensive against West Germany. Now they can reactivate their agents of influence. Now they can again expect their strategy to succeed, to bring them credits and technology from the West and to lead to the reunification of Germany and the break-up of the NATO alliance, and to allow them to exert more pressure on the West for unilateral disarmament... .

The Soviet strategists' primary interim objectives will include the following:

❒ To divide the American nation.
❒ To increase pressure for defence cuts.
❒ To increase tension between the United States and its allies.
❒ To reactivate the anti-military movements in Britain and West Germany.
❒ To reactivate the nuclear freeze movement in the United States '. ∎

Memorandum to the CIA: APRIL 1985

AN ASSESSMENT OF THE INVITATION TO
BILLY GRAHAM TO PREACH IN SOVIET CHURCHES
DURING HIS SECOND VISIT TO THE USSR

[Television documentary shown on American television networks on 5 March 1985].

᛫ This was an extraordinary, moving and impressive event with serious political and strategic implications. The spectacle was arranged in masterly fashion by the Soviet authorities, by KGB-controlled Russian Orthodox priests like **Patriarch Pimen** and by Soviet strategists including **Georgiy Arbatov**, the Director of the Institute for the Study of the USA and Canada, **Boris Ponomarëv**, a member of the Politburo of the Party, and **Yuriy Zhukov**, the head of the Soviet Peace Committee with whom the Reverend Graham had a number of meetings. The congregation was a carefully selected one.

Besides the traditional, genuine old women believers, the congregation also included an influx of young Komsomols and members of the *druzhiny* (Soviet vigilantes). The presence of Komsomol members was indirectly revealed when it was stated that the authorities had invited Soviet students to the ceremony in the Siberian church. The invitation to Graham, the royal treatment afforded him, the boldness of the initiators of the spectacle and the publicity surrounding it, all clearly indicated that the Soviet strategists were after big stakes.

So what was the true meaning and purpose of this spectacle?

(a) It was undertaken to impress the Western audience and particularly Western Christians, Catholic and Protestant, with the alleged growth of religious freedom in the Union of Soviet Socialist Republics.

(b) In essence, it followed the lines of Stalin's demonstrations of tolerance of the Church during the Second World War.

(c) It was an indication and element of the Soviet 'liberalisation' and political offensive predicted by this analyst. In wartime, religious relaxation was used to secure the Western alliance and to help the Soviet war effort. Today it is being used in another kind of war – to serve the political strategy of disarming the West.

d) Another purpose was to strengthen the credibility of the Russian high priest as a genuine shepherd, on a par with Western priests and as a moral authority;

(e) It was intended to prepare the ground for similar invitations and mass visits of other senior Western priests to the USSR and particularly for a visit by the Pope;

(f) Its ultimate purpose was to promote cooperation and a united front between the Soviet churches and Western Christians, Catholic and Protestant, to support nuclear disarmament and to exploit the trend revealed in the pastoral letter of the Catholic Bishops.

The Soviet strategists may well succeed in their manipulation of the Western churches because:

(1) Soviet priests are controlled and directed by the KGB and the Soviet strat-

egists and their participation is a deception which serves the strategy of unilateral Western disarmament and convergence; and:

(2) Western priests, as demonstrated by the Billy Graham visit, are unaware of the true activist rôle of the Soviet high priests and of the true purpose of religious relaxation in the Soviet Union[68] [9]. ∎

---

68 *Editor's Note:* In 1993, the Archbishop of Canterbury and the Bishop of Oxford paid a visit to Russia, Armenia and Georgia. In Armenia, they met the Armenian President, **Ter-Petrosyan**, whom, they were informed, has translated the Psalms into contemporary Armenian. In Tbilisi, the British churchmen were greeted warmly by **Catholicos-Patriarch Ilya II**, accompanied by other Georgian bishops. **MVD General Eduard Shevardnadze**, who received the British visitors personally, also attended a reception given by the Archbishop of Canterbury in the Georgian capital. According to a 'line' disseminated by Georgian sources, Shevardnadze was 'baptised a Christian in 1992, when he took the Christian name of George'. When Shevardnadze was filmed by a British documentary film producer in 1993, an icon was placed immediately behind Shevardnadze's shoulder, so that it appeared in most of the footage [*source:* director's personal communication to the Editor]. However Georgians traditionally place their icons in the top right-hand corner of the room. Shevardnadze's 'conversion', like Ter-Petrosyan's translation of the Psalms into modern Armenian, and rumours of Gorbachëv's 'conversion to Christianity' which followed Billy Graham's visits to the USSR and circulated in Washington in 1985, is false – designed to hoodwink the West in general and Western clerics in particular. Shevardnadze's interesting image as a 'born-again Christian' believing in God hardly chimes, for instance, with his statement in the Georgian parliament on 6 August 1993 that '*My* word should be law for everybody' [*See also Note 72, pages 203-204*; broadcast by SNARK, Yerevan, cited in FBIS-SOV-93-151, 9 August 1993]. On 22 March 1995, the Russian Defence Minister, Pavel Grachev – while leading a Russian military delegation which 'negotiated' a renewable 25-year military agreement between Russia and Georgia under which key Georgian military infrastructure is placed in Russian hands and which, according to a statement by Shevardnadze to the Georgian Parliament, would not require ratification – was baptised into the Georgian Orthodox Church in the village of Ananuri in the Dusheti District. Grachev was baptised by a Father Teymuraz, while the Georgian Defence Minister, Bardiko Nadibaidze, a Russian using a Georgian name, said to be 'an old friend' of Pavel Grachev, became his godfather. The news of General Grachev's baptism was confirmed by officials of the Georgian Patriarchate. [*Sources:* ITAR-TASS, Moscow, in Russian, 1611 GMT, 22 March 1995, cited by BBC Monitoring Service, 24 March 1995, SU/2260 F/2].

Memorandum to the CIA: AUGUST 1985

THE DANGER FOR THE WEST:
AN ASSESSMENT OF THE RISE OF MIKHAIL GORBACHEV,
THE ROLE OF 'LIBERALISATION' IN SOVIET STRATEGY,
AND ITS GRAVE IMPLICATIONS FOR THE WEST

‘ The speedy appointment of Mikhail Gorbachëv as the Party leader[69] confirms this analyst's earlier conclusion about the cessation of power struggles in the Soviet leadership and the solution of the succession problem by the selection of the leader in advance by the Politburo.

Gorbachëv was selected, coached and prepared for this appointment by the late Suslov and Andropov and by Ponomarëv and Gromyko in the same way as Dubcek was chosen for the Czechoslovak leadership. Gorbachëv's speech and other indications confirm the Author's earlier analysis about forthcoming Soviet 'liberalisation' which has been in preparation during the past two decades under Shelepin and Andropov. Gorbachëv was selected as the 'new generation' representative because of his decisiveness, his demeanour and, above all, because he has been well groomed for implementing the 'liberalisation strategy'. Another factor favouring his selection was his non-involvement in Stalin's repression.

There are no valid grounds for favourable illusions or for any euphoria in the West over Gorbachëv's appointment and the coming 'liberalisation'. In fact, these developments may present a grave challenge and a serious test for the United States' leadership and for the West. **The 'liberalisation' will not be spontaneous and nor will it be genuine. It will be a calculated 'liberalisation' patterned along the lines of the Czechoslovak 'democratisation' which was rehearsed in 1968. It will be** *initiated from above and will be guided and controlled by the KGB and the Party apparatus.* The 'liberalisation' will include the following elements:

(a) Economic reforms to decentralise the Soviet economy and to introduce profit incentives along the lines of those in Hungary and China. Since Gorbachëv is a Soviet agricultural expert, one can expect a reorganisation of the *kolkhozy* or collective farms into *sovkhozy* or state farms. In fact, Beria was already planning the liquidation of the *kolkhozy* in 1953.

(b) Religious relaxation along the lines of Stalin's relaxation during the Second World War. The recent sensational Soviet invitation to the Reverend Billy Graham to preach in Soviet churches indicates that the Soviet strategists have already introduced this element without waiting for the formal installation of Gorbachëv as General Secretary of the Party.

(c) Permission for Jewish émigrés to leave the USSR.

(d) Relaxation of travel restrictions to allow Soviet citizens to make visits abroad. This will be done in part to impress the West with the Soviet Government's compliance with the Helsinki agreements .

69 *Editor's Note:* See the Author's prediction that Gorbachëv had been selected to succeed Chernenko in the extract from his Memorandum to the CIA dated **4 July 1984,** on pages 8 and 183 of the present work; and in the excerpt from his Memorandum dated **January 1985,** on page 185.

(e) Some relaxations for Soviet intellectuals and cultural defectors. Soviet writers and producers will be permitted to write books and produce plays on controversial subjects. Cultural defectors, musicians and dancers will be allowed to perform in the USSR and to travel and perform abroad, thus getting the best of both worlds. One can expect that an amnesty will be declared for the so-called 'dissidents'.

(f) Some apparent reductions in the military budget and the transfer of some military funds to improve the state of the economy.

THE NEW PHASE OF SOVIET TOTALITARIANISM: THE DOMESTIC ASPECT

This 'liberalisation' has become possible because the Soviet system has been strengthened economically, partly by Western credits and technology, and politically, partly because of *détente*. It has now reached a new 'mature' phase of socialism.

'Liberalisation' will change the Soviet régime into a new form of totalitarianism, characterised by two critical changes:

○ **A broader political base**, and
○ **Increased political activism.**

It is, however, *a false, cosmetic liberalisation*. For example, the alleged religious relaxation is a spectacle produced and managed by the KGB and the high priests of the church who are KGB agents assigned to fulfill the strategy.

The same applies to the so-called dissidents who are under KGB control, along the lines of Dzerzhinskiy's infamous 'Trust' provocation in the 1920s.

Domestically, the 'liberalisation' does not affect the leading rôle of the Party or the foundations of the Communist totalitarian system. In fact, it is designed to strengthen them and to make them more viable, in just the same way as Lenin's New Economic Policy did in the 1920s.

THE DANGERS OF ' LIBERALISATION':
SOVIET STRATEGIC DESIGNS AGAINST THE WEST

'Liberalisation' is dangerous for the West not because of its domestic features, but because of its foreign policy implications and its strategic designs against the Western democracies. 'Liberalisation' is a part of the Soviet strategy against the West:

○ First of all, it is a significant component of the overall Soviet strategy to deceive, to influence and to disarm the West through manoeuvres and through political means. If presented and advertised by the innocent and uninitiated media as a far-reaching, radical change in the Communist system, the 'liberalisation' will allow the Communist leaders immediately to regain the political initiative and to revive the political and diplomatic *détente* which was so disastrous for the West and so beneficial to the Communists in the past.

○ The charismatic personality of Gorbachëv may play an important rôle in the over-reaction of the Western media. The record of the Western media in their reactions to and in their assessments of Soviet leaders has been very poor.

In the past, the then head of the KGB, Shelepin, was characterised as a 'young Turk'; while later on, Andropov was described as a 'closet liberal'. Gorbachëv has already been presented by the media, ludicrously, as the Soviet 'Jack Kennedy'.

THE OBJECTIVES OF THE POLITICAL OFFENSIVE

The Soviet 'liberalisation' is a key component of the strategy of the whole Communist Bloc, and particularly of Poland and East Germany, against the West. The main objective is to launch a political offensive against the United States in Europe by changing the political and military situation.

This strategy is designed to accomplish the following:

○ To bring about a 'German Confederation' of East and West Germany and withdrawal from both the Warsaw Pact and NATO.

○ To break up NATO and force a United States withdrawal from Europe.

NEW OPPORTUNITIES

One can expect that, in order to accomplish their disguised objectives, a similar 'liberalisation' will be introduced in Poland and East Germany. Presented and advertised as a new reality in Europe, the Soviet, Polish and East German 'liberalisations' will have a stunning and mesmerising effect on both West Europeans and Americans. The resulting confusion will be exploited by the Soviet, Polish and East German leaders through their activist diplomacy, especially towards West Germany.

Czechoslovak, Hungarian and Romanian leaders may actively contribute to this strategy. The Communist strategists, who are encouraged by anti-NATO and anti-American trends, especially among socialists in West Germany, Britain and Greece, will try to exploit their 'liberalisation' in order to develop united front cooperation with conservatives and social democrats against military blocs in Europe.

The alleged religious relaxation will be exploited by the Communist churches to establish a similar united front operation against NATO with Catholics, Protestants and other Christians in Western Europe. The 'liberalisation' will become a powerful catalyst for revitalising anti-war movements in Western Europe and particularly in West Germany, Britain, Belgium and the Netherlands.

THE ROLE OF THE KGB: ITS COVERT OPERATIONS AND AGENTS OF INFLUENCE

During this political offensive, the KGB and the special services of other Communist states will use their intelligence potential and run both overt and covert operations to secure specific strategic objectives, especially through the manipulation of pacifists. Sabotage operations against NATO installations in Western Europe will increase.

A significant activist rôle will be played by Soviet agents of influence in the execution of the strategy. They will include politicians, scientists, priests and members of the media. In this analyst's opinion, Western counter-espionage services underestimate the intelligence potential of the Communist countries in Europe, especially their agents of influence. According to this analysis, the following developments are indicative of the beginning of the political offensive in Western Europe:

(a) The sudden invitation to the Foreign Minister of West Germany, Hans Dietrich Genscher, to visit Poland and the USSR.

(b) The visit of Andrei Gromyko and his entourage to the Vatican. (The visit took place after claims had been made that the KGB and the Soviets were implicated in the attempt on the Pope's life. This analyst regards the claims as groundless but he wonders why these Soviet officials should have been welcomed in the Vatican).

(c) The planned visit of Mikhail Gorbachëv to France and the visit of Vitaliy Vorotnikov, a member of the Politburo, to Yugoslavia.

It is significant that the Soviets initiated their offensive *before* the formal installation of Gorbachëv as Party leader. **This indicates that the execution of the strategy is in the hands of the apparatus and its strategists and, furthermore, that the strategists consider timing to be of the essence of the strategy.**

'LIBERALISATION' AND ITS IMPACT ON STRATEGIC NEGOTIATIONS:
STRATEGIC DESIGNS AGAINST THE UNITED STATES' MILITARY POSTURE

The 'liberalisation' in the USSR, Poland and East Germany will be used actively by Soviet strategists to undermine and destabilise American military power and its military programmes, including the Strategic Defence Initiative and the military budget.

It will be a new ball game in the negotiations in Geneva. The 'liberalisation' will unleash a Pandora's box of varied political pressures on the US negotiators both domestically and from the allies. The Soviets will try to exploit the 'liberalisation' theme to extract concessions damaging to US interests. One can expect that Gorbachëv will come up with some startling strategic initiatives about arms reductions and/or the withdrawal of a number of Soviet missiles from Eastern Europe along the lines of Khrushchev's reductions of Soviet troops in January 1960.

These proposals will be designed to disturb and undermine the US military posture, to bring about greater pressure for reductions in the military budget, to influence the US-Soviet strategic negotiations in the Soviet Union's own interest and to undermine the US Strategic Defence Initiative [SDI].

One can also expect the dispatch by the KGB of false defectors with disinformation **or even the arrangement by the KGB of a calculated mishap leading to the breaking of their code by the United States which would influence the US negotiating position.** One can further expect the activation of Soviet agents of influence among their scientists to undermine US military programmes, especially the SDI.

Already the well-known Director of the Institute for the Study of the USA and Canada, Georgiy Arbatov, and a Soviet space expert have developed active contacts with the Dean of Notre Dame College and members of the media in an attempt to kill the programme[70]. The rôle of Arbatov was revealed by his participation in a

70 *Editor's Note:* The Author explains in this work that in the late 1980s, the KGB despatched its most experienced operatives to the United States to conduct unpublicised Embassy briefings with members of the American political, scientific, intellectual and economic élite. These briefings laid the basis for a rapid expansion of intensive contacts between Soviet/Russian builders of influence and the American élite – an activity which Gorbachëv subsequently continued through 'new' structures such as the Gorbachëv Foundation/USA (with 'global' initiatives such as the 'Global Security Project') and International Green Cross (of which Gorbachëv has made himself President, and which exploits global environmentalism as a dimension of the strategy. Its ultimate purpose is an attack on private property). The International Foreign Policy Association, established by Shevardnadze ostensibly to enlist support from the US élite for initiatives mainly in Georgia, is a parallel influence-building operation administered in conjunction with the Gorbachëv Foundation/USA from a common office in San Francisco [*see Note 22, page 43*]. Concerning space-related 'convergence', '*The New York Times*' reported on 7th April 1993 that 'The White House has ordered NASA to work with the Russians in designing a smaller and cheaper space station'. NASA Administrator Daniel Goldin said that 'Russian participation would be coordinated by the East-West Space Science Center at the University of Maryland under the leadership of **Dr Roald Z. Sagdeyev**... now living part of the time in the United States'.

conference on 'A Nuclear Winter' *which was actually arranged by Arbatov* in collaboration with the Dean of Notre Dame College. This fact was revealed in a programme on the Cable News Network on 14 January 1985.

'LIBERALISATION' AS PART OF THE STRATEGY
OF THE INTERNATIONAL COMMUNIST MOVEMENT

'Liberalisation' is also an important part of the strategy of the *international* Communist movement. It provides broad opportunities for the Communist Parties in Western Europe and gives them new political ammunition to revive their fortunes and to increase their influence and power. 'Liberalisation' removes the stigma of the discredited, repressive Stalinist practices of the Soviet régime and its satellites. The stigma has been an obstacle to Communist propaganda and has kept the West European Communist Parties in isolation.

'Liberalisation' will change the situation significantly. The hungry Soviet revolutionary was a pathetic caricature and a laughing stock. The well-fed revolutionary with a 'human face' and a nice Western-style suit makes for more effective propaganda. 'Liberalisation' will provide grounds for the revival of 'Euro-Communism' or variants which eschew the word 'Communism'. It will provide a new basis for the establishment of a united front with social democrats. **It further increases opportunities to isolate the conservatives and to bring about a swing of the political pendulum away from the conservatives in Western Europe and elsewhere.**

The class struggle is not dead: it will be waged in new and more effective, activist forms. The 'liberalised' régimes will establish a more attractive model for emulation. 'Euro-Communist' association with the 'liberalisation' and its manipulation will increase the chances of Euro-Communists entering governments. The covert activities of the Communist intelligence services in Western Europe will be stepped up. **These activities will include the secret assassination of leading anti-Communists who are perceived as obstacles to the strategy. Other activities will include the recruitment and blackmailing of conservative and socialist politicians and the use of agents of influence to bring about united front governments.**

THE WESTERN RESPONSE TO 'LIBERALISATION' AND THE POLITICAL
OFFENSIVE IN WESTERN EUROPE: THE PROBLEM FOR THE LEADERSHIP OF THE WEST

The 'liberalisation' in the USSR, Poland and East Germany may set off a chain reaction in the West and inflict irreparable damage particularly on the NATO countries and the US military posture, unless its true nature and rôle in Communist strategy are realised. The 'liberalisation' and its strategic manipulations, combined with overt and covert Communist operations, will also present problems for the leadership of the West.

It will be aimed at confusing the Western leaders, splitting the West European allies from the United States and then splitting the people from their elected leaders. The leaders who are taken in by the 'liberalisation' can be expected to make erroneous decisions, albeit unwittingly, in the interests of the Communists.

The only way to provide effective leadership and to maintain public trust in these circumstance is to explain to the public frankly the essence and dangers of 'liberalisation'. It is vital to refute erroneous views about the so-called crisis of the Soviet régime. **It is time to realise the strength and the political potential of the present active, mature totalitarian state which is committed to world conquest through political means and offensives. It is also time to extract the right lessons from the erroneous Western over-reaction to 'liberalisation' and to view the situation coolly, assessing both the pluses and the minuses for the West.**

There is an urgent need for quiet consultation between the United States and their European allies on the dangers of the new situation.

THE NEED TO REBUILD THE US INTELLIGENCE AND COUNTER-INTELLIGENCE POTENTIAL

The present reality is that the West has allowed itself to be disarmed politically in the face of the Communist political offensive. The CIA lost many of its vital assets in 1967 and through the Watergate scandal. Its potential for overt and covert operations to defend the United States, NATO and Western Europe from a Communist political offensive has been much reduced. The West European services are no better prepared to detect and deal with KGB agents of influence. There is an urgent need to restore the intelligence potential of the West.

THE VITAL NEED TO PRESERVE US AND NATO MILITARY STRENGTH

Although the United States is politically unprepared for a Communist political offensive, it has increased its military strength and the deterrent is working. The SDI and advanced American technology would make the country even more secure: hence the Soviet campaign to undermine them. The military strength of the United States and NATO are the West's principal assets which prevent Soviet adventurism and which may stall the present political offensive. No illusions about 'liberalisation' in the Communist countries should be allowed to affect these military assets.

Otherwise the United States will become a 'paper tiger' in the eyes of the Communist countries, setting off a chain of risky and unpredictable events.

ABOUT THE SUMMIT MEETING

There is a danger that participation by the United States in a Summit Meeting will give more credibility to Gorbachëv and the strategists' aspirations.

Three considerations should be kept in mind:

(1) The United States should not provide grounds for the Communist side to manipulate US participation as signifying approval of Gorbachëv's policies;

(2) The United States should not be taken in by Gorbachëv's plans for 'liberalisation' in the Soviet Union; and:

(3) The United States should take into account the possible danger to the life of the President, as in the case of his earlier visit to China. There is a definite risk in summits outside the United States if the Soviet strategists regard the President as a real obstacle to their strategy. This warning will remain valid for future leaders'. ■

Memorandum to the CIA: 12 NOVEMBER 1985

THE SUMMIT MEETING

' The previous policy of the US President of rejecting *détente* with the Soviets while stimulating American economic recovery has been successful. It isolated the Soviets both in the United States and in Western Europe, and held up Soviet domestic 'reform'. The present US intention of holding systematic summits with the Soviet leader, Mikhail Gorbachëv, appears to be an attractive public relations gimmick but would be a strategic error detrimental to US national interests.

It would be a move towards restoration of full *détente* with the Soviets similar to that of Willi Brandt's *détente* of 1970. It would be like inviting a fox into the chicken coop. Furthermore it will allow the Soviets to regain the political initiative and to **unleash a Pandora's box of Soviet offensives both domestically and abroad**. It would also allow the Soviets to proceed with their economic reforms and to launch their offensive in Western Europe against NATO...'. ■

Memorandum to the CIA: 21 NOVEMBER 1985

AN ASSESSMENT OF THE SUMMIT MEETING:
A STRATEGIC MISCALCULATION WITH LONG-TERM CONSEQUENCES FOR THE UNITED STATES

• Because US and Soviet strategic perceptions and commitments are radically different, the Summit and the future direction it has set, namely a slide back into *détente*, will not bring peace to the West and in the long run will be detrimental to the United States' strategic interests.

US policymakers have forgotten the main lesson of 70 years' experience with the Communist threat – that the most effective way to stop Soviet expansion is not *détente* but keeping the pressure up.

In this analyst's opinion, the Soviets have again tricked the United States just as they previously tricked Presidents Nixon and Carter.

By waging an impressive public relations campaign, they created the impression that their main objective was a ban on the Strategic Defence Initiative. Their main objective in fact was to return to *détente* with the United States; and they have achieved it. **The Communist strategists realise that they cannot defeat the United States by military means but they are convinced they can win politically under conditions of** *détente***.** The President's five years of continuing pressure on the Soviets put them on the defensive and created obstacles to the execution of their political strategy. It was this pressure that brought them to Geneva.

For a successful outcome of their conflict with the West, the Soviets count primarily on their political strategy of economic 'reform' and 'convergence' with the West *on their terms*, and not primarily on military strength. Thus the return to *détente* is more important to them than a ban on the Strategic Defence Initiative which may or may not become a problem in ten years or more.

The following considerations indicate that by returning to *détente*, the United States will make strategic miscalculations which may surpass those unfortunately committed by Presidents Nixon and Carter:

(1) The Soviets regard *détente* as the most effective form of acute struggle with the capitalist West, in which they enjoy advantages. They demonstrated this by exploiting *détente* under Presidents Nixon and Carter.

(2) The primary advantage to the Soviets is that *détente* gives them access to the media and the political opposition in the West and allows them to employ their political and intelligence potential, particularly their agents of influence, their front organisations and their sabotage agents against NATO.

The West has no such advantage because it has no access to genuine opposition in the USSR, which has been immobilised, and because it dissolved its own political potential in 1967 and during Watergate. Ironically, the West only has access to the KGB-controlled 'dissident movement'.

(3) A return to *détente* allows the Soviets to carry out their economic reforms and to regain the initiative in the execution of their political strategy against the West.

(4) A return to *détente* provides the Soviets with opportunities to increase their influence and their pressure for military budget cuts and the dismantling of the 'military-industrial complex' and NATO. In the event of a US economic slump, pressure on the military will increase.

(5) A return to *détente* undercuts the anti-Communists in the West and reduces the chances of conservative parties winning future elections in West Germany, Britain, France and the United States.

It is ironic that all this should result from the actions of a conservative President. However, the Communist strategists always take particular delight in taking advantage of anti-Communist leaders, as in the case of the conservative President Richard Nixon[71].

(6) A return to *détente* will improve the President's image as a peacemaker only for a limited period of time, because the damaging consequences of his miscalculations will reveal themselves to the public over the longer run⁹. ∎

---

71 *Author's Note:* And of course the Conservative Margaret Thatcher.

Memorandum to the CIA: DECEMBER 1985

GORBACHEV HAS LAUNCHED A POLITICAL OFFENSIVE:
THE NEED TO EXPOSE 'HIS' STRATEGY AND COVERT OPERATIONS

' Somehow the Western media have an uncanny capacity to detect, expose and attack covert operations of the United States – but not those of the Soviet Union. Granted that apartheid in South Africa must be terminated, it is nevertheless still paramount to define the Communist strategic threat and to identify Soviet covert operations.... Now that it is apparent that Gorbachëv has launched a political offensive, one can expect that the next logical step will be Communist covert action projects through their surrogate guerrilla movements against the **South African** régime, and against **Israel** by exploiting the Palestine issue.

Anti-American and anti-NATO campaigns will be stepped up in Europe. The essence of these covert operations is to attack the United States' system of alliances in Africa, the Middle East and Western Europe.

In order to accomplish the dissolution or severe weakening of NATO, the Soviets will exploit their coming economic reforms and manipulate the political opposition in Eastern Europe, particularly in Poland and East Germany...'. ■

EDITOR'S NOTE:

The document presented on pages 199-212 as a Postscript, a few copies of which circulated in the United States in **late 1991**, came into the Editor's hands independently of the main text, which was of course not made available in its entirety until the arrangements for the publication of this book had been finalised.

The document contains a powerful summary of Anatoliy Golitsyn's background and of the Memoranda submitted to the Central Intelligence Agency [CIA] over many years and now cleared for publication. It addresses the essence of the Author's analysis, an explanation of the Soviets' Leninist long-range strategy, information about the application of Communist deception theory, exposure of the use of controlled 'democrats' practising 'democratism' and other deception devices such as 'false equivalence', the trickery surrounding the apparent surrender of power by the Communists, the meaning and hidden purpose of provisional 'independence' for the national Republics, an expression of concern at the West's ignorance of the strategy and its consequent failure to understand its significance and aggressive intent, and warnings about the implementation of the strategy and its implications for the West.

The Editor felt that this important document, which certainly helped clarify his own thinking, should be added to the manuscript, and accordingly included it with the proofs. The Author consented to its incorporation, and it is presented here with the following subheadings [page references *in bold italic type*]:

THE LONG-RANGE DECEPTION STRATEGY

POSTSCRIPT

Anatoliy Golitsyn's

Summary of his
Analysis of the

SOVIET LONG-RANGE
DECEPTION STRATEGY

And the world's slide towards
the 'Second October Revolution'

THE LONG-RANGE DECEPTION STRATEGY

SUMMARY OF THE AUTHOR'S BACKGROUND, WORK AND PURPOSE
The Author defected to the United States in December 1961 after 16 years' service in the KGB. He had also been a member of the Communist Party since 1945. He is a graduate of the counter-intelligence faculty of the High Intelligence School in Moscow and of the University of Marxism-Leninism. He completed a correspondence course with the High Diplomatic School.

In 1959 he graduated with a law degree from a four-year course at the KGB Institute (subsequently the KGB Academy) in Moscow. From 1959 to 1960, at a time when the present long-range Soviet strategy was being formulated and the KGB was being reorganised to play its part in it, he served as a senior analyst in the NATO section of the Information Department of the Soviet intelligence service.

He served in Vienna and Helsinki on counter-intelligence assignments from 1953 to 1955, and from 1960 to 1961, respectively. His contribution to Western security has been officially recognised by the American and British Governments.

Since 1962, he has studied Communist affairs and East-West relations in terms of Soviet political strategy and has given his assessments to the Central Intelligence Agency [CIA] and other Western intelligence and security services. In 1984 he published 'New Lies for Old', a study of Soviet strategic disinformation,

He also prepared a book entitled 'The Birth of Perestroika', covering the period in Soviet history between 1946 and 1960, in which the present long-range Communist political strategy was formulated. He has continued to keep the CIA informed of his views in a series of Memoranda on this long-range deception strategy, of which 'perestroika' is an advanced phase.

Since his assessments have not influenced American policymaking, he requested clearance from the Central Intelligence Agency to publish these Memoranda in the present work 'The Perestroika Deception'.

In 'New Lies for Old', and in his Memoranda to the CIA, the Author predicted that the Communist strategists would **go beyond Marx and Lenin** and introduce economic and political 'reforms' – a false 'liberalisation' – in the USSR and Eastern Europe. He predicted the legalisation of Solidarity in Poland, the return of 'democratisation' in Czechoslovakia, and the removal of the Berlin Wall. These and many other predictions were borne out by events. They were accurate because they reflected the Author's knowledge and study of the long-range strategy finalised in 1958-60, of which 'perestroika' is the logical manifestation.

SEVEN KEYS TO UNDERSTANDING WHAT THE SOVIETS ARE UP TO
These Memoranda provide seven simple keys to understanding the long-range deception strategy masterminded in Moscow. They can be summarised as follows:

1. The strategy applies, innovatively, the lessons of Lenin's experience with his 'New Economic Policy' [NEP] to the entire Communist Bloc.
2. It involves intensive preparations for the use of the Communist Bloc's political and security potential.

3. The strategy focuses in particular upon the creation of controlled 'political opposition' elements by the KGB and the security services of the other Communist countries. These elements were trained to implement 'democratism' – the creation and maintenance of the illusion of Western democracy.

4. The strategy applies Lenin's ideas on the 'forging of new and old forms' for the development of socialism (i.e., Communism), and the achievement of Communist supremacy. Chicherin's ideas, in a letter to Lenin, on the creation of false 'representative institutions' by the admission of non-Communist members, are implemented.

5. The strategy further deploys the new 'controlled opposition' elements for the creation of revised 'democratic' and ostensibly 'non-Communist' structures.

6. Lenin's experience in giving fictitious political 'independence' to the Far Eastern and Georgian Republics is repeated, on a much more extensive scale.

7. The strategy encompasses a new, secret, deadly anti-Western strategic formula which *uses the Bloc's full potential* in its execution.

THE MAIN OBJECTIVE OF LENIN'S NEW ECONOMIC POLICY [NEP] STRATEGY

The main objective of Lenin's strategy under the New Economic Policy was to induce the West to create favourable conditions for 'building socialism' in Soviet Russia, and for strengthening it as the base for global revolution (*'Weltoktober'*) by extending recognition to the Soviet régime and reviving its economy through trade, credits, technology transfer and Western specialist assistance.

The main objectives of the *'perestroika'* stage of the long-range strategy are:

(a) To induce Western responses which will accelerate the process of Communist renewal and the transformation of Communist régimes into attractive models of 'socialism with a human face'.

(b) To create favourable conditions for Communist world hegemony through the long-envisaged 'convergence' of the two systems. Lenin offered concessions to foreign and home-grown capitalists. The strategists behind *'perestroika'* emphasise joint ventures. This device facilitates confiscation at a later date; and in the meantime, joint ventures can become bridges for the promotion of 'convergence' – which is to be achieved on Moscow's terms.

Because of the narrow political base of his régime, Lenin limited his so-called 'New Economic Policy' to economic reform. But the *'perestroika'* strategists, drawing on their political and security potential, have incorporated political as well as economic reforms in the offensive. These facilitate the execution of the intensified anti-Western strategy upon which they have embarked.

Lenin employed activist diplomacy to swing the unfavourable balance of power in his favour, and to prevent the emergence of a European anti-Soviet coalition. Exploiting the differences which had emerged between the victorious Western allies and the defeated Germans, he concluded the Rapallo Treaty with Germany.

The *'perestroika'* strategists have also resorted to activist diplomacy – exploiting the contradictions between the United States, Japan, Germany and other European countries. They are exploiting the 'changes' in Eastern Europe, the removal of the Berlin Wall and the reunification issue, with a view to neutralising West Germany and dissolving NATO. They are concealing their intention to exploit the new 'democratic' image which they have manufactured, and the political potential of their renewed régimes, to promote 'restructuring' in Western Europe, through the European Community, and also – indeed especially so – in the United States.

SOVIET STRATEGY MATURES FROM ONE TO TWO DIMENSIONS

Formerly, the application of Soviet political and security potential operated on only one dimension: the Soviet security services, and those they controlled, used their political and security potential repressively against their own populations.

But now the employment of the political and security potential has two dimensions: *domestic* and *international*. The *domestic* dimension involves the use of this potential to broaden the base of the Communist Parties, and to create 'non-Communist', 'democratic' and 'nationalist' structures – replacing Lenin's 'dictatorship of the proletariat' with a 'new form' – the 'state of the whole people' – exploiting the introduction of deceptive, controlled democracy. Now that the West has accepted this deceptive, controlled democracy as genuine, this process is almost complete.

The *international* element comprises the aggressive use of the political and security potential of the whole Bloc in the execution of the Communists' anti-Western strategy. Given the growth of this potential and the Bloc's military power, the design of the strategy is broader, more comprehensive, more aggressive and more realistic than was the case with Lenin's early anti-Western strategy under the New Economic Policy. For Lenin's strategy was based upon the creation of united fronts between Communist and socialist parties. The design of *'perestroika'* is based upon the deployment of the Bloc's political and security potential for the practical promotion of 'convergence' on Soviet terms between the (now masked) Communist system and the Western democracies.

Given the maturity of the old Communist régimes, the strength of their political and security potential and the long period of preparation of controlled 'political opposition', these régimes are in a position to allow representatives of controlled 'non-Communist' parties a third, a half, or even more of the seats in their governments and parliaments, so as to present these institutions as 'representative' and 'democratic'. It should be noted that Chicherin's letter to Lenin was held as a state secret until its publication in 1962 – that is to say, *shortly after* the adoption of the long-range deception strategy.

The deployment of controlled 'political opposition' has rendered possible the introduction of deceptive 'non-Communist' and 'democratic' structures. Even so-called 'free' elections do not pose a problem for the Communist Parties. Because of their secret partnership with the 'opposition', the Communist Parties are invariably in a winning position. It is *their* candidates – whether Communist or 'non-Communist' – who *always* win, since all the non-Communist candidates and 'parties' are controlled. No other truly independent candidates exist. This is the new statecraft of the Communist Parties and their security services. They are using a new form for the broader development of socialism.

The introduction of 'democratism', which can be defined as the creation and maintenance of the illusion of Western democracy, controlled by the Communists and the security services – allows the Communist Parties to broaden their political base and, in accordance with a decision of the 22nd Party Congress held in October 1961, to replace the outlived concept of the 'dictatorship of the proletariat' with the revised concept of 'the state of the whole people', while maintaining the Communists' power and strengthening their actual leading rôle.

But while exercising this leading rôle, they have made themselves 'invisible' – even though we can see clearly indeed that the key players are 'former' Party and KGB officials and their appointees.

The Communists have succeeded in concealing from the West that the 'non-Communist' parties are secret partners of the Communists, not *alternatives* or *rivals* to them, and that the new power structures, despite their apparently democratic form, are in reality structures which have been made more viable and effective, introduced by the Communist Parties – that is to say, from above – with a broader base.

Because of this Communist control, the 'former' Soviet Bloc 'democracies' are not true democracies and cannot become so in the future. To imagine otherwise is to indulge in wishful-thinking. The earlier acceptance of false 'political opposition' by the West as genuine, has led logically, and as was intended, to the contemporary environment of uncritical acceptance of this deceptive 'democracy' ('democratism') as true democracy.

PARTNERSHIP BETWEEN THE OLD AND NEW GENERATIONS OF LEADERS
The turnover from one generation of leaders of the 'old' Communist Bloc to another has indeed followed a logical pattern – but one which has been lost to those in the West who have scant knowledge of, or who have forgotten, the teachings and lessons of Lenin. In general (with a few notable/notorious exceptions), the old leaders have resigned without a struggle. Those who were arrested were usually spared, on the grounds of old age or ill-health.

It was under the old generation of leaders, of course, that the 'reforms' were prepared – under Brezhnev and Andropov in the Soviet Union; under Kadar in Hungary; under Honecker in East Germany, for instance. It was this generation which had formulated, created and developed the controlled 'political opposition' method, and which had even gone to the lengths of appearing to persecute the early manifestations of such 'opposition' in order to buttress the controlled 'dissidents'' credibility. Since these new 'non-Communist' leaders are the secret partners of the Communists, there is, self-evidently, no animosity between them.

It has therefore been quite logical for the new President of Czechoslovakia to advise the President of the United States to support Gorbachëv and to bankroll 'perestroika', to accept a Communist as his Minister of Defence or, when asked whether or not his country would remain within the then overtly existing Communist alliance, to reply: 'If a totalitarian system is dismantled, some peculiarities remain[72]. Some

72 *Editor's Note:* In August 1993, Eduard Shevardnadze summarised some of the 'peculiarities which remain' in Georgia: 'It takes dozens of years to build a democratic state... a democratic society. The election of a parliament or even of the head of state, or the chairman of the parliament and even the president **does not mean that this is a democratic state**. We have just started on the road leading to a democratic statehood...' [Continued on page 204]:

things I cannot discuss with 'The New York Times' before I discuss them with President Gorbachëv in Moscow'. And it was logical that the new Czechoslovak Foreign Minister should have favoured the revision of 'obsolete strategic conceptions' and suggest the withdrawal of both Soviet and American troops from Europe.

It was logical for the new Polish 'non-Communist' Prime Minister to suggest that Soviet troops should remain in Poland for the time being to provide 'protection'. It was logical that Walesa should have declared that he wanted a Communist as Poland's President or, as a potential candidate himself to that high office, should have said that 'we want to cooperate constructively with the Communist authorities'.

It was logical that Walesa should have urged Solidarity voters to support 'liberal' Communist leaders like General Kiszczak who, together with General Jaruzelski, imposed martial law in 1981, placing Walesa for public consumption purposes under house arrest and 'forcing' Solidarity underground. And it was logical that it should have been General Kiszczak who negotiated the agreement providing for the 'free elections' which in fact enabled the 'non-Communist' Solidarity to enter parliament as the 'opposition'.

Furthermore, it was logical that, despite the drastic changes in the leadership, there should have been no significant revelations about secret agents of the security services among the former 'dissidents' who have become leading figures in the 'democratic', 'non-Communist' and 'nationalist' structures. The explanation is that the new leaders have a common interest with the Communist strategists and their security services in keeping the files secret.

So long as these secrets are not revealed, and by and large they will not be, the Communist Parties will retain their monopoly of power in practice. As John Lenczowski put it in 'The Los Angeles Times' of 11 January 1989, 'for all the increased openness in these countries, a great deal remains secret. And where there is secrecy, there is, perforce, uncertainty'.

FALSE 'INDEPENDENCE' OF THE SOVIET REPUBLICS

The present Communist strategists are concealing that it is they who are now creating 'independent' Republics – repeating on a much broader scale Lenin's experience with the Far Eastern and Georgian Republics, and also Stalin's deceptive dissolution of the Comintern in 1943. The strategists are concealing the secret coordination that exists, and will continue to exist, between Moscow and the 'nationalist' leaders of these newly 'independent' Republics. There has been ample time, and every oppor-

72 [Continued from page 203]: '... Deviations, certain deviations, for instance, **strengthening the power in order to save the main thing**, the most important achievement... I remember very well... When I worked here in the past, once I noticed just a pile of rubbish in the suburbs of Tbilisi. I would summon the people responsible and tell them: as from tomorrow you are not at your job any longer, and we used to expel people from the Party... I used to fly in a helicopter over Tbilisi... and if I noticed a pile of inert materials, the officials responsible would get a strong reprimand the following day... That was the way we worked at the time. **I do not know whether it is good or bad**... At the present stage... in a certain sense, **compulsion is also necessary.** I mean that democracy, real and true national democracy, must **compel antidemocratic forces to take into account the interests of society and the state**'. And in case the message was not clear enough, Shevardnadze told the Georgian Parliament on 6th August 1993 that **'My word should be law for everybody'** [see also Note 68, page 187]. It is interesting, in the light of all this, to re-read in the January-February 1983 issue of 'Problems of Communism', formerly published by the US Government, that 'Shevardnadze, as First Secretary of the Georgian Party organization, has been, by all accounts, a determined opponent of corruption, and has been sensitive to public opinion in Georgia'. His 'anti-corruption' drive involved the arbitrary arrest and imprisonment of over 100,000 people.

tunity, to prepare for this coordination in advance. Given such coordination, the fragmentation of the Soviet Empire will not be real or lasting, as the West assumes, but fictional. This is not true self-determination, but the use of 'national' forms in the execution of a common Communist strategy along lines pioneered by Lenin.

CENTRAL PURPOSES OF THE STRATEGY

The central domestic purpose of the strategy and the final phase of 'perestroika' is to renew the régimes in the Soviet Union and other Communist countries, and to convert them into states of 'mature socialism with a human face' in order to promote the external strategy of 'convergence'. These régimes must be 'acceptable' to the West for 'convergence' purposes. Thus the strategy goes far beyond domestic political restructuring, since it is aimed at the 'restructuring' or 're-shoeing' of the West – the 'reform' of Western attitudes and policies – and ultimately at the peaceful conquest of the United States and Western Europe from within.

The essence of the special manoeuvre within this strategy is the creation of secretly controlled opposition movements and the use and manipulation of them in a transition to a spectrum of new 'democratic' or 'democratist', 'non-Communist' and 'nationalist' power structures which will remain Communist-controlled in practice. It is these renewed régimes which are intended to achieve the global hegemony of Communism by means of 'convergence' on Communist terms of the 'former' Communist and non-Communist systems.

THE WEST'S FAILURE TO UNDERSTAND THE LENINIST PROGRAMME

The West has failed to comprehend the deceptive, controlled nature of the new 'democratic' and 'non-Communist' structures which have been introduced in the USSR and Eastern Europe. The West is jubilant that former so-called 'dissidents', seen as members of the 'persecuted political opposition', are now becoming presidents, premiers, members of government and parliament, and ambassadors in these new structures. **For the Communists have succeeded in concealing from the West that this so-called 'political opposition' of 'dissidents' has been created, brought up and guided by the Bloc's Communist Parties and security services during the long period of preparation for 'perestroika'.** The Bloc's political and security potential have been fully deployed in the interests of the strategy.

NEW 'DEMOCRATS' REMAIN COMMITTED TO 'SOCIALISM' (COMMUNISM)

Gorbachëv and his strategists are not true democrats and never will be. They remain committed to socialism and Communism. They are a new, smoother generation of revolutionaries who are using 'democratic' reforms as a new method, based on Leninist principles, of achieving final victory.

The Communist strategists appreciated that they could not implement their strategy of 'convergence' using the old, obsolete, Stalinist, Communist Party structure and dormant institutions like the old Soviet parliament. But they do believe that they can carry it out using new, revitalised, 'democratic' structures.

They are therefore reorganising the party system, the Presidency and the legislature to give them more power and prestige and at the same time greater likeness to their American counterparts. Meanwhile the Communist Party *appears* to be taking a back seat, relegated to the shadows.

However in reality, the Communist Party has not surrendered its real monopoly of power. On the contrary, it has broadened it by handing power to its members in the Presidency and the legislative organs, for the purpose of executing the strategy of *'perestroika'* and 'convergence'. Greater presidential powers are needed in order to carry this strategy throughout the world.

This is not a transfer of power from the Party to the President. The President remains a member of and an instrument of the Party, the executor of its strategy. He is not the Pope or Luther. He does not impose his will on the Party; he is fulfilling the Party's will. The ultimate decision-making power rests with the Politburo, the Party apparatus and their strategists.

Although the end of the Party's monopoly is proclaimed, **the Party apparatus remains in being and is still being run mainly by the same old-timers**.

The Party apparatus, though less visible, will continue to provide guidance to Party members in the reformed institutions. The Party not only retains a vast organisation, but has long experience, including periods of illegal operation under the Tsarist régime and in those territories which fell under German occupation in the Second World War. It will have no difficulty in adjusting to the environment of a fictional 'multi-Party system' which in practice it and the strategists will control.

MIMICKING THE AMERICAN SYSTEM, TO CREATE 'EQUIVALENCE'
All the apparent structural-political reforms – the apparently 'strong' Presidency, the new and livelier Congress, the talk of a National Security Council and of 'oversight' of the KGB and the creation of a 'loyal opposition' – are being implemented with the emphasis on their similarity to the American system. They should all be seen in the context of the devious strategy of 'convergence'.

This explains the introduction of the pretence of 'opposition', the calculated, heated and often televised arguments between old-style conformists and apparently Western-style members of the legislature like Yeltsin on the subject of the KGB and sensitive issues such as the future of the national Republics.

It also explains the emergence of groups of Russian nationalists, inheritors of the Slavophile tradition, Stalinists and even anti-Semites represented in *'Pamyat'* ['memory']: all are controlled by the Party and are being used in the interests of the strategy to play on Western hopes and fears so as to ensure continued Western support for the régime for 'fear' of a worse alternative coming to power.

MONOPOLY OF POWER 'SURRENDERED' IN ORDER TO PROMOTE THE STRATEGY
The Party will continue to exercise its leading strategic rôle through its members in the Presidency, government, the legislature, and the new political groupings and parties and national fronts. Even those 'reform Communists' who are seemingly calling for a reduction in the Party's rôle and for the introduction of a 'multi-Party system', are in fact fulfilling the instructions of the Party's strategists.

This, then, is the essence of the apparent 'surrender' by the Communist Party of its monopoly, and of the associated 'reforms'. The execution of the strategy of *'per-*

estroika' and 'convergence' is not governed by any laws or rules. On the contrary, it represents a skilful application of the Soviet political potential in its totality. The strategists realise that they cannot openly march to victory under Lenin's banner, or even use the word 'convergence' while Lenin remains unburied. They may in fact bury him with full honours, while in practice they continue to follow his devious ideas, as they make their final assault on the 'capitalist' West.

HOW THIS SITUATION AROSE

The crucial period, when the gap in Western strategic intelligence opened up, was between 1958 and 1960. At that time, Western intelligence services were unable to acquire reliable information concerning the adoption of the long-range strategy and the programme of strategic disinformation, because they were deeply penetrated by the KGB and their main sources in the USSR and China were compromised.

Self-evidently, KGB penetration in the United States did not begin with the Walker ring. The Central Intelligence Agency was already penetrated in 1958 – by both the KGB and Chinese intelligence. In 1958, the Agency lost its most important source, Colonel Popov of Soviet Military Intelligence [GRU], who could have provided strategic information had he not been compromised by KGB penetration, arrested by the KGB, and burned alive in the GRU's crematorium furnace.

ACCUMULATED MISCONCEPTIONS IN THE WEST

As fundamental misconceptions about Soviet policy have accumulated in Western Foreign Ministries, intelligence services and 'think-tanks', they have generated a vicious circle of bureaucratic vested interests which make the correction of the misconceptions difficult, if not impossible. The confusion caused by Soviet strategic disinformation, the vested interests of Western bureaucracies in now long-accepted misconceptions, and the consequent lack of proper strategic criteria for evaluating what the Soviet Communists and their Chinese allies are implementing, have inflicted serious damage on Western assessments of Communist developments, and on the capacity of the West to evaluate them correctly.

With few exceptions, Western experts fail to comprehend the strategic continuity behind these developments. They accumulate facts but are unable to see their strategic interaction, and are thus unable to build them into a coherent strategic picture. They continue to analyse events in terms of outdated, inapplicable Stalinist concepts such as continuing power struggles. This was notably the case in respect of Western interpretations of Gorbachëv's rise to power, the removal of his alleged rivals, and his assumption of the Presidency.

Accordingly, the introduction of *'perestroika'* was misinterpreted as a strictly domestic campaign by Gorbachëv himself to overcome the economic and political deficiencies of the Soviet Union. This attitude overlooked the reality that *'perestroika'* amounted in fact to a broad strategic assault on the Western mindset – to a Leninist 'reshoeing' of the West designed to alter Western attitudes, to facilitate the abolition of the 'image' of the enemy, and to inveigle the West into signing bilateral treaties, supporting broad inter-bloc 'collective security' arrangements (despite the 'abolition of the *image* of the enemy'), the entry of East European and CIS states into the European Union and other devices intended to establish 'irreversible' Soviet hegemony through 'convergence' with the West on Communist terms.

Some Western experts have gone to the extreme of interpreting the emergence of Gorbachëv and *'perestroika'*, in typically Western terms, as spontaneous, positive developments pushing the Soviet régime towards capitalism and Western-style democracy. These people have seen Gorbachëv as an independent innovator facing genuine resistance from the Party bureaucracy and the military. In other words, they bought the illusion that there is fundamental conflict within the Soviet structures over reforms and policies.

Ignorant of the Leninist roots and origins of *'perestroika'*, they failed to comprehend that it is a logical, advanced phase of Communist strategy. They have been unable to understand the essence of *'perestroika'*, the objectives of *'perestroika'* or its dangers as an element of the design for the achievement of global Communist supremacy – as an element of *'Weltoktober'*, or the Second October Revolution. They have been impressed by the drama of *'perestroika'*, but have been unable to appreciate its Leninist dialectical logic or dynamics, and its consequent revolutionary potential and intent. Essentially, too many Western analysts and observers fail to understand Leninist dialectics. Because of this vacuum at the core of their perceptions, Western experts failed to warn policymakers, **President Reagan**, **Chancellor Kohl** and the British Prime Minister, **Mrs Thatcher** (especially), about the implications and dangers of Western support for Gorbachëv and for *'perestroika'*.

As a consequence, the conservative leaderships of the West have failed to understand the essence of *'perestroika'*, and have signalled a wrong direction to their supporters – leading them and their countries towards a nightmare crisis because of their misguided support for Gorbachëv. Conservatives are confused about Gorbachëv and *'perestroika'*. Their old assumptions have been upset. They are out of ideas. They have lost perspective. In short, they are floundering.

By contrast, the Soviet long-range strategists have a coherent framework within which to pursue their objectives. And they are taking precautions to ensure that the crisis of confusion among conservative forces will not be temporary. On the contrary, practical measures are in hand to prevent any recovery of perspective, which would lead to the true purposes of 'restructuring' being understood in time. These measures of Soviet political warfare involve, in particular:

❑ Neutralising anti-Communist influence, especially within the conservative parties, as an important factor in the political life and orientation of the United States, Germany, France and Britain.

❑ Securing the victory of the radical Left in the next US presidential elections in 1992, and victories for the Socialist and Labour Parties in elections to be held in Germany, France and Britain in the 1990s.

To the extent that the conservatives in these countries have been neutralised, their parties' policies have moved in tandem with Soviet policies.

American policymakers, and especially the conservatives in both the Republican and Democratic Parties, were unable, despite their long experience with Communist duplicity and treachery, to grasp the intentions behind the new manoeuvres of the Communist strategists. So they rushed recklessly ahead to commit the West to helping 'perestroika', which is contrary to their interests. It is sad to observe the contemporary jubilation of American and West European conservatives who are cheering 'perestroika' without realising that it is intended to bring about their own political and even physical demise. Liberal support for 'perestroika' is understandable, but even I was surprised at the extent of support among the conservative forces[73,74].

THE APPROPRIATE RESPONSE TO THE CHALLENGE

Two possible responses to the aforementioned aggressive, but hidden, Communist strategy, are possible. One is that adopted by Kerensky and Vice-President Wallace, namely to ignore the challenge and thus to court disaster. The alternative response would be that of Churchill and Truman, namely to recognise the challenge and to face it down. Unfortunately, Reagan and Thatcher have displayed the naïveté of Kerensky and Wallace. It is vital that their strategic blunder should be corrected. If the new American leadership fails to change course and to correct this error, it will face responsibility for the progressive loss of Western Europe to socialism (Communism) and, ultimately, for the end of the great American experiment with democracy.

The moral basis for a reversal of the American response and for recommending a rejection of cooperation with the Soviet strategy are simple. A system which has murdered 20 million of its own people (50 million, if the loss of life in China under Communism is included), which has raped its intellectuals, and which has brought suffering and misery to the peoples of the Soviet Empire, does not deserve to be renewed. The American people are under no moral obligation to help with the resurrection of such a plainly evil system. The pragmatic basis for a revised US response to 'perestroika' is the need to protect and preserve the American system from 'restructuring' preparatory to 'convergence' with the 'reformed' Soviet system, and to save the American people from the blood baths and re-education camps which such 'convergence' will eventually bring about, of which the West currently has no conception.

Unfortunately, the active engagement of the Administration of President Bush in support of Gorbachëv and 'perestroika' shows that the Administration has failed to comprehend the strategy underlying 'perestroika', and is blind to hostile Communist intentions, and to the dangers implicit in them. The Bush Administration did in fact undertake what was billed as a 'reassessment' of 'perestroika'. But that process produced a classic failure of comprehension, and may even have reinforced US official illusions about Moscow's intentions.

73 *Author's Note:* It is possible that eventually the conservatives will recover. There are already indications that the recovery has begun. Senators Wallop and Lugar have both criticised the Clinton Administration's policy towards Russia. Senator Lugar specifically suggested after revelation of the Ames case that the policy of partnership with Russia was mistaken and should be re-examined.

74 *Editor's Note:* Following the Republicans' landslide victory in the mid-term elections in November 1994, prominent Congressional voices, led by Senator Lugar working in cooperation with like-minded influential Democratic Party leaders, started to question key elements of US and Western policy such as the subordination of NATO to the United Nations, let alone to the CSCE – now the OSCE – as agitated for ahead of the Budapest summit meeting held on 5-6 December, by Moscow. A review of the United States' posture towards the former Soviet Bloc reportedly took place in November 1994.

Certainly, instead of rectifying the fundamental error committed by President Reagan's Government when it euphorically and uncritically embraced Gorbachëv and *'perestroika'*, the Administration of President George Bush has gravely compounded President Reagan's errors and has gone further by fully adopting the recommendations and scenario propounded by Brzezinski and Genscher as the Western response to the 'changes' in the USSR and Eastern Europe. By doing so, it has set the West on a disastrously mistaken course.

The meaning of developments in the (formerly) Communist world is misunderstood, and the intentions behind Communist initiatives have been misinterpreted. Enemies are accepted and treated as though they have suddenly, overnight, become allies of the West. The Western countries have responded enthusiastically, without realising the potential damage which will be inflicted upon their democratic systems. Continuing Western blindness allows the Soviet strategists to turn everything in the West on its head. **The truth is being turned inside out.** This blindness, upon which the strategists have of course all along been relying, has become a gravely destabilising factor affecting international relations, Western diplomacy, trade, economics, military strategy and budgets, election processes, the media, national cohesion and Western societies generally.

THE UNITED STATES IS BEING DIMINISHED

The blindness of the American leadership élite is diminishing the rôle of the United States as the leader of the Western world, and is offering the Soviets fresh openings enabling them to manipulate erroneous and naïve perceptions of *'perestroika'*, to the detriment of the Western alliances. The distinction between the US vision of an enlarged Europe based upon Western values, and the Soviet vision of a neutral socialist Europe stretching from the Atlantic to the Urals, has been completely lost from sight[75,76].

75 *Editor's Note:* Under the Single European Act and the Maastricht Treaty with its intergovernmental accords, no EC/EU Member State may claim intrinsic national interests any longer in key areas, such as foreign policy. On the contrary, such interests are held 'in common' by the Member States plus the Commission; and it is for that 'collective' to decide what the interests of the European Union are as a whole. These are liable to be acceptable to Moscow, given the binding obligations assumed by the individual EU countries towards Russia under the terms of their new bilateral treaties.

76 *Editor's Note:* The phrases 'From the Atlantic to the Urals', 'From the Atlantic to Vladivostok' and 'From Vancouver to Vladivostok' are interchangeable in the strategists' lexicon. In the course of his Nobel Peace Prize Lecture, delivered in Oslo in June **1992**, Gorbachëv said: **'Our** [*sic*] vision of the European space from the Atlantic to the Urals is not that of a closed system. Since it includes the Soviet Union [*sic*], which reaches to the shores of the Pacific, it goes beyond nominal geographical boundaries'. Note that Gorbachëv, who had been out of office for six months, referred to the **Soviet Union**, not Russia. In an interview on Moscow Television on 19 November 1991, Eduard Shevardnadze continued speaking as though he was still Soviet Foreign Minister: 'I think that the idea of a Common European Home, the building of a united Europe, and I would like to underline today, of great Europe, the building of Great Europe, great, united Europe, from the Atlantic to the Urals, from the Atlantic to Vladivostok, *including all our territory*, most probably a European-Asian space, this project is inevitable. I am sure that we will come to building a united military space as well. To say more precisely: we will build a united Europe, whose security will be based on the principles of collective security. Precisely, collective security'. These statements by key implementers of the strategy reflect the central strategic objective of asserting 'irreversible' Russian/Soviet hegemony over Eurasia, thus establishing the primary geographical component of the intended World Government.

To sum up, US blindness in helping *'perestroika'* in the USSR and Eastern Europe shows that the Bush Administration does not realise the strategic and political implications of such a policy for the United States and Western Europe. This blindness will end in disillusionment following the collapse of US long-term expectations, and may facilitate the final victory of the Soviet strategy of 'convergence' through political means.

WESTERN PROSPECTS SIGNIFICANTLY UNDERMINED
The blindness of the United States and the West generally to Soviet strategy, its uncritical acceptance of the authenticity of deceptive, controlled 'pseudo-democracy' ('democratism'), and its support for *'perestroika'*, have given the Soviets significant advantages and have shortened the life expectancies of the Western democracies. Ignorant of aggressive Communist intentions, the Western democracies are now acutely vulnerable to the entry into their countries of the political and security potential of the renewed Communist régimes. This potential consists of the 'non-Communist' governments, the new political parties, the members of the new parliaments, renewed trade unions, prominent churchmen and intellectuals, and the leaders of the new 'non-Communist', 'democratic' structures in the newly 'independent' 'nationalist' 'ex'-Soviet states. It is a potential which has been systematically retrained, inspired and revitalised in the context of the success of *'perestroika'* and its uncritical acceptance by the West.

THEY WILL RETAIN THE UPPER HAND UNTIL WE COME TO OUR SENSES
Until the West abandons its simplistic thinking, penetrates mentally the complexities of the 'changes' which have taken place in the Communist world, and comes to terms with the Leninist dialectic driving those 'changes', the Communist strategists will retain the upper hand. This critical state of affairs demands urgent rethinking of the West's response to the strategy of *'perestroika'*, and its dangers for the West. That is the main and urgent priority. This review will take courage and statesmanship of the highest order. The following issues might be addressed:

First of all, Western governments should put an end to the confusion, euphoria and destabilisation of their societies by admitting their mistake, disengaging from their support for *'perestroika'*, and exposing its dangers. They should concentrate on strengthening their alliances, upon addressing their domestic problems, and on developing an effective counter-strategy to *'perestroika'*.

Secondly, the Vatican should reverse its mistaken support for the renewal of the Communist régimes in the USSR and Eastern Europe. The statement by the late Pope Pius XII concerning **the incompatibility and irreconcilability of Communism and religion** is as correct as ever. The Vatican should reaffirm this dictum and should use its influence and its 'divisions' to defend Western values from the new, deadly but 'hidden' Communist assault.

Thirdly, Western industrialists and financiers should reverse their mistaken involvement in joint ventures with the Communists, thereby financing the revival of their main political adversaries, supplying them ill-advisedly with new technology, and wasting time and money on operations that will ultimately be taxed to death, confiscated, or both.

In the fourth place, free Western trade unions, especially the AFL-CIO, should wake up from their illusions concerning the new 'non-Communist' unions in the Communist countries, and should not walk into the trap they have laid.

Fifthly, the political élite in Western Europe and the United States should rethink its unquestioning support for *'perestroika'* and for concepts which flow from it such as 'collective security' and the 'enlargement' of the EC through the entry of East European and CIS states.

In the sixth place, the Western media should reconsider its biased presentation of *'perestroika'*, should penetrate the façade of *'glasnost'* and the new 'non-Communist' structures, and should provide much more realistic and objective accounts of the 'changes' implemented in the Communist countries, and their meaning and implications for the West.

Finally the United States should correct the grave mistake it made when it weakened and degutted its intelligence and counter-intelligence services, taking away the Central Intelligence Agency's *policy formulation rôle* ahead of the so-called 'end of the Cold War'. Instead of bragging that they won the 'Cold War' – in fulfilment of Sun Tzu's warning that an adversary's objective should be to 'pretend inferiority and encourage the enemy's arrogance' – the United States must belatedly understand that in fact it 'lost' the Cold War, as soon as the West began to offer enthusiastic support for the *'perestroika'* deception, and to regard it as serving the West's best interests.

The American intelligence and counter-intelligence services should now be radically rebuilt in order to counteract the aggressive deployment against the West of the Communists' full political and security potential.

And Western counter-intelligence must find effective ways, as a matter of particular urgency, of dealing with Communist agents of influence operating without constraint throughout the West. ∎

EDITOR'S NOTE:

In June 1994, the Author requested that the following two Memoranda be included with the preceding text. The first Memorandum – 'THE COST OF MISPLACED TRUST', filed with the Central Intelligence Agency on 27 September 1993 following the murder of the CIA operative, Fred Woodruff, outside Tbilisi – dealt with events in Georgia and Azerbaijan, the return to power of **Shevardnadze** and **Aliyev**, and the meaning of their return. The second of these Memoranda – filed with the CIA on 28 April 1992 – is entitled: 'WARNING TO THE CIA, THE FBI AND THE US INTELLIGENCE COMMUNITY CONCERNING THE FORTHCOMING CAMPAIGN EXPLOITING THE ALLEGED DISCLOSURE OF KGB FILES'. **In this Memorandum, the Author warned the CIA that the KGB would release information from its files selectively and instrumentally, in pursuit of the strategy's objectives.** This Leninist technique is called 'revealing state secrets in the interests of strategy'. He also reflected on who really 'won' the Cold War. ∎

ADDENDUM

FURTHER RELEVANT MEMORANDA TO THE CIA

1. The cost of misplaced trust.

2. Warning to the CIA, the FBI and the US intelligence community concerning the forthcoming disinformation campaign through the alleged disclosure of KGB files.

3. Destruction through KGB penetration of the Central Intelligence Agency of its capacity to interpret developments in Russia and China correctly, taking their strategy and disinformation into account.

The events in Chechnya explained in terms of Russian strategy.

The Kremlin's objectives and the Chechnya crisis.

The urgent need to reconsider prevailing assumptions about Russia and China.

4. Control of political events in Russia.

Memorandum to the CIA: 27 SEPTEMBER 1993

For the attention of: The Director of Central Intelligence

THE COST OF MISPLACED TRUST

The tragic murder of **Mr Fred Woodruff** in Georgia is striking evidence of the price the US and other Western governments will pay for involving themselves in complex situations in the former USSR which they do not understand because they have never taken adequate account of Soviet strategy. As a fellow citizen of Mr Woodruff and as a former colleague of his in that both of us have worked for the CIA, I deplore the fact that American lives should be put at risk and lost in an apparent effort to cooperate with the Georgian security authorities under Shevardnadze. As I stated in my Memorandum to the Agency in March 1989, Shevardnadze was for many years the Communist Party boss and Minister of Internal Affairs in Georgia. As a member of the former Soviet Politburo and as Gorbachëv's Foreign Minister he was chosen to play an active role in creating, developing and carrying out the long-range Soviet strategy of *'perestroika'* about which I have written at such length. His alleged conversion to democratic views is spurious. Trust in his good faith is misplaced and support for him and his régime in Georgia is mistaken. It is tragic that Mr Woodruff's life, and perhaps the lives of other Americans in future, should be lost in the pursuit of an erroneous policy. If the CIA had paid any serious attention to my earlier Memoranda, Mr Woodruff would not have been in Georgia to be murdered.

The roughly simultaneous re-emergence of **Shevardnadze** as the leader of Georgia with its internal conflict and of **Aliyev** as the leader of Muslim Azerbaijan in conflict with the Christian Armenians is no coincidence. As stated in my Memorandum of March 1990, Aliyev was for many years the KGB Minister and Party boss in Azerbaijan and, like Shevardnadze, a Politburo member. The restoration to power in these two Republics with strongly anti-Communist populations of former Communist Party bosses who were and still are partners in executing the Soviet strategy of *'perestroika'* shows that Communist influence and power are still alive and strong in the Republics despite their alleged moves towards democracy.

The continuing existence of this Communist power is a further indication that the Soviet-manufactured strategy is still in operation. Shevardnadze and Aliyev owe their positions, not to the popular will, but to concealed support from their former colleagues in the Soviet Government, the Communist Party infrastructure, the KGB's successor organisations and the army whose combined influence remains intact despite organisational changes and the alleged independence of the Republics.

Why have Shevardnadze and Aliyev re-emerged in their leading positions? In the first place they are there to reassert control over the conflicts in their Republics. Secondly they are there to implement the Sino-Soviet strategy *vis-à-vis* Iran and the Arab world outlined in my Memorandum of 26 March 1992 [*see pages 149-153*][77]. **This**

77 *Author's Note:* They are also there to help implement the strategy *vis-à-vis* the United States and NATO, as is implied by Shevardnadze's recent visit to the United States, and the Georgian Foreign Minister's visit to NATO headquarters in Brussels.

entails involving Western countries on the side of the Georgians and Armenians while involving Turkey, Iran and Arab countries *inter alia* on the side of the Turkic and Muslim Azers. The longer-term purpose of this manoeuvre is, through the Muslims of the former USSR, to consolidate concealed Russian influence over Islamic fundamentalism to complement that being openly sought by the Chinese Communists.

This Sino-Soviet strategy is based on the experience of Iran where the Islamic fundamentalists came to power. As an anti-American and anti-Western movement, Islamic fundamentalism offers obvious possibilities for undermining the pro-western régimes in Saudi Arabia and the Gulf. The Chinese Communists are openly supporting and supplying the Iranian Government.

Under concealed Russian guidance, the Muslims of the former USSR, especially the Azers, will seek to cooperate and ally themselves with Muslims in Iran and the Arab states while Russia maintains its open policy of cooperation and partnership with the West. In this way China openly and Russia secretly will jointly attempt to swing the balance of power in their favour in the highly strategic, oil-producing Arab/Iranian areas of the Middle East.

It is disturbing that, like the CIA, the FBI is involving itself in the former Soviet Union. Since the FBI understands no more than the CIA about Soviet strategy and CIS affairs, it too will pay a high price for its involvement.

The Russian and Soviet 'security organs' have been reorganised and renamed many times in their history without these changes significantly affecting their personnel, their mentality or their operations. The recent reorganisation and alleged reform of the KGB is no exception. When Lenin's New Economic Policy with its limited toleration of domestic and foreign capitalism was introduced in the 1920s, the KGB's predecessor set up a new department, which became known as the Economic Department, to deal with smuggling, currency offences, black market operations and other economic crimes. In order to control the activities of domestic and foreign capitalists the Economic Department resorted to recruiting Western entrepreneurs by blackmail or other means. In his original report to the British, the GRU defector Walter Krivitsky stated that five or six out of every ten Western businessmen in the USSR were recruited by the Soviets.

In the US context it was the Economic Department that recruited Armand Hammer and others. The department provided the Soviet service with some of its best legal and illegal *Rezidents* like Vassili Zarubin, former illegal and legal *Rezident* in Europe and the United States, Yevgeniy Mitskevich, former *Rezident* in Italy, and Aleksandr Orlov, former *Rezident* in Germany and France. All of them, while serving abroad, ran agents recruited by the Economic Department. With the adoption of the new strategy in 1959 the KGB re-established the Economic Department as the Anti-Contraband Department under Sergey Fedoseyev.

This department arrested possible future Soviet entrepreneurs and blackmailed foreign diplomats and officials engaged in currency offences or black market dealings. It was as a result of his recruitment of an American diplomat or intelligence officer in the USSR while in this department that Fedoseyev was promoted to head the American Department of the KGB's Second Chief Directorate.

In parallel with the Economic Department, the Soviet Ministry of the Interior maintained a department known as the OBKhS which was responsible for uncovering theft and embezzlement of state property and which developed an extensive network of secret agents in the criminal world. No doubt, with the present acceptance of domestic and foreign capitalism in the C.I.S., the successors to the Economic Department and the OBKhS will energetically expand their agent networks among domestic and foreign entrepreneurs and criminals[78].

The attitude of the FBI and the C.I.S. intelligence authorities to their liaison will differ significantly. The FBI will approach it in good faith expecting sincere C.I.S. cooperation in crime-busting. The C.I.S. authorities however will see the liaison in the context of *their strategy which has not been and will not be revealed to the West*. The C.I.S. authorities will seek to exploit their liaison with the FBI and other Western services for the following purposes and along these lines:

1. To control and, when not cooperating with them, to fight criminal operators in their own territories in their national interests;

2. To maintain their liaisons at a credible level they will supply them with tit-bits of genuine information, some of them juicy, BUT;

3. They will continue to study FBI, CIA and other Western officials as targets for recruitment and will approach them when appropriate. They will not hesitate to murder all whom they see as a serious threat to their strategy or operations;

4. They will seek to exploit the new situation of 'openness' to send their own agent-running officers involved in criminal and economic activities abroad as illegals to build up their own networks along the lines of the Italian mafia which they know and understand. In this way they will seek to build up their penetration of and influence in the economic, financial and government sectors in the West. They will use this influence to assist their strategy of convergence with the West;

5. Their official liaisons with Western agencies will provide a useful degree of protection for and feedback on their undeclared agent-running activities.

In the light of the above, I recommend that the FBI, the CIA and other agencies should brief their officials before they leave for the C.I.S. that:

(a) They will be studied for possible recruitment and may be approached;

(b) If, in the course of their duties in the C.I.S., they should pick up significant information indicating that the C.I.S. authorities are acting in the manner described above they should be wary of discussing it locally but should if possible return to headquarters and report it in person.

Without adequate briefing on these lines, Western officials in the C.I.S. will be sitting ducks. I request that the new Director of the FBI and the Head of the Counter-Intelligence Staff in the CIA be informed of the contents of this Memorandum. ∎

---

78 *Editor's Note:* The use of structures ostensibly established to combat corruption and organised crime as cover for controlled criminal operations is well established. For instance, Claire Sterling writes in *'Crime without Frontiers'* [Little, Brown and Company (UK) Limited, London, 1994, pages 79-80]: '[The Azerbaijani state mafia], headed by the Soviet Union's First Deputy Prime Minister [KGB General] Gaidar Aliyev, a full member of the Soviet Politburo – restored to power in Azerbaijan in 1993 – presided over a 'petroleum mafia', a 'fishing mafia', a 'fruit and vegetable mafia', a 'caviar mafia', a 'railroad mafia', an 'export mafia', a 'customs mafia' and a 'militia mafia' operating inside the Interior Ministry's Division for Fighting Violators of Socialist Property and Speculation'.

Memorandum to the CIA: 28 APRIL 1992

From: ANATOLIY GOLITSYN

WARNING TO THE CIA, THE FBI AND THE US INTELLIGENCE COMMUNITY CONCERNING THE FORTHCOMING DISINFORMATION CAMPAIGN EXPLOITING THE ALLEGED DISCLOSURE OF KGB FILES
[The disclosure of state secrets in the interests of strategy]

According to this assessment, disclosures about the contents of KGB files will not be the spontaneous acts of individual former KGB officers but a planned and calculated disinformation campaign or, more precisely, a covert joint operation by the relabelled intelligence services of the Commonwealth of Independent States (CIS) and Arbatov's Institute for the Study of the United States and Canada. This covert operation will be combined with other active measures and the use of agents of influence among movie-makers, scholars and journalists in the United States and Europe.

The new leadership of the CIS will make available for this campaign the necessary technical facilities and the services of the best scriptwriters and the best experts in documentary photomontage whose techniques are on the same plane as the legendary Sergey Eisenstein.

The main purpose of the campaign will not be to enlighten the West by clearing up the mysteries of the KGB's primary Cold War operations or by revealing the true identities of the KGB s important agents or its false defectors. Its objective will be to discredit the US Presidency, the CIA and the FBI in the eyes of American and world public opinion in order to generate pressure for the further weakening of the American special services if not for their complete abolition and replacement by new emasculated or nominal services. A further objective will be to discredit the remaining anti-Communist politicians and experts, to extinguish their residual influence in the US Administration and political parties, and to prevent its revival.

The successors to the KGB have no intention of revealing the whole truth contained in KGB files but only such half-truths as will enable them to manipulate American public opinion to suit their purposes as described above. Since the Watergate hearings the CIA and the FBI have destroyed many files and have lost much of their counter-intelligence memory. This has impaired their ability to apprehend manipulation of disclosures about the KGB. A recent example illustrates the point.

Several 'former' KGB officers visited the United States to meet and exchange views with their CIA counterparts. The Russian group included a certain **Zvezdenkov**. The visit was treated in the US press simply as a public relations affair. It escaped the notice of the press and apparently of the CIA and the FBI that Zvezdenkov was the man who investigated and sent to his death Petr Popov, the most valuable agent the Central Intelligence Agency ever ran in the GRU. **The successors to the KGB did not reveal this fact: the CIA and the FBI seemed to have forgotten it**. We are left in the dark as to why Zvezdenkov should have been sent to the United States. Similar partial revelations and manipulation of them can be expected on more important matters in the future.

This joint covert operation should be viewed as the opening shot in a widespread CIS offensive to implement the strategy of convergence with the United States. The CIS strategists reckon that they will only be able to approach the objective of World Government if they can first drastically weaken the US Presidency, the CIA and the FBI and eliminate from the US political scene any lingering anti-Communism and any residual doubts and misgivings about their allegedly reformed system.

These strategists and the new intelligence services of the CIS enjoy significant advantages over the CIA and the FBI which will favour the success of their operations. To understand this one must first reject certain assumptions and illusions which have become widespread in the atmosphere of optimism and euphoria engendered in the West by the changes in the former Soviet Union.

In the first place, the leaders of the CIS and their military and political forces do not regard themselves as having been defeated[79]. On the contrary, they have discarded the old, discredited Stalinist form of Communist organisation and replaced it, in accordance with the decisions of the 22nd Party Congress in 1961, with a new, more viable form of organisation, the 'state of the whole people', which has far greater potential for achieving convergence with the West. They have broadened the powers of the national Republics and created a provisional form of federal union, the CIS, in which, contrary to well propagated myths, the unifying bonds will prove to be stronger, more natural and healthier than before.

Secondly, they have launched political and economic reforms intended to convert their Republics and the CIS as a whole into modern technological societies. They regard this transformation as part of another October Revolution. The first October Revolution failed to broaden into world revolution because the world was scared by Soviet terror. The second revolution is being attempted through the introduction and manipulation of a spurious form of Western-style democracy ('democratism') and market economy environment.

The strategists behind these 'changes' believe that the second revolution can lead to successful convergence with the West *on their terms*. Their confidence in victory is based upon the fact that the West has accepted the reforms they have engineered as representing genuine progress towards democracy, and is committing itself to financing the new course adopted by the former Soviet Union.

The CIS leaders and strategists are well aware that blind Western acceptance of the new course as genuinely democratic is largely attributable to the KGB which prepared and introduced KGB-controlled political opposition and 'perestroika' into the former Soviet system. It was because of their successes in preparing and carrying out this programme that successive leaders of the KGB were elevated by Andropov to the leadership of the Party, and Chebrikov and Kryuchkov to membership of the Politburo. The KGB officers and veterans who created the Association of Foreign Intelligence Veterans regard themselves and are regarded by the leaders of the CIS not as the losers but as the victors of the Cold War.

They are in no doubt that they outwitted the Western intelligence services

---

79 *Author's Note:* If they were defeated, why are they still demanding to be treated as a superpower and why are the alleged victors in the Cold War competing with one another in offering the 'defeated' party concessions?

because, through their covert operations, they succeeded in concealing from them that the so-called political opposition in the USSR was in fact under KGB control: the political and economic reforms implemented in the former USSR which the KGB played a large part in organising are now accepted and financed by the West in the mistaken belief that they represent true progress towards a democratic capitalist system. The KGB won the intelligence war with the American, British, West German and French Governments through penetration agents like the atomic spies and the Walker ring, through plants like 'TOPHAT', 'FEDORA', 'KITTYHAWK' and 'FAREWELL', and through false defectors like Yurchenko and others[80].

The campaign of partial disclosure of KGB files is a continuation of the struggle with the CIA and the FBI and is intended to destroy their reputations and effectiveness once and for all.

As Russian sources have disclosed, the first important stories based on material from the KGB files will deal with the Soviet atomic spies in the United States, the Kennedy assassination and the Iranian revolution. A film documentary on Soviet defectors is also planned. This choice of subjects underlines the warning given in this Memorandum. All these subjects will provide ample opportunities through selective 'documentary' disclosures to revive old controversies and create new ones whether on nuclear disarmament, CIA involvement in the Kennedy assassination, the CIA's rôle in Iran or the authenticity of Yuriy Nosenko's defection.

The new CIS intelligence services are determined to exploit to the full all available scope for manipulating information on both the known and the unsolved penetrations of the United States. Their task is simplified by the following factors:

1. The CIA weakened its own capacity to shape events in the interests of US policy when it chose in 1967 to disclose its political assets among US student organisations and Western intellectuals.

2. The Watergate hearings further weakened the CIA and the FBI by exposing additional assets and capabilities. The main fatality was the destruction of effective counter-intelligence within the CIA and the loss of its research and analytical capabilities and files.

3. The FBI's counter-intelligence has never understood the KGB's political rôle in the execution of Soviet strategy or its use of new methods, in particular strategic disinformation. The primary cause of this failure has been the FBI's acceptance of KGB-controlled plants as genuine sources.

4. The intelligence and counter-intelligence services of Britain, France and Germany are in no position to help the American services to counter the forthcoming disinformation campaign because they have been weakened by KGB penetration, both resolved and unsolved.

5. The Western media, film-makers and scholars have all been confused by

---

80 *Author's Note:* The Ames case confirms that the KGB won the intelligence war. **The victors in an intelligence war control information and disinformation: the losers lack accurate information and take their decisions on a false basis**. The Ames case shows how blind and bankrupt is the American policy of aid to the 'new' régime in Russia. Such aid permits the new KGB to finance and expand their intelligence activities and to be more generous in paying their agents in the United States and Europe. American dollars would be more wisely spent on improving the quality of the United States' own intelligence services, leaving the KGB with no alternative but to pay their agents in roubles.

the 'changes' in the former Soviet Union. They have accepted the 'changes' at face value as spontaneous and genuine, and have overlooked their strategic implications for the United States and the West generally. In their confusion, they accept uncritically the veracity of statements made by former KGB officers which inevitably lead them to adopt revisionist views concerning past CIA operations.

6. The ignorance and confusion prevailing among members of the US Congress about the changes in the former USSR induce them to pass harmful legislation to weaken the CIA and other elements of the intelligence community, and to reduce their budgets and capabilities.

CONCLUSION

Unless addressed, these factors will leave the Central Intelligence Agency, the Federal Bureau of Investigation and the intelligence community as a whole unprepared and vulnerable in the face of the coming disinformation campaign. There is accordingly an urgent need for a CIA counteraction programme to be added to the priorities already defined by the new Director of Central Intelligence. The CIA, the FBI and other components of the intelligence community should create a special research and advisory staff of experts, both old and new, to assess and counteract the campaign.

The most suitable candidate to take charge of such a staff would be **Newton S. Miler**, the last of the counter-intelligence Mohicans, who was being trained by the late **James Jesus Angleton** as his successor and who possesses the necessary experience and determination. ■

Memorandum to the CIA: **1 FEBRUARY 1995**

For the attention of: Admiral William O Studeman,
Acting Director, Central Intelligence Agency

DESTRUCTION THROUGH KGB PENETRATION OF THE CENTRAL INTELLIGENCE AGENCY OF ITS CAPACITY TO INTERPRET DEVELOPMENTS IN RUSSIA AND CHINA CORRECTLY, TAKING THEIR STRATEGY AND DISINFORMATION INTO ACCOUNT

THE EVENTS IN CHECHNYA EXPLAINED IN TERMS OF RUSSIAN STRATEGY

THE KREMLIN'S OBJECTIVES AND THE CHECHNYA CRISIS

THE URGENT NEED TO RECONSIDER PREVAILING ASSUMPTIONS ABOUT RUSSIA AND CHINA

In my Memorandum dated 1st October 1993[81], and in earlier Memoranda, I concluded that the confrontations between Gorbachëv and Ligachev, between Gorbachëv and Yeltsin (the August 1991 'coup') and between Yeltsin and the Russian parliament in March and September 1993 were all contrived and controlled by the Kremlin strategists in pursuit of their strategic objectives. I suggested that the Central Intelligence Agency should review *all their information from all sources* on these events with a view to improving their assessments of them and determining which of their sources were being used by the Russians to feed disinformation to them. Because of its relevance, a complete copy of my Memorandum of 1 October 1993 is enclosed [*see pages 235-237 of the present work*].

When I was preparing that Memorandum I was unaware that Aldrich Hazen Ames had, since 1985, been passing to his Soviet and Russian masters all the information to which he had access on the CIA's secret sources in the USSR and the CIS. It remains to be established whether the agents whose identities Ames disclosed to the Russians were genuine agents of the Central Intelligence Agency, or whether they were themselves Russian-controlled.

Penetration of the CIA by the KGB in the late 1950s compromised genuine CIA agents such as the GRU Lieutenant-Colonel Petr Popov. Accordingly, the CIA failed to understand the significance of the new political strategy which had been developed for the entire Communist bloc and movement, including China, when it was adopted in 1958-60. Penetration also explains why the Agency failed to detect the political disinformation employed in support of the new strategy in its initial

81 The Memorandum dated 1 October 1993 was appended to the present Memorandum, and is reproduced here on pages 235-237. In addition to its relevance to the Author's submission of 1 February 1995, it may be read in conjunction with his Memoranda and observations dated 26 March and 12 October 1993 [*see pages 162-163*], addressing the 'confrontation' between Yeltsin and the Congress of Peoples' Deputies in March and the new type of 'Reichstag Fire' of October that year. CIA clearance of the material appearing on pages 221-237 was provided in early April 1995.

phase, and why it failed to realise that new models for the structure of Communist societies were envisaged as replacements for the existing Soviet Communist model. As far as the USSR was concerned, the official intention to carry out such a change was publicly announced to the world by the Twenty-Second CPSU Congress in November 1961 which called for the replacement of the concept of the 'dictatorship of the proletariat' by the model of the 'state of the whole people'[82].

For the next 25 years, the CIA persisted in identifying Soviet disinformation with Soviet 'active measures' – which were interpreted in the narrow sense of meaning, for example, character assassination and the circulation of forged Western documents. **By ignoring the existence and dimension of joint Sino-Soviet strategic political deception, the CIA condemned itself to further extraordinary failures.** The most important was the failure to detect the continuation of Sino-Soviet strategic coordination behind the smokescreen of the Sino-Soviet 'split'. Accepting the false premise of real hostility between the Soviet Union and China, successive US Governments actively negotiated agreements with the USSR in the early 1960s 'playing the China card', and with China in the 1970s 'playing the Soviet card'. A further critical failure on the part of the Agency was the acceptance of Sakharov and other Soviet 'dissidents' as genuine opponents of the Soviet system – whereas in fact they were acting as controlled exponents and instruments of Soviet strategy.

The Central Intelligence Agency's penetration by Ames, and possibly others – we shall see – contemporaneously with the introduction of 'perestroika' in the 'former' USSR, explains the absence of genuine secret intelligence reaching the Agency on the subject. It explains why the CIA did not foresee 'perestroika', why it did not detect the deception behind it and why it misinterpreted 'perestroika' as representing the emergence of the prospect of real democracy in Russia, rather than the contrived arrival of ➧

82 *Editor's Note:* Official announcement of the new course was preceded and accompanied by explicit statements by Aleksandr Shelepin, Chairman of the Committee of State Security [KGB], that the Party lives and breathes inside the KGB, the key instrument for implementing the strategy, and *vice versa*. The KGB, as Golitsyn explains in *'New Lies for Old'* and in the present work, was reorganised under Shelepin in order to enable it to realise the full political potential of the state's resources in the pursuit of the long-range strategy of preparing for 'convergence' with the West in order to dominate and control it. In a speech before the 22nd Party Congress [as reported in *'Izvestia'* on 28 October 1961] Shelepin said that 'the state security agencies have been reorganised, have been cut down substantially, relieved of functions not proper to them.... **The Party has assigned a large contingent of Party, Soviet and Young Communist league [Komsomol] workers to positions in them. The State Security Committee and its local agencies now have well-trained, competent cadres who are supremely devoted to the Party.... The *entire activity* of the agencies of the State Security Committee is now *under the continual supervision of the Party and Government*.... The Party has restored true Leninist style and methods of work in the State Security agencies... An exceptionally big rôle is being played in the activities of the agencies of the State Security Committee by the Party organisations, which have taken a worthy and fitting place in all our work'.** In an address before the 21st Party Congress two years earlier, Shelepin, in announcing the intended reorganisation of the KGB for strategic purposes along the lines explained by Golitsyn, revealed that the Chekists would 'endeavour to restore and introduce into all our activity the style and methods of work of the splendid Bolshevik Dzerzhinskiy' [*'Pravda'*, 5 February 1959]. In addition to confirming Golitsyn's explanation of how the KGB was mobilised for strategic purposes along the lines originally pioneered for Lenin by Dzerzhinskiy, Shelepin's statements before the 22nd CPSU Congress confirmed the effective integration of the Party within the KGB – or, to put it another way, that the Party and the KGB share the same bloodstream. Note, too, that Shelepin made it clear that the *'entire activity'* of the KGB would be under the *continual supervision of the Party and Government*. 'Continual' means that there is to be no end to such supervision. Therefore, it is illogical to assume, as some Western experts do, that, while the KGB lives on in new guises, the Party has truly 'disappeared'.

the 'state of the whole people' as envisaged and planned for by the Soviet strategy formulated and introduced in 1958-60.

The final objective of this strategy is Sino-Russian world domination, which means – self-evidently – that it is therefore fundamentally hostile to the West. In the absence of any warning to this effect from secret intelligence sources, US policymakers rashly accepted that 'perestroika' was a spontaneous political development and that first Gorbachëv and subsequently Yeltsin were (and remain, irrespective of their blatantly incompatible actions) genuine reformers. In reality both have faithfully carried out the strategy laid down in 1958-60, as subsequently elaborated. Yeltsin's fitful, unconvincing professions of his 'commitment' to democratic reform, which Western policymakers find so comforting, and his willingness to 'cooperate' with the West, are no more than temporary expedients, in the classic Leninist tradition, which serve to conceal his allegiance to the strategy.

Deprived by Ames, and possibly others, of genuine secret intelligence concerning internal Russian politics, US policymakers have continued to accept uncritically the interpretation of events projected by open sources including the Russian and Western media and, in particular, by the expert communicators spawned by Arbatov's Institute for the Study of the USA and Canada.

In my Memorandum of 1 October 1993, I suggested that the collective leadership of the Russian strategists – who represent the ultimate authority when decisions have to be made on such issues as who serves as President and what policies he pursues – might be using the National Security Council as their main decision-making instrument. *The New York Times'* asserted on 20 and 22 January 1995 that this body, which it described as a 'semi-Politburo', seemed to be running the country and was calling the shots on Chechnya.

In a letter to a publisher dated 12 October 1993[83] I explained my view that the collective leadership had various options at their disposal in connection with the matter of who should occupy the Presidency. The first option, which they exercised, was to appoint a Communist, Gorbachëv, to introduce 'perestroika'. Their second option was to arrange for the continuation of 'perestroika' under a 'democratic' leader, Yeltsin, whom they selected and groomed for the purpose, and who was elected because he had appeared to 'renounce' his Communism[84] and strategic purpose.

---

83 See the Author's observations on page 163, which are condensed from a letter to the Editor.

84 *Editor's Note:* At the 28th CPSU Congress held in July 1990, Yeltsin in fact laid down a political strategy for the Communist Party, which was to be splintered into 'democratist' parties of every apparent political complexion, during the phase when 'capitalism' was to be discredited, while in practice retaining control of the new political environment under the 'state of the whole people'. 'In a democratic state', he proclaimed on 6 July, 'a changeover to a multiparty system is **inevitable**. Various political parties are gradually being formed in our country. At the same time, a fundamental renewal of the CPSU is **inevitable**. It is necessary to organisationally codify all the platforms that exist in the CPSU and to give every Communist time for self-determination [i.e., to chose which label to play 'democratism' under – *Ed.*]... The Party should divest itself of all State functions... a parliamentary-type Party will emerge. Only this type of Party... will be able to be a leading Party and to win elections for one or other of **its** [*sic*] factions. With the development of democratic movements in the country and the further radicalisation of restructuring, it will be possible for this alliance to become *the vanguard of society in actual fact*. This will provide a broad social base for the renewal of society, erect a barrier against attacks by the conservatives [by which Yeltsin did *not* mean 'old-guard' 'conservative' Communists – *Ed.*], and guarantee the **irreversibility of restructuring**'.

Failing to appreciate the true Leninist nature of the new Russian political structure and Yeltsin's rôle within it, Western leaders, with exaggerated expectations of Russian 'progress towards democracy', committed themselves to supporting Yeltsin – believing mistakenly that he was sincere and that he enjoyed a relatively free hand as President to pursue 'reformist' policies. As a consequence, Western policy became the captive of the Kremlin strategists, of whom Yeltsin is just one.

Just as the Party and the KGB controlled the literary debate between 'liberals' like Tvardovskiy and 'conservatives' like Kochetov in the 1960s, so today the strategists control Zhirinovskiy on the one hand and leading reformers on the other[85]. They also control the military. By deliberately creating setbacks to the progress of reform, the strategists can play on Western fears of the 'Zhirinovskiy factor' or the possibilities of a military coup to extract yet further concessions from the gullible West which, because of its failure to understand the true nature and motivation of Soviet/Russian strategy, finds itself with no alternative but to continue supporting Yeltsin or whoever else may for the time being purport to represent the 'forces of reform'. Yeltsin and members of his Government routinely 'play the Zhirinovskiy card' in their contacts with Western leaders like Kohl, and with other influential individuals. At a lower level, 'ex'-Soviet 'parliamentarians' are busy influencing their counterparts, especially in Europe, to believe that uncontrolled 'reformist' forces are genuinely emerging in Russia[86] (and the other 'ex'-Soviet Republics). **They are not:** the strategists in, and associated with, the National Security Council, are in control.

THE EVENTS IN CHECHNYA EXPLAINED IN TERMS OF RUSSIAN STRATEGY
The events in Chechnya, like the events of August 1991 and October 1993, have been deliberately staged largely for Western consumption by the Kremlin strategists in the pursuit of their objectives[87]. One indication of this is the timing of the events. Chechnya declared its independence from Russia in 1991[88]. Yet for three years the Russians did not react, other than ineffectually. Why did they do so only at the end of 1994?

Independence for Chechnya is a wholly artificial concept. Although my own ➡

85 *Editor's Note:* Likewise, individuals selected for prominent positions as 'reformers' in the 'former' USSR may resurface in a contrasting rôle later. A conspicuous example of such seamless switching is the recent career of Mr Tedo Japaridze, who took up his post as Georgia's Ambassador to Washington in the first quarter of 1995. Prior to Shevardnadze's arrival in Tbilisi in March 1992, Japaridze had served as Deputy Foreign Minister under President Zviad Gamsakhurdia, who was removed to make way for Shevardnadze.
86 *Editor's Note:* In this task, the 'ex'-Soviet 'democratists' are routinely assisted by Western Governments. In Britain, for instance, the Foreign Office is associated with an all-party parliamentary organisation called The Future of Europe Trust, which provides platforms for establishing contacts with European 'parliamentarians', including representatives from the 'ex'-Soviet Bloc. At a conference held in London in May 1993, the organisation welcomed many democratist 'parliamentarians', including Georgiy Gavrilin, Secretary of the Central Committee of the Russian Union of Youth, Anatoly Liabiedzka, President of the Association of Young Political Leaders of Belarus and Revaz S Adamia, Secretary of the Parliamentary Commission on Defence and National Security of the Georgian Parliament, who said he belonged to a 'Green party'.
87 *Editor's Note:* During period of Lenin's 'Trust' scam in the 1920s, the Soviets timed the blowing up of police stations to coincide with prearranged visits by anti-Bolshevik émigré opposition leaders, in order to convince them that opposition to the Communists continued on the ground. The staging of spectacular destructive spectacles is therefore nothing new. Today, though, they are televised for global consumption.
88 *Editor's Note:* It was former Soviet Air Force General Dzhokhar Dudayev *himself* who, at the Chechen All-National Congress which met in Grozny in November 1990, called for the establishment of a sovereign Chechen Republic. Writing in *'The Washington Post'* [10 March 1995], Dudayev rewrote history, stating that this mandate was 'handed to me' by the Congress.

sympathies are for the Chechens, their territory has no direct access to the outside world. (Dr Brzezinski's recent comparison between Chechnya and Puerto Rico is inapposite). The Chechens lost half their numbers in exile under Stalin. By 1994 50% of the population of Chechnya were ethnic Russians. Russians control the pipeline to Novorossiisk, giving them powerful leverage in the area. Given these circumstances the idea of a serious Chechen independence struggle is a non-starter.

Equally artificial is the Russian choice of method for dealing with Chechen aspirations. The Yeltsin Government inherited over 70 years' worth of Soviet experience of dealing politically and militarily with nationalist opposition in the Republics. Yet it chose to wield an enormous military sledgehammer to crack a small nut in Chechnya, when the only rational way to handle the situation would have been the path of negotiation leading to a peaceful settlement as in the case of Tatarstan.

In earlier Memoranda I suggested that the confrontation between Yeltsin and his then Vice-President Rutskoi and the parliamentary Speaker Khasbulatov – a confrontation which culminated in the televised bombardment of the 'White House' in Moscow [a new kind of 'Reichstag Fire': see page 163] was contrived by the strategists with Rutskoi and Khasbulatov playing the rôle of provocateurs. The release and amnesty granted to Rutskoi and Khasbulatov after a ludicrously truncated period of imprisonment was consistent with their having played such a provocative rôle.

Frequent press mentions during December 1994, in the Chechnyan context, of Khasbulatov, himself a Chechen, provided a possible pointer to provocation there: he could well have played a rôle behind the scenes as an adviser to the 'Chechen fighters'. Another pointer to the likelihood of provocation is Dzhokhar Dudayev's own background. Like Shevardnadze in Georgia and Aliyev in Azerbaijan, Dudayev is a 'former' Communist. He is also a former Soviet Air Force General[89].

The conduct of the Chechnyan operation raises a number of questions. For instance: why, given the vast military and secret police experience at their disposal, did the Russians choose to despatch into Chechnya in the first place, inexperienced young Soviet army draftees who put up a poor performance in front of Western television cameras? Why were the Russian special forces who, for example, captured General Pal Maleter during the Hungarian upheaval of 1956, too inept to capture any of the Chechen leaders? How did the Chechen fighters come to be so well armed? Why did the army and Ministry of the Interior troops not take immediate action to surround the city of Grozny and cut off the one route which remained available for the movement of Chechen fighters and supplies in and out of the city centre?

Why, with their huge preponderance of fire power, did it take the Russians so long to capture the Presidential Palace, the symbolic centre of Chechen resistance? Why, before the Palace fell, were its Chechen defenders, according to their own accounts, allowed to leave, taking their Russian prisoners with them, so that they were free to continue the struggle elsewhere? Why was the bombardment of buildings in the centre of Grozny conducted with what Chancellor Kohl described as 'senseless madness'? And why, as the Chechen fighters 'took to the hills', was a local

89 *Editor's Note:* One of Dudayev's close associates, Usman Imaev, who served first as the Chechen Minister of Justice and later as President of the National Bank of the Chechen Republic, was previously a senior military intelligence officer in the Soviet Embassy in Mozambique.

guerrilla leader willing to receive a Western journalist in his own home in a moun-
tain village without disguise, providing his full name and a history of his family?
[*The New York Times*, 20 January 1995][90].

I am sceptical about much of the Western press and television coverage of
Chechnya. In the first place, coverage was restricted by various factors. For example,
Western access to Russian troops engaged in the operation was severely limited
according to John Dancey, the NBC News correspondent in Moscow, speaking on
the Donahue-Pozner Program on 12 January 1995. The bombardment itself was a
powerful disincentive to intrusive journalism, and reporters obviously cannot be
blamed for their inability to provide a coherent account of the fighting which took
place in the centre of Grozny.

The important general point is that Western press and TV representatives
reported the events as Westerners observing what they took to be a real conflict in a
free society. It is not their fault that they were not briefed concerning the possibilities
of provocation along Communist lines. Hence they were not looking for evidence of
mock confrontations, faked casualties or planted information. The prominent Western reporters themselves, though courageous, appeared young and lacking in experience as war correspondents.

Nevertheless, some revealing items surfaced in the coverage. For example,
The New York Times reported on 15 January that 'some of the *least serious*' of the
Chechen fighters 'would parade before the cameras' at the Minutka traffic circle.
That report prompted questions as to how many *serious* Chechen fighters were actu-
ally involved in action against Russian troops. Another report insisted that 'the last
Western reporters' had left the area of the Presidential Palace, where the 'murderous
fighting' was concentrated and that Chechen fighters were no longer able to move
easily to the south of the city in order to brief journalists about what was happening.
It seems therefore that there were no Western eyewitnesses of the 'final battle' for the
Palace, and that much of the evidence on the fighting was derived from Chechen
fighters, whose reliability the reporters were in no position to assess.

Two Western reporters were killed during these events. Though these deaths
were reported as accidental, the fact is that the Russians would have no compunction
about eliminating Western journalists if they thought they might be liable to expose
their provocation. It was no coincidence that 40 Russian rockets were targeted at, and
hit, Minutka Circle – which up to that moment had been favoured for meetings
between journalists and fighters. Almost certainly, Russian officers who told journalists that they had arrived in Grozny without maps were briefed to tell this tall story.
A Russian General who was shown on television going through photographs taken
by reporters, said the pictures they had taken were useful because they helped him to
assess what was going on in Grozny. In all likelihood, he was checking to make sure
that the photographs taken by the reporters conveyed the images the Russians
wanted conveyed for international public consumption.

90 *Editor's Note:* And why, on 16 December 1994, did General Ivan Babichev permit a gathering of
local women to 'block' – in front of Western TV cameras – an armoured column of paratroopers, elements of the 19th Motor-Rifle Division and some Interior Ministry forces, which stretched back to the
horizon? The General declared that it would be a 'crime' to use force against unarmed old ladies.
After this televised show of military 'irresolution', Babichev presided over the sacking of Grozny.

The spectacular and continuous bombardment of buildings in the centre of Grozny, many of them probably empty, struck me as deliberately designed to monopolise television cameras, replicating in many ways the 'Reichstag Fire' bombardment of the 'White House' in Moscow in October 1993.

Inevitably, the detonation of so much high explosive was accompanied by casualties. But the actual number of casualties was probably limited by the departure of many inhabitants of the centre of Grozny before the bombardment started in earnest. As early as 7 January 1995, the Red Cross reported that 350,000 people had fled from the fighting, a figure equivalent to over 80% of the population of Grozny. It would be interesting to know to what extent the authorities encouraged or arranged the evacuation of central Grozny before the bombardment began.

Verification of casualty numbers is the most difficult problem. According to Dudayev, cited in 'The New York Times' of 12 January, 18,000 Chechens had already died, a figure which the reporter said 'seems exaggerated'. Casualty figures for the Russian army quoted in 'The New York Times' of 17 January varied from 400 to 800 killed. Again there is no knowing whether these figures were exaggerated or minimised. The Russian authorities are reported to have delayed the admission of European observers interested in verifying numbers. Even if they were eventually to arrive on the scene, such observers would be unlikely to be able to check the numbers allegedly buried in mass graves. Total casualties will probably never be known with any certainty. From the Kremlin strategists' point of view, casualties are inevitable during this kind of operation and a necessary price to pay for the attainment of defined strategic objectives.

THE KREMLIN'S OBJECTIVES AND THE CHECHNYA CRISIS

The timing of the Chechnyan crisis is an essential key to understanding the strategic objectives which underlie it. The crisis followed closely on the Republican Congressional victory, with its possible consequence of a reversal in the US military rundown. Contrived and televised Russian military bungling during the Chechnyan campaign has sent a strong message to the West that Russian military leaders are divided amongst themselves and that there is widespread incompetence and low morale in the army – factors which demonstrate that it can be discounted as a serious military adversary for the foreseeable future.

This message is intended to influence US Congressional debate on the subject of Russia's military potential and the size of US forces required to maintain a balance with it. The message can also be used as a pretext for deepening the partnership between the US and Russian armed forces by seeking American advice and help in 'reforming', reorganising and retraining the Russian army in order to enable it to serve a 'democratic' system[91].

The events in Chechnya have enabled the Russians to play especially on European fears of destabilisation in Russia and the development there of an internal 'Bosnian situation'. These fears have injected a further boost to the European desire for partnership with the 'democratic forces' in Russia in developing democratic solu-

91 *Editor's Note:* Television images of Russian tanks displaying the Soviet Red Flag with its hammer and sickle motif (for instance, on BBC TV News on 10 April 1995) dialectically reinforce such signals.

THE PERESTROIKA DECEPTION

tions to Russian problems. European hopes of promoting real democracy in Russia will of course prove illusory. The Russians will use the partnership to ease their entry into European institutions as a rightful member of the 'European House', a house which over the longer term they intend to dominate.

Given continuing Russian influence and leverage in Eastern Europe, East European and eventually Russian involvement in NATO are in the long term Russian strategic interest in accordance with Sun Tzu's principle of 'entering the enemy's camp unopposed'. Though for different reasons, I share the view expressed by a writer in 'The New York Times' of 11 January 1995 that **East European membership would mean the ruin of NATO**. The ruin of NATO is a long-term Russian objective, towards the achievement of which much progress has already been made. The televised spectacle of Russian barbarity in Chechnya has aroused apprehension in neighbouring states of comparable Russian military operations against themselves, thereby strengthening the argument that former members of the Warsaw Pact should be admitted to membership of NATO[92]. Yeltsin's firmly expressed opposition to their membership and his Foreign Minister's ambivalence (see, for instance, 'The New York Times' of 20 January 1995) can be read as possible preludes to a dramatic 'change' in Russian policy, perhaps under a new government[93].

Furthermore, the reassertion of Kremlin control over Chechnya through massive military intervention (which, despite the calculated impression of bungling, achieved its objective, thereby itself revealing the contrived nature of the televised 'bungling'), the spectacular, televised destruction of buildings in Grozny and the publicity surrounding the level of casualties, have sent the strongest possible signals to genuine would-be Muslim and non-Muslim secessionists in Chechnya and other Republics that secessionism is a very dangerous game. The strategists may well have chosen Chechnya for their demonstration of force specifically because real secessionism can be more easily contained in that territory than in others.

It would also be consistent with the strategists' method that the publicised impression of Yeltsin's inept handling of the Chechnyan situation was intended in part to help destroy suspicions that Russian leaders are capable of implementing a long-range strategy, as this Author has consistently contended that they do. For the strategists, it is particularly important to keep obscuring this fact, even though it is largely beyond Western comprehension, since belated Western understanding of strategic continuity would inevitably lead to the far-reaching reassessment of Soviet-Chinese strategy and objectives which they seek to preclude.

Just as consistently, the Russian scenario for Chechnya provides for a peace-

92 *Editor's Note:* The 'NATO expansion' dialectic works as follows. Moscow has been feigning opposition to the suggestion that NATO should expand to embrace East European countries (which are under overtly Communist or 'neo'-Communist control, and which collaborate secretly with the Russians). The West is bending over backwards to 'placate' Moscow on this score. But against the background of the televised images of Grozny's destruction, the argument that NATO should expand to provide these countries with protection appears unanswerable to confused Western policymakers who do not stop to ask why they might need protection from the West's friendly 'partner', Russia. The strategic objective, coordinated in secret between Moscow and the East European capitals, is irreversible penetration of NATO – the enemy's camp – in accordance with the teachings of Sun Tzu.
93 *Editor's Note:* This would be represented in the West as a 'triumph' for Western diplomacy, after the model of US self-flattery once Washington had persuaded itself that it had 'won the Cold War'.

ful solution of the Chechnyan problem under either Yeltsin or his successor. Khasbulatov might emerge as a new Chechnyan leader just as Shevardnadze and Aliyev
emerged in Georgia and Azerbaijan respectively. Although at present there is obvious European revulsion against Russian brutality in Chechnya, given a peaceful
solution and the associated psychological sense of 'relief', European and Arab capital
could be attracted to help finance the reconstruction of Grozny and to undertake
investment in the Caucasian oil industry.

In my letter of 12 October 1993 I referred to the military/nationalist option as
the third course upon which the Kremlin strategists might embark in future to adjust
the style and leadership of a new government if, for example, Yeltsin was considered
to have exhausted his usefulness in extracting concessions from the West. In this context, the Chechnyan 'crisis' can be seen not as a likely cause of a military coup, but as
a possible planned prelude to a change of government. The new government might
be military or nationalist. Certain indications that this is envisaged, are apparent.

It should be remembered, too, that the emergence of 'perestroika' in Russia
was accompanied by the tightening of military and political control in China, starting
with the Tienanmen Square episode. Far from being coincidental, this was the result
of a joint Sino-Soviet decision – confirmed during Gorbachëv's visit immediately
ahead of the Tienanmen Square provocation – that, while one main pillar of the
Leninist world was engaged in 'perestroika', the other should be held under firm control. Similarly, the introduction of a Chinese version of 'perestroika', which may be
expected in China after the death of Deng, would be a probable reason for a tightening of control in Russia[95].

Since an outright military or nationalist government might prejudice the flow
of Western aid and the continued 'cooperation' with the West which furthers the
strategists' interests, it is more likely that the Kremlin strategists will opt for a hybrid
solution involving, for example, a new President and Commander-in-Chief with a
military background and a 'reformist' Prime Minister, in the context of overtly
tighter KGB control. The President would be presented as a guarantee of Russian stability while the Prime Minister's task would be to ensure the continued flow of Western aid and the continuation of cooperative operations. The transition might be
brought about, for example, by the resignation of Yeltsin on health grounds and/or
through elections, due anyway in 1996, for which the strategists would have chosen
and groomed their presidential candidate. In this way, 'legitimacy' could be preserved and the election could be used as further 'proof' that democracy, cherished by
the West, was 'working' in Russia (albeit in step with increasing authoritarianism)[96].

95 Editor's Note: While these additional Memoranda were being incorporated in this book during the first
week of April 1995, the legislation to reorganise and 'strengthen' the intelligence services which is the subject of Note 35 on page 98, was signed by President Boris Yeltsin. The Federal Security Service [FSB] was
'empowered' to search homes without warrants, to run its own jails and independent 'criminal' investigations, to operate under cover of other official agencies, to bug telephones and intercept mail (with 'court
permission'), and to operate abroad. Summarising the situation, Sergei Karaganov, Deputy Director of the
Institute of Europe of the Academy of Sciences, an adviser to President Yeltsin, said that 'Russia is moving
towards a mixed democratic [sic], semi-authoritarian model, with the strengthening of elements of a police
state'. A new postage stamp bears the image of Stalin ['The Sunday Times', London, 9 April 1995].

96 Editor's Note: The minimal extent of any risk to the 'cooperation' element of the 'cooperation-blackmail'
equation that the strategists may have run during their Chechnya provocation was soon made clear when,

[Note 96 continued on page 230:]

THE URGENT NEED TO RECONSIDER
PREVAILING ASSUMPTIONS ABOUT RUSSIA AND CHINA

(1) In the political arena:

The failure of US policymakers to comprehend the veiled aggressiveness and hostility towards the United States inherent in Sino-Russian strategy and the belief that the political and economic reforms in Russia and the partial introduction of capitalism in China have foreshadowed these countries' development into real democracies, have eroded the effectiveness of US policies in the foreign affairs, defence, intelligence and counter-intelligence fields. US policymakers have recklessly accepted the premise that Russia and China are no longer their enemies, but are rather potential allies and partners fully deserving of US support. Only countries like Iran, Iraq and North Korea – which (ironically, in this context) work secretly with Russia and China – are still considered potential adversaries.

A particularly alarming indication of the extent to which US foreign policy has become degraded is Washington's willingness to consider the admission of Russia and other former Warsaw Pact countries into NATO – an alliance which provided the United States and its allies with effective protection from these countries for many years. **This policy jeopardises the security of the United States, gravely threatens the security of Western Europe, and undermines the United States' rôle as the leader of the developed world.**

US policymakers should urgently re-examine their assumptions about the 'progress' of Russia and China 'towards democracy'. They should take account of Sino-Russian strategy and should recognise that the long-term strategic, political and economic threat comes from a Sino-Russian axis and associated participants like North Korea, Iran, Iraq and Syria. **The Russian and Chinese leaders are still committed to their objective of world domination and believe that, disguised as 'democrats', in accordance with Leninist teaching, they will be able to achieve it.**

The Ames case has provided a conspicuous reminder of the Kremlin's veiled but continuing hostility towards the United States and its institutions, and of Russian determination to dominate them. It is extraordinary that the US Administration has managed to ignore the political implications of the Ames case – continuing to claim success for its Russian policy and conducting business as usual with the Kremlin as if the Ames case, and its ominous implications, were of no significance.

[**Note 95**: *Continued from page 229:*] after implying distaste for the Russians' behaviour in Chechnya and raising the prospect that President Clinton might refuse to visit Moscow during the celebrations in May 1995 of the end of the Second World War in Europe, the President's entourage soon advised the press that US-Russian relations were so important, that the visit might still proceed. Then *'The New York Times'* reported on 17 March 1995 that President Yeltsin had told foreign editors: 'We want to arrange a program so that in Red Square [*sic*], there will be a military parade, but without any military equipment'. Russian officials were reported to have said that the Red Square parade would consist of some 2,500 Second World War veterans, and would be preceded by religious ceremonies. A *separate parade*, involving troops and modern armaments, was being planned for Poklonnaya Hill in the north of Moscow, some distance from Red Square, and Mr Clinton would not be asked to attend that parade. The striking feature of this report was the contempt Russian officials thus revealed for the American official mentality, which they judged so feckless as to be willing to accept the US President's presence at the innocuous parade, even though plans for the real military parade had been made publicly known. Nor did *'The New York Times'* reporter see any irony in the announcement of the Poklonnaya Hill event.

The United States should reassert its rôle as the leader of the world, explaining the long term strategic threat to its NATO allies and Japan and reinforcing its traditional alliances with them. To continue ignoring the innumerable indications of Leninist deception will add cumulatively to the scale of the tragedy the world faces.

(2) In the defence arena:

False and naïve assumptions about Russian and Chinese 'progress towards democracy' and about their 'friendship towards the United States' threaten defence policy. The threat is not just associated with reduced military budgets but also with the matter of priorities. US involvement in regional and local conflicts in Somalia, Bosnia and Haiti, on the basis that 'the Cold War is over', and in fighting drug cartels in Latin America, distracts attention from the real strategic threat from Russia and China.

Worse still, the US military appear to have been accepting the new military doctrines of their Russian counterparts uncritically and at face value and are engaged in cooperation and partnership with them over nuclear disarmament and in other respects, without taking into account Sino-Russian strategy and the deception imperative which accompanies it. The US Secretary of Defense, Mr Perry[96], even pays tribute to Sakharov's 'wise advice' concerning the desirability of American-Russian partnership, not realising that Sakharov was the unacknowledged spokesman of the Soviet strategists who was never a friend of the US military and whose writings, as I have argued at length elsewhere, made it clear that he saw East-West partnership leading to East-West *convergence* and **eventual world government on Communist terms**, which is the strategists' objective. It should be remembered that soon after the adoption of the Sino-Soviet strategy formulated in 1958-60, Mao, one of its main authors, uttered words to the effect that 'We should pull the United States' nuclear teeth and turn it into a paper tiger'.

The US military should pull back from partnership with both the Russian and the Chinese armed forces and should revert to regarding them as their long-term adversaries rather than unwittingly helping them to implement their strategy.

(3) In the intelligence arena:

The effectiveness of the Central Intelligence Agency was eroded by disclosures about its methods during the Congressional hearings in the mid-1970s. In the 1980s its covert capabilities were significantly reduced. It lost its main human sources in the USSR and Russia in 1985, as a result of Ames' treachery. It is vulnerable to 'exposure' operations designed to discredit it once and for all, at a time when the future of the US intelligence community is under review.

96 *Editor's Note:* On 17 March 1993, the Gorbachëv Foundation/USA circulated a document about its 'Global Security Project' which revealed that a paper entitled *'A new Concept of Cooperative Security'* prepared by Mr William Perry *et al*, would serve as the basis for discussion in a Working Group convened under the auspices of the 'Global Security Project'. The Project, which issued its Final Report in October 1994, was 'developed... with the active involvement of Mr Mikhail Gorbachëv [and]... specifically with Georgiy Shaknazarov, Director of Global Programs for the Foundation'. Shaknazarov spent the greater part of his career working within the CPSU Central Committee apparatus in the Socialist Countries Department, is President of the Russian Association of Political Sciences and was Vice-President of the International Political Sciences Association [*see also Note 23, page 43*].

In the final years of the period known as the Cold War, analysts from the Central Intelligence Agency, the National Security Agency and the Defense Intelligence Agency, especially experts concerned with satellite photography, paid close attention to the dangers of Soviet political and military disinformation and camouflage (*maskirovka*). It would appear that these analysts have for some reason forgotten about disinformation, or else have chosen to assume that the 'reformed' Russian military and intelligence services have abandoned such practices. This view is mistaken.

The former Director of Central Intelligence, Mr William Webster, placed it on record that, because of the changes which he thought had taken place in the USSR, the Agency now relied to a much greater extent than previously, on Russian official and press sources. This rash decision was also mistaken.

The Ames case has shown that the 'heirs' of the KGB continued successfully to implement the KGB's operations to penetrate vital centres of the US Government. Likewise, Russian political and military deception operations have continued under the new 'democratic', system, with certain modifications.

Now, the pseudo-democratic institutions adopted under Soviet *'perestroika'* are employed to manipulate the perceptions and conclusions of the Western media concerning staged confrontations in Russia such as the August 1991 'coup', the battle between Yeltsin and the Russian parliament in October 1993 and the Chechnya crisis of 1994-95. **American military and intelligence analysts, having accepted democratic 'reforms' in Russia as genuine, have lowered their guard with respect to disinformation and have failed to detect its continuation.**

These staged confrontations in the former USSR will continue to occur for as long as their true deceptive nature and intent remains undetected. And their continuation will foster growing Western confusion over perceptions of events in Russia and China. This confusion is intended to reinforce the West's continuing failure to apprehend the scope and scale of the long term strategic threat to the free world.

The US Congress is pressing, meanwhile, for a redefinition of US intelligence priorities. Since US policymakers and Congress accept the false premise that Russia is 'moving towards democracy', the prevailing view is that intelligence coverage of Russia should be reduced or dropped.

Furthermore, on the unreliable premise that Russia is a potential ally, the FBI and the CIA are deepening their unwise partnerships with their Russian counterparts over such issues as tackling nuclear terrorism.

Similar tendencies to reduce the coverage of, while expanding partnership with, China may be expected when China embarks upon its own form of *'perestroika'*.

For the intelligence professional, the Ames case was nothing less than an intelligence Pearl Harbor which proved beyond all question that Russia remains the main adversary of the Central Intelligence Agency, while definitively exposing the falsehood of Arbatov's claim that Russia is no longer an enemy of the United States. To draw any other conclusion is to ignore reality and to risk further jeopardising the security of the United States and the West.

Because Russia and China are secretly hostile to the United States in particular and the West in general, they should remain intelligence priorities.

More specifically:

☐ **The Central Intelligence Agency should be strengthened to deal with the threat to the West represented by the joint Russian-Chinese strategy.**

☐ *The quality and content of the CIA's intelligence analysis needs to be drastically improved.* Analysts should abandon reliance on conventional media interpretations of events in Russia and China, should grasp the problem of strategic disinformation by its roots and should seek once and for all to uncover the workings of Sino-Russian strategic coordination.

☐ Analysts with the Central Intelligence Agency, the National Security Agency and the Defense Intelligence Agency should re-examine their assumptions about Russia and China and should set about offering policymakers fresh, more realistic assessments of strategic disinformation, informed by their immersion in the literature of the Leninist dialectical political method.

☐ The covert action capability of the Central Intelligence Agency should be rebuilt in the light of the Sino-Russian threat.

(4) In respect of counter-intelligence:

Acceptance by the Federal Bureau of Investigation in the early 1960s of the Soviet intelligence plants 'FEDORA' and 'TOPHAT' eroded the effectiveness of the FBI's counter-intelligence and severely damaged its relations with the Central Intelligence Agency's counter-intelligence under James Jesus Angleton.

Further damage was inflicted upon the FBI's counter-intelligence capabilities by the Church Committee's public hearings in the mid-1970s. At the same time, counter-intelligence in the CIA was all but destroyed by the forced resignations of Angleton and his chief of operations, Scotty Miler. Their departure destroyed any chance of US counter-intelligence recovering from the disasters of the 1970s.

Following their departure, the CIA adopted an anti-counter-intelligence culture. Systematic analysis of the case histories of and information from important defector and other sources was discontinued. Attempts to neutralise penetration of the Agency were scorned and condemned. What little remained of counter-intelligence became ineffectual.

The KGB and its 'heirs' took advantage of the CIA's weakness to penetrate key areas of its Soviet Division, using Howard and Ames. Congress, the FBI and the CIA are now trying to prevent any recurrence of the Ames case by focusing on defensive measures such as background checks and greater vigilance over the personal behaviour and financial circumstances of intelligence staff. But that is not enough. To such work should be added comparative study of the case histories of, and information derived from, all secret sources on Russia: those compromised by Ames and those which were not compromised by his activities. Such a study might uncover further penetration of CIA and would throw light upon the information which the Russian service fed to the CIA and the FBI in order to influence US policy and perceptions in the interests of their strategy. But such a study can only be undertaken to advantage if the strategy and its deception lines are taken into account.

US counter-intelligence within the FBI, the CIA and the DIA should re-examine assumptions about Russia, China and former members of the Warsaw Pact and their intelligence services. It should then embark upon a proper study to achieve an understanding of Sino-Russian strategy and the rôle within it of the intelligence and strategic disinformation services and their agents of influence both in their own territory and in the West. Until such an analysis has been successfully completed, any 'reinvention' of US counter-intelligence will be unrealistic, even counter-productive – and counter-intelligence work will remain superficial.

But once the study has been completed, the revised understanding which results from it should be shared with the counter-intelligence services of the NATO allies and Japan. Only then will Western counter-intelligence stand any chance of recovering its effectiveness. It will become possible, once again, to identify and monitor agents of influence working in the political and defence areas in the West, who are secretly promoting Sino-Russian strategy. In this connection, counter-intelligence should make a special study of the use of political, scientific, industrial and commercial US-Russian joint ventures and foundations as cover for espionage and for exerting political influence.

Before my analysis, warnings and recommendations are rejected as ridiculous, it should be recalled that the predictions I made in the early 1980s about a forthcoming liberalisation of the Soviet system were dismissed at the time as absurd.

But in a recent book entitled 'Wedge: the Secret War between the FBI and CIA', [New York, Alfred Knopf, 1994, pages. 407-408], Mark Riebling has drawn attention to the accuracy of my predictions. One reason for their accuracy was that they were based on the inside knowledge I acquired before my defection at the end of 1961. This knowledge covered the KGB's rôle in the newly adopted political strategy[98], the KGB's successes in penetrating, in particular, Western intelligence services and the Soviet intelligentsia, and the opportunities provided by these successes to implement strategic deception operations successfully.

I request that copies of this Memorandum should be sent to the Chiefs of the Federal Bureau of Investigation, the National Security Agency and the Defense Intelligence Agency. Respectfully,

ANATOLIY GOLITSYN

THE FOLLOWING MEMORANDUM DATED 1 OCTOBER 1993 WAS ATTACHED TO THIS PRESENTATION: ☛

---

98 *See Note 82, page 222.*

Memorandum to the CIA: **1 OCTOBER 1993**

For the attention of: The Director of Central Intelligence

CONTROL OF POLITICAL EVENTS IN RUSSIA

The so-called crisis in Moscow initiated by Yeltsin's dissolution of the Russian parliament on 21 September was another blatant example of a prearranged and controlled political manoeuvre. Among the signs of this were:

1. The hint dropped to the Secretary of State a week beforehand by the Soviet Foreign Minister, Andrei Kozyrev, that Yeltsin had some kind of 'event' in mind. The Secretary of State later admitted that he did not pay enough attention to it.

2. Yeltsin's relaxed appearance when announcing the dissolution of the parliament, his withdrawal to his dacha afterwards and his appearance on the Moscow streets the following morning accompanied by his Defence and Interior Ministers.

3. The absence from the Moscow streets during the first two days of the crisis of any significant display of strength by the security forces.

4. The relaxed behaviour of Rutskoi and Khasbulatov, and their failure to follow through with any significant measures to carry out their decisions. According to an eyewitness *'New York Times'* report datelined 22 September, 'there was none of the frantic bustle associated with high-stakes political confrontation' in the parliament building. Rutskoi was reported to have left the building, although 'he was sure to return to his command post before long, if only for security's sake' [*sic!*].

5. The desultory display of support for Rutskoi and Khasbulatov demonstrated by a relatively small crowd outside the 'White House', which obligingly erected token knee-high barricades in the streets.

6. *'The New York Times'* of 24 September reported that the rest of Russia was quiet: 'There were no reports of violence or even a strike in support of the legislators'.

7. The Defence Ministry issued a statement to the effect that parliament was planning to 'attack' the Ministry. Despite this, the 'volunteers' outside the 'White House' and the guards inside it were reported to have handed over most of their arms without a struggle.

8. Two incidents were reported up to 26 September which allegedly involved shooting and fatalities. The following points about them were noteworthy: first, the reports were attributed to Russian Government sources; secondly, the incidents were said to have occurred, not in the immediate vicinity of the 'White House', but at the CIS military command and at the GRU, where observation by independent Western sources could have been excluded.

9. General Pavel Grachev was reported as saying that he had tightened security in the army and had established special units to prevent terrorist or provocative actions by servicemen. Significantly, Grachev did not refer to the army's Political Directorate, which is responsible for morale and disciplinary matters.

10. Sergei Rogov, the Deputy Director of Arbatov's Institute for the Study of the USA and Canada, commented attributably to *'The New York Times'* on the 'very nasty consequences' which might flow from rivalry between Grachev and Achalov or Achilov. This remark was significant in two respects: First, Rogov was commenting on the *Russian Army*, not on his proper field of study, namely *the US and Canadian armed forces*; and secondly, he was doing so in a manner which might be considered off-limits even in a mature democracy for someone in a semi-official position speaking at a time of crisis. I have commented in earlier Memoranda about the role of Arbatov's Institute in the evolution and presentation of 'perestroika' strategy.

The immediate response of the West to the events of September was to reconfirm its support for Yeltsin, and to condone his unconstitutional behaviour in dissolving parliament. The events coincided with the Group of Seven meeting and with the annual meetings of the International Monetary Fund and the World Bank at which the provision of further aid to Russia was on the agenda. The US Senate hastened, in the face of Yeltsin's closure of the legislature, to pass a foreign aid bill containing $2.5 billion of US taxpayers' money for Moscow.

The American media presented these events as a further confrontation and crisis in the Russian system, and the American establishment treated them as such. The President and the Administration were taken by surprise. Reporters asked why there had been no warning of the crisis from the intelligence services. Experts on Russian affairs debated the crisis on television. All these debates were conducted on the basis of a common acceptance that the events in Moscow were spontaneous political developments. As I have argued in previous Memoranda, they were nothing of the sort. There is no parallel between the interplay of independent political forces in America and the West on the one hand. and 'perestroika' and Russian political evolution on the other. 'Perestroika' and Russian political evolution have all along been deliberately contrived and controlled.

In my book 'New Lies for Old' [1984] it was shown that, on the basis of a study of Soviet strategy and disinformation, accurate predictions could be made concerning the forthcoming liberalisation of the Soviet system, and of the course that it would take. Accurate predictions concerning events in the context of the new fake 'democratist' political set-up in the CIS can also be made, once it is recognised that the system is being manipulated by the political élite of 'former' Communists who are extending the strategy of which they were the architects.

Gorbachëv, Yeltsin, Rutskoi and Khasbulatov are all members of this élite, which contains the group I have referred to in successive Memoranda as the Russian strategists. The élite were responsible for returning Shevardnadze and Aliyev to power in Georgia and Azerbaijan. They are also responsible for planning and conducting the Leninist evolution of the political system and the way it operates, including the occurrence, and recurrence, of political 'crisis'.

The élite is the ultimate authority on which Yeltsin's position rests: it provides the collective leadership of which he is a member and which decides, among other things, how long he should serve as President. The élite has to have some mechanism at its disposal through which such decisions can be reached and through which controlled political events can be coordinated. It is essential to the success of the strategy that this mechanism should be well concealed from the West. I lack the facilities to study how it might be operating. The likelihood is, however, that it functions under cover of some openly acknowledged body. The National Security Council might be a candidate for investigation as a possible front for this secret mechanism.

In the light of the indications I have given that the September and earlier events were contrived and controlled, I recommend that CIA analysts of CIS affairs and counter-intelligence staff should together take a new look, on an all-source basis, at the detailed record of the confrontations between Gorbachëv and Ligachev, between Gorbachëv and Yeltsin and between Yeltsin and the parliament in March and September 1993 – paying close attention to their timing in relation to meetings or decisions in the West concerning the provision of support and how the West could provide aid to Russia and the 'former' Soviet Union. I am confident that they will find in each case anomalies, discrepancies, disinformation and indications of Russian control and the use of confrontations to attain strategic objectives. These include gaining acceptance of first Gorbachëv and then Yeltsin as genuine reformers and partners of the West, exploitation of the new treaty-based relationships with key Western countries and 'cooperation' in the furtherance of geopolitical ends, and ensuring the continued availability of massive flows of economic assistance through the open-ended transfer of resources from Western taxpayers to the strategists.

I believe that, if such a re-examination were to be carried out, US intelligence assessments would benefit and that the intelligence community would be less prone to be surprised by events in Russia, as they have been in recent years.

I also believe that recognition of the degree to which political events in the 'former' Soviet Union are controlled, and analysis of them along the lines suggested, would throw up useful criteria for judging which channels of information – overt and covert, human and technical – are being employed by the political, intelligence and security authorities of the 'former' USSR as channels for feeding disinformation to the West to suit their political purposes. Pointers would be provided identifying agents of influence, particularly among experts and commentators on Russian affairs, who have Russian and East European backgrounds. Lastly I suggest that analysts with all-source access should be briefed to look out for indications of the existence of the secret strategic control and coordination mechanism. ∎

INDEX

Pages 1-237

Index

Designed by Christopher Story FRSA. Print production by Lithofax Limited, 108 Horseferry Road, Westminster, London SW1P 2EF, United Kingdom. *Telephone:* 0171-222 3836.

• Lenin and Chicherin were not the only sources of inspiration for the revival of strategic disinformation [by the Soviet régime]. The ancient Chinese treatise on strategy and deception, Sun Tzu's 'The Art of War', translated into Russian by N.I. Konrad in 1950 (shortly after the Communist victory in China), was translated into German in 1957 by the Soviet specialist Y.I. Sidorenko, with a foreword by the Soviet military strategist and historian General Razin. It was published in East Germany by the East German Ministry of Defense and was prescribed for study in East German military academies. A new translation and other studies of Sun Tzu were published in Peking in 1957 and 1958 and in Shanghai in 1959. Mao is known to have been influenced by Sun Tzu in his conduct of the civil war.

This intense official interest in Sun Tzu on the part of both the Soviets and the Chinese at the very time when the new policy and strategy were being formulated is a good indication that the Chinese probably made a positive contribution to their formulation.

The strategy of strengthening the Communist Bloc while presenting an appearance of Communist disunity is neatly expressed in Sun Tzu's aphorisms:

○ All warfare is based on deception. Therefore, when capable,
feign incapacity; when active, inactivity.
○ Offer the enemy a bait to lure him; feign disorder and strike him.
○ One who wishes to appear to be weak in order to make his enemy
arrogant must be extremely strong. Only then can he feign weakness •.

ANATOLIY GOLITSYN, 'New Lies for Old', 1984; 1986 edition by Wheatsheaf Books Ltd, Brighton, Sussex, England, pages 42-43. Sun Tzu quotations from 'The Art of War', translated by Samuel B Griffith, Oxford University Press, London, Oxford and New York 1963.

• [Russia's main enemy is] the creation of a global dictatorship by the West under the crafty label "New World Order" •.
ALEKSANDR RUTSKOI, cited in 'The Sunday Times,' London, 9 April 1995.
This revealing remark dialectically accuses the West of precisely the objective pursued secretly by the Russian-Chinese strategists, as explained by Anatoliy Golitsyn. It is well known that pathological liars accuse their enemies of harbouring intentions which are in fact their own. Even Rutskoi's own fellow 'ex'-Communists admit to the objective of merging, and therefore abolishing, nation states, in accordance with Lenin's teaching that 'we set ourselves the ultimate aim of destroying the state' ['State and Revolution', International Publishers, New York, 1961 Edition, page 68], and the long-range Leninist programme for the establishment of World Government which is authoritatively expressed in the following official statements:

• The transition step to the "New World Order" involves merging the newly captive nations into regional governments •.
PETRENKO, F., AND POPOV, V., 'Soviet Foreign Policy, Objectives and Principles'
Progress Publishers, Moscow, 1985.

• The more states are intertwined with one another, the more durable will be the net of their relationships •.
ANDREI KOZYREV, Russian Foreign Minister, cited in 'Frankfurter Allgemeine Zeitung', 8 January 1995, quoting what Kozyrev had earlier told 'Frankfurter Rundschau'.

SOVIET
ANALYST
AN INTELLIGENCE COMMENTARY

SOVIET ANALYST, An Intelligence Commentary, provides a necessary antidote to fashionable, consensus and confused Western thinking about developments in the so-called 'former' Soviet Bloc countries. Applying the analytical methodology explained by **Anatoliy Golitsyn** in *'New Lies for Old'* and *'The Perestroika Deception'*, this publication, which was established in 1972, reviews the activities of the Leninist policymakers from the perspective of the implementation of their long-range strategy. It focuses on the steady progress they are making towards the realisation by stealth of their global revolutionary objectives through the progressive weakening and integration of nation states and their piecemeal replacement by intricate 'cooperative' cross-border structures that are intended to form the framework of a World Government.

This 'New World *Social* Order' [*see below*] will, by definition, be a global dictatorship. Those in the West who are collaborating, whether as agents of influence or unwittingly, with the Russian strategists in the furtherance of their secret strategy of 'cooperation-blackmail', recklessly imperil the future of Western civilisation.

It was President George Bush who re-popularised the phrase 'New World Order'. Other purveyors of this phrase include Dr Henry Kissinger, who has remarked: 'NAFTA is a major stepping-stone to the New World Order'. And speaking at a United Nations Ambassadors' Dinner on 14 September 1994, Mr David Rockefeller observed: 'This present "window of opportunity" during which a truly peaceful and interdependent world order might be built, will not be open for long. Already there are powerful forces at work that threaten to destroy all our hopes and efforts to erect an enduring structure of global cooperation'.

But the Soviets have a different phrase to describe their extraordinary global control objective. In 1932, William Z Foster, the leader of the Communist Party USA, wrote in his book *'Toward Soviet America'* that the objective of Communism was the establishment of a 'New World *Social* Order'. In 1985, two Soviet *apparatchiks*, F Petrenko and V Popov, explained [in *'Soviet Foreign Policy, Objectives and Principles'*, Progress Publishers, Moscow] that 'the transition step to the "New World Order" involves merging the newly captive nations into regional governments'. In 1942, Stalin wrote: 'As growing numbers of nations fall to the revolution, it becomes possible to reunite them under a Communist world régime' [International Publishers, New York]. The focus of SOVIET ANALYST is *the Soviet-Chinese version of the 'New World Order'*, which includes the adjective *'Social'* – meaning Communist. This objective has not changed.

Published by Christopher Story, Editor of *'The Perestroika Deception'*, SOVIET ANALYST circulates world-wide among professional analysts, official agencies, embassies and the diplomatic profession, intelligence communities and informed observers. SOVIET ANALYST is published on a prepaid annual subscription basis [for ten issues per Volume/series] by **World Reports Limited, 108 Horseferry Road, Westminster, London SW1P 2EF, United Kingdom.** *Telephone:* **0171-222 3836;** *Facsimile:* **0171-233 0175.** *Subscription price details on request.* ∎